Secession on Trial

The post–Civil War treason prosecution of Confederate president Jefferson Davis (1865–1869) was seen as a test case on the major constitutional question that animated the Civil War: the constitutionality of secession. The case never went to trial, however, because it threatened to undercut the meaning and significance of Union victory. This book describes the interactions of the lawyers working on both sides of the Davis case, who saw its potential to disrupt the battlefield's verdict against secession. In the aftermath of the Civil War, America was engaged in a wide-ranging debate over the legitimacy and effectiveness of war as a method of legal adjudication. Instead of risking the "wrong" outcome in the highly volatile Davis case, the Supreme Court took the opportunity to pronounce secession unconstitutional in another case, *Texas v. White* (1869), in a single, perfunctory paragraph.

Cynthia Nicoletti is an associate professor of law at the University of Virginia. She holds a BA, an MA, and a PhD from the University of Virginia and a JD from Harvard Law School. She is a member of the American Society for Legal History and the Society of Civil War Historians. Her dissertation, on which this book is based, won the William Nelson Cromwell Prize and the Hay-Nicolay Dissertation Award.

T0384651

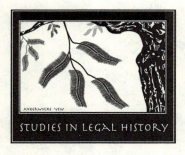

See the Studies in Legal History series website at
http://studiesinlegalhistory.org/

Studies in Legal History

EDITORS

Sarah Barringer Gordon, University of Pennsylvania
Holly Brewer, University of Maryland, College Park
Michael Lobban, London School of Economics and Political Science
Reuel Schiller, University of California, Hastings College of the Law

Also in the series:

Secession on Trial

The Treason Prosecution of Jefferson Davis

CYNTHIA NICOLETTI
University of Virginia Law School

CAMBRIDGE
UNIVERSITY PRESS

CAMBRIDGE
UNIVERSITY PRESS

One Liberty Plaza, 20th Floor, New York, NY 10006, USA

Cambridge University Press is part of the University of Cambridge.

It furthers the University's mission by disseminating knowledge in the pursuit of education, learning, and research at the highest international levels of excellence.

www.cambridge.org
Information on this title: www.cambridge.org/9781108401531
DOI: 10.1017/9781108233941

© Cynthia Nicoletti 2017

First published 2017

Printed in the United States of America by Sheridan Books, Inc.

A catalogue record for this publication is available from the British Library.

Library of Congress Cataloging-in-Publication Data
Names: Nicoletti, Cynthia, author.
Title: Secession on trial: the treason prosecution of Jefferson Davis / Cynthia Nicoletti.
Description: New York: Cambridge University Press, 2017. |
Series: Studies in legal history |
Includes bibliographical references and index.
Identifiers: LCCN 2017009820 | ISBN 9781108415521 (hardback) |
ISBN 9781108401531 (paperback)
Subjects: LCSH: Davis, Jefferson, 1808–1889 – Trials, litigation, etc. |
Trials (Treason) – United States. | Secession – United States – History. |
United States – History – Civil War, 1861–1865. |
BISAC: HISTORY / United States / 19th Century.
Classification: LCC KF223.D3855 N53 2017 | DDC 345.73/0231–dc23
LC record available at https://lccn.loc.gov/2017009820

ISBN 978-1-108-41552-1 Hardback
ISBN 978-1-108-40153-1 Paperback

To my mother and the memory of my father

Contents

Acknowledgments

This is probably not the book one should write before tenure. It was, and is, something of a controversial project, although I have lost some perspective on this fact over time. Secession, in any of its guises, is fraught, and I live with the worry that the reader will assume I wrote this book as a kind of advocacy piece for the secessionists' cause. That was not my motive.

I wrote this book because I think it has an important story to tell, and it is one that hasn't been told before. Most of the histories of the Civil War and Reconstruction that have been written in my lifetime tend to focus on the "heroes" of the story: those whose views accord the most with our own. Such a lens is necessarily distorting. In reading this history, especially in the aggregate, it's hard to understand why the beliefs of the Radical Republicans – so smart, so familiar, so *modern* – did not immediately prevail over contrary ideology. Without studying the ideas and actions of those who espoused the opposite points of view – views that we now find distasteful – it is almost impossible to answer the question of why history looks the way it does. History is often a give-and-take between people with radically different ideas, and telling it well requires the historian to engage seriously with those on both sides of an issue. That is why this book spends so much time exploring – and, frankly, humanizing – people whom we might say were on the "wrong side" of history. The secessionists were smart, passionate, and devoted to their cause – and that made a difference in the world. It was a world populated by Charles O'Conor as well as Thaddeus Stevens, and if we want to understand more about that world, we need to pay attention to both of them.

Clearly, prudence was not my primary guiding principle in writing this book. *Secession on Trial* is the product of (a) my own stubbornness, and (b) my inability to sustain a long-term interest in anything that doesn't make me feel hopelessly morally conflicted. So be it. I don't know how I feel about O'Conor; I both admire and fear him. I also don't know how I feel about law's tortured relationship with war as explored in this book. Americans certainly stretched the law beyond what it should bear in the 1860s, but in the end I don't think we could live with any other outcome. To paraphrase the decidedly mediocre legal thinker B. J. Sage, "Perhaps what was, was right."

Secession on Trial has been a long time in the making, and I have accumulated many debts. I benefited from a great deal of help and encouragement as I was writing this book. Three law school deans, Jim Rosenblatt of the Mississippi College School of Law, Paul Mahoney, and Risa Goluboff of the University of Virginia Law School gave me institutional support while I worked on this project, for which I am grateful.

A number of very generous historians from around the country offered invaluable feedback, including Bill Blair, Al Brophy, Kris Collins, Laura Edwards, John Gordan, Mark Graber, Sally Hadden, Taja-Nia Henderson, Morton Horwitz, Tim Huebner, Carrie Janney, Kelly Kennington, Elizabeth Leonard, Jon Lurie, Maeva Marcus, Patti Minter, Nick Parrillo, Mike Ross, David Seipp, Jed Shugerman, Barbara Welke, Jim Whitman, Diana Williams, Owen Williams, and John Fabian Witt. Pamela Haag helped me to restructure the book completely – at a time when I felt hopelessly stuck. She also helped me to write like my best (nonlawyer) self. I will be forever grateful.

It is truly a joy to work among a group of such talented legal historians as the ones at UVA. I am proud – and a little awed – that my colleagues include Ted White, Paul Halliday, Gordon Hylton, Molly Brady, Jessica Lowe, and Risa Goluboff. Jessica Lowe has proven to be a great friend and colleague, particularly during the year I visited at UVA. I don't think I have ever learned more (or had more fun) than when we taught the American Legal History course together. When I started teaching, the legal history circle at UVA also included Chuck McCurdy. As one of my advisers, Chuck nurtured this project when it was nothing more than the germ of a wacky idea. I am certain that Chuck didn't know quite what to make of me, a student who insisted on writing about secession and state sovereignty ideology at every turn. Chuck advised my undergraduate thesis long before he was saddled – a second time – with Jefferson Davis and secessionist theory, this time in extended dissertation form. But I would not be moved, and Chuck always encouraged me. He believed in my ability to say something new and interesting, however provocative. Chuck's only benchmark was the quality of the work, and for that I am more thankful than I can say.

Beyond the inner circle of legal historians, my colleagues at UVA Law School proved to be no less helpful. George Rutherglen read the entire manuscript and offered invaluable advice about how to make the prose more literary. If the reader encounters a felicitous phrase in the book, it is likely due either to pure happenstance or to George. Ruth Mason helped me to find a title, a task with which I had been struggling for years. I had quite despaired of finding one I could live with, until her intervention. Kerry Abrams, Barb Armacost, Charles Barzun, Michael Collins, Anne Coughlin, Ashley Deeks, John Duffy, Kim Ferzan, Kim Forde-Mazrui, Brandon Garrett, Rachel Harmon, Andrew Hayashi, Debbie Hellman, Toby Heytens, Julia Mahoney, Dan Ortiz, Mildred Robinson, Rich Schragger, John Setear, Mila Versteeg, Annie Woolhandler, and George Yin offered invaluable support and advice along the way.

A great many archivists and librarians helped me to piece this story together. There are far too many for me to name, but Lynda Crist at the Papers of Jefferson Davis at Rice University and John Coski at the Museum of the Confederacy deserve special thanks. At UVA, Leslie Ashbrook and Loren Moulds went above and beyond when I was in the final stages of manuscript production. Barbie Selby and Allison White helped me to track down many sources when I was a graduate student, and when I returned to UVA as a faculty member I quickly discovered that there is no better resource for a scholar than the wonderful – and legendary – team of UVA law reference librarians. Leslie Ashbrook, Ben Doherty, Kristin Glover, Micheal Klepper, Kent Olson, and Cathy Palombi helped me in countless ways. I owe a great debt to Stephen Parks of the Mississippi College Law Library – and now the chief law librarian of the state of Mississippi. Stephen is amazingly talented and this book would never have happened if not for his help. My thanks to all.

A group of fantastic research assistants, including Anna Casey, MO Eckel, Stephanie Evans, Carling Hughes, Gresham Kay, Jordan Naftalis, Ethan Scapellati, Caitlin Shea, and James West, contributed immensely to this book. Thanks also to my faculty assistants, Brenda Guy and Donna-Maria Green.

Many history professors at UVA nurtured this project, including Edward Ayers, Michael Holt, Joseph Kett, Duane Osheim, Peter Onuf, Sophie Rosenfeld, Mark Thomas, and Olivier Zunz. Other friends who helped with this project include Meredith Aden, Mike Caires, Allison Elias, Elizabeth Fitton, Shauna Hanley, Keith Harris, Christoph Henkel, Phillip Herrington, Bob Jackson, Jamila Jefferson-Jones, Larry Logue, Mason Lowe, Stephanie Hunter McMahon, Katy Meier, Victoria Meyer, Amanda Mushal, Sean Nalty, Scott Nesbit, Rob Rakove, Laura Phillips Sawyer, Logan Sawyer, Sarah Seo, Rachel Shelden, and Kid Wongshrichanalai.

Risa Goluboff read the manuscript – in its entirety – several times: once when it was an unwieldy dissertation, and again (and then again) when it was a slightly-more-wieldy book manuscript. Risa's comments were always astute, and the answers to her insightful queries revealed themselves in stages. Risa's comments are the kind you cannot absorb all at once, because she understands your project better than you do yourself. I owe her an immense debt; a number of the hard-won revelations I achieved in rewriting the manuscript are due to her input. She is, quite simply, the best reader I have ever had, which doesn't bode well for her ability to avoid my manuscripts in the future.

Sally Gordon is also this kind of reader. Completing the manuscript under Sally's editorship at Cambridge University Press was a challenge (in the best sense) and a joy. She was both patient and encouraging. When we started working together, I did not see the potential good book lurking in the dissertation. Let's just say I was resigned to the idea that the book would be a mess – I thought I was destined to be vaguely unhappy with it. Sally helped me to see its potential, and to deepen the book's insights at times when I thought that I had wrested everything I could from the material. Sally helped me to uncover hidden layers.

My largest debt is owed to my adviser (and now colleague), Gary Gallagher. I am sure that when I was student, I was unable to appreciate how rare it is to have someone like him in my corner. He insisted that I challenge the established wisdom. He taught me to trust what I saw in the archives rather than in the historiography, and to ignore the trendy and listen instead to my own voice. What he valued was boldness, accuracy, and diligent research. These have been my touchstones. Whatever else one can say about *Secession on Trial*, it is not derivative, and that is due to Gary's influence.

This book is dedicated to my parents, Robert and Eleanor Nicoletti. My interest in the constitutional history of the Civil War – and in secessionist thought – took hold when I was in high school. This was decidedly weird, since I was a New Yorker whose first American relatives arrived in the United States in the decade after the Civil War's conclusion. I was also a girl. The interest took hold nonetheless, and my parents encouraged it even when they did not fully understand it. They were the first ones who believed in me, and their belief persisted even when circumstances probably did not warrant it. But that's the way it is with parents, and I am grateful for their love and support.

Introduction

> The inherent inconsistency of a double allegiance has always shown itself
> as soon as stern and testing cases have presented themselves.
>
> – Francis Lieber, "Amendments to the Constitution," 1865

A scant three months after the conclusion of the Civil War, New York
legal scholar John Codman Hurd wrote his friend Francis Lieber, a
prominent law and political science professor at Columbia University,
to complain that the "defeated" principle of states' rights continued
to stalk national politics. Hurd warned, "It looks as if the question
of State Rights in our practical politics [is] about to make new trouble."[1] Three years later, the two correspondents still feared that the
specter of state sovereignty would rise to plague the nation again.[2]
Lieber had recently given a number of talks extolling the virtues of a
powerful national government but feared that his speeches had fallen

---

[1] John C. Hurd to Francis Lieber, July 23, 1865, Box 12, Francis Lieber Papers,
Huntington Library, San Marino, CA (repository hereafter cited as HEHL). Originally
from Boston, Hurd had moved to New York, where he authored a famous treatise on the law of slavery, published in 1858. *Dictionary of American Biography*
(New York: Scribner's, 1928).

[2] The terminology about federalism in the nineteenth century is often frustratingly
vague. Michael Les Benedict equates the term "state sovereignty" with the compact theory of the Union, but a belief in state sovereignty is not incompatible with
the idea that the national government is also sovereign. See Michael Les Benedict,
"Preserving Federalism: Reconstruction and the Waite Court," *Supreme Court
Review*, 1978: 39, 41.

on deaf ears.[3] He told Hurd frankly, "I wholly agree with you that we have to go through that whole struggle and plague of that abominable state-rights fudge again. Every one must do his part. My son writes to me from New Orleans that literally people who are not for worshipping state sovereignty are looked upon as benighted fools." Given this state of affairs, Lieber urged Hurd to publish works that promoted the national government, believing that such public discourse was necessary to convince the American people to embrace a vigorous nationalism. Most white Southerners, and even many Northerners, according to Lieber, still needed to be convinced to abandon their belief in state sovereignty.[4]

New York attorney and diarist George Templeton Strong agreed with Lieber. He set forth in his diary his worry that ex-Confederates had not yielded in their adherence to state sovereignty and secession. Strong even feared the possibility of another Southern secession and attendant war. Strong wrote, "The First Southern War may prove not the last," and he predicted that "there may well be another sectional war within three years." To combat this tendency toward disintegration, Strong recommended a harsh program of Reconstruction, one that would not be constrained by constitutional niceties. "We must not be too nice and scrupulous about the Constitution in dealing with these barbaric, half-subdued rebel communities," he wrote, "or we shall soon find that there is no Constitution left."[5] As Lieber, Hurd, and Strong feared in the uncertain aftermath of the Civil War, the war itself had not entirely routed the spirit of secessionism in the United States.

Historians have debated the extent to which the Civil War transformed the antebellum federal system, but they have universally assumed that the war led inexorably to the demise of secession as a constitutional argument. While most historians have acknowledged that a robust debate about the nature of the Union and the ultimate locus of sovereignty flourished in American political discourse until

[3] See Frank Friedel, *Francis Lieber: Nineteenth-Century Liberal* (Baton Rouge: Louisiana State University Press, 1947), 387–417.
[4] Francis Lieber to John C. Hurd, August 10, 1868, John Codman Hurd Papers, Boston Athenaeum, Boston.
[5] George Templeton Strong, *Diary of George Templeton Strong*, ed. Allan Nevins and Milton Halsey Thomas, 4 vols. (New York: Macmillan, 1952), 4: 92, 99, 75.

1861, historians and legal scholars have long asserted that the doctrine of state secession immediately vanished from public dialogue with the triumph of the Union army at Appomattox.[6] James McPherson, for example, wrote that although historians debate the larger meaning of the war, "certain large consequences of the war seem clear. Secession and slavery were killed, never to be revived during the century and a quarter since Appomattox." Beginning with the first professional histories of the Civil War, historians have contended that the Civil War foreclosed any future debate about secession's constitutionality.[7] The death of secession at Appomattox has become something of an adage in historical writing, often baldly declared in a throwaway line or

---

[6] There is some disagreement among scholars on the pre-war status of secession arguments. See, e.g., Samuel H. Beer, *To Make a Nation: The Rediscovery of American Federalism* (Cambridge, MA: Belknap Press of Harvard University Press, 1993).

[7] James M. McPherson, *Battle Cry of Freedom* (New York: Oxford University Press, 1988), 859. Further examples are essentially everywhere. See, e.g., William A. Dunning, *Essays on the Civil War and Reconstruction* (New York: Macmillan, 1898), 304; John W. Burgess, *Reconstruction and the Constitution, 1866–1876* (New York: Scribner's, 1905), 54; James G. Randall, *Constitutional Problems under Lincoln* (1926; repr., Urbana: University of Illinois Press, 1964), 522; Andrew C. McLaughlin, *A Constitutional History of the United States* (New York: Appleton-Century, 1936), vii; Harold M. Hyman, *A More Perfect Union: The Impact of the Civil War and Reconstruction on the Constitution* (Boston: Houghton Mifflin, 1975), 284–85, 368; Kenneth Stampp, "The Concept of a Perpetual Union," *Journal of American History* 65 (June 1978): 5, 6; Brooks D. Simpson, *America's Civil War* (Wheeling, IL: Harlan Davidson, 1996), 4, 217; Phillip S. Paludan, *A Covenant with Death: The Constitution, Law, and Equality in the Civil War Era* (Urbana: University of Illinois Press, 1975), 98, 225; Alfred H. Kelly, Winfred A. Harbison, and Herman Belz, *The American Constitution: Its Origins and Development* (New York: W. W. Norton, 1991), 317; Arthur J. Jacobson, Bernhard Schlink, and Virginia Cooper, *Weimar: A Jurisprudence of Crisis* (Berkeley: University of California Press, 2000), 217; Bernard Schwartz, *From Confederation to Nation: The American Constitution, 1835–1877* (Baltimore: Johns Hopkins University Press, 1973), 133; Bernard Schwartz, *A History of the Supreme Court* (Oxford: Oxford University Press, 1993), 134; Bernard Schwartz, *A Commentary on the Constitution of the United States*, 5 vols. (New York: Macmillan, 1963), 1: 41; Bruce Ackerman, *We the People: Transformations*, 2 vols. (Cambridge, MA: Belknap Press of Harvard University Press, 1998), 2: 22; Daniel Farber, *Lincoln's Constitution* (Chicago: University of Chicago Press, 2003), 78; Michael Stokes Paulsen, "The Civil War as Constitutional Interpretation," *University of Chicago Law Review* 71 (Spring 2004): 716; Akhil Amar, "Of Sovereignty and Federalism," *Yale Law Journal* 96 (June 1987): 1512 n. 341 and accompanying text. See also Norman W. Spaulding, "Constitution as Countermonument: Federalism, Reconstruction, and the Problem of Collective Memory," *Columbia Law Review* 103 (December 2003): 2019; Daniel Elazar, "Civil War and the Preservation of American Federalism," *Publius* 1 (1971): 47, 56.

treated as an unspoken assumption that nonetheless undergirds the analysis but never thoroughly examined.

Scholars of the period have wrangled over the degree of change occasioned by the Civil War, primarily focusing their attention on the formal transfer of governmental authority from the states to the nation that occurred with the ratification of the postwar constitutional amendments.[8] If debate about the extent to which the Civil War altered the antebellum federal system has flourished, scholars have taken it as given that, at the very least, the war unequivocally established the unconstitutionality of the extreme state sovereignty position espoused by the defeated Confederates. In their account, the nation that emerged out of the Civil War was at least assured of its basic integrity.

Drawing on the insights of constitutional scholars, other historians have argued that the Civil War established a united, fully grown, and powerfully aggressive American nation, one that "emerged from the war with a confirmed sense of destiny."[9] Robert Wiebe's classic Progressive Era synthesis, *The Search for Order*, tellingly described the "true legacy of the war" as a "new United States, stretched from ocean to ocean, filled out, and bound together [that] had miraculously appeared" as a result of the war.[10] Under this interpretation, the Civil

---

[8] Most of these battles are about change and continuity and the degree to which the postbellum constitutional amendments were "radical" or "conservative." See Hyman, *A More Perfect Union*; Michael Les Benedict, *Preserving the Constitution: Essays on Politics and the Constitution in the Reconstruction Era* (New York: Fordham University Press, 2006); Michael Les Benedict, *A Compromise of Principle: Congressional Republicans and Reconstruction, 1863–1869* (New York: W. W. Norton, 1974); Michael Vorenberg, *Final Freedom: The Civil War, the Abolition of Slavery, and the Thirteenth Amendment* (Cambridge: Cambridge University Press, 2001), 109–10, 132–35; Ackerman, *We the People*; Herman Belz, *Emancipation and Equal Rights: Politics and Constitutionalism in the Civil War Era* (New York: W. W. Norton, 1978); Paludan, *A Covenant with Death*; Robert Kaczorowski, "To Begin the Nation Anew: Congress, Citizenship, and Civil Rights after the Civil War," and Robert Kaczorowski, "Revolutionary Constitutionalism in the Era of the Civil War and Reconstruction," *New York University Law Review* 61 (1986): 863. Historian G. Edward White noted recently that this debate still dominates the field. G. Edward White, *Law in American History, Volume II: From Reconstruction through the 1920s* (New York: Oxford University Press, 2016), 7.

[9] Robert Penn Warren, *The Legacy of the Civil War* (New York: Random House, 1961), 46.

[10] Robert H. Wiebe, *The Search for Order, 1877–1920* (New York: Hill and Wang, 1967), 11. This is a dominant theme in scholarship about the legacy of the Civil War. See Charles Royster, *The Destructive War: William Tecumseh Sherman, Stonewall Jackson, and the Americans* (New York: Knopf, 1991), 371; Richard

War created a new America, one empowered by its triumph over the forces of disintegration.

This book has a different story to tell. The Civil War did not definitively resolve the question of secession's constitutionality. The validity of secession remained at base a *legal* question, and in the war's immediate aftermath, Americans engaged in a national dialogue about whether they could permit the blunt instrument of military victory to substitute for the judgment of a court of law in resolving the issue. As Christopher Tomlins has argued, nineteenth-century Americans looked to the law as their source of stability and national purpose. By the beginning of the century, "law [had become] *the* paradigmatic discourse explaining life in America, the principal source of life's 'facts.' "[11] The Civil War shook Americans' belief in the primacy of the rule of law to its foundations.[12] In the months following the war's conclusion, the U.S. government sought to mitigate the war's disruption of the regular legal process by selecting a test case that would provide a final determination of secession's constitutionality and the war's legitimacy.

The case selected was a high-profile one that would capture the attention of the nation: Confederate president Jefferson Davis's treason prosecution. The government could easily make out a prima facie case that Davis had committed treason by levying war against the United States. It was widely anticipated that Davis would defend his suit by arguing that the secession of his home state of Mississippi had

Bensel, *Yankee Leviathan: The Origins of Central State Authority in America, 1859–1877* (Cambridge: Cambridge University Press, 1990), 2; Heather Cox Richardson, *West from Appomattox: The Reconstruction of America after the Civil War* (New Haven: Yale University Press, 2007), 31, 37, 39; George Frederickson, *The Inner Civil War: Northern Intellectuals and the Crisis of the Union* (New York: Harper Torchbooks, 1965); Louis Menand, *The Metaphysical Club* (New York: Farrar, Straus and Giroux, 2001), x; McPherson, *Battle Cry of Freedom*, 859.

[11] Christopher L. Tomlins, *Law, Labor, and Ideology in the Early American Republic* (Cambridge: Cambridge University Press, 1993), 21. See also Perry Miller, *The Life of the Mind in America: From the Revolution to the Civil War* (New York: Harcourt, Brace & World, 1965); Laura F. Edwards, *The People and Their Peace* (Chapel Hill: University of North Carolina Press, 2009), 66–67, particularly n. 4, noting the dominance of legal thought in the South.

[12] See William Wiecek, *The Lost World of Classical Legal Thought: Law and Ideology in America, 1886–1937* (New York: Oxford University Press, 1998), 79; Phillip S. Paludan, "The American Civil War Considered as a Crisis in Law and Order," *American Historical Review* 77 (October 1972): 1013.

removed his U.S. citizenship and his duty of loyalty to the Union, thus rendering him incapable of committing treason against the United States. His conviction would definitively resolve the secession issue in the Union's favor.

And yet Davis was never tried. Neither Davis nor any other Confederate was punished for treason following the Civil War. Davis's fate was constantly discussed in the newspapers, and the American public – and indeed the wider world – saw his case as the forum in which secession, the "great question of the war," would receive a legal hearing.[13] The government and the other actors in Davis's case operated against a backdrop of intense public scrutiny. Because of the high profile of the case, the United States government proceeded cautiously, wanting to ensure that the verdict would be seen as a legitimate legal pronouncement on treason and the right of secession. Over the angry objections of many in Congress, the Johnson administration – on the advice of Attorney General James Speed – refused to relax any of the procedural rules governing the conduct of federal criminal trials. Speed worried about the disruptive effect of the war and would not tinker with the rule of law. In his opinion, altering the legal system during this vulnerable period merely to ensure the proper outcome in the Davis case would unmoor the United States from its foundations. For this reason, Speed rejected the possibility of conducting Davis's trial before a military commission and instead determined to hold trial before a federal jury in the place where Davis had committed his crimes: the former Confederate capital of Richmond, Virginia.[14]

Once it was decided that Davis's trial was to take place in Richmond, it became increasingly clear that the government would face considerable trouble convicting Davis on a treason charge. Trusting Davis's fate to a Virginia jury was an invitation to jury nullification. Federal jurors were required to swear unbroken loyalty to the United States, and Davis's federal jury pool was the first in American history to include African Americans. Still, there could be no guarantee that Confederate sympathizers would not find their way onto the jury and refuse to convict their former president. Instead of supplying a legal endorsement of the Union's victory, Davis's case could provide a backdoor vindication

---

[13] Quotation is from the *New York Times*, February 9, 1867.
[14] This was constitutionally required. U.S. Const. art. III, § 2; amend. VI.

of the right of secession and thus undercut the results of the war. As the possibility of ensuring the proper outcome in Davis's case seemed more remote, the government's attorneys groped for a way to avoid the issue of secession in Davis's case without signaling to the country that they feared putting him on trial. They opted for delay, hoping that a solution would somehow present itself.

Davis's attorneys were equally hesitant about forcing the case to come to trial, knowing that not only the principle of secession but also their client's life would be at stake.[15] At the same time, they sought to turn the government's concerns about secession's possible vindication to their own advantage. To induce the government to drop the prosecution, they overstated their own confidence in winning an acquittal. Chief Justice Salmon P. Chase, who presided over the federal circuit court in Richmond, along with District Judge John C. Underwood, seemed similarly reluctant to entrust Davis's fate to a jury. With all parties equally determined not to proceed to trial, the case dragged on without resolution for almost four years, until Davis's attorneys moved to quash the indictment in December 1868 on the grounds that the newly ratified Fourteenth Amendment barred the prosecution of Confederate officials for treason. When the two judges split on the merits of the defense's argument, the question was certified to the Supreme Court for resolution. Later that month, however, President Andrew Johnson issued a universal amnesty proclamation, relieving all former Confederates from prosecution. Accordingly, the momentous issues of Davis's treason and the legitimacy of the Confederate war effort were left unsettled precisely because their resolution might prove so explosive. Just a few months later, the Supreme Court

---

[15] In advancing this argument, I depart from most writing about Davis's case. In a true "Lost Cause" vein, many writers have emphasized that Davis himself wanted to see his case go to trial to vindicate the principle of secession. See Lloyd T. Everett, "The 'Case of Jefferson Davis': Why No Trial," *Tyler's Quarterly Magazine and Genealogical Magazine* 29 (1947): 94, 110–14; Horace Henry Hagan, "United States vs. Jefferson Davis," *Sewanee Review Quarterly* 25 (1917): 220; Eberhard P. Deutsch, "*United States v. Jefferson Davis*: Constitutional Issues in the Trial for Treason," *American Bar Association Journal* 52 (February 1966): 139, and *American Bar Association Journal* 52 (March 1966): 263, 264 [two parts]; Charles Adams, *When in the Course of Human Events: Arguing the Case for Southern Secession* (Lanham, MO: Rowman & Littlefield, 2000); Charles M. Blackford, *The Trial and Trials of Jefferson Davis: Paper Read to the Virginia Bar Association* (Richmond, VA: John T. West, 1900), 39.

delivered a perfunctory pronouncement against the constitutionality of secession in a far less volatile context, quietly declaring the nation to be "an indestructible Union composed of indestructible states" in *Texas v. White,* a case involving the repayment of government bonds.[16]

As the public, both North and South, regarded Davis as a symbol of the defeated Confederacy, Davis's guilt or innocence would have stood as a pronouncement on the legality of secession and the worthiness of the Confederate cause.[17] His case had the potential to undercut the moral weight of Union victory. It could have disturbed the verdict of the war.

My analysis of the Davis case focuses not on Davis himself but on the lawyers who participated in it, both on the side of the prosecution and on the defense. The eventual determination of Davis's fate owed much to the wrangling of the primary attorneys who labored on his case: William Evarts and Richard Henry Dana for the prosecution, and Charles O'Conor for the defense. Distracted by other, more promising career opportunities and unnerved by the possibility of secession's vindication, which only seemed to increase with the passage of time, lead prosecutor William Evarts failed to take charge of the prosecution and instead tried to extricate himself from the miserable business of serving as counsel of record in a potentially catastrophic case. O'Conor, by contrast, feigned confidence in secession's vindication in order to increase the pressure on the prosecution. As these lawyers shaped and reacted against developments in the trial to ensure the best possible outcome for their clients, their interaction and maneuvering provides a window onto the operations of high-level attorneys in nineteenth-century America. By focusing on Evarts's and O'Conor's litigation strategy and its day-to-day unfolding and progression, this book demonstrates how smart and aggressive lawyering outside the courtroom worked to Davis's advantage. Embedded in my analysis is an argument for the centrality of the strengths and foibles of individual

---

[16] Texas v. White, 74 U.S. 700 (1868).

[17] See Anne Sarah Rubin, *A Shattered Nation: The Rise and Fall of the Confederacy, 1861–1868* (Chapel Hill: University of North Carolina Press, 2005), 201–7, discussing Davis's image as a martyr for the defeated Confederacy; Carl Schurz, *Reminiscences of Carl Schurz,* ed. Frederic Bancroft and William A. Dunning, 3 vols. (Garden City, NY: Doubleday, Page, 1907), 3: 143; Nina Silber, *Romance of Reunion* (Chapel Hill: University of North Carolina Press, 1993), 29.

lawyers, as well as that of larger social and legal forces, in resolving the constitutionality of secession.

As much as this book focuses on secession and the legal significance of the Civil War, it takes place during Reconstruction and explains how secession's murky legal status became intimately bound up with the shaky theoretical foundations of Reconstruction policy.[18] Maintaining a federal military presence in order to protect the rights of freedpeople in the former Confederate states seemingly transgressed the constitutional limits on federal authority over state affairs. Military Reconstruction was premised on the idea that the rebellion had disrupted the normal constitutional status of the Southern states within the Union. As some legal theorists argued, Union victory entitled the federal government to treat the states of the former Confederacy like conquered provinces. Conquest could be effected only if the Southern states had managed to remove themselves from the federal Union and had constituted a separate nation during the war. Such a theory seemed tacitly to endorse secession, and many Americans believed that the U.S. government would have to abandon its military Reconstruction policy if it hoped to establish the illegality of secession. Indeed, the leading proponent of "Radical Reconstruction" and the conquest theory of Reconstruction, Congressman Thaddeus Stevens, lent credence to this argument.[19] He offered to represent Davis in his treason trial

[18] For more on the different theories on which Reconstruction was premised, see Eric L. McKitrick, *Andrew Johnson and Reconstruction* (Chicago: University of Chicago Press, 1960); Burgess, *Reconstruction and the Constitution*; Benedict, *Preserving the Constitution*; Gregory Downs, *After Appomattox* (Cambridge, MA: Harvard University Press, 2015).

[19] Radical Reconstruction, implemented by the "Radical" wing of the Republican Party after it wrested power from the president, was the most far-reaching and racially egalitarian program of Reconstruction put forth in the post–Civil War period. Unlike President Johnson's far more limited plan to readmit the states of the former Confederacy to the Union without fundamentally overhauling their social structure, the Radical Republicans intended to dismantle white supremacy and possibly redistribute property from former masters to former slaves through the Reconstruction process. Owing to its ambitious scope, Radical Reconstruction also disrupted the ordinary operation of the federal system in the United States by placing the states of the former Confederacy under the direct military supervision of the federal government. This aspect of the Radicals' plan was known as "military Reconstruction" – the product of four Military Reconstruction Acts passed over President Johnson's veto beginning in March 1867. These topics will be explored in greater depth in Chapter 8.

in the hope that a vindication of secession would, ironically, act to strengthen the theoretical basis of Radical Reconstruction.

In the aftermath of the American Civil War, Americans engaged in an ongoing public debate about the validity of permitting the outcome of a war to substitute for a legal judgment on the constitutionality of secession. For many Americans, both Northern and Southern, the Civil War exposed the troubling thinness of the nation's commitment to the rule of law and revealed that Americans were willing to betray their most deeply held beliefs in order to guard against the disintegration of the Union. The war seemed to demonstrate that the ordinary legal process was too narrow to provide a definitive resolution of the most deeply divisive and most important legal disputes in American society. The most difficult questions were simply too volatile to be contained in a court of law. For others, the war served as the most active – and therefore the most legitimate – means of constitution making in a democratic society, as the people of the United States had put their very lives on the line for the vindication of Unionist or secessionist principles. If the judgment of a court of law could be permitted to overturn the victory sealed by the death of 700,000 men, they had no way to make sense of the suffering occasioned by the war.[20]

Although the Civil War had surely substituted violence for the calm and deliberative processes of law, it had also involved the people in the lawmaking process in an immediate and tangible way.[21] Nineteenth-century Americans remained despondent about the implications of war as law, even though they recognized that the Civil War had functioned as a form of lawmaking, the ultimate method of "popular constitutionalism." The national conversation about the meaning of the Civil War and its resolution of the secession issue forced Americans

---

[20] On efforts to make sense of the suffering and death brought on by the war, see Drew G. Faust, *This Republic of Suffering: Death and the American Civil War* (New York: Knopf, 2008); Royster, *The Destructive War*; and, in a roundabout way, James Q. Whitman, *The Verdict of Battle: The Law of Victory and the Making of Modern War* (Cambridge, MA: Harvard University Press, 2012).

[21] For more on popular constitutionalism, see Ackerman, *We the People*; Larry D. Kramer, *The People Themselves: Popular Constitutionalism and Judicial Review* (Oxford: Oxford University Press, 2004); Daniel Hamilton, "Popular Constitutionalism in the Civil War: A Trial Run," *Chicago-Kent Law Review* 81 (2006): 979. My assessment of popular constitutionalism through the mechanism of civil war is far less sanguine than these treatments.

to confront the unsettling realization that they had allowed a violent conflict to provide the final determination of the most divisive legal issue in their society.[22]

In telling this story of secession's lingering postwar career, this book focuses on a wider and less well known cast of characters than those who populate most constitutional histories of the period. Many of the protagonists of this story were not in political power, and they challenged the Unionist point of view. I also seek to broaden our traditional focus on the courts and Congress, as the major actors in this book are lawyers, scholars, thinkers, and members of the general public. By expanding the scope of the study to include others besides the Republicans in the halls of Congress and on the Supreme Court, a far murkier and less straightforward picture emerges of the war's immediate significance.

The nation that came out of the chaos of the Civil War was mired in doubt and uncertainty about its future. In 1860, at the start of the war, the nation had been only eighty years removed from the Revolution. The United States was still very much an experiment and the Union fragile. Although only Southerners had actually attempted secession, other plans to break the Union apart circulated in American political discourse. Rumors spread of plots to annex Canada, to break off the western states to form a separate confederacy, and to form an independent nation in the Midwest. New York City mayor Fernando Wood advocated the city's secession from both the state and the nation, and other New Yorkers pressed for the secession and subsequent confederation of New York and New Jersey.[23] The Civil War demonstrated the federal government's willingness to keep the Union together at all costs, but military victory alone did not silence all concerns about the permanency of the American political arrangement. The war's meaning became fully apparent only with the passage of time, and Americans would continue to work out its larger significance in the decades to come.

---

[22] See Whitman, *Verdict of Battle*, for a discussion of how war functioned as a method of lawmaking throughout history. Whitman counts the Civil War as a turning point in the history of warfare. For more on this topic, see Chapter 4.

[23] See Cynthia Nicoletti, "The New York City Secession Movement," master's thesis, University of Virginia, 2004; Cynthia Nicoletti, "Reimagining the Union: Centralization, Balance, and the Forces of History in the Aftermath of the Civil War" (in press).

Scholarly attention to the Davis case and its potential to undermine the outcome of the Civil War has been surprisingly minimal, given the importance of the issue.[24] The explanation for this is twofold. First, most historians who have written about the legal history of the Civil War have approached the legal questions raised throughout the war from a legal realist perspective. Most of the existing literature treats law as though it *has* to derive ineluctably from politics, particularly when it comes to a political event so cataclysmic as the Civil War. From a modern, realist perspective, all law is endlessly manipulable and simply reifies political determinations. In the aftermath of the war, Americans engaged in a national discussion about the relationship between law and politics, and they were conflicted about how and whether the law should merely reflect the results of the battlefield. They both strategically deployed *and* believed themselves to be constrained by law. As this book will reveal, nineteenth-century

---

[24] See Roy F. Nichols, "United States vs. Jefferson Davis, 1865–1869," *American Historical Review* 31 (January 1926): 266, 267. Nichols's wonderfully rich article traces delays in the prosecution of the case but generally does not connect the case to the larger issues it implicated. See also John Fabian Witt, *Lincoln's Code: The Laws of War in American History* (New York: Free Press, 2012), chapter 10; Charles Fairman, *Reconstruction and Reunion*, 2 vols. (New York: Macmillan, 1971), 1: 607–12; William A. Blair, *Why Didn't the North Hang Some Rebels?* (Milwaukee: Marquette University Press, 2004); William A. Blair, *With Malice toward Some: Treason and Loyalty in the Civil War Era* (Chapel Hill: University of North Carolina Press, 2014), particularly chapter 8; Jonathan W. White, "The Trial of Jefferson Davis and the Americanization of Treason Law," in *Constitutionalism in the Approach and Aftermath of the Civil War*, ed. Paul D. Moreno and Johnathan O'Neill (New York: Fordham University Press, 2013); William J. Cooper, *Jefferson Davis, American* (New York: Vintage Books, 2000), 576–626, all of which deal with the Davis case in some detail, but not its subversive potential. David W. Blight's *Race and Reunion: The Civil War in American Memory* (Cambridge, MA: Harvard University Press, 2001), 57–59, also discusses the efforts of Horace Greeley and other Northerners to secure Davis's release on bail, and Joan E. Cashin's *First Lady of the Confederacy: Varina Davis's Civil War* (Cambridge, MA: Belknap Press of Harvard University Press, 2006) touches briefly on Varina Davis's clever, unstinting, and ultimately successful efforts to ensure Davis's freedom. Other works that touch on the possible endorsement of secession in Davis's case are unfortunately informed by a strong Lost Cause sensibility, which leads the authors to begin with the presumption of secession's constitutionality and the illegitimacy of the Union war effort. See Adams, *When in the Course of Human Events*, 178, 185; Clint Johnson, *Pursuit: The Chase, Capture, Persecution, and Surprising Release of Confederate President Jefferson Davis* (New York: Citadel Press Books, 2008), 260–61; Thomas DiLorenzo, *The Real Lincoln: A New Look at Abraham Lincoln, His Agenda, and an Unnecessary War* (New York: Three Rivers Press, 2002).

Americans considered the law to be partially autonomous even in the aftermath of the Civil War. For them, it was not endlessly malleable. Second, there is something especially and persistently frightening about contemplating the possibility that the law might not match the results of the war in the volatile context of the secession issue. This has deterred and indeed continues to deter Americans from entertaining the notion that secession might have been legal. This book, 150 years after the war, raises questions that we still find uncomfortable to confront.

A word about structure: in telling this story, I proceed in roughly chronological fashion, tracing Jefferson Davis's trial from the call for his arrest in the spring of 1865 to the government's abandonment of his prosecution in 1869 and the Supreme Court's halfhearted effort to settle the secession question in *Texas v. White* in April of that year. The chronology unfolds more slowly in the earlier portions of the book, which focus on the complicated web of actors and events that surrounded Davis's trial in 1865, than it does in the later chapters. Interspersed throughout are several chapters (2, 4, 9, and 12) that are emphatically nonchronological and thus break the narrative. They do so for two distinct purposes. Chapters 2 and 9 provide backstory on the lawyers (Chapter 2) and judges (Chapter 9) involved in the Davis case. Chapters 4 and 12 pull back from the case itself to explore the larger questions of how Civil War–era Americans thought about the legitimacy of war as a method of legal adjudication (Chapter 4) and how Unionist legal thinkers sought to harmonize the decision to treat the Confederacy as a separate legal entity under international law with the illegitimacy of secession under the U.S. Constitution (Chapter 12).

Advocacy of secession was not a morally neutral position during the sectional crisis. Secessionist theory was inextricably bound up with white supremacy and racial hierarchy. Secessionists espoused theories of state sovereignty to insulate the institution of slavery and state-sponsored racial inequality from federal control. The secessionists chronicled in this book were, to a man, proponents of racial slavery and black inferiority. Secessionist theory and state sovereignty arguments were never advanced as merely academic positions: they were actively deployed to defend slavery. As Abraham Lincoln pointed out in 1861, slavery was indeed the cause of the conflict; and the state's right to define human beings as property was the only one that white Southerners sought to protect by seceding.[25]

But it is also important to recognize that secessionist theory was not *merely* an empty vessel into which racists channeled their venom. Southerners seized on state sovereignty ideology to present a legal theory that would prevent national interference with the state institution of slavery and the maintenance of white supremacy, but they came to believe in that theory in its own right.[26] In the course of repeatedly crafting and articulating proslavery arguments based on state sovereignty constitutionalism, secessionists came to believe deeply and sincerely in the desirability of limited government and the logic of the compact theory of the Union, even though these principles remained inextricably entangled with the issue of slavery.

There is no right of secession specified in the United States Constitution. Both secessionists and perpetual Unionists were able to agree on this much. But did the Constitution contain an implicit *legal* (i.e., nonrevolutionary) right permitting the states to withdraw from the federal government? Secessionists drew a sharp distinction between a right of revolution, a right held under natural law and therefore in some sense *extralegal*, and a right of secession, which they argued was granted by the U.S. Constitution – the foundational document of American government.[27] According to secessionist theory, the Union was a revocable compact, made by the ultimate political sovereign in

[25] See Abraham Lincoln, "First Inaugural Address" and "Second Inaugural Address," in Lincoln, *This Fiery Trial: The Speeches and Writings of Abraham Lincoln*, ed. William E. Gienapp (New York: Oxford University Press, 2002), 88, 220. A strain of historical argument insists that Northerners and Southerners also wrangled over economic issues such as the protective tariff, but the protectionist strategies to which Southerners objected in 1828 and again in 1860 also tracked slaveholding economic interests. See Frank Taussig, *The Tariff History of the United States* (New York: Putnam's Sons, 1910); Richard Ellis, *The Union at Risk: Jacksonian Democracy, States' Rights and the Nullification Crisis* (New York: Oxford University Press, 1987).

[26] Psychological studies confirm the intuition that individuals come to believe in the arguments they advance. See Daryl Bem, "An Experimental Analysis of Self Persuasion," *Journal of Experimental Psychology* 1 (1965): 199; Erwin Chemerinsky, "Protecting Lawyers from Their Profession: Redefining the Lawyer's Role," *Journal of the Legal Profession* 5 (1980): 31. My thanks to John Monahan for this citation.

[27] See Abraham Lincoln, Message to Congress, July 4, 1861, in Lincoln, *This Fiery Trial*, 101. Lincoln specifically denominated secession a revolutionary right.

the United States: not the states as corporate entities themselves but the people within their respective states. In their formulation, the federal Union was a government of limited powers, and it possessed only the authority granted by the Constitution. The remainder of sovereign authority was reserved to the states. The federal government was the creature of the states and existed only because it was useful for carrying out what the states could not accomplish individually: war and diplomacy, interstate and international commerce, the postal service, and the organization of federal territories. As the states – or more accurately, the people within the states – retained the ultimate authority in the United States, they could withdraw from the Union if and when the federal government transgressed the limits on its powers as granted by the Constitution.[28] Alternatively, they could simply exit when they believed that the Union no longer served their needs.

State sovereignty theorists argued that the right of secession was implicit in the Constitution and the circumstances surrounding its adoption. The states, they argued, had individually declared their independence and contracted to form an alliance that would help them fend off the British during the Revolution. This alliance became a formal Union with the adoption of the Articles of Confederation in 1781. The Articles affirmed that "each state retains its sovereignty, freedom, and independence," reserving to the states the powers not expressly delegated to the federal government. They also declared the Union formed under its auspices to be "perpetual."[29] When it became clear that the central government did not possess enough power to govern effectively, the states again convened, to write the Constitution. Although the delegates to the constitutional convention – representing the states in their individual capacities – were empowered only to modify the Articles, in Philadelphia they decided to make more radical changes and write an entirely new constitution. The new constitution, according to the secessionists, signified a new compact and a new Union, which still reserved all nondelegated powers to the states as the ultimate sovereign, but increased the powers of the general government.

---

[28] According to secessionists, Lincoln had exceeded the limits on federal power by rejecting the *Dred Scott* decision and pledging to outlaw slavery in the territories.
[29] Articles of Confederation of 1781, art. II, preamble.

The old Articles of Confederation had declared the Union formed thereunder to be perpetual, and secessionists argued that the states had seceded from the old Union to form the new compact under the new U.S. Constitution. Accordingly, despite the Articles' declaration of perpetuity, the people within the states, as the ultimate sovereign, had revoked their assent to the initial compact and formed another.

According to the secessionist formulation, the present Union was therefore *created* through secession. In support of the contention that the Articles of Confederation and the Constitution had formed two distinct American Unions, secessionists pointed out that under Article VII, the new Constitution became effective when ratified by nine of the thirteen states, forming a Union among the states so ratifying the same.[30] This clause underscored the point that the Union did not consist of the people of the United States as an aggregated whole, as the people of four of the states could remain separate from the other nine. Indeed, North Carolina and Rhode Island remained outside the Union for a year after the new Constitution went into effect. What was more, New York's ratifying convention declared that "the powers of the government may be reassumed by the people [presumably within the states], whensoever it shall become necessary to their happiness."[31] The Constitution was formed by the people within each individual state rather than in the aggregate, and since the Union had been formed by secession despite the Articles' declaration of the Union's perpetuity, the states could again secede whenever they so desired.[32]

[30] U.S. Const. art. VII.
[31] "Ratification of the Constitution by the State of New York," July 26, 1788, available at http://avalon.law.yale.edu/18th_century/ratny.asp (accessed November 1, 2016). This language would not necessarily support a right of secession. It could be read as permitting a right of revolution instead, as in the Declaration of Independence, which states that "whenever any form of government becomes destructive of these ends, it is the right of the people to alter or to abolish it." Declaration of Independence, para. 2 (U.S. 1776). But secessionists relied on it to argue that there was a reserved right to secede in the states. See Jefferson Davis, *Rise and Fall of the Confederate Government*, 2 vols. (New York: D. Appleton, 1881).
[32] This discussion of the right of secession is drawn primarily from Davis, *Rise and Fall*, 1: 86–168, and John C. Calhoun, "A Discourse on the Constitution and Government of the United States," in John C. Calhoun, *A Disquisition on Government and Selections from the Discourse* (Indianapolis: Hackett Publishing, 1995), 85–104. See also Alexander H. Stephens, *A Constitutional View of the Late War between the States*, 2 vols. (Philadelphia: National Publishing, 1868, 1870), and Albert T. Bledsoe, *Is Davis a Traitor?* (Baltimore: Innes and Company, 1866).

Perpetual Unionists contended instead that the ultimate sovereign in the United States was the people in the aggregate. As the nation's foremost perpetual Unionist thinker, Abraham Lincoln, stated in his first Inaugural Address, secession simply could not exist as a legal right, because "perpetuity is implied, if not expressed, in the fundamental law of all national governments." A nation, of necessity, could not contain the seeds of its own destruction and permit secession at will. Jurist Joseph Story reiterated this point, condemning "the baneful practice of secession, ... which is subversive of all the principles of order and regular government, and which leads directly to public convulsions, and the ruin of republican institutions."[33] Furthermore, even if the Union were a compact between states, it did not follow that one party to the compact could break it without the consent of the others. Perpetual Unionists rejected the theory that the states (or the people within their respective states) were the constituent sovereign in America. Rather, the people of the United States in the aggregate were the true sovereign; it was the people who had made both the federal and state governments to suit their needs.

Lincoln dismissed the theory that the Union formed under the Articles of Confederation constituted a distinct entity from the one that came into being with the ratification of the Constitution. The Articles had declared the Union to be perpetual, and the Constitution merely refined the government already in place, cementing "a more perfect Union." If the Constitution had contained a right of secession, thus permitting the compact to be broken, it would have rendered the Union *less* perfect than it had been under the Articles, "having lost the vital element of perpetuity." Lincoln and fellow perpetual Unionist Daniel Webster also spoke of the affective ties of Union, which served to bind the nation together. By the time of the Civil War, the Union was not just the product of logic; eighty years removed from the Revolution, it was a collectively imagined community.[34]

[33] Joseph Story, *Commentaries on the Constitution of the United States*, 3 vols. (Boston: Hilliard, Gray, 1833), 2: §833.

[34] Daniel Webster, "The Seventh of March Speech," March 7, 1850, available at www .dartmouth.edu/~dwebster/speeches/seventh-march.html (accessed April 12, 2017). See also Benedict Anderson, *Imagined Communities: Reflections on the Origin and Spread of Nationalism* (London: Verso, 1983); David Potter, "The Historian's Use of Nationalism and Vice Versa," *American Historical Review* 67 (1962): 924.

The debate over the ultimate locus of sovereignty and the existence of the states' right to withdraw from the Union surfaced in several significant crises during the antebellum period.[35] By 1860, however, states' rights arguments were almost exclusively associated with the protection of Southern proslavery interests.[36] Lincoln's election in the fall of that year on a platform that pledged to halt slavery's expansion touched off a firestorm of secession.[37]

Led by South Carolina, eleven Southern states seceded from the Union and formed an independent Confederacy in 1860 and 1861, leading directly to civil war. Animated by a widespread Southern secession movement to preserve the institution of slavery, the war demonstrated Northerners' commitment to maintain the Union intact.[38] Nevertheless, it remained necessary for Northerners and Southerners to determine the war's ultimate legal significance in the wake of Union military victory.

In 1865, Americans were unsure whether Union victory in the field would stand as the definitive pronouncement of secession's illegality or whether Davis's case would provide an alternate answer to that question.

[35] These included the passage of the Virginia and Kentucky Resolutions in 1798–99, the Hartford Convention in 1814, the Nullification Crisis in 1832–33, and the decades-long struggle over federal power to ban slavery in the territories. There is a vast literature here; good basic works include Don E. Fehrenbacher, *Constitutions and Constitutionalism in the Slaveholding South* (Athens: University of Georgia Press, 1989); Stampp, "The Concept of a Perpetual Union"; Harold M. Hyman and William M. Wiecek, *Equal Justice under Law: Constitutional Development, 1835–1875* (New York: Harper & Row, 1982); Paul Finkelman, *An Imperfect Union: Slavery, Federalism, and Comity* (Chapel Hill: University of North Carolina Press, 1981).

[36] This book points to several counterexamples, however, including efforts by antislavery activists to enact personal liberty laws in Northern states and the proslavery arguments in *Lemmon v. People*, advocating for a national right of transit (with one's slaves) through a free state; see Chapter 2.

[37] Republican Party Platform of 1860, § 8, in *National Party Platforms*, ed. Kirk H. Porter (New York: Macmillan, 1924), 55. See also Dwight Dumond, ed., *Southern Editorials on Secession* (New York: Century, 1931), and Howard Perkins, ed., *Northern Editorials on Secession*, 2 vols. (Gloucester, MA: Peter Smith, 1964). Secessionists believed that the federal government could not limit slavery in the territories, because in doing so the federal government would promote the interests of some of the states at the expense of the others. The federal government was merely the agent of the sovereign states, as *Dred Scott* had established. See Dred Scott v. Sandford, 60 U.S. 393, 448 (1857).

[38] See Gary W. Gallagher, *The Union War* (Cambridge, MA: Harvard University Press, 2011).

The war had prevented the disintegration of the Union, but many feared that the "verdict" of the war would not survive a legal challenge in a regularly constituted court of law. The nation had yet to determine what the final legal settlement of Appomattox would be. In the pages that follow, we will rediscover how that process took place.

I

The Imprisoner's Dilemma

The Union army reached the Confederate capital of Richmond on April 2, 1865, a Sunday. Jefferson Davis, the president of the Confederacy, received the news of the city's imminent collapse while worshipping at St. Paul's Church. Davis fled the city and traveled south, hoping to reach Texas and then begin a phase of nontraditional guerrilla warfare against the Union forces. Davis never made it to Texas, however. Events outpaced him. As he made his way south, Davis received word of Robert E. Lee's surrender at Appomattox – and later, of President Abraham Lincoln's assassination at Ford's Theatre. Thereafter, an angry nation was out for blood. The Bureau of Military Justice, headed by Judge Advocate General Joseph Holt, hastily convened a military commission to unravel the conspiracy to assassinate the president. The new president, Andrew Johnson, accused Davis, Alabama senator Clement Clay, and other Confederate officials of involvement in the plot and put a price on their heads.[1]

Federal cavalrymen caught up with Davis in Irwinville, Georgia, on May 10. His surrender was ignominious, to say the least. For the rest of his life Davis was dogged by reports that he had been captured

---

[1] Presidential Proclamation 131, May 2, 1865, in Andrew Johnson, *The Papers of Andrew Johnson*, ed. Paul Bergeron, 16 vols. (Knoxville: University of Tennessee Press, 1967–69), 8: 15–16. See also *New York Times*, May 26, 1865; William J. Cooper, *Jefferson Davis, American* (New York: Vintage Books, 2000) 374–75; Varina Davis, *Jefferson Davis, Ex-President of the Confederate States: A Memoir*, 2 vols. (New York: Belford, 1890), 2: 582–635; Jefferson Davis, *Rise and Fall of the Confederate Government*, 2 vols. (New York: Appleton, 1881), 2: 701–2.

FIGURE 1.1 Jefferson Davis in his cell at Fort Monroe. Library of Congress.

while trying to escape disguised in women's clothing, which he passionately and repeatedly disputed. Once in federal custody, Davis was transported by rail and then by boat to a federal prison at Fort Monroe, Virginia (Figure 1.1). Conditions at the prison were initially very harsh, so much so that Davis's friends and family feared his imminent death.

After being thrust into office after Lincoln's assassination on April 15, President Johnson had repeatedly spoken of his resolve to deal harshly with traitors. Johnson was determined to cement the battlefield's resolution of the secession question with a judicial decision condemning treason and thus confirming the permanence of the federal Union. He told an Indiana delegation on April 21 that "treason must be made odious.... [T]he American people should be educated and taught what is crime, and that treason is a crime, and the highest crime known to the law and the Constitution."[2] There was no reason to doubt his commitment. In the heady atmosphere of Union victory and the charged aftermath of Lincoln's death, it must have seemed like the easiest task in the world to convict Jefferson Davis of treason. The facts were not in doubt: Davis had indeed served as president of the

---

[2] Andrew Johnson, "Speech to Indiana Delegation," April 21, 1865, in Johnson, *Papers of Andrew Johnson*, 7: 612.

Confederacy and, in that capacity, had led great armies against the United States. There could hardly be any dispute that Davis had thus "levied war" against the United States within the meaning of Article III of the U.S. Constitution.[3] At that time, his trial and conviction seemed to be a foregone conclusion.

Once the government had Davis in custody, the president was immediately deluged with demands that he *do something* with the prisoner. The *New York Freeman's Journal and Catholic Register* queried: "They have got the elephant, now. What will they do with him?"[4] Davis was seen by both North and South as a symbol of the defeated Confederacy, and Johnson's decision about Davis's fate was, in some sense, a proxy for his plans for the reconstruction of the United States. Would Johnson show mercy or vengeance to his defeated countrymen?

Many voices preferred vengeance. Elizabeth Irvin of Centralia, Indiana, sent the president a photograph of her dead son Joshua along with a poignant note, telling him that Joshua had been "starved and tortured" at Andersonville Prison because of Davis's orders. If Johnson ever felt inclined toward mercy, she begged him to remember Joshua Irvin and the "ten thousand [others] that Jefferson Davis had willfully put to death." Mrs. Irvin demanded to know whether the president would "pardon [Davis] or give him his due[.] [P]ay them in their own coin or not."[5] Mrs. Irvin was not alone in recommending that Johnson deal harshly with Davis. An Illinois rope maker asked for the privilege of "making the rope, free of charge, with which to hang the scoundrel." Another group of citizens wanted the "Arch Traitor instigator and head Leader of the great Rebellion hanged untill [*sic*] he is Dead

---

[3] Article III, § 3, of the U.S. Constitution defines treason against the United States as "levying war against them, or in adhering to their enemies, giving them aid and comfort." U.S. Const. art. III, § 3.

[4] *Freeman's Journal and Catholic Register*, May 20, 1865. The pro-Davis coverage in this northern paper prompted Davis to write the editor, James A. McMaster, a note of thanks. "It is a great comfort to me," he wrote, "that justice and constitutional right is and can be so boldly vindicated as it now is in your periodical." Jefferson Davis to James A. McMaster, September 18, 1867, James A. McMaster Papers, University of Notre Dame, South Bend, Indiana. The *Freeman's Journal*'s pro-Confederate views had gotten McMaster in trouble before: the paper had been banned from the public mail and McMaster had been imprisoned briefly in late 1861.

[5] Elizabeth Irvin to Andrew Johnson, [month missing] 26, 1865, Indiana Petitions, Box 250, Jefferson Davis Amnesty Papers, Record Group 94, National Archives, Washington, DC (repository hereafter cited as NA-DC).

Dead Dead," and several proposed that Johnson hold off on executing Davis and instead parade him through the United States in the women's clothing in which he had supposedly been captured, adding that he could charge members of the general public for the privilege of seeing Davis thus attired.[6]

At the same time, Johnson received numerous pleas for compassion from writers who emphasized that pardoning the Confederate president would help to reunite the country. Mercy in Davis's case, they believed, would help bring the white South back into the national fold. A group of women from Iberville, Louisiana, acknowledged that Johnson was motivated by a sense of "imperative duty" in seeking to prosecute Davis, but insisted that the government could not punish Davis vicariously for the sins of the Confederacy. Davis was no more guilty than any other individual, they declared. In their opinion, Johnson could win ex-Confederates back to the Union if he spared Davis. "The people of the South crave your clemency and pardon for Mr. Davis," they wrote. "Such a magnanimous favor at your hands would fill with lasting gratitude the heart of the nation."[7] Mrs. James McKellen of Memphis told Johnson that leniency toward Davis would help to put the pieces of the Union back together: "Magnanimity, Mr. Johnson, should characterize the triumphant party. Kindness to Mr. Davis, more than aught-else would do more to reconcile our distracted and *devastated* country, than all the *Battles* lost and won."[8]

The Italian patriot Giuseppe Garibaldi, who participated in Italy's unification movement, also sounded the theme of mercy. Garibaldi and a group of Italians visited the United States in 1865 to petition on Davis's behalf. They linked the Confederate cause to the nationalist movement in their own country and pleaded with Johnson to spare

[6] Ben H. Goodno to Andrew Johnson, May 6, 1865, Illinois Petitions, Box 249, Jefferson Davis Amnesty Papers, NA-DC; Lilla C. Sibby to Andrew Johnson, May 23, 1865, Massachusetts Petitions, Box 249, ibid.; Samuel Smith to Andrew Johnson, May 19, 1865, New York Petitions, Box 249, ibid.; Elisha Farnham to Andrew Johnson, May 13, 1865, Connecticut Petitions, Box 250, ibid.; J. P. Longfellow and thirteen others, November 1865, Indiana Petitions, Box 250, ibid.

[7] Petition of the Ladies of Iberville, Louisiana, to Andrew Johnson, n.d., Box 246, Louisiana Petitions, Jefferson Davis Amnesty Papers, NA-DC.

[8] Mrs. James McKellan to Andrew Johnson, April 18, 1865, Tennessee Petitions, Box 247, Jefferson Davis Amnesty Papers, NA-DC (original emphasis). See also St. Louis Petitioners to Andrew Johnson, May 17, 1865, Missouri Petitions, Box 250, ibid.; H. S. Julian to Andrew Johnson, June 27, 1866, Kentucky Petitions, Box 246, ibid.

Davis. The delegation drew an unflattering comparison between punishing Davis and the murderous actions of Lincoln's assassins, insisting that "the death of President Lincoln plunged us into mourning, but the execution of Davis would make us blush. We cannot comprehend through what necessity the justice of a great and victorious people could imitate the vengeance of an assassin."[9]

As Johnson's visit from Garibaldi illustrates, the nation – and indeed the wider world – was focused on Davis's case and understood its magnitude. The topic was at the forefront of the national consciousness, and the national (and international) press reported on Jefferson Davis's fate on an almost daily basis. As the world recognized, Davis's case was to be the first and most important treason prosecution to come out of the Civil War and would definitively establish secession's illegitimacy. By convicting Davis of treason and rejecting the contention that secession removed his duty of loyalty to the United States, the government would secure a judicial confirmation of the war's outcome. The cause of secession would be defeated, both practically and legally. Then, once Davis was convicted, other cases would follow. A large number of Confederates, including Robert E. Lee and most of Jefferson Davis's cabinet, were indicted after the war, but their trials were put on hold awaiting the outcome of Davis's case.

Indeed, it seemed as though Union victory would be incomplete without a test case to determine, once and for all, that secession was a legal nullity and did not excuse Confederate acts of war. The *Boston Daily Advertiser* reprinted a letter from Louis Blanc, who had participated in the French Rebellion of 1848, in which Blanc insisted that Davis's trial would put the legal theory of the Union cause to the test. Blanc argued that the U.S. government could not pardon Davis without trial, because such a policy would be tantamount to admitting that "he had a right to attack the Union, sword in hand." In Blanc's estimation, a trial was necessary to establish the righteousness of the Northern theory of the perpetual Union. "There is no middle ground,"

---

[9] "Jefferson Davis: The Italians Interceding in His Behalf," *Philadelphia Inquirer*, October 26, 1865; "The Italians and Mr. Davis," *Augusta Constitutionalist*, November 3, 1865. See Andre M. Fleche, *The Revolution of 1861: The American Civil War in the Age of Nationalist Conflict* (Chapel Hill: University of North Carolina Press, 2012), and Don H. Doyle, *The Cause of All Nations: An International History of the American Civil War* (New York: Basic Books, 2015), for more on the Civil War in an international context.

Blanc wrote. "If Jefferson Davis is innocent, then it is the government of the United States which is guilty; if secession has not been rebellion, then the North in stifling it as such, has committed a crime."[10]

In a similar spirit, the *New York Times* welcomed the prospect of a thorough legal hearing on the right of secession. In the Davis case, "the arguments, alike for the prosecution and the defence, will involve the most comprehensive and searching inquest into the constitutional authority of the Government, and the relations of individual States thereto, that has probably ever been made since the foundation of the Union." The paper welcomed the opportunity to thrash out this question in a spirit of calm objectivity, with arguments to be presented by some of the ablest constitutional lawyers in the country. According to the *Times*, Davis's prosecution could serve as a test case to secure a definitive legal pronouncement on the validity of secession.[11] England's *Law Magazine* declared that Davis's trial would settle the long-standing question of the nature of the Union. His prosecution would allow "the legal authorities of the United States to discuss fully and accurately the real powers and limits of the much-misunderstood Constitution as to the various States considered in relation to each other, and to the Union as a whole."[12]

Elijah Nashua of Iowa insisted that Davis's prosecution was necessary in order to prove that secession was indeed unconstitutional and that might had not simply prevailed over right. If the United States was to be seen as a permanent nation in the eyes of the world, it had to have the capacity to punish treason. "As grateful beings that carnage and bloodshed, has subsided in our country, that forse [*sic*] and arms have decided in favor of liberty and freedom," he wrote, "we take this method of assisting to punish traitors, if there be such a crime of treason, if not, our breasts have been bared for might instead of right."[13] The *Philadelphia Inquirer* echoed these sentiments, insisting that it was necessary to hold a trial "to render traitors infamous, and to have it judicially settled that Secession is illegal."[14]

---

[10] "Punishing Treason," *Boston Daily Advertiser*, July 25, 1865.

[11] "The Approaching Trial of Jefferson Davis," *New York Times*, May 24, 1866.

[12] R. E. F., "The Trial of Jefferson Davis," *Law Magazine and Law Review* 21 (1866): 258, 271–72.

[13] Elijah Nashua to Andrew Johnson, December 16, 1865, Iowa Petitions, Box 250, Jefferson Davis Amnesty Papers, NA-DC.

[14] "Jeff. Davis and Other Criminals," *Philadelphia Inquirer*, December 7, 1865.

But the high stakes of the Davis trial were also worrisome, as Andrew Johnson quickly recognized. If Davis's conviction would cement the righteousness of the Union cause and the perpetuity of the federal Union, his acquittal would signal the opposite. Edwin D. Morgan, former governor of New York, wrote to the president to urge him to consider carefully before trying Davis in a civil tribunal. Morgan's objections stemmed from his concern that Davis's counsel would "reviv[e] the Doctrine of State Sovereignty as a constitutional defence of Davis," and that raising these issues would "demoralize the public mind and weaken our position. Even should he be convicted, the case would be carried up [to the Supreme Court on appeal], in all probability." Morgan noted that the disloyal (Copperhead) press in New York City was already insisting that no treasonous activity had taken place – that Davis had simply obeyed the order of his rightful sovereign, the state of Mississippi.[15]

Morgan's proposed solution was that the government should forgo conducting Davis's trial before a civil court. To avoid reopening the secession issue, Morgan recommended that the government try him before a military commission for violations of the law of war.[16] Private J. Baldwin also advised the president to try "Jeff Davis under the war power [i.e., before a military tribunal] if the Civil power that had already indicted him was not competent to convict him. These men have trampled on civil law," he wrote, so Davis should not be afforded the privilege of invoking that law. Union veteran John Varennes agreed that "the arch-rebel Jefferson Davis should be punished for his many crimes" by a military tribunal. Varennes worried that Davis would be likely to escape punishment by a civil tribunal if he raised the constitutionality of secession as his defense. "There is great danger that if

---

15 For more on the Copperheads, see Jennifer L. Weber, *Copperheads: The Rise and Fall of Lincoln's Opponents in the North* (New York: Oxford University Press, 2006), and Joel H. Silbey, *A Respectable Minority: The Democratic Party in the Civil War Era, 1860–1868* (New York: W. W. Norton, 1977).

16 E. D. Morgan to Andrew Johnson, May 31, 1865, Jefferson Davis Case File, Record Group 60, National Archives, College Park, Maryland (repository hereafter cited as NA-CP) [original letter not found; copy on file at the Papers of Jefferson Davis, Rice University, Houston]. Morgan argued that Davis had violated the law of war in permitting the massacre of African American soldiers at Fort Pillow and planning the burning of New York City, in addition to his complicity in Lincoln's assassination and the cruel treatment of Union prisoners of war.

tried by a civil court, secessionists may get on the Jury and that consequently he may be acquitted or the Jury may disagree," Varennes reasoned. Varennes requested that President Johnson convene a court-martial – "the only proper way to try this blood stained fiend" – to ensure Davis's execution.[17]

While Johnson fielded suggestions about Davis's fate, Davis's closest confidante, his wife, Varina, immediately mobilized support. In May, she began contacting some of the most prominent lawyers in the United States, urging them to take on her husband's defense. Along with Virginia Clay, whose husband, Clement, joined Jefferson Davis in federal custody at Fort Monroe, Varina Davis began a letter-writing campaign to prominent Northerners who might be willing to defend Davis on a charge of treason. Just before their separation following her husband's capture, he had told her to engage, if at all possible, New York attorney Charles O'Conor as defense counsel. Varina contacted O'Conor, along with *New York Tribune* editor Horace Greeley, Jeremiah Black (who had served as attorney general under James Buchanan), and Maryland senator Reverdy Johnson.[18]

Davis's case sparked O'Conor's interest, and he signed on as the leader of the Davis defense team. For O'Conor, the case was attractive because it seemed to implicate the most troublesome constitutional question of the war. The legality of secession could be invoked at Davis's

[17] Henry Proctor to Andrew Johnson, May 18, 1865, Massachusetts Petitions, Box 250, Jefferson Davis Amnesty Papers, NA-DC; J. Baldwin to Andrew Johnson, June 18, 1865, New Jersey Petitions, Box 250, ibid.; Petition of John J. Varennes to the Senate, May 18, 1866, Records of the Senate, Record Group 46, NA-DC.

[18] V. Davis, *Jefferson Davis, Ex-President of the Confederate States*, 2: 647, 702, 780–81; Virginia Clay-Clopton, *A Belle of the Fifties* (New York: Doubleday, Page, 1905), 289–92. While Davis languished, his wife tirelessly campaigned on his behalf throughout his long imprisonment, imploring the assistance of anyone who might be of help to her. She corresponded with Davis's attorneys, directing his defense when Davis was unable to do so, and begged friends and nonacquaintances alike to help her plead with President Johnson for Davis's release on parole owing to his poor health. Davis often expressed his gratitude for her love and support in his letters to Varina, which were the only letters he was allowed to write. According to Joan Cashin, Varina Davis's biographer, Varina and Jefferson Davis's sometimes rocky relationship was at its best during his imprisonment; after his release, she writes, he reneged on "the companionate marriage he seemed to promise in his prison letters." Joan E. Cashin, *First Lady of the Confederacy: Varina Davis's Civil War* (Cambridge, MA: Belknap Press of Harvard University Press, 2006), 186. Cashin does not otherwise discuss Varina Davis's dedicated efforts to secure her husband's release.

treason trial to show that Davis was not a citizen of the United States
and therefore did not commit treason. O'Conor regarded Davis's case as
an opportunity to confront the government's theory of perpetual Union
in a forum that would command the attention of the American people.
Jeremiah Black, who agreed to act as Clement Clay's lawyer, also recognized the magnitude of the constitutional questions implicated by the
case. Davis's trial could undermine the verdict of the battlefield.

Judge George Washington Woodward, chief justice of the
Pennsylvania Supreme Court, wrote to Black in May to highlight the
issues the case would raise.[19] Woodward considered Davis's conviction
far from a sure thing, and speculated that the trial might serve to vindicate the Confederate view of secession:

The doctrine of State Rights will have a severe test and may find a strange
vindication in that trial. Secession has yet to be defined. Hitherto it has been
a toy of politicians and they have dodged everything like a definition.... But
is secession treason? That's a grand question. If it is not, war in support of it
cannot be. If the right to withdraw existed, it must have included the right
of defense, so that levying war to defend a confederacy founded in secession
could not be levying war against the Govt of US. But this is on the assumption
that Secession is something less than treason, which I neither aver not deny.
Spero clarionem lucem.[20] It will have to be defined and made plain, unless
indeed we continue to set aside all law and administer only drumbeat justice.[21]

Reverdy Johnson, a senator from Maryland and an eminent attorney, hoped that Davis's prosecution would act as a test case so that
"the courts might decide whether there was a right of secession and

---

[19] Black's pro-Southern leanings were no secret, although he never defended the legality
      of secession. As attorney general under President James Buchanan, Black had issued
      an opinion arguing that the president had neither power to recognize a state's seces-
      sion, nor to use coercive force to bring a recalcitrant state back to the Union. In fact,
      Black had argued, an attempt on the part of the federal government to coerce a state
      "would be ipso facto an expulsion of such State from the Union. And if Congress
      shall break up the present Union, by unconstitutionally putting strife and enmity and
      armed hostility between different sections of the country, instead of the domestic
      tranquility which the Constitution was meant to insure, will not all the States be
      absolved from their federal obligations?" Jeremiah Black, "Power of the President in
      Executing the Laws," *Opinions of the Attorney General* 8 (1860): 516, 525.
[20] Loosely translated, "I hope the issue will be illuminated."
[21] G. W. Woodward to Jeremiah Black, May 28, 1865, Reel 22, Jeremiah Black Papers,
      Manuscripts Division, Library of Congress [microfilm edition]; (Manuscripts
      Division, Library of Congress, hereafter cited as LC). By "drumbeat justice,"
      Woodward meant military justice.

whether, after the close of an insurrection which was so great that it was necessary to treat those engaged in it as public enemies, they stood, as to a charge of treason, as subjects of another nation."[22]

After accepting Varina Davis's request to head the Davis defense, Charles O'Conor recruited other notable attorneys for the team. They included George Shea and James T. Brady, also from New York; William B. Reed of Philadelphia; George William Brown and Thomas G. Pratt from Maryland; James Lyons, Robert Ould, and John Randolph Tucker from Virginia; George Pugh of Ohio; Burton Harrison of Mississippi (and later New York); and B. J. Sage of New Orleans. The state of Mississippi appointed three lawyers, Robert Lowry, Giles Hillyer, and Charles Hooker, to assist in Davis's defense. O'Conor also collaborated closely with Jeremiah Black and corresponded informally with Philip Phillips of Alabama and Thomas F. Bayard of Delaware about the case.[23] Perhaps most astonishingly, Varina Davis's personal plea touched Republican newspaper editor Horace Greeley, who thereafter sought to aid her in securing Davis's release. He was later joined by Gerrit Smith, the Radical abolitionist who had underwritten John Brown's 1859 raid on Harpers Ferry. Both Greeley and Smith believed that the nation would be best served by a merciful stance toward former Confederates. In their opinion, treason prosecutions would only halt the reconstruction process.

O'Conor assembled a massive defense team, but he was its sole director. He orchestrated the Davis defense without much input from anyone else, and his considerations in putting together the team were more strategic than collaborative. He recruited attorneys who possessed expertise that might prove valuable in the course of Davis's trial. For instance, he urged Varina Davis to retain James Brady for Davis's defense. Brady, well known for his skill before a criminal jury, would complement O'Conor's own more cerebral and less affable qualities, were the case to go to trial. Even more important, hiring Brady would

---

[22] Bernard C. Steiner, *Life of Reverdy Johnson* (Baltimore: Norman, Remington, 1914), 156.

[23] Davis did not suffer from a dearth of well-connected supporters. Reverdy Johnson of Maryland and Caleb Cushing of Massachusetts both stated that they would have offered their services had Davis found himself without good counsel. See Reverdy Johnson to G. A. Chaires, May 15, 1866, in Jefferson Davis, *Jefferson Davis, Constitutionalist: His Letters, Papers, and Speeches*, ed. Dunbar Rowland, 10 vols. (Jackson: Mississippi Department of Archives and Records, 1923), 9: 415; Caleb Cushing to Franklin Pierce, July 3, 1865, Box 95, Caleb Cushing Papers, LC.

prevent him from working for the prosecution. As O'Conor told Varina Davis, "Unless retained for Mr. D[avis], [Brady] will probably appear for the government on any trial in a civil Court that may be ordered."

Neutralizing Brady as a possible adversary was more crucial than securing his services. O'Conor believed that the "liberal fee" Brady would demand and "probably not do anything for" would be money well spent, as it would "insure us against what some persons would regard as a calamity i.e. his appearance on a trial against Mr. D." Although O'Conor could not be sure of the exact particulars of Brady's politics, it was clear "he is not a Republican," and therefore he could be counted on to serve willingly and effectively as defense counsel.[24] Brady had supported the Union cause throughout the Civil War, but he chose to defend Davis without compensation. Upon Brady's untimely death in 1869, O'Conor praised him for his devotion to Davis's cause, recalling that when Davis "was summoned to a[n] ... ordeal, at once ... James T. Brady appeared as his defender.... He thought that courts, juries, and the gallows were unfit weapons of war; he deemed them most unfitting accompaniments of the peace which arms had won."[25] Brady, in O'Conor's opinion, had been content to leave secession's determination to the field of battle, rather than reviving the question in a postbellum court.

Most of the other members of the defense team were either committed secessionists or were noted for their anti-administration activities during the Civil War. William B. Reed had defended prominent Philadelphians charged with engaging in treason during the war, as O'Conor had done in New York. Reed had also endorsed secession and spoken out against the centralizing tendencies of the war. He predicted that "when the South is conquered, the lines of the states ... are to be

---

[24] Charles O'Conor to Varina Davis, October 7, 1865, Box 24, Jefferson Davis Papers, Museum of the Confederacy, Richmond, Virginia (repository hereafter cited as MC). Brady was well known for his work as defense counsel for Union General Daniel E. Sickles, who was tried for murdering his wife's lover. During the Sickles trial, Brady had become friends with co-counsel Edwin Stanton, whom O'Conor feared might now prevail on Brady to represent the prosecution. See "James T. Brady," in *Kings of Fortune, or the Triumphs and Achievements of Noble, Self-Made Men*, ed. Walter Houghton (Chicago: Loomis National Library Association, 1888), 467.

[25] *In Memoriam: James T. Brady* (New York: Transcript Association, 1869), 31. Brady had run for New York governor in 1860 on a ticket that also supported John C. Breckinridge for the presidency. During the war, he aligned himself with the War Democrats. *New York Times*, August 9, 1860.

rubbed out." His actions had prompted a Unionist mob to surround his house in Pennsylvania until a servant floated an American flag from the window.[26] George William Brown, the former mayor of Baltimore, had tried (and failed) to instigate Maryland's secession from the Union in 1861. Both he and former Maryland governor Thomas G. Pratt suffered military imprisonment as a result of their disloyal activities.[27]

Ohio lawyer George Pugh had been at the forefront of treason litigation during the Civil War. Pugh had unsuccessfully represented the notorious Ohio Copperhead Clement Vallandigham (a personal friend of Pugh's) in his prosecution for treason, and had even run on Vallandigham's failed gubernatorial ticket as lieutenant governor in 1863. Before working on Vallandigham's case, Pugh had defended James W. Chenoweth, an Ohio man who had sold military supplies to the Confederate government, in a treason prosecution in the federal circuit court in Ohio.[28]

---

[26] William B. Reed, *A Northern Plea for Peace* (London: Henry F. Mackintosh, 1863), 17. See also Russell F. Weigley, "The Border City in Civil War, 1854–1865," in Russell Weigley, ed., *Philadelphia: A 300-Year History* (New York: W. W. Norton, 1982), 402–3; Sidney George Fisher, *A Philadelphia Perspective: The Diary of Sidney George Fisher Covering the Years 1834–1871*, ed. Nicholas B. Wainright (Philadelphia: Historical Society of Pennsylvania, 1967), 439; Arnold Schankman, "William B. Reed and the Civil War," *Pennsylvania History* 39 (1972): 455, 460–62; Joanna D. Cowden, *"Heaven Will Frown on Such as Cause as This": Six Democrats Who Opposed Lincoln's War* (Lanham, MD: University Press of America, 2001), 95–125; James Buchanan to William B. Reed, September 23, 1865, Reel 51, James Buchanan Papers, LC [microfilm edition].

[27] See William A. Blair, *With Malice toward Some: Treason and Loyalty in the Civil War Era* (Chapel Hill: University of North Carolina Press, 2014), chapters 2, 6, 7. Another member of the team, Thomas Bayard, was a Peace Democrat who won election to the Senate in 1869. For more on these lawyers, see Cynthia Nicoletti, "Strategic Litigation and the Death of Reconstruction," in *Signposts: New Directions in Southern Legal History*, ed. Sally E. Hadden and Patricia H. Minter (Athens: University of Georgia Press, 2013).

[28] In Chenoweth's case, Pugh successfully contended that English precedent forbade the treason prosecution of any person who had merely given "aid and comfort" to *domestic* enemies of the United States. Upholding Pugh's motion to quash the indictment, Justice Noah Swayne found that in a domestic insurrection, as opposed to a foreign war, a defendant could be prosecuted only for directly levying war against the United States, and not for merely supporting the country's internal enemies. *Chenoweth* is discussed in Ex parte Vallandigham, 28 F. Cas. 874 (C.C.S.D. Ohio 1863) (No. 16,816), and in the *Washington National Intelligencer*, May 13, 1862. See also Carl B. Swisher, *History of the Supreme Court of the United States: The Taney Period, 1836–64* (New York: Macmillan, 1974), 952–53. Willard Hurst's *The Law of Treason in the United States* (Westport, CT: Greenwood Press, 1971), 262,

Southern members of the defense team included Philip Phillips, whose wife, Eugenia, had been imprisoned in Union-occupied New Orleans for disloyal outbursts, and prominent Virginia lawyers James Lyons and Robert Ould. Ould had served as an exchange agent for Confederate and Union POWs during the war, and in that capacity had gained a great deal of knowledge about the application of international law to the Confederacy as a wartime belligerent, which would prove useful in the Davis case.[29] O'Conor also secured the services of B. J. Sage, who had authored a pamphlet defending the right of secession, titled *Davis and Lee: A Protest against the Attempt of the Yankee Radicals to Have Them and Other Confederate Chiefs Murdered*, in the summer of 1865. Sage later reported that O'Conor had hired him on the strength of his pamphlet, which the senior attorney had characterized as "an admirably prepared and overwhelmingly conclusive brief for Davis's defence."[30]

Faced with difficult choices about Davis's ultimate fate, President Johnson surveyed his options during the summer of 1865. Before his untimely death, President Lincoln had remarked that Davis's flight from Richmond in April was a good thing because it forestalled the political and legal difficulties that might attend a high-profile treason prosecution. "I'm bound to oppose the escape of Jeff. Davis," Lincoln had reportedly told General William T. Sherman, "but if you could

gives a brief synopsis of the case. It was not entirely clear whether Justice Swayne's decision interpreted the language of the Constitution or merely the statutory language of the Crimes Act of 1790, which punished "any person or persons, owing allegiance to the United States of America, [who] shall levy war against them, or shall adhere to their enemies, giving them aid and comfort." Crimes Act of 1790, 1 Stat. 112, § 1 (1790). After debating whether the decision was constitutional or statutory, the Confiscation Act of 1862 fixed the problem by defining, as a crime less than treason, "engag[ing] in, or giv[ing] aid and comfort to, any such existing rebellion or insurrection," punishable by imprisonment, fine, or confiscation of slaves. Confiscation Act of 1862, 12 Stat. 589, § 2 (1862). See *Congressional Globe*, 37th Cong., 2d sess., March 16, 1862, 2166–67. See also U.S. v. Greathouse, 26 F. Cas. 18, 22–23 (C.C.N.D. Ca. 1863) (No. 15,254).

[29] See John Fabian Witt, *Lincoln's Code: The Laws of War in American History* (New York: Free Press, 2012), chapter 9.

[30] B. J. Sage, *Davis and Lee: a Protest against the Attempt of the Yankee Radicals to Have Them and Other Confederate Chiefs Murdered* (London: C. Mitchell & Co., 1865); B. J. Sage, "Some Great Constitutional Questions," *Southern Historical Society Papers* 12 (1884): 485, 488; Charles O'Conor to B. J. Sage, December 10, 1865, reproduced in B. J. Sage, *The Republic of Republics* (Philadelphia: William W. Harding, 1878), iv. This letter appeared only in the book's 1878 edition.

manage to have him slip out unbeknownst-like, I guess it wouldn't hurt me much!"[31]

Johnson soon had occasion to reflect on the wisdom of Lincoln's inclination to let Davis go and allow the triumph of the Union army to stand as the last word on secession. Throughout the summer of 1865, Johnson met repeatedly with his cabinet to discuss how they would deal with Jefferson Davis. Johnson had promised to "make treason odious," and he was determined that Davis's would be the first – and most important – prosecution. There were a several options on the table: Davis could be charged with treason, a civil crime (laid out in the Constitution – the domestic law – of the United States), or with violations of the law of war. Davis's alleged war crimes stemmed from his supposed participation in the Lincoln assassination and from his responsibility for the cruel conditions Union POWs had endured at Andersonville prison.[32] The particular charge also related to the forum in which his case would be heard – military or civil. Davis's conviction was virtually assured if the trial were to be conducted in a military court, where the procedural protections of the Bill of Rights, including trial by jury, were suspended. The jury would also be composed of U.S. soldiers, who would harbor great antipathy for Davis.

In the summer of 1865, it was not entirely clear whether military commissions were competent to hear civil cases.[33] Could a military court hear a treason prosecution? Prior to the Civil War, there was a vague general understanding that military courts had cognizance

---

[31] "Interview between Gen. Sherman and Chief-Justice Chase," *New York Times*, July 4, 1865; Salmon P. Chase to Kate Chase Sprague, May 5, 1865, in Salmon P. Chase, *The Salmon P. Chase Papers*, ed. John Niven, 5 vols. (Kent, OH: Kent State University Press, 1993), 5: 38.

[32] See Francis Lieber, *Instructions for the Government of Armies of the United States in the Field: Originally Issued as General Orders No. 100, Adjutant General's Office, 1863* (Washington, DC: Government Printing Office, 1898), art. 148, 56. As discussed in Chapter 12, what was known as the Lieber Code was a document drafted in the midst of the war at President Lincoln's instigation. It purported to codify the laws of war, but in crafting the document, Francis Lieber altered generally agreed-upon principles to accord with the Union's legal position in the Civil War. The code, once completed, was issued to the Union army as General Orders No. 100.

[33] In Ex parte Milligan, 71 U.S. 2 (1866), decided a year later, the Supreme Court held that military commissions could not continue to operate in areas where the courts were open after "actual war" had ceased. But *Milligan* arguably did not apply in the states of the former Confederacy, such as Virginia, where Davis was likely to be tried. See more on military versus civil jurisdiction in Chapter 9.

over military crimes (including violations of the law of war), while civil courts had sole jurisdiction over civil offenses, such as treason charges.[34] But there was disagreement on this subject.[35] Postwar legal thinkers hashed out a consensus on these difficult issues with Davis's case firmly in mind.

The cabinet first took up the topic of Davis's fate on July 18. The president was looking for a quick consensus, and, according to Secretary of the Navy Gideon Welles, Johnson "did not conceal his anxiety that we should come to some determination. But we got none." At the initial cabinet meeting, Secretary of War Edwin M. Stanton recalled "a great diversity of opinion in the matter as to whether Davis should be tried first for the crime of high treason."[36] Stanton and Secretary of State William H. Seward emerged as Davis's most zealous opponents, arguing strenuously in favor of trying Davis before a military commission, primarily for his alleged role in Lincoln's assassination and secondarily for the crime of treason. Seward emphasized that a military trial was necessary, as "he had no confidence in the proceeding before a civil court." It seemed unlikely to him that civil jurors could be counted on to convict Davis. Seward and Stanton also believed that it would be better to delay the trial for some time, in order to determine whether the newly created Archive Office – presided over by legal scholar Francis Lieber – could turn up evidence in the Confederate records of Davis's active involvement in Lincoln's assassination. Welles remarked that "it was evident these two intended there should be no result at this time and the talk became discursive." Welles himself urged that Davis should be tried quickly and only in a

---

[34] See Isaac Maltby, *A Treatise on Courts Martial and Military Law* (Boston, 1813), 55; Stephen V. Benét, *A Treatise on Military Law and the Practice of Courts-Martial*, 5th ed. (New York: D. Van Nostrand, 1866), 110; William C. DeHart, *Observations on Military Law and the Constitution and the Practice of Courts Martial* (New York: D. Appleton, 1863), 15–16. See also Marty Lederman, "The 'Law' of the Lincoln Assassination," available at https://papers.ssrn.com/sol3/papers .cfm?abstract_id=2854195.

[35] The attorney general authored an opinion addressing this issue. James Speed, "Trial of Jefferson Davis," *Opinions of the Attorney General* 11 (1866): 411. See Chapter 6 for more on Speed's opinion.

[36] *Impeachment Investigation: Testimony Taken before the Judiciary Committee of the House of Representatives in the Investigation of the Charges against Andrew Johnson* (Washington, DC: Government Printing Office, 1867), 397 (testimony of Edwin M. Stanton).

civil proceeding on the charge of treason rather than for the president's murder. The first meeting accordingly ended in deadlock.[37]

The cabinet continued the discussion less than a week later. Johnson again pressed his advisers to reach a definitive decision about Davis's fate, polling the cabinet members as to their individual opinions. The cabinet members were still divided in their judgment about whether Davis should be charged with treason or with war crimes, whether the trial should be held before a military or a civil court, and where such a trial should take place. Seward was focused on achieving the right outcome. He insisted that Davis's trial had to be conducted before a military commission, before a jury of military officials, as "there could be no conviction of such a man, for any offense, before any civil tribunal." He also believed Davis should be tried before a military commission whether he was charged with war crimes or with civil offenses. Stanton thought that Davis could be tried in a military court for treason, but that it would be preferable to hold his trial in a civil court. Postmaster General William Dennison maintained that Davis had to be tried in military court if any evidence surfaced that indicated his involvement in the Lincoln murder, but that otherwise Davis should face treason charges only in civil court, as a military commission could try only cases arising under the law of war. Dennison did not offer an opinion about where such a civil trial should take place and was willing to leave that determination to the attorney general. Treasury secretary Hugh McCulloch believed that Davis should eventually be tried only in civil court, but he wanted to postpone the trial and the discussion about the trial until public outrage had died down and calm prevailed.

Welles again argued "emphatically for the civil court and an arraignment for treason – for an early institution of proceedings – and was willing the trial should take place in Virginia" even if it meant that Davis would not be convicted. Applying the law with neutrality and regularity was of paramount importance. "If our laws or system were defective," he argued, "it was well to bring them to a test." Secretary of the Interior James Harlan disagreed, believing it would be foolhardy to try Davis before a civil court "unless satisfied there would be a

[37] Gideon Welles, *Diary of Gideon Welles*, ed. Edgar Thaddeus Welles, 3 vols. (Boston: Houghton Mifflin, 1911) 2: 335–36.

conviction. If there was a doubt, he wanted a military commission." If Davis were tried and not convicted, Harlan argued, the result "would be most calamitous." It would be better to pardon him immediately than run such a risk. Attorney General James Speed wanted the trial to be a civil one, for treason, but believed that the trial should be postponed until the rebellion had been fully suppressed and a state of peace reigned in the United States. A military commission, in his view, could only be empowered to try violations of the law of war. The cabinet also worried over the poor state of Davis's health, fearing public outrage if Davis should die in the government's care.[38] Yet again Johnson's cabinet reached no conclusions about Davis's fate.

After the initial trial and execution of Lincoln's assassins in June and July of 1865, the government sought to turn up evidence of Davis's participation in planning the Lincoln assassination or his direct involvement in the abuse and neglect of Union prisoners of war at Andersonville. Judge Advocate General Joseph Holt of the Bureau of Military Justice and Francis Lieber, who sifted through the Confederate archives, were charged with the responsibility of finding evidence of Davis's role in Lincoln's murder. Nothing concrete emerged. In the summer and fall of that year, Holt latched on to the shaky assurances of a con man, Sanford Conover, who promised that he could tie Davis to the assassination plot. Conover's testimony later unraveled, however. Witnesses were unable to provide any evidence that Davis had ordered or ever discussed the murder.[39]

Linking Davis to Andersonville also proved to be a nonstarter. The government tried and executed Andersonville commandant Henry Wirz for his role in the supervision of the prison camp, but Wirz steadfastly refused to implicate Davis. Wirz's trial was by military commission, and he told his accusers that he had informed his superiors of the need for more supplies in order to alleviate the horrors of Andersonville. The Confederate government was unable to provide

---

[38] Welles, *Diary of Gideon Welles*, 2: 337–39.

[39] See Depositions of Witnesses, vol. 92, Joseph Holt Papers, LC; Elizabeth D. Leonard, *Lincoln's Avengers: Justice, Revenge, and Reunion after the Civil War* (New York: W. W. Norton, 2004); Carman Cumming, *The Devil's Game: The Civil War Intrigues of Charles A. Dunham* (Urbana: University of Illinois Press, 2004), 145; Seymour J. Frank, "The Conspiracy to Implicate the Confederate Leaders in Lincoln's Assassination," *Mississippi Valley Historical Review* 40 (March 1954): 629.

these, given the extent of privation on the Confederate home front, and Wirz maintained that Davis had no involvement with the care of Andersonville's prisoners.[40]

If the plan to charge Davis with war crimes looked shaky, what remained certain was the Johnson administration's ability to make out a prima facie case against Davis for treason. For four years, almost every official action Davis had undertaken as Confederate president had been for the purpose of levying war against the United States. By the late summer and fall of 1865, after having met with his cabinet, President Johnson had committed to the task of trying Davis for treason. As he told a group of South Carolinians gathered at the White House to petition on behalf of the jailed Confederates, he considered a test case to establish the illegality of secession necessary. To affirm its authority and legitimacy as a nation, the United States would have to prove its case off the battlefield. Johnson told the petitioners that "if treason were committed there ought to be some test to determine the power of the government to punish the crime." A court case would determine that the rebellion had been an illegal act on the part of the Confederate states and not merely a military contest between two validly constituted parties. "Looking at the government as we do," Johnson asserted, "the laws violated and an attempt made at the life of the nation, there should be a vindication of the government and the constitution."[41]

Although Johnson had resolved to move forward with a treason prosecution, he had decided on very little else. The cabinet was divided, and Johnson would not act boldly on his own. The case was too just perilous. With no indication that the cabinet could agree on a course of action, Attorney General Speed decided to move forward

[40] Louis Schade (Wirz's attorney) to "the American Public," April 4, 1867, reprinted in James Madison Page, *The True Story of Andersonville Prison* (New York: Neale Publishing, 1908), 234–42. See also Jefferson Davis, *Andersonville and Other War-prisons* (New York: Belford, 1890), 15–16; George Shea, *Jefferson Davis: A Statement concerning the Imputed Special Causes of His Imprisonment by the Government of the United States, and of His Tardy Release by Due Process of Law* (London: Edward Stanford, 1877), 8–9; Charles O'Conor to William Preston Johnson, December 30, 1865, and George Shea to Charles O'Conor, January 6, 1867, Box 24, Jefferson Davis Papers, MC.

[41] Andrew Johnson, "Exchange with South Carolina Convention Delegates," October 13, 1865, in Johnson, *Papers of Andrew Johnson*, 9: 236.

independently. When the cabinet consulted on the Davis matter on August 22, Speed announced that he had retained two well-known lawyers from outside his office to direct the treason prosecution: William M. Evarts of New York City, and John H. Clifford of New Bedford, Massachusetts, with Evarts taking the lead. Evarts and Clifford were to be assisted by Lucius Chandler, the U.S. attorney for Virginia, and would also receive guidance from the attorney general himself.[42]

With this decision, the two lead attorneys for the Davis prosecution and defense (William Evarts and Charles O'Conor) were in place. In the course of the next three and a half years, Davis's fate would depend on their ability to outmaneuver one another in the complicated legal and political tangle over the decision to try Davis for treason and thus test the war's resolution of the secession question.

---

[42] Chandler was to be assisted initially by Lovell H. Rousseau, a Kentucky Unionist general who became military governor of Louisiana in 1865 and dropped out of the case very quickly. See Joseph G. Dawson III, "General Lovell F. Rousseau and Louisiana Reconstruction," *Louisiana History* 20 (Fall 1979): 373–91.

2

Two Lions of the New York Bar

The leading lawyers on both sides of the Davis case, William Evarts and Charles O'Conor, were two of the most respected attorneys in the country. At the time of the founding of the New York Bar Association in 1870, William Evarts "was easily the most prominent member of the bar, with the exception of Charles O'Conor."[1] The two also had a long history. When they signed on to work on the Davis case, they had known each other for many years, and their association continued for many more after the case concluded. O'Conor and Evarts both fought against the wave of corruption infecting the New York bench and bar in the 1860s and '70s as the heads of two rival voluntary associations of lawyers – O'Conor's New York Law Institute and Evarts's New York Bar Association.[2] Evarts and O'Conor worked together on a few cases and opposed each other in many more, including several

[1] Theron G. Strong, *Landmarks of a Lawyer's Lifetime* (New York: Dodd, Mead, 1914), 191. Evarts's biographer, Chester Barrows, considered Evarts's rivalry with Charles O'Conor to be the most important professional relationship of his career and devoted a chapter to the interactions between the two attorneys. See Chester L. Barrows, *William M. Evarts: Lawyer, Diplomat, Statesman* (Chapel Hill: University of North Carolina Press, 1941), chapter 6.

[2] Their reform efforts against corruption included the prosecution of executives and politicians in the Erie Railroad scandal and the Tweed Ring. See Charles Francis Adams, *The Erie Railroad Row Considered as an Episode in Court* (Boston: Little, Brown, 1868), and Charles Francis Adams, *Chapters of Erie and Other Essays* (New York: H. Holt, 1886); George Martin, *Causes and Conflicts: The Centennial History of the Association of the Bar of the City of New York, 1870–1970* (New York: Fordham University Press, 1997).

high-profile ones, such as *Lemmon v. New York*, the Parish Will Case, the Metropolitan Police Case, and the disputed electoral contest of 1876.[3]

The two men held opposing political viewpoints, but they remained friendly and respected each other's abilities. On O'Conor's death, Evarts spoke admiringly of O'Conor's "manly strength, skill and courage" and even remarked on his fortitude in adhering to his anti-Union political beliefs in the face of great opposition in the North during the Civil War.[4] For his part, O'Conor recommended Evarts's services to potential clients, assuring one that Evarts would "bring forward every possible point, present every possible argument the case admits of."[5] At a dinner O'Conor hosted in Evarts's honor in the thick of the Davis prosecution, O'Conor – as the keynote speaker – praised his rival's "ripe scholarship, profound sagacity, [and] skill in the adaptation of means to ends made perfectly." More to the point, O'Conor described Evarts to Jefferson Davis as a formidable opponent, calling him "as good a lawyer as any to be found in the [Republican] party if indeed he be not decidedly the best" (Figure 2.1).[6]

At the time of his retainer, Evarts was one of the most renowned lawyers in New York City and had gained national prominence based on his work as a lawyer and his skills as a witty and persuasive public orator. Perhaps more important, Evarts also possessed strong credentials as an advocate on behalf of the Republican cause. He had argued several important pro-Union and antislavery cases throughout his career, including *Lemmon v. New York* in 1859, involving the right of a state to prohibit slaves from passing through the state in transit; the *Savannah* case in 1861, prosecuting Confederate privateers; and the

[3] See Lemmon v. People, 20 N.Y. 562 (1860); Delafield v. Parish (the Parish Will Case), 25 N.Y. 9 (1862); People ex rel. Wood v. Draper (Metropolitan Police Case), 15 N.Y. 532 (1857). See also letters between O'Conor and Evarts relating to the Parish Will Case, August 28, September 3, 20, and undated, 1860, folder 288, Box 13, Evarts Family Papers, Beinecke Library, Yale University, New Haven, CT (repository hereafter cited as Yale).
[4] *In Memory of Charles O'Conor* (New York: n.p., 1884), 40–48.
[5] William M. Evarts, *Arguments and Speeches of William Maxwell Evarts*, ed. Sherman Evarts, 3 vols. (New York: Macmillan, 1919), 1: xiii.
[6] "Banquet to Hon Wm. M. Evarts," *New York Times*, November 18, 1868; Charles O'Conor to Jefferson Davis, October 2, 1867, Box 24, Jefferson Davis Papers, MC.

FIGURE 2.1 Lead prosecutor William Evarts. Library of Congress.

1863 *Prize Cases*, a Supreme Court case establishing the president's authority to proclaim the blockade against the Confederate states.[7]

At age forty-seven, Evarts had cemented his reputation as an advocate and was beginning to look toward a political career. When Chief

---

[7] Lemmon v. People, 20 N.Y. at 562; A. F. Warburton, *Trial of the Officers and Crew of the Schooner Savannah* (New York: Notable Trials Library, 1997); The Prize Cases, 67 U.S. 635 (1862).

Justice Roger Taney's death opened up a seat on the Supreme Court in late 1864, Evarts believed that he might be the next appointee. Confiding to his friend Richard Henry Dana that "a good deal of interest has been spontaneously shown here to put me in the place on public grounds, by persons of the highest political influence," Evarts concluded that "aside from Gov. Chase [who secured the nomination] I am justified in thinking that many things occur to make me a very prominent, if not the most prominent candidate."[8]

Politics were in Evarts's blood, as he hailed from the prominent Sherman family. His mother, Mehetabel Sherman Evarts, was the daughter of Roger Sherman, a signer of the Declaration of Independence. Other members of the family included distinguished jurists Ebenezer Rockwood Hoar and George F. Hoar, William Evarts's first cousins, and General William T. Sherman and Senator John Sherman, who were related to Evarts more distantly. Evarts's father, Jeremiah, also enjoyed some degree of fame as a Puritan missionary and theologian and a staunch advocate on behalf of American Indians. In the early nineteenth century, Jeremiah Evarts had labored to stem the tide of Unitarianism rising in New England, favoring the more orthodox Congregationalism. His son William Maxwell Evarts, born in Boston in 1818, grew up well connected but not wealthy. The family sank into poverty when Jeremiah Evarts died in 1831, when William was only thirteen. Still, young Evarts showed a good deal of promise as a scholar by winning a place at Boston Latin School, where he reportedly astonished his classmates with his command of Latin. Evarts later entered Yale College, his father's alma mater, which was paid for by two wealthy uncles. At Yale, Evarts hobnobbed with other elite young men, joining the secret Skull and Bones society, and developed a true talent for debate and public speaking. After graduation, Evarts decided to become an attorney and spent a year studying law privately in Windsor, Vermont.[9]

Evarts then enrolled at Harvard Law School, at a time when the vast majority of lawyers were not formally trained. After graduating from law school in 1840, Evarts moved to New York City, where he

[8] William Evarts to Richard Henry Dana, October 15, 1864, Box 16, Dana Family Papers, Massachusetts Historical Society, Boston (repository hereafter cited as MHS). See also Barrows, *William M. Evarts*, 125–26.
[9] Barrows, *William M. Evarts*.

partnered with several other lawyers and opened a small firm. Evarts had come to New York with a letter of introduction from Justice Joseph Story to Chancellor James Kent that immediately gained him entry into the upper echelon of the New York bar. He soon formed a friendship with elite lawyer Daniel Lord (later of the law firm Lord, Day, and Lord), whom Evarts had met in his Yale days. As one historian put it, "It was an easy beginning."[10]

As a lawyer, Evarts was a generalist. He possessed a philosophical orientation, which led him to try to fit the issues raised by his cases into larger jurisprudential frameworks. He was better suited to persuading judges than juries and was at his best in appellate practice. Evarts was able to earn a large income from his legal work, and he counted Wall Street bankers, merchants, and insurance companies among his clients. His biographer estimated his annual income at a staggering $75,000 – about 2.3 million in today's dollars.[11] Personally, Evarts was known to be engaging, friendly, and mild mannered, qualities that won him a wide circle of friends.

Evarts also got in on the ground floor of the Republican Party in New York in 1855. In the party, Evarts connected with and eventually befriended William Seward, who spearheaded the party's development in the state. Evarts was more moderate than his friend Seward, and counted himself as a moderate Republican throughout his life. During the 1850s he strongly opposed the extension of slavery in the territories, but he did not count himself as an abolitionist. Indeed, Evarts drew fire from the Radical wing of the Republican party for the speech he had given at Castle Garden in New York in 1850, in which he defended the constitutionality of the recently proposed fugitive slave law.[12] In the speech, Evarts urged his audience to consider the duties Northern citizens owed to their Southern counterparts to maintain interstate comity and to keep the Union intact. Returning fugitive slaves to their masters was a requirement of the Constitution, and Evarts warned his listeners that "he who strikes at *a* law, strikes at *the* law."[13]

---

[10] Martin, *Causes and Conflicts*, 24.
[11] See www.measuringworth.com (accessed November 1, 2016).
[12] Barrows, *William M. Evarts*, 41.
[13] William Maxwell Evarts, "Speech at the Union Meeting in Castle Garden," in Evarts, *Arguments and Speeches*, 2: 433.

Whatever ground Evarts lost with antislavery Republicans in his Castle Garden speech, he more than regained with his participation in the *Lemmon* case on the eve of the Civil War. In *Lemmon v. New York*, Evarts was pitted against Charles O'Conor. The two lawyers battled in the New York Court of Appeals over the scope and possible extension of the recent *Dred Scott* decision. New York had enacted a statute that freed slaves who were brought into the state voluntarily, even if their sojourn in New York was a temporary one undertaken in the course of an interstate journey with their master. *Dred Scott* had prohibited the federal government from outlawing slavery in the territories, but *Lemmon* raised the question of whether the free *states* could interfere with a slaveholder's right to travel unimpeded throughout the United States – with the unfree status of his human property intact.[14] The Lemmons were Virginia residents who had temporarily brought their slaves with them to New York while en route to Texas.[15] A New York judge freed the slaves pursuant to a writ of habeas corpus filed on their behalf. In the court of appeals, Evarts, who was retained as counsel for the state of New York, argued that *Dred Scott* could not be read to support a federal right of uninterrupted transit (as a benefit of national citizenship) for slaveholders through a free state.

It was permissible for the state to refuse to tolerate slavery within its borders. Slavery was a status contrary to the law of nature, Evarts insisted, and thus needed positive law to support it. No such positive law existed in New York, which, by default, meant that slaves became free on entering the state. Furthermore, Evarts argued, skirting closer to

[14] *Dred Scott* had held that neither Congress nor the territorial legislatures could constitutionally bar slavery in the federal territories. Lincoln, in his 1858 "House Divided" speech, had worried that the next step would be to exalt the right to own slaves to such an extent as to prevent the states from banning the institution. *Lemmon* showed that Lincoln's fears were well grounded. Abraham Lincoln, "House Divided Speech," in Lincoln, *This Fiery Trial: The Speeches and Writings of Abraham Lincoln*, ed. William E. Gienapp (New York: Oxford University Press, 2002), 43. For an analysis of the case and the role of the lawyers who argued it, see Paul Finkelman, *An Imperfect Union: Slavery, Federalism, and Comity* (Chapel Hill: University of North Carolina Press, 1981), 296–313; John D. Gordan III, "The Lemmon Slave Case," *Report of the Historical Society of the Courts of the State of New York* 4 (2006): 1; available at www.courts.state.ny.us/history/pdf/HSNLVol.4.pdf (accessed November 1, 2016).

[15] Before the interstate railroad came to Texas, a trip by steamboat to New York, and then to Texas, was in fact the easiest route from Virginia to Texas.

undercutting some of the arguments he had ventured at Castle Garden in 1850, principles of comity did not require the free states to recognize slave status "existing abroad." It was perfectly permissible for New York to prefer the freedom guaranteed to individuals by the law of nations, which coincided with the domestic policy of the state, to a "foreign municipal law [of the slave states] of force against right." For Evarts, maintaining the unfree status of the Lemmons' slaves in these circumstances would violate the sovereignty of the state of New York. As he argued, "The Federal Constitution and legislation under it have, in principle and theory, no concern with the domestic institutions … within the several States," unless the Constitution prescribed an exception, as it had in the Fugitive Slave Clause. There was no countervailing federal principle that would overcome New York's profreedom directive.[16] Evarts won the case, which O'Conor had planned to appeal to the Supreme Court of the United States when the Civil War intervened.

Throughout the war, Evarts devoted much of his energy to supporting the Union cause in court, defending the government's legal position on the status of the Confederacy in several notable cases. These included the 1861 case of the *Savannah* privateers, in which Confederate blockade runners were prosecuted in New York for the crime of piracy. The crew of the *Savannah* contended that they were not guilty of piracy, as their privateering actions had the sanction of the Confederate government. Until the Civil War, the United States had declined to ratify the Declaration of Paris (1856), which banned privateering.[17] In the case of the *Savannah*, the government maintained that the blockade runners were guilty of piracy, regardless of the applicability of the Declaration of Paris in America. This was because the Confederate government was a nullity and thus incapable of ratifying the lawless acts of the defendants by granting letters of marque. The Confederacy was itself an illegitimate band of marauders.[18]

[16] Lemmon v. People, 20 N.Y. at 592–99 (1860) (oral argument of William M. Evarts). The Fugitive Slave Clause did not apply here because the owners brought the slaves into New York voluntarily.
[17] The United States acceded to the Declaration of Paris only in 1861, owing to the fact that the Confederacy relied on privateers and the Union did not.
[18] See John Fabian Witt, *Lincoln's Code: The Laws of War in American History* (New York: Free Press, 2012), chapter 5; Mark Weitz, *The Confederacy on Trial: The Piracy and Sequestration Cases of 1861* (Lawrence: University Press of Kansas, 2005).

In the course of laying out the government's position, Evarts argued that the federal courts were bound to instruct the jury in conformity with the Lincoln administration's views on the Confederacy's nonexistence. In other words, sanction from the Confederate government would not insulate the defendants from a piracy charge. In fact, Evarts characterized contrary judicial instructions as potential incursions on the president's executive power to recognize foreign nations. Evarts argued that the courts could not deviate from the political branches' position and independently confer some kind of semiofficial status on the Confederacy. "I have never heard it proposed," he maintained, "as a view either of public or domestic law, that when a Government has declined to recognize a nation, it was within the jurisdiction of a Court of that Government to determine differently, and reverse the decision of the political power."[19]

After the war, Evarts continued his advocacy on behalf of the Union in both the Davis case and in the Alabama Claims international arbitration.[20] In the flush of Union victory and the trial and conviction of the Lincoln assassins, securing a conviction against Davis when and if the case did go to trial did not actually strike Evarts as a very difficult task. The opportunity to vindicate the principles of the Republican Party and Union victory in a court of law undoubtedly led Evarts to accept the government's retainer in the Davis case. Representing the government in such a high-profile case on such an important topic – Evarts quoted the *New York Herald*, which termed it "the greatest criminal trial of the age" – was a very attractive prospect.[21] Had Evarts won a treason conviction against Davis and confirmed the legitimacy of the Union war effort, he certainly would have cemented his reputation as one of the foremost attorneys in the country.

---

[19] Warburton, *Trial of the Officers and Crew of the Schooner Savannah*, 193. To the embarrassment of the federal government, the case resulted in a hung jury and the privateers were set free. For more information on the case and the New York jury's refusal to convict, see Weitz, *The Confederacy on Trial*; John D. Gordan III, "The Trial of the Officers and Crew of the Schooner 'Savannah,'" *Yearbook 1983 Supreme Court Historical Society* (1983): 31.

[20] See Adrian Cook, *The Alabama Claims: American Politics and Anglo-American Relations, 1865–1872* (Ithaca: Cornell University Press, 1975).

[21] *New York Herald*, October 28, 1865; William Evarts to John Clifford, November 11, 1865, Papers August–December 1865, John H. Clifford Papers, MHS. Defense counsel also quoted the same headline. Charles O'Conor to Jefferson Davis, April 18, 1868, Box 24, Jefferson Davis Papers, MC.

In fact, Evarts was a conservative choice on the government's part. He was solidly pro-government but hardly a Radical. Evarts was selected to represent the government in the Davis case on the recommendation of William Seward, who advised Attorney General Speed to retain his friend. His co-counsel John Clifford also came recommended by Seward and Edwin Stanton. The attorney general's decision to retain private outside counsel to direct the case was not an unusual one. Prior to the organization of the Department of Justice in 1870, few lawyers worked in the attorney general's office. The attorney general himself typically considered it his job to argue cases on behalf of the government only in the Supreme Court. The federal government did employ local U.S. attorneys throughout the United States to prosecute the government's interests in the local federal courts, but their efforts were often supplemented by outside counsel in complex or high-profile cases.[22]

Speed did not consult the president before offering Evarts and Clifford the retainer. His decision was somewhat controversial within the cabinet, so Speed presented it as a fait accompli. Secretary Welles thought Evarts and Clifford to be poor choices for a jury trial, counting them "both learned and able counsel before the court, but not as distinguished for success with a jury." Welles found them both too tepid, especially compared with former Union general (and well-known Radical Republican) Benjamin Butler. In Welles's opinion, Butler possessed the necessary mettle to prosecute Davis, not based on his qualities "as a politician or statesman, but because he possesses great ability, courage, strength, I may add audacity, as a lawyer."[23] Butler was bold, to be sure, but he was also known to be self-aggrandizing and unpleasant to work with, and the cabinet quickly dismissed the notion of retaining him.

[22] Luther A. Huston, *The Department of Justice* (New York: Frederick A. Praeger, 1967), 90; Homer Cummings and Carl McFarland, *Federal Justice: Chapters in the History of Justice and the Federal Executive* (New York: Macmillan, 1927), 188–229; Arthur J. Dodge, Origin and Development of the Office of the Attorney General, H.R. Doc. No. 70-510, at 10–11 (1929). See also Jed Shugerman, "The Creation of the Department of Justice," *Stanford Law Review* 66 (2014): 121, and Robert J. Kaczorowski, *The Politics of Judicial Interpretation: The Federal Courts, the Department of Justice and Civil Rights, 1866–1876* (New York: Oceana Publications, 1985), esp. 79–99, for a discussion of how the Department of Justice functioned in its early years to enforce the Reconstruction-era civil rights statutes.

[23] Welles, *Diary of Gideon Welles*, 2: 367–68.

The decision to retain the placid Evarts over the more fiery Butler had tangible consequences. Butler would not have permitted procedural constraints to prevent Davis's conviction and punishment. Butler met with President Johnson to discuss the problem of the Davis trial in 1865. At the conference, Johnson expressed concern that the American public might erupt in fury if Davis were convicted "by a negro jury in Virginia," even if the trial took place in a regularly constituted civil court. "Such a trial," Johnson worried, "continuing perhaps at great length and occupying the public mind, might cause great bitterness of feeling especially in the South."[24]

Butler brushed these concerns aside. Rather than pursuing a civil trial, he proposed convening a military commission to try Davis, on the theory that the state of Virginia remained under military control. The commission would consist of nine U.S. generals, with Butler himself in charge. If Davis advanced a pro-secession argument in mounting his defense, Butler would answer: "All of us sitting here have fought four years to decide those questions in the negative, and therefore it would be useless to have them argued here." Butler said he would permit Davis to appeal to the Supreme Court after his certain conviction by the military commission, as he believed that the Court could be counted on to rubber stamp the military commission's ruling and thereby provide a "definitive" legal pronouncement against the constitutionality of secession.[25]

Thus, Butler would have pursued Davis's conviction with single-minded zeal. Evarts's retainer, in contrast, represented a far more cautious approach by the government. Indeed, Evarts and Clifford understood their assignment as limited in scope: they were to proceed against Davis only on a treason charge in a civil court.[26] Speed did not instruct them to prepare for a military trial, or even to weigh the

---

[24] Benjamin Butler, *Butler's Book: Autobiography and Reminiscences of Major-General Benjamin F. Butler* (Boston: A. M. Thayer, 1892), 915–18.

[25] Butler, *Butler's Book*, 915–18. Butler did not lay out a plan to have the case reviewed on appeal by the Supreme Court, but in *Ex parte Vallandigham*, 68 U.S. 243 (1863), the Supreme Court had decided that no appeal could be taken from a military commission directly to the Supreme Court. See also *Ex parte Milligan*, 71 U.S. 2 (1866), in which the defendant appealed his military conviction to the federal circuit court and from there to the Supreme Court, as permitted by the Habeas Corpus Act of 1863.

[26] *Impeachment Investigation: Testimony Taken before the Judiciary Committee of the House of Representatives in the Investigation of the Charges against Andrew Johnson* (Washington, DC: Government Printing Office, 1867), 653 (testimony of William Evarts).

benefits and drawbacks of trial before a military tribunal against those of a regular civil trial. As Evarts confirmed in testimony given in the House of Representatives in 1867, "My whole connection with the subject, were with reference to a judicial trial in a civil court. I never regarded myself as having been asked to represent the government or advise it at all on the question of a military trial, and I have no doubt I truly understood my position."[27]

Charles O'Conor's advocacy on behalf of Jefferson Davis was very different in kind: it was unrestrained, creative, energetic – and above all, successful. At the time he took on the role as Davis's lead lawyer, O'Conor had earned a reputation as "leader of the New York bar" and was probably the most famous attorney in the country (Figure 2.2).[28] His friend Samuel J. Tilden lauded him as "the greatest jurist among all the English-speaking race."[29] This lofty status was not the passive product of an elite existence: it reflected a steely determination. O'Conor had been a scrapper from an early age. Born in Manhattan in 1804, O'Conor had grown up very poor, the son of a well-educated but impoverished Irish Catholic immigrant who had fallen on hard times soon after coming to the United States. Rather than attending college or law school, O'Conor learned at home from his father and then read law in an office for several years. On passing the New York bar in 1824, O'Conor sought to open his own practice, but he did not have enough money to purchase the necessary law books until a benefactor agreed to endorse a note that enabled him to buy them on credit.

O'Conor's professional stature grew over time, and his contemporaries credited his rise to his inexhaustible energy and comprehensive knowledge of special pleading rules, which he put to good use in a wide

---

[27] *Impeachment Investigation*, 653 (testimony of William Evarts).
[28] Henry Ellsworth Gregory, "Charles O'Conor," in *Great American Lawyers*, ed. William Draper Lewis, 8 vols. (Philadelphia: John C. Winston, 1907), 5: 84; Strong, *Landmarks of a Lawyer's Lifetime*, 217. While abroad in Rome in late 1869, O'Conor himself admitted in his diary that he was "strangely enough denominated ... the 'great' American lawyer, 'leader of the bar,' etc." Charles O'Conor diary, December 23, 1869, quoted in Charles W. Sloane, "Charles O'Conor: Some Incidents of His Life, From His Private Papers, Parts I & II," *United States Catholic Historical Magazine* 4 (1891): 225–50, 396–429, 420.
[29] Samuel Tilden to Patrick Ford, May 13, 1884, in Samuel Tilden, *Letters and Literary Memorials of Samuel J. Tilden*, 2 vols. (New York: Harper Brothers, 1908), 2: 643.

FIGURE 2.2 Lead defense attorney Charles O'Conor. Library of Congress.

array of cases in his highly diversified law practice.[30] His considerable
fortune came primarily from his work on a number of high-profile
probate cases, but his reputation as a great advocate became firmly
cemented with his work on the notorious Forrest divorce case in the
early 1850s, in which he represented Catherine Sinclair, the estranged

[30] His talent with special pleading rules led O'Conor to oppose the code reform movement, once telling David Dudley Field that "under your code, Mr. Field, the plaintiff
comes into court and tells his story like one old woman and the defendant comes in
and tells his story like another old woman." *Chicago Legal News* 44 (1912): 144.

wife of noted stage actor Edwin Forrest.[31] After his work on the Davis case, O'Conor went on to lead the prosecution of the Tweed Ring in the 1870s, along with his friend Samuel Tilden, and he represented Tilden in the electoral dispute arising out of the presidential contest of 1876.[32] In the New York of the late 1860s, O'Conor was somewhat unique among the men at the height of the increasingly rarefied legal profession, in that he had never attended college, let alone law school, and did not hail from a privileged background.[33] If O'Conor's humble

[31] O'Conor's fortune in the 1860 census was listed as $150,000; it was $450,000 (including both real and personal property) in the 1870 census. Charles O'Conor, United States Eighth Census (1860), New York County, New York (see "1860 United States Federal Census," Ancestry.com, http://search.ancestry.com/search/db.aspx?dbid=7667, accessed November 1, 2016); Charles O'Conor, United States Ninth Census (1870), New York County, New York (see "1870 United States Federal Census," Ancestry.com, http://search.ancestry.com/search/db.aspx?dbid=7163, accessed November 1, 2016). Some of his more famous will cases included the Jumel Will Case, the Mason Will Case, the Parish Will Case, and the Lispenard Will Case. As Bruce Kimball points out, O'Conor's high fees may have been inflated, and shifty accounting in such cases seems to have been the norm rather than the exception. Bruce A. Kimball, *The Inception of Modern Professional Education: C. C. Langdell, 1826–1906* (Chapel Hill: University of North Carolina Press, 2009), 78–81; Bruce A. Kimball and R. Blake Brown, "'The Highest Legal Ability in the Nation: Langdell on Wall Street, 1855–1870," *Law and Social Inquiry* 29 (Winter 2004): 39, 94–100.

[32] Samuel Tilden, *The New York City "Ring": Its Origin, Maturity and Fall Discussed* (New York: J. Polemus, 1873); Charles O'Conor, *Peculation Triumphant: Being the Record of a Four Years' Campaign against Official Malversation in the City of New York* (New York: John Polemus, 1875); Michael F. Holt, *By One Vote: The Disputed Presidential Election of 1876* (Lawrence: University Press of Kansas, 2008), 226.

[33] See Wayne K. Hobson, "Symbol of the New Profession: Emergence of the Large Law Firm, 1870–1915," and Robert W. Gordon, "'The Ideal and the Actual in the Law': Fantasies and Practices of New York City Lawyers, 1870–1910," in *The New High Priests: Lawyers in Post–Civil War America*, ed. Gerald Gawalt (Westport, CT: Greenwood Press, 1984), 3–28, 51–74. Despite O'Conor's vaunted reputation in the nineteenth century, his name is obscure today. Scholarly interest in O'Conor has been very minimal; there is no full-length biography of him. Perhaps this is owing to the unpopularity of his reactionary views on race, or to the fact that O'Conor's career at the bar did not conform to the accepted model for an elite lawyer, who would have attended an elite law school, hailed from a middle-class Protestant background, practiced in a law firm rather than as a sole practitioner, endorsed legal modernizing reforms such as code pleading, and espoused generally progressive political beliefs. Charles Warren's highbrow *History of the American Bar*, published in 1911, reveals how much O'Conor's reputation had suffered by the early twentieth century. Tellingly, Warren mentions O'Conor just once, in passing, a fact that prompted one contemporary reviewer to note the difference between the popular perception of the eminent figures at the bar and the scholarly inattention to men such as O'Conor, writing that "no one would suspect from reading the book that Charles O'Conor is

beginnings made him an anomaly among elite New York lawyers, they also endeared him to the large Irish working-class community in the city, who regarded O'Conor as something of a hero.[34]

Throughout the course of his long career, O'Conor had argued many important cases, but his high stature in the legal profession had not translated into a political career – nor did he want it to. O'Conor had served in public office only as the U.S. attorney for the Southern District of New York in the 1850s and as a delegate to the New York constitutional convention in the 1840s, where he had notoriously opposed the Married Women's Property Act.[35] In 1860 O'Conor squelched rumors of a run for the vice presidency, and some years later he declined a third-party nomination for president. In 1865, at age sixty-one, O'Conor had announced his retirement but remained as busy in his law practice as ever.

He was a spare man of average height with a grim visage, a slow, deliberate style of speaking, and a somewhat forbidding manner that did not endear him to his fellow attorneys or gain him any points with juries. It was widely acknowledged that his skill as an attorney stemmed from his prodigious attention to detail, indefatigable devotion to research, and knowledge of the arcane history of the common law, rather than a dynamic courtroom presence and an ability to connect with jurors. When he was once asked how he had achieved his considerable success, he replied with a single word: "Study."[36]

O'Conor's forbidding manner was accompanied by a bitingly acerbic wit, which contributed to his frosty public reputation. Best-selling author Matthew Hale Smith wrote that he possessed "a quiet, almost cold manner" and an "inexorable logic," and fellow attorney Joseph

still considered by the laity to be the greatest lawyer that New York has ever seen." Roger Foster, review of *History of the American Bar* by Charles Warren, *American Historical Review* 17 (April 1912): 616–18, 618; Charles Warren, *History of the American Bar* (Boston: Little, Brown, 1911), 409.

[34] See Florence Gibson, *The Attitudes of the New York Irish toward State and National Affairs, 1848–1892* (New York: AMS Press, 1951), 286, on O'Conor's exalted status in the Irish American community.

[35] See Norma Basch, *In the Eyes of the Law: Women, Marriage, and Property in Nineteenth-Century New York* (Ithaca: Cornell University Press, 1982), 152–56.

[36] Van Vechten Veeder, ed., *Legal Masterpieces: Specimens of Argumentation and Exposition by Eminent Lawyers*, 2 vols. (Chicago: Callahan, 1912), 2: 820.

Choate likened him to "a machine of steel springs and hard rubber."[37] Even O'Conor's good friend Samuel Tilden considered him somewhat difficult to get along with, describing him as "a man of extensive and accurate legal learning, of an acuteness of reason somewhat excessive even for the higher uses of his profession – of great mental activity – indefatigable, vehement and sarcastic in controversy – remarked at the bar as able rather than wise, and remarkable for want of tact."[38] O'Conor himself admitted that he lacked the ability to compromise; he declined a presidential nomination in 1872 because of his "love of absolute independence which cannot now be maintained in public office."[39]

O'Conor's single-minded devotion to purpose served him well in the Davis case. From the beginning, O'Conor threw himself wholeheartedly into his advocacy on Davis's behalf, and as one biographer recounts, he determined to "make [his representation] the crowning professional achievement of his life."[40] On receiving letters from Varina Davis, Virginia Clay, and their supporters begging for his assistance in May 1865, O'Conor had immediately volunteered his services.[41] O'Conor later wryly explained to John C. Breckinridge that he had taken on the task of representing Davis "for the purpose of saving my country from the reproach of unanimity."[42]

In truth, O'Conor's reasons for taking on Davis's defense went far beyond sheer orneriness and nonconformist tendencies, although he certainly possessed those qualities. O'Conor's advocacy on Davis's behalf stemmed from his own conservative political sensibilities.

[37] Matthew Hale Smith, *Sunshine and Shadow in New York* (Hartford, CT: J. B. Burr, 1869), 534; Choate quoted in Edward J. McGuire, "The Catholic Bar of New York from 1808–1908," *United States Catholic Historical Society: Historical Records and Studies* 5, Part 1 (November 1907): 414, 420. See Eric Foner, *Reconstruction: America's Unfinished Revolution, 1863–1877* (New York: Harper and Row, 1988), 477, for an account of the appeal of Smith's work, which contrasted the living conditions of the rich and the poor in New York.

[38] Samuel Tilden to an unknown correspondent (probably John Bigelow), January 15, 1853, Charles O'Conor Papers, Miscellaneous Manuscripts, Manuscripts Division, New York Public Library, New York (repository hereafter cited as NYPL).

[39] *Columbus Daily Enquirer*, September 8, 1872.

[40] Hamilton W. Mabie, ed., *The Portrait Gallery of Eminent Lawyers* (New York: Shea and Jenner, 1880), 314; Smith, *Sunshine and Shadow in New York*, 535–36.

[41] Charles O'Conor to Jefferson Davis, June 2, 1865, Box 24, Davis Papers, MC.

[42] Charles O'Conor to John C. Breckinridge, July 5, 1865, Breckinridge-Marshall Papers, Filson Historical Society, Louisville, KY. See also Charles O'Conor to Franklin Pierce, July 5, 1865, Reel 3, Franklin Pierce Papers, LC [microform edition].

O'Conor shared many of Davis's political views, including a belief in the inherent inferiority of African Americans and the attendant benefits of the institution of racial slavery. In late 1859 he delivered a speech at the New York Academy of Music in which he justified the institution of slavery and condemned Northern antislavery zealots for threatening the integrity of the Union with their strong abolitionist rhetoric. In that speech O'Conor asserted that African Americans had been "assigned by nature" to servitude. Thus, he claimed, it was "not an injustice to leave the negro in the condition in which nature has placed him, and for which he alone is adapted. Fitted only for a state of pupilage, our slave system gives him a master to govern him and to supply his deficiencies: in this there is no injustice."[43]

O'Conor established his proslavery credentials in two famous slavery cases in New York's highest court: *Jack v. Martin* (1835) and *Lemmon v. New York* (1860).[44] O'Conor won *Jack v. Martin* in the New York Court of Errors, arguing that the state could not bar its citizens from owning slaves who resided in other states. Even more prominent was O'Conor's participation in the *Lemmon* case, in which he appeared for the state of Virginia and against opposing counsel William Evarts. In *Lemmon*, O'Conor sought to turn some of the most established wisdom about the law of slavery on its head. He assailed Lord Mansfield's famous dictum in the 1772 English *Somerset* case, which set forth the maxim that slavery was an unnatural status unrecognized by the common law that could only be legalized by express statutory authorization. Mansfield's declaration caused, in O'Conor's punchy prose, "negro-philism [to be] in raptures with him ever since." O'Conor's gift for withering sarcasm was used to devastating effect when he characterized Mansfield's lauded precept as "a bald inconsequential truism" and scorned the supposedly liberty-giving character of English common law. "English ... air," he stated, "had not its true enfranchising purity till drawn through the nostrils of a negro. White slaves had long respired it without their status being at all affected."[45]

---

[43] Charles O'Conor, *Negro Slavery Not Unjust* (New York: Van Evrie, 1859). See also Nathaniel Macon to Charles O'Conor, August 24, 1860, in Nathaniel Macon, *Letters to Chas. O'Conor: The Destruction of the Union Is Emancipation* (Philadelphia: John Campbell, 1862).

[44] Jack v. Martin, 12 Wend. 311 (N.Y. Sup. Ct. 1834); Jack v. Martin, 14 Wend. 507 (N.Y. 1835). Lemmon v. People, 20 N.Y. at 562.

[45] Lemmon v. People, 20 N.Y. at 568, 566 (oral argument of Charles O'Conor).

O'Conor's defense of slavery in the Academy of Music speech came on the heels of his argument in *Lemmon,* and critics accused him of shilling for his client rather than expressing his own honestly held beliefs. At an anti-O'Conor rally organized by New York's African American community, speaker Jeremiah Powers questioned the sincerity of O'Conor's beliefs, maintaining that the hateful sentiments O'Conor had expressed at the Academy of Music stemmed from his advocacy in the *Lemmon* case. "Even if Charles O'Conor was not paid for that speech," Powers insisted, "he is to be paid for the slave speech he made for the State of Virginia in the Lemmon Slave Case; and he had to dance to the music there, or he didn't know whether Virginia would pay him."[46] Politician George Washington Clark also chastised O'Conor for the "unblushing boldness" of his racist beliefs, arguing that as an Irish American who had himself experienced anti-Catholic and anti-Irish prejudice, he should have sympathized with African Americans.[47] Given the discrepancy between O'Conor's opinions and the antislavery viewpoints of reform-minded Irishmen Daniel O'Connell and Jonathan Swift, Clark could not bring himself to believe that O'Conor actually meant what he said. In Clark's opinion, O'Conor must have acted merely to advance the cause of the slaveholders in the *Lemmon* case. "Can it be," Clark queried, "that this newly-fledged champion of human bondage, is from the same Emerald Isle where repose the ashes of Dean Swift?"[48]

O'Conor's proslavery sentiments were sincere, however, and they led him to align himself with the Southern wing of the Democratic Party, even to the extent of accepting Southern separatism during the sectional crisis. He subscribed to the compact theory of the Union, asserting that the states were "independent nations, ... co-equal members of a Confederacy," but he did not embrace the doctrine of secession

---

[46] "The Anti-O'Conor Meeting," *Weekly Anglo-African* (New York), January 28, 1860.
[47] After O'Conor's death, a biographer commented on this inability to analogize the plight of the Irish to that of African Americans: "One would suppose that a person of such tender sensibilities ... would have had some sympathy with the four millions of black slaves in this country at that time. On the contrary, he always admired, and defended the system of human slavery, and thought its subjects very reprehensible for trying to run away from it. This in an Irishman and a lawyer seems anomalous." Irving Browne, "Charles O'Conor," *Green Bag* 7 (1895): 1–11, 83–92, 85.
[48] George Washington Clark, *Refutation of Mr. Charles O'Connor's Defence of Slavery before the Union Meeting in New York and before the Court of Appeals in Albany* (Rochester, NY: published by the author, 1860), 3, 17.

unequivocally. He believed that the Southern states were justified in exercising "the sacred right of revolution" and exiting the Union, but maintained that "as a mere point in jurisprudence, the 'right of secession' cannot exist," because the Union was an organic entity, and, as such, retained the right and the obligation to defend and maintain its own existence and integrity.[49]

However, O'Conor also insisted that there was no practical distinction between the right of revolution and the purported right of secession, and that the national government could not and should not "pin [the Union] together with bayonets." According to O'Conor, the founders understood that "the Central government in the very nature of things, could never wage war against any rebel State for the purpose of reducing it to subjection and holding it captive as a delinquent." It was thus futile to argue against the right of secession when there was no possible way for the federal government to stop resistant states from exercising it: "It is an axiom that in the action of States the power to do a thing without the danger of being coerced to retract, is not practically distinguishable from the right to do it." For O'Conor, the "only important question" that remained was whether the election of a Republican president in 1860 had threatened the Southern states to such an extent as to justify their withdrawal from the Union. Unsurprisingly, he answered this query in the affirmative. Because "the moral odium or sentiment of conscientious aversion [toward slavery] must find its way into the action of the central government," he said, the South would eventually suffer harm by remaining within the United States. "Whenever the virtuous haters acquire sufficient power," O'Conor wrote, "the unhappy hated must become the subject of hourly insult and daily oppression."[50]

O'Conor also drew an unflattering analogy between the subservient position of the South under Republican rule in Washington and the long-standing oppression of Ireland under English rule. He predicted that Lincoln and the Republicans would try to divide Southerners against each other, such that "every expectant of office or of profit in any form under his administration, would seek and obtain his favor by action toward their fellow citizens precisely as the Orangemen of Ireland in the worst period of Irish history treated that class of their fellow subjects who were loyal to the peculiar interests of their

---

[49] O'Conor quoted in Sloane, "Charles O'Conor," 413–14.
[50] Sloane, "Charles O'Conor," 414.

native land, or adhered to the prevailing faith." Because, as O'Conor put it, these evils "are in their nature intolerable," he understood and approved of the South's decision to exit the Union.[51] Long after the Civil War, he still linked the Confederate cause to Ireland's troubles, suggesting "[Thaddeus] Kosciusko failed and [Robert] Emmet perished" as an appropriate epigraph for Davis's pro-secession polemic *The Rise and Fall of the Confederate Government*.[52]

These issues hit home for O'Conor. For him, the issue of Southern independence and the "oppression" of the South in the United States was bound up with Ireland's subordinate relationship with England. O'Conor's father, Thomas O'Connor,[53] had come to the United States in 1801, forced to leave Ireland because of his participation in the failed rebellion of 1798.[54] According to one newspaper

---

[51] Sloane, "Charles O'Conor," 415.

[52] Charles O'Conor to Jefferson Davis, July 28, 1881, Jefferson Davis Papers, Alabama Department of Archives and History, Montgomery (repository hereafter cited as ADAH). Thaddeus Kosciusko was a Polish patriot who fought in the American Revolution; Robert Emmet was an Irish nationalist who was killed in the aftermath of the 1798 uprising against English rule. Emmet's brother, Thomas Addis Emmet, emigrated to the United States and became a noted New York attorney. He was a good friend of O'Conor's father, and O'Conor participated in various presentations to honor Emmet for his actions on behalf of oppressed Irish Catholics in America. See Thomas Addis Emmet, *Memoir of Thomas Addis and Robert Emmet*, 2 vols. (New York: Emmet Press, 1915), 1: 464–66, 539.

[53] Charles O'Conor adopted the spelling of his name with one *n* upon visiting Ireland for the first time in 1841, and discovering that his great-grandfather, Charles O'Conor of Belanagare, a noted Irish scholar of the eighteenth century, had changed the spelling of his name from O'Connor to O'Conor after researching O'Con[n]or family history. Charles O'Conor (of New York) wrote in his diary, "His son Charles, my grandfather, adhered to the method of spelling the name which he had learned in his youth; and hence the difference." Hence also the difference between the spelling of Charles O'Conor and Thomas O'Connor. "Notes and Comments," *United States Catholic Historical Society: Historical Records and Studies* 12 (1918): 136, 136–37. See also Charles P. Daly, "Charles O'Conor: His Professional Life and Character," *Magazine of American History* 13 (June 1885): 513, 527.

[54] On Thomas O'Connor, see *Irish-American* (New York), May 24, 1884. For more information about the rebellion of 1798 and the O'Connors' involvement in it, see Thomas Pakenham, *The Year of Liberty: The History of the Great Irish Rebellion of 1798* (New York: Random House, 1969); Charles Owen O'Conor, *O'Conor Don, The O'Conors of Connaught: An Historical Memoir* (Dublin: Hodges, Figgis, 1891), 47–78, 292–308, 319; John O. Ranelagh, *A Short History of Ireland* (Cambridge: Cambridge University Press, 1983), 3. For more on O'Connor's move to America, see Charles O'Conor, *Letters of Charles O'Conor of Belangare: A Catholic Voice in Eighteenth-Century Ireland*, ed. Robert E. Ward, John F. Wrynn, SJ, and Catherine Coogan Ward (Washington, DC: Catholic University of America Press, 1988);

report, the elder O'Connor had spent the three intervening years in a Scottish prison along with the other Irish patriots (or rebels), which could well have contributed to Charles O'Conor's empathy for Jefferson Davis.[55] Arriving in New York City with a fairly substantial inheritance, Thomas O'Connor tried to establish a colony for expatriate Irishmen on land he purchased in Genesee (now Steuben) County in the western part of New York.[56] He moved with his wife and newborn son to that uncharted wilderness, where the young Charles remembered Indian raids and attacks by wild animals. The experiment lasted five years and ended in bankruptcy, and the son recalled gloomy days spent with his parents in debtors' prison as a young child.[57] After his release, the elder O'Connor turned to his pen for a living, publishing *The Shamrock or Hibernian Chronicle*, the first newspaper in the United States to promulgate a specifically Irish Catholic viewpoint.[58] His home in New York City also became a haven for the aging refugees of the 1798 Irish Rebellion, whom Charles O'Conor met as a child.

Thomas O'Connor passed his abiding concerns on to his son, who devoted much of his spare time to Irish causes and felt keenly the effects of anti-Irish and anti-Catholic prejudice in the United States. When asked whether his ethnicity had helped him in his career, O'Conor emphatically countered: "By no means. So far from being an advantage, the reputation of being an Irishman and a Catholic has been to

Thomas O'Connor to Charles O'Conor (of Stowe), July 5, 1815, and February 9, 1816, items 880–81, Stowe Manuscripts, HEHL.

[55] *Irish-American* (New York), May 24, 1884. This is likely an apocryphal report, as there is no other record of this imprisonment. United Irishman Arthur O'Connor and his brother Roger were imprisoned at Fort George, which may have led to the confusion. See Clifford Conner, *Arthur O'Connor* (New York: iUniverse, 2009).

[56] Sloane, "Charles O'Conor," 227.

[57] Thomas O'Connor is listed in the 1810 census in debtors' prison. Thomas O'Connor household, United States Third Census (1810), New York County, New York ("1810 United States Federal Census," Ancestry.com, http://search.ancestry.com/search/db.aspx?dbid=7613, accessed April 11, 2017). See Mabie, *The Portrait Gallery of Eminent Lawyers*, 215, on O'Conor's childhood recollections of the prison's "gloominess." See also O'Conor, *The O'Conors of Connaught*, 304–5, and Bruce Mann, *Republic of Debtors* (Cambridge, MA: Harvard University Press, 2002), on life in the New York debtors' prison.

[58] Thomas F. Meehan, "New York's First Catholic Newspaper," *United States Catholic Historical Society: Historical Records and Studies* 3 (1903): 115, 118. Charles O'Conor to Joseph Maria Finotti, February 25, 1867, in Joseph M. Finotti, *Bibliographia Catholica Americana* (New York: Catholic Publication House, 1872), 209–10.

me a most serious political, social, and professional disadvantage."[59] O'Conor was a benefactor of many Catholic causes as well, including the founding of his local church, St. Elizabeth's, in Fort Washington (now Washington Heights), and the construction of St. Patrick's (new) Cathedral on Fifth Avenue.[60] For O'Conor, Irish and Catholic identity ran together, and he often conflated the two.[61]

O'Conor's pro-Irish fervor translated into a pro-Southern sensibility, which in turn caused him to view the Civil War as an unparalleled calamity in American history. This was not only because it had cemented the dominance of the Republican Party and the destruction of Southern slave society, but also because it had led Americans to substitute the imperative of force for the rule of law. O'Conor regarded the Civil War as a great tragedy, referring to it as "that disastrous event ... which divided this great Republic, and from a band of united brothers converted our people into two great warring nations."[62] During the

---

[59] John Bigelow, "Some Recollections of Charles O'Conor," *Century Magazine* 29 (March 1885): 725, 732.

[60] See John M. Farley, *History of St. Patrick's Cathedral* (New York: Society for the Propagation of Faith, 1908), 235, and Henry A. Brann, "A Few Chapters in Church History: St. Elizabeth's Church," *United States Catholic Historical Society: Historical Records and Studies* 6 (February 1911): 63, for information on O'Conor's involvement in the establishment of Catholic churches in New York. For information on O'Conor's interest in Irish history, see "Charles O'Conor's Will," *New York Herald*, May 30, 1884, and O'Conor, *The O'Conors of Connaught*, xx. Discussion of O'Conor's continuing association with the exiled Irish patriots of 1798, such as Wolfe Tone, William Sampson, and Thomas Moore, can be found in his correspondence with Charles P. Daly: Charles O'Conor to Charles P. Daly, March 7, 1864, and June 27, 1864, Box 4; May 21, 1879, Box 5, Charles P. Daly Papers, NYPL, and in Luke Gibbons, "Republicanism and Radical Memory: The O'Conors, O'Carolan and the United Irishmen," in *Revolution, Counter-Revolution, and Union: Ireland in the 1790s*, ed. Jim Smyth (New York: Cambridge University Press, 2000), 211–27; "Notes and Comments," *United States Catholic Historical Society*, 138. For information on O'Conor's involvement in the banquet for John Mitchel and in various St. Patrick's Day's celebrations, see *New York Times*, December 20, 1853 [John Mitchel], and Charles O'Conor to John I. Binnys, March 15, 1844, folder 25, Box 1, Thomas F. Madigan Papers, NYPL; Charles O'Conor, Robert Emmett, and Charles M. Connolly to Samuel Tilden, May 9, 1848, Box 4, Samuel J. Tilden Papers, NYPL; and Charles Delany to Thomas O'Connor, February 23, 1848, Thomas O'Conor Miscellaneous Manuscripts, New-York Historical Society, New York (repository hereafter cited as NYHS) [St. Patrick's Day celebrations].

[61] Sloane, "Charles O'Conor," 239; see also Frederic R. Coudert, "Memorial of Charles O'Conor," in *Addresses: Historical – Political – Sociological* (New York: G. P. Putnam's Sons, 1905), 206.

[62] Association of the Bar of New York, *In Memoriam: James T. Brady* (New York: Baker, Voorhis, 1869), 28.

Civil War, O'Conor's sympathy with the Confederate cause led him
to embrace the peace wing of the Democratic Party, opposing General
George B. McClellan's presidential nomination by the Democratic
Party in 1864 because of McClellan's avowed prowar stance.[63]

In spite of the extremism of these beliefs, the New York legal community still respected O'Conor's abilities as a lawyer.[64] The patrician
lawyer George Templeton Strong found himself both frustrated and
a little mesmerized by O'Conor. After O'Conor's Academy of Music
speech, which Strong attended, he wrote in his diary: "Were I an
Abolitionist I would so crush O'Conor that he should never shew his
head among civilized Northerners again. But I'm not an Abolitionist –
and O'Conor was half right." In 1865, on hearing that O'Conor had
agreed to represent Davis, Strong called O'Conor a "maleficent ...
Copperhead" who had misused "his great talent and learning to
weaken the national cause and to uphold the cause of secession and
slave breeding, all through these years of war."[65]

The *San Francisco Elevator*, an African American newspaper, also
reacted to the announcement of O'Conor's role in the Davis case with
both alarm and grudging respect. The paper warned its readers that
O'Conor was both "as great a traitor as Jeff Davis" and "as unscrupu-
lous as a politician as he is able as a lawyer." But O'Conor was undeniably talented, which meant that "Jeff. Davis will have an advocate
who will use all his power to effect the liberation of his client: and the
Administration will require all the ability they can command to contend with him."[66] O'Conor's pro-Confederate views even caused a rift

[63] Daly, "Charles O'Conor," 514–16.
[64] A rumor floated in 1864 that O'Conor endorsed a plan to divide the Union still further and create a distinct "Republic of Ontario," which would consist of New York,
Pennsylvania, New Jersey, and Delaware. Even his friend William Wilkins Glenn,
himself a Copperhead, called O'Conor an "ultra-secessionist" and marveled at the
fact that O'Conor continued to retain high public favor in New York: "So much for a
man whom everyone respects and who is regarded as one of the very best men in the
North." William Wilkins Glenn, *Between North and South: A Maryland Journalist
Views the Civil War*, ed. Bayly Ellen Marks and Mark Norton Schatz (Cranbury,
NJ: Associated University Presses, 1976), 218.
[65] George Templeton Strong, *Diary of George Templeton Strong*, ed. Allan Nevins and
Milton Halsey Thomas, 4 vols. (New York: Macmillan, 1952) 2: 479, 3: 310, 4: 85.
[66] *San Francisco Elevator*, June 16, 1865. Despite O'Conor's Confederate sympathies, some ex-Confederates still distrusted his ability to represent Davis – and his
cause – effectively. One Virginian present at the grand jury indictment of Davis in
1866 wrote: "Reed of Philadelphia, O'Connor [*sic*] of New York and others, who

in his friendship with fellow (War) Democrat Judge Charles P. Daly, who reported, "My views were so opposed to his upon the subject of slavery, and upon the war, that I saw little of him for some years; not, in fact, until [O'Conor's serious] illness in 1875."[67]

To be sure, O'Conor was not alone among New Yorkers – particularly in the Irish community – in harboring pro-Confederate sentiments.[68] The city became something of a hotbed of disloyalty throughout the war, and New York seemed awash in pro-Davis sympathy following Appomattox.[69] Not only did several of Davis's most prominent attorneys hail from New York (O'Conor, James Brady, and George Shea – all Irish Americans), but the city's Copperhead papers also published a number of pro-Confederate editorials.[70] This led the Democratic *Herald* to complain that city's "rebel press … glorif[ied] Davis and Booth." In July 1865, a group of Davis supporters gathered on Broad Street, where a supportive letter from Mayor C. Godfrey Gunther was read aloud. The Broad Street meeting attendees openly defended the right of secession, forcefully predicting that Davis's trial would prove "the secession cause was right, and entitled to sympathies of the world."[71] They also took action to ensure that outcome, forming a committee to meet with O'Conor and to raise funds to defray the costs of Davis's representation.

have undertaken his defence, men who, during the War, have suffered, at home, for conscience sake, but who have not been reared in Davis' political school, who are consequently unfamiliar, to a great degree, with these strongest points, on which the justification of his conduct during our struggle, must greatly depend." David Lee Powell to Elizabeth Lewis Dabney Saunders, June 8, 1866, Section 40, Saunders Family Papers, Virginia Historical Society, Richmond (repository hereafter cited as VHS).

[67] Daly, "Charles O'Conor," 532–33.

[68] Gibson, *The Attitudes of the New York Irish*.

[69] See Cynthia Nicoletti, "The New York City Secession Movement," master's thesis, University of Virginia, 2004; Iver Bernstein, *The New York City Draft Riots* (New York: Oxford University Press, 1990).

[70] Brady's father emigrated to America in 1812, and Shea was born in Ireland and came to the United States as a baby. Edward J. McGuire, "The Catholic Bar of New York from 1808–1908," *United States Catholic Historical Society: Historical Records and Studies* 5, Part 1 (November 1907): 414–25, 418–19; Mary Rogers Cabot, *Annals of Brattleboro, 1681–1895*, 2 vols. (Brattleboro, VT: E. L. Hildreth, 1922), 2: 954–55; John Mitchel to Varina Davis, November 1, 1865, Samuel Richey Collection, Miami University of Ohio, Oxford, OH; *New York Daily News*, August 30, 1865.

[71] *New York Herald*, May 19, 1865; *New York Times*, August 5, 1865; *Washington National Intelligencer*, August 2, 1865.

O'Conor would accept no compensation for his services, although he did receive money from former Confederate diplomat James M. Mason to cover expenses and the costs of hiring additional counsel.[72] As Horace Greeley deduced, "Mr. O'Conor no longer needs practice or money, [and so he] has taken up this case from a deep conviction of right and duty." Indeed, O'Conor's disillusionment with what he perceived as the degeneracy of legal and constitutional values after the Civil War led him to agree to represent Davis.[73] He saw the trial as an opportunity to mitigate the progress of this evil.[74] O'Conor worried that war had allowed violence to triumph over the rule of law and saw his advocacy on Davis's behalf as a way of counteracting that tendency.

[72] Charles O'Conor to James M. Mason, July 9, 1865, vol. 8, James Mason Papers, LC. See also Charles O'Conor to Thales Lindsley, July 21, 1865, Charles O'Conor Papers, Houghton Library, Harvard University, Cambridge, MA (repository hereafter cited as HU). See Robert W. Gordon, "The Independence of Lawyers," *Boston University Law Review* 68 (1988): 1, 40 (noting that "historically lawyers have sacrificed income repeatedly" in order to pursue civic-minded cases and projects, although the lawyers who have made this choice have tended to be wealthy).

[73] O'Conor considered some aspects of the Constitution to be unamendable and spearheaded a movement to rescind New York and New Jersey's ratification of the Fourteenth and Fifteenth Amendments. For him, the Reconstruction Amendments were invalid, both because of their irregular ratification and because they sought to do away with the core principles of the U.S. Constitution. See John Harrison, "The Lawfulness of the Reconstruction Amendments," *University of Chicago Law Review* 68 (2001): 375, for a discussion of the irregularities of the ratification of the Reconstruction amendments, and Michael Vorenberg, *Final Freedom: The Civil War, the Abolition of Slavery, and the Thirteenth Amendment* (Cambridge: Cambridge University Press, 2001), 107–12, on the nineteenth-century idea of an unamendable constitution. See also Cynthia Nicoletti, "Strategic Litigation and the Death of Reconstruction," in *Signposts: New Directions in Southern Legal History*, ed. Sally E. Hadden and Patricia H. Minter (Athens: University of Georgia Press, 2013), 264, for information about O'Conor's attempts – along with a cadre of other lawyers – to get the Supreme Court to overturn Congress's program of Reconstruction.

[74] Horace Greeley to Varina Davis, June 27, 1865, Box 24, Jefferson Davis Papers, MC. See also Charles O'Conor to John Randolph Tucker, December 26, 1868, folder 19, Box 2, Tucker Family Papers, Southern Historical Collection, University of North Carolina, Chapel Hill (repository hereafter cited as SHC); Charles O'Conor to Fr. Joseph M. Finotti, March 16, 1876, folder 10, Box 2, Joseph Maria Finotti Papers, Georgetown University Special Collections Library, Washington, DC; Charles O'Conor to Robert McKinley Ormsby, October 7, 1867, Charles O'Conor Papers, HU; Charles O'Conor to Gerrit Smith, November 10, 1873, Reel 14, Gerrit Smith Papers, LC [microfilm edition].

3

O'Conor's Bluff

Upon Charles O'Conor's death in 1884, the *New York Times* published an unflattering biographical sketch of the deceased lawyer. The *Times* had been critical of O'Conor and his unsavory political sentiments throughout his life, and the biography described O'Conor as cold and calculating, a slave to "formal logic." The paper illustrated this point by highlighting O'Conor's actions in the Davis trial as an example of his willingness to sacrifice the interests of his own client in the service of his larger agenda. According to the *Times*, at the time of Davis's trial, "Mr. O'Conor went down to defend Jefferson Davis full of confidence in his ability to prove, by flawless logic, that the Southern States had the right to secede, which was decided against them at Appomattox." Arriving in Virginia, he was "immensely disgusted to find his client more solicitous not to be hanged than to have the validity of his position established, and willing to accept a compromise which illogically put him at liberty without giving his counsel an opportunity to argue the main question."[1]

In this, the *Times* was mistaken. O'Conor would have been pleased by the *Times* editorial nonetheless, because it perfectly reproduced O'Conor's public statements about the trial. It reflected what he *wanted* the public to think.

O'Conor did not intend to use Davis's case to test the legality of secession. He considered the risk too great and the likely payoff too

---

[1] *New York Times*, May 14, 1884.

small. As he well understood, there was no guarantee that the federal court in Virginia would acquit Davis and thereby vindicate secession. But there was also no assurance that it would convict him. So O'Conor embarked on a high-stakes bluff. For four years, O'Conor kept up a bold façade, proclaiming his eagerness to prove the legality of secession, in full possession of the understanding that the prosecutors feared an undesirable outcome even more than he did. He recognized that from their perspective, a serious defense of secession was deeply troubling: it had the potential to shatter the fragile postwar settlement achieved at Appomattox. It could undermine the verdict of the battlefield. O'Conor seized the advantage and openly challenged the government to test secession's constitutionality by trying Davis for treason.

Sustaining this posture allowed O'Conor to pressure the prosecution, which caused the government's lawyers to hesitate for so long that it became politically infeasible to try Davis. O'Conor's plan was based on secrecy: he carefully concealed his true hopes for the eventual dismissal of the case. This success has misled historians, who have concluded – wrongly – that O'Conor was determined to vindicate the right of secession in Davis's case, and have accordingly missed the extent to which O'Conor engineered the ultimate disposition of the case.[2] O'Conor's behind-the-scenes actions, set forth in his private, coded correspondence with Varina and Jefferson Davis, demonstrates how shrewd maneuvering to counter an opponent's actions was an important but vastly underappreciated aspect of nineteenth-century legal practice.[3]

---

[2] See William J. Cooper, *Jefferson Davis, American* (New York: Vintage Books, 2000), 605; William C. Davis, *Jefferson Davis: The Man and His Hour* (Baton Rouge: Louisiana State University Press, 1991), 651–63; Roy F. Nichols, "United States vs. Jefferson Davis, 1865–1869," *American Historical Review* 31 (1926): 266, 271; Lloyd T. Everett, "The 'Case of Jefferson Davis': Why No Trial," *Tyler's Quarterly Magazine and Genealogical Magazine* 29 (1947): 114; Henry Hagan, "United States vs. Jefferson Davis," *Sewanee Review Quarterly* 25 (1917): 220; Charles Adams, *When in the Course of Human Events: Arguing the Case for Southern Secession* (Lanham, MO: Rowman & Littlefield Publishers, 2000), 177–92; Clint Johnson, *Pursuit: The Chase, Capture, Persecution, and Surprising Release of Confederate President Jefferson Davis* (New York: Citadel Press Books, 2008), 210–80.

[3] On the legal profession in the nineteenth century, see Robert W. Gordon, "'The Ideal and the Actual in the Law': Fantasies and Practices of New York City Lawyers, 1870–1910," in *The New High Priests: Lawyers in Post-Civil War America*, ed. Gerald Gawalt (Westport, CT: Greenwood Press, 1984); Bruce A. Kimball, *The Inception of*

If Charles O'Conor's paramount goal was to ensure that Davis's case did not come to trial, initially Davis himself had different priorities. Davis hoped a trial would vindicate the Confederate cause and the legitimacy of secession. In fact, Davis had planned a test case about the constitutionality of secession before the war broke out in 1861. He had lingered in Washington for a full week after his resignation from the Senate following Mississippi's secession in January, hoping to be arrested.[4] A "test case" in 1865 was a much riskier proposition than it might have been in 1861. It was no longer merely a theoretical question. Now, Davis faced the death penalty if convicted of treason – and the deaths of 700,000 Americans in the intervening Civil War made the likelihood of secession's vindication much more remote. Davis nonetheless "desire[d] to confront [his] accusers" and to have his day in court. Davis's private secretary Burton Harrison reported in 1866 that the delays proved "a great disappointment to the chief, – he has all along earnestly desired a trial, confident … [that] the world and posterity would see the thing in its right light, if the court and jury did not."[5]

For this reason, Davis steadfastly refused to apply for a pardon. Pardon would have presented Andrew Johnson with a graceful solution to the difficult problems Davis's trial presented.[6] Robert E. Lee had applied for a pardon as early as June 1865, and had taken the loyalty oath that October.[7] But Davis would not follow suit, because,

Modern Professional Education: C. C. Langdell, 1826–1906 (Chapel Hill: University of North Carolina Press, 2009), 78–81; Bruce A. Kimball and R. Blake Brown, "'The Highest Legal Ability in the Nation: Langdell on Wall Street, 1855–1870," *Law and Social Inquiry* 29 (Winter 2004): 94–100; George Martin, *Causes and Conflicts: The Centennial History of the Association of the Bar of the City of New York, 1870–1970* (New York: Fordham University Press, 1997).

[4] Varina Davis, *Jefferson Davis, Ex-President of the Confederate States: A Memoir*, 2 vols. (New York: Belford Company, 1890), 2: 2–3.

[5] Jefferson Davis, undated notes [written during imprisonment], Box 24, Davis Papers, MC; Burton Harrison to Mother, June 13, 1866, in James Elliot Walmsley, "Some Unpublished Letters of Burton N. Harrison," *Publications of the Mississippi Historical Society* 8 (1904): 82.

[6] See Eric L. McKitrick, *Andrew Johnson and Reconstruction* (Chicago: University of Chicago Press, 1960), for a discussion of how pardoning formed the basis of Johnson's Reconstruction policy. See also Jonathan T. Dorris, *Pardon and Amnesty under Lincoln and Johnson* (Chapel Hill: University of North Carolina, 1953).

[7] "Pieces of History: General Robert E. Lee's Parole and Citizenship," *Prologue Magazine* 37 (Spring 2005); www.archives.gov/publications/prologue/2005/spring/piece-lee.html (accessed April 28, 2017).

as one of his friends put it, "what has he done to ask pardon for?"[8] Intermediaries, such as the Christian missionary Paul Bagley, attempted to broker a deal between Davis and President Johnson, but neither would budge. Johnson refused to commit in advance to pardoning Davis. Bagley urged Davis to acknowledge that the "God of Battles" had given an answer to the secession question that no court of law could overturn. Davis should not now expect to "raise it from the dead and bring it to the bar and acquit it or its *exponent, yourself.*" Davis would not cooperate, however. As Varina Davis said, he "could not honestly express the contrition he did not feel."[9]

Davis soldiered on, determined to martyr himself for the Confederate cause. At Fort Monroe, he smuggled letters to his friend and fellow prisoner Clement Clay, pouring out his hopes and fears for the future. In tiny print on scraps of paper, Davis told Clay that he believed that the government would entomb him in the prison and never bring him to trial unless they could be certain of his conviction. But he hoped to defend the Confederate cause, even if he suffered the penalty of death as a result. Davis believed firmly that secession was a complete defense to the "charge of Treason, as defined by the Constn," but he doubted that a court would vindicate him. Davis understood that Union victory would be enough of an adjudication of the secession question for many. In his view, the Republicans in Congress would use a trial to "degrade our cause in person," and he remained ready to meet the challenge. "I have lived for my country," he wrote melodramatically, "and have risked on many occasions my life in her service, [so] it may therefore be pardonable of me to say I am now willing to die for our sacred cause." Davis assured Clay that he planned to "make my death more useful to my country than my life has been." Although his family would suffer without his presence as a husband and father, he would leave them a spotless legacy instead. "The thought of my Wife and

[8] F. R. Lubbock to Varina Davis, April 6, 1867, Box 24, Jefferson Davis Papers, MC.
[9] Paul Bagley to Jefferson Davis, April 27, 1867, and May 1, 1867, in Jefferson Davis, *Jefferson Davis, Constitutionalist: His Letters, Papers, and Speeches*, ed. Dunbar Rowland, 10 vols. (Jackson: Mississippi Department of Archives and Records, 1923), 7: 96–99; V. Davis, *Jefferson Davis, Ex-President of the Confederate States*, 2: 817. See also Paul Bagley to Andrew Johnson, August 29 and 31, 1867, and Paul Bagley to Jefferson Davis, August 31, 1867, in Jefferson Davis, *Jefferson Davis, Constitutionalist: His Letters, Papers, and Speeches*, ed. Dunbar Rowland, 10 vols. (Jackson: Mississippi Department of Archives and Records, 1923) 7: 126–29.

little children left alone in the world and without the means of support bows my heart to the depths of sorrow," he wrote, "but I will at least leave them a name which truthfully cannot be tarnished and hope that calumny will be exposed for the benefit of their only inheritance."[10]

Ironically, because of his imprisonment Davis became a martyr for the cause of secession and won back the affection of many white Southerners he had alienated during the war. Davis's popularity had plummeted over the course of the war, due to privation on the home front and losses on the battlefield, but "as a prisoner Davis became a symbol for the lost Confederacy."[11] Former Supreme Court justice John Campbell, who was also imprisoned after the war, was annoyed that Davis had managed to redeem himself in the eyes of the Confederate people. Campbell groused that "if the authorities were aware … of the complete success [Davis] had in estranging from him every one whose opinion was worth having; and how the United States were assisted by his faults and deficiencies in administration they would let him go."[12]

Jefferson Davis might have enjoyed martyrdom (or at least the idea of it), but his wife, Varina, was far more practical. In her memoir of her husband, written in the 1890s, she reported that her husband would have welcomed death after the war, "but for the charges he was waiting to rebut before a lawful tribunal on earth." But when the actual prospect of his trial loomed before them, she gently told Davis that "your expectations will [not] be fully realised in the matter of your trial." In her estimation, his enemies would find a way of ensuring a conviction. They would not allow his case to disrupt the verdict of the war. Varina Davis was far more concerned about saving her husband's

---

[10] Jefferson Davis to Clement Clay, two letters, n.d., Box 5, Clement Clay Papers, Duke University Library, Durham, NC (repository hereafter cited as DU). One letter was written in December of 1865, and the other in the spring of 1866 before Clay's release from Fort Monroe in April. See Jefferson Davis, *The Papers of Jefferson Davis*, ed. Lynda L. Crist, 14 vols. (Baton Rouge: Louisiana State University Press, 1971–2014), 12: 66 n. 1, for a discussion of the date of the first letter; Jefferson Davis to Varina Howell Davis, December 26 or 28, 1865, in J. Davis, *Papers of Jefferson Davis* 12: 82. See also Jefferson Davis to Varina Howell Davis, January 28, 1866, in J. Davis, *Papers of Jefferson Davis*, 12: 106–8.

[11] Cooper, *Jefferson Davis, American*, 595.

[12] John A. Campbell to Anne Campbell, September 7, 1865, Box 1, Campbell Family Papers, SHC.

life and in ensuring that their children grew up with a father than in securing a verdict in favor of secession.[13]

Like Varina, Charles O'Conor insisted that Davis put his survival above a quixotic vindication of the Confederacy and its supposed virtues. And despite his flirtation with martyrdom for the Lost Cause,[14] Davis never countermanded his attorney's instructions, nor even expressed dissatisfaction with O'Conor's strategy.[15] Davis reported to former Confederate diplomat James M. Mason, who funneled money to O'Conor to cover the costs of the defense, that he was entirely happy with O'Conor's representation. Davis and his wife also remained on friendly terms with O'Conor until the latter's death in 1884. They corresponded regularly over the years and the Davises expressed gratitude for O'Conor's zealous representation.[16] Both Jefferson and Varina Davis acknowledged that O'Conor "was a tower of strength to us, to whom we owed more than can be expressed."[17]

O'Conor's paramount duty, as he saw it, was to save Davis's life. He knew that a trial might result in Davis's conviction and hanging.

---

[13] V. Davis, *Jefferson Davis, Ex-President of the Confederate States*, 2: 767–68; Varina Howell Davis to Jefferson Davis, February 8, 1866, Jefferson Davis Papers, University of Alabama Library, Tuscaloosa.

[14] The Lost Cause ideology, which took hold among ex-Confederates after the Civil War, posited that the Confederate struggle had been a noble one, animated by constitutional principles instead of racism and fought, against overwhelming odds, by fiercely brave Confederate soldiers. For more, see David W. Blight, *Race and Reunion: The Civil War in American Memory* (Cambridge, MA: Harvard University Press, 2001), and Caroline E. Janney, *Remembering the Civil War* (Chapel Hill: University of North Carolina Press, 2013).

[15] Davis's responses to O'Conor's suggestions are unfortunately impossible to reconstruct, as Davis's letters to O'Conor have not survived. O'Conor directed in his will that a "rough little box" of papers in his study pertaining to his representation of Davis should be "carefully preserved" because of their historical value, but they have not been seen again since his death, despite my efforts to track them down. See *New York Tribune*, May 28, 1884; personal correspondence with Roderic Sloane and Buzz Roddy, October 13 and November 18, 2006. But Davis's acquiescence in O'Conor's strategy can be inferred from his actions, particularly with regard to O'Conor's plans for combating the probable consequences of Andrew Johnson's impeachment; see Chapter 13.

[16] Davis confirmed that "Charles O'Conor of New York is attentive and diligent in regard to the case." Jefferson Davis to James M. Mason, April 16, 1868, in J. Davis, *Papers of Jefferson Davis*, 12: 289; Jefferson Davis to C. S. Sloane, December 7, 1875, Jefferson Davis Papers, Mississippi Department of Archives and History, Jackson; C. S. Sloane to Jefferson Davis, December 11, 1875, Jefferson Davis Papers, ADAH. The Davises kept in touch with O'Conor and his family long after their professional relationship ended in 1869.

[17] V. Davis, *Jefferson Davis, Ex-President of the Confederate States*, 2: 647.

Weighing Davis's life in the balance, O'Conor judged a trial to be too risky and never wavered in his conviction that Davis would be best served by a dismissal of the prosecution. He could allow the results of the battlefield to stand.

But O'Conor's ultimate aim remained secret – necessarily so. It would undermine his client's bargaining power with the Johnson administration to reveal that Davis (or rather, his attorney) would just as soon avoid a trial. His plan to use the secession argument instrumentally was best kept close to the vest. Always a cagey tactician, O'Conor kept quiet about his litigation strategy, even refusing to divulge details of his plan to his co-counsel, whom he viewed essentially as subordinates rather than collaborators.[18] He discussed his true intentions with only three people: Jefferson and Varina Davis and, for a time, Clement Clay's defense lawyer, former attorney general Jeremiah Black.

Instead of sharing his own thoughts, O'Conor sought to divine those of his opposing counsel to exploit the government's vulnerabilities. He reflected on the internal politics of the Johnson administration, seeking to discern which political forces might influence Johnson, his cabinet, the attorney general, and the outside prosecutors hired by the attorney general's office. He also surveyed congressional politics and sought to determine just how much power the president held vis-à-vis the Radical Republicans in Congress. Alliances and political dynamics shifted constantly during Reconstruction, and O'Conor stayed on top of them, hoping to figure out where the next front would develop in the battle to save Davis's life before the crisis was upon him.

O'Conor made as thorough a study as he could of the government's legal strategy in planning his own. He read legal treatises written by Lincoln administration insiders, especially those that discussed

---

[18] One observer even referred to junior counsel George Shea as O'Conor's lapdog, who "fetch[ed] and carried just as Mr. O'Conor directed him." William Wilkins Glenn, *Between North and South: A Maryland Journalist Views the Civil War*, ed. Bayly Ellen Marks and Mark Norton Schatz (Cranbury, NJ: Associated University Presses, 1976), 286–87. O'Conor's co-counsel occasionally chafed at his opacity and unwillingness to keep them informed about the progress of the case. See William B. Reed to James Lyons, November 1, 1868, Reel 3, Lyons Family Papers, VHS [microfilm edition]; William B. Reed to Robert Ould, April 2, 1868, Carrington Correspondence, Letters 1865–1873, Isaac Carrington Papers, DU. See also Charles O'Conor to James M. Mason, June 15, 1866, Box 1, Colin McRae Papers, ADAH.

the legal status of the Confederate government under international and domestic law. He perused the international law treatise by legal scholar Henry Halleck, who served as Lincoln's chief of staff, as well as War Department solicitor William Whiting's book, which set forth "his lucubrations touching law as connected with rebellion, insurrection, prize, treason etc."[19] Whiting's treatise proved particularly enlightening: it gave O'Conor a veritable blueprint of the difficulties the government would face in bringing Davis to trial. Armed with this information, O'Conor planned his own trial strategy knowing that the government feared the prospect of jury trial in Virginia just as much as, if not more than, he did.

Whiting had concluded that treason prosecutions arising out of the Civil War would probably prove ineffectual, absent modifications to the federal statutes that regulated jury trials. Whiting's treatise recognized that Confederates' genuine belief in the legitimacy of secession presented an almost insurmountable barrier in the federal government's pursuit of treason convictions. A judge's instruction condemning secession would likely be ignored by a jury in the rebellious states, even after the war's conclusion, because a judge "would have no power to root out from the jury their honest belief, that obedience to the laws of their own seceding State is not, and cannot be, treason." In Whiting's estimation, no jury drawn from the former Confederate states, as required by the Sixth Amendment, would convict: "How improbable is it that any jury of twelve men will be found to take away the lives or estates of their associates, when some of the jurymen themselves, or their friends and relatives or debtors, are involved in the same offence!"[20]

Unionist treatises such as Whiting's were valuable. What information O'Conor could not glean directly from them he gathered by savvy and conjecture, based on his experience as a high-powered lawyer and an astute political observer. O'Conor explained to confidante James Mason that he discussed the case with those he trusted and "watch[ed] as closely as practicable the movements and outgivings of those in

[19] Charles O'Conor to Ward Hill Lamon, November 5, 1867, Ward Hill Lamon Papers, HEHL.
[20] William Whiting, *The War Powers of the President, and the Legislative Powers of Congress in Relation to Rebellion, Treason and Slavery* (Boston: John L. Shorey, 1862), 124, 126, 127. Whiting authored several treatises while War Department solicitor, all offering a similar opinion.

power."[21] He quickly surmised that the decision about whether to go to trial rested on political considerations, and he learned that confusion reigned among Johnson and his law officers on the matter. At one point, he even hinted that he had gleaned information from an inside source – an "abolitionist soldier on the spot."[22]

O'Conor was correct in his assessment of the political confusion surrounding the Davis matter on the other side. There was no consensus about whether Davis should be tried for treason or for violations of the law of war; whether his trial should be conducted before a military commission or before a federal court; and, most crucially, whether the government should risk trying him at all. Radicals clamored loudly for Davis's trial and death, while moderates feared that Davis's execution might alienate the white South and eliminate any hope of sectional reconciliation. Johnson held the ultimate power to decide whether to move forward with Davis's trial, but he hesitated, both because of the potential outcry from ex-Confederates and their Northern allies, and also because he worried that Davis might be acquitted. Johnson had begun to doubt the wisdom of reexamining the verdict the Union army had rendered against secession. At the same time, he understood that Davis's release would signal the weakness of the administration and expose to the world the president's fear that secession might be vindicated. This put him between a rock and a hard place.

O'Conor focused his attention on Johnson's cabinet. In his view, most of the cabinet was cautious. The president enjoyed the support of the majority of his cabinet officers when he retreated from his initial fervent determination to punish treason, but O'Conor speculated that dissenting voices in the cabinet – particularly Secretary of State William Seward, and, possibly, Secretary of War William Stanton – continued to demand Davis's blood. O'Conor believed that Seward hated Davis with an almost demonic obsession and sought to orchestrate Davis's demise through any devious means at his disposal. O'Conor was convinced, for instance, that Seward tried to intercept his correspondence with Davis in the hope of learning the defense's strategy. Accordingly, O'Conor remained secretive and guarded – always

---

[21] Charles O'Conor to James M. Mason, August 16, 1865, vol. 8, James Mason Papers, LC.
[22] Charles O'Conor to William Wilkins Glenn, February 28, 1866, Box 3, John Glenn Papers, Maryland Historical Society, Baltimore (repository hereafter cited as MdHS).

referring to his supposed adversary Seward not by name but instead by inventive serpentine metaphors – when writing to Davis, and even then he sent letters by circuitous routes.[23] Despite his uncanny ability to see into the deadlock within the Johnson cabinet, O'Conor was wrong to lay such intrigue at Seward's door. Seward eventually emerged as the strongest proponent of a military trial within the cabinet, but he did not conspire against Davis as O'Conor imagined.[24] In O'Conor's opinion, Seward kept the possibility of prosecution alive over time, endlessly needling the president to ensure that the case would remain active.

[23] Charles O'Conor to Thomas G. Pratt, John W. Garrett, and William Wilkins Glenn, November 27, 1868, Box 77, Robert Garrett Papers, LC (my thanks to the Garrett family for allowing me the use of the collection); Charles O'Conor to Burton Harrison, July 13, 1866, Box 6, Burton Harrison Papers, LC; Charles O'Conor to Thomas F. Bayard, April 14, 1868, vol. 12, Bayard Family Papers, LC; Charles O'Conor to Jefferson Davis, April 19, 26, 1868, Box 24, Davis Papers, MC. See George Parsons Lathrop, "The Bailing of Jefferson Davis," *Century Magazine* 33 (February 1887): 636, 638, for confirmation of O'Conor's belief in Seward's enmity.

[24] There is no evidence that Seward did act underhandedly in the Davis prosecution by stealing O'Conor's correspondence or conspiring against Davis. He did not follow the progress of the case closely, although he did track Davis's movements when he left the United States to settle in Canada immediately after his release on bail in 1867, instructing the U.S. consul in Toronto to be prepared to return Davis to the United States by force if it became "necessary to secure his presence at Washington." D. Thurston to William H. Seward, May 3, 1867, Dispatches from U.S. Consuls in Toronto, 1864–1906, Public Archives of Canada, Ottawa, ON. The reasons for O'Conor's belief in Seward's enmity are not entirely clear, but O'Conor and Seward had clashed before in New York over the issue of slavery. Additionally, during the war Seward was widely regarded among the more conservative members of the legal profession as willing to manipulate legal doctrine to ensure a favorable legal outcome for the Lincoln administration. Lastly, the fact that Seward had been attacked and almost killed by Lincoln's assassins contributed to O'Conor's stubborn belief that Seward harbored a desire to punish Davis for his supposed involvement in the plot. See Frederick W. Seward, *Seward at Washington, as Senator and Secretary of State: A Memoir of His Life, with Selections from His Letters* (New York: Derby and Miller, 1891), 446; John Fabian Witt, *Lincoln's Code: The Laws of War in American History* (New York: Free Press, 2012), chapter 5; John M. Taylor, *William Henry Seward: Lincoln's Right Hand* (New York: Harper Collins, 2001), 243–50. Jefferson Davis agreed with O'Conor's assessment of Seward's malevolence, despite the fact that he and Seward had formed a friendship in the 1850s when once, during a bad snowstorm, Seward had sent a nurse by sleigh to attend Varina Davis during an illness. See Cooper, *Jefferson Davis, American*, 262; Jefferson Davis to Dudley Mann, November 4, 1868, in J. Davis, *Papers of Jefferson Davis*, 12: 325; and Francis Preston Blair Sr. to Andrew Johnson, August 8, 1865, folder 10, Box 13, Blair-Lee Papers, Princeton University Library, Princeton, NJ, for confirmation of the Davises' own belief in Seward's nefariousness.

O'Conor calculated that Johnson and most of the other cabinet officers, including the attorney general, were vacillating about making a decision. The president had quickly regretted his promise to make treason odious, fearing an uproar in the South if he actually punished Jefferson Davis. The cabinet members refused to give in to intemperate demands for Davis's blood but also would not risk censure by dropping the prosecution. Because of their inaction, responsibility for the case passed to lower-level legal officers.[25]

Outside of the White House, O'Conor surmised that no one political faction in Washington possessed enough power to force its agenda on the others. And because Johnson was reluctant to act decisively, Davis's fate was in limbo. O'Conor relied on these competing considerations to keep the prosecution at bay. "That the prosecution of Jefferson Davis should get the go-by is an almost universal opinion," he concluded. "The President thinks so. The Attorney General, the Chief Justice, Thad Stevens, even poor Underwood and Chandler the District Attorney of Virginia think so," although no one was willing to proclaim this view publicly.[26] No one wanted to acknowledge that the "wrong" verdict in Davis's case could disrupt the Union victory.

This was O'Conor's bluff, and his overall strategy. Throughout 1865, however, the treason defense took a backseat to a more immediate, pressing matter: ensuring that his client remained alive in the short term. O'Conor feared for Davis's life on two distinct fronts: conditions at Fort Monroe had caused his health to fail, and the government had also threatened to try Davis before a military commission for offenses against the laws of war. If the government carried out that threat, it was very likely that Davis would meet the same fate as Lincoln's assassins: summary execution.

O'Conor's first order of business was securing Davis's release on bail or parole pending trial. He initially appealed directly to the president, as Davis was being held in military custody at Fort Monroe,

---

[25] See Charles O'Conor to E. M. Stanton, May 31, 1865, in J. Davis, *Jefferson Davis: Constitutionalist*, 7: 27; Charles O'Conor to Thomas F. Bayard, October 19, 1867, in *Tyler's Quarterly Magazine* 29 (October 1947): 182.

[26] Charles O'Conor to Thomas F. Bayard, October 19, 1867, reprinted in *Tyler's Quarterly Magazine* 29 (October 1947): 182.

despite the fact that he was not yet officially charged with an offense, either military or civil.[27] Reminding Johnson that Davis's poor health might "become in effect, an infliction of the death-penalty," O'Conor proposed that Davis be arraigned and then admitted to bail before a civil judge. O'Conor pledged his own fortune, offering to "enter into a recognizance for his appearance to any amount, not exceeding my whole estate. It may be placed at $1 or 200,000 or even a higher sum if desired." If the government did not trust that Davis would reappear for trial, O'Conor recommended that restrictions be placed on Davis's movements, or even that he be released into O'Conor's personal custody. He suggested that Davis might be confined to his estate "in the rural part of [Manhattan]."[28] Johnson refused to release Davis or to move him to another prison, but in response to O'Conor's pleas and Varina Davis's emotional appeals to the president, the administration moderated the harshest conditions of Davis's imprisonment.

Meanwhile, in the short term, O'Conor was determined at all costs to prevent a military trial, convinced that a military commission would summarily convict Davis and then order his execution. The threat of a military trial lay in a charge that Davis had violated the law of war – either for his supposed participation in Abraham Lincoln's assassination or for the horrific conditions at Andersonville prison.[29] Although some of the president's advisers had argued that Davis could be tried for the civil crime of treason by military commission, this view won few adherents in the cabinet.

To combat the possibility of a military trial, O'Conor called a strategy session in New York City in July 1865. In addition to O'Conor, former president Franklin Pierce (in whose cabinet Davis had served

[27] Until formally indicted on a treason charge, he was not within the cognizance of a federal court. See Chapters 7 and 9 for more on Davis's indictment and release on bail.
[28] Charles O'Conor to Andrew Johnson, November 1, 1865, in Andrew Johnson, *The Papers of Andrew Johnson*, ed. Paul Bergeron, 16 vols. (Knoxville: University of Tennessee Press, 1967–69), 9: 322. O'Conor lived in Fort Washington, now Washington Heights, in the northern part of Manhattan, where his land spanned several city blocks. See Major and Crapp, "Map of That Part of the City of New York North of 155th Street" (New York: 1865), Maps Division, NYPL.
[29] See Francis Lieber, *Instructions for the Government of Armies of the United States in the Field: Originally Issued as General Orders No. 100, Adjutant General's Office, 1863* (Washington, DC: Government Printing Office, 1898), art. 75–76, 148.

as secretary of war) and Jeremiah Black were in attendance.[30] Military trials were already under way. In the wake of the Lincoln assassination, Judge Advocate Joseph Holt had convened the Bureau of Military Justice, which conducted quick and cursory trials of Mary Surratt and the other conspirators to Lincoln's murder, who were condemned and executed by early July 1865.[31] Determined to link Davis and other Confederate leaders to the assassination plot, Holt searched for evidence that Davis had ordered Confederate agents in Canada (led by Clement Clay) to kill the president. Clay was to provide the crucial evidentiary link between Davis and the Lincoln assassins.[32] In addition, the government also searched for proof that Davis had ordered Henry Wirz and his superior, John Winder, to deprive Andersonville's Union prisoners of basic necessities. The government, according to Davis, went so far as to offer a Wirz a deal the night before his hanging: his life in exchange for testimony against Davis.[33]

O'Conor's advice with regard to military commissions remained unwavering: Davis and his team should do nothing until the government made a definite move to try him in such an irregular manner. The furor for summary trials would die down quickly, he predicted. O'Conor certainly believed that the Surratt trial and "the Wirz tragedy" were gross miscarriages of justice, but he refused to allow Davis's supporters to be involved publicly with either. He feared that association with Wirz or with the assassins would taint Davis's reputation, thereby reducing his chances of avoiding trial. "If we should send

---

[30] Charles O'Conor to Jeremiah Black, July 18, 1865, Reel 22, Jeremiah Black Papers, LC [microfilm edition]; Charles O'Conor to Franklin Pierce, July 15, 18, 1865, Reel 3, Franklin Pierce Papers, LC [microfilm edition].

[31] U.S. War Department, *The War of the Rebellion: A Compilation of the Official Records of the Union and Confederate Armies*, 128 vols. (Washington, DC: Government Printing Office, 1880–1901), ser. 2, 8: 696–700. See also Elizabeth D. Leonard, *Lincoln's Avengers: Justice, Revenge, and Reunion after the Civil War* (New York: W. W. Norton, 2004); and Elizabeth D. Leonard, *Lincoln's Forgotten Ally: Judge Advocate General Joseph Holt of Kentucky* (Chapel Hill: University of North Carolina Press, 2011).

[32] See Leonard, *Lincoln's Forgotten Ally*, 204–5; Clement Clay to Virginia Clay, November 11, December 3, 1865, Box 5, Clement Clay Papers, DU.

[33] See Louis Schade (Wirz's attorney) to "the American Public," April 4, 1867, reprinted in James Madison Page, *The True Story of Andersonville Prison* (New York: Neale Publishing, 1908), 234–42. Jefferson Davis claimed to have verified this story with both Schade and Father F. E. Boyle, Wirz's confessor. See Jefferson Davis, *Andersonville and Other War-prisons* (New York: Belford and Company, 1890), 15–16.

Counsel to defend Wirz," he warned Varina Davis, "it would leak out
that we had done so, and from that moment Mr. Davis would in effect
be on trial."[34] Despite his admonition, O'Conor secretly found lawyers to defend Wirz's superior, General John Winder, who died before
trial. He paid their fees, eliciting a promise of their silence on the matter, and somehow managed to keep the news of his involvement from
becoming public.[35] From O'Conor's perspective, Davis's trial should
focus only on the issue of treason, without the added complication
of possible violations of the law of war. He instructed Varina Davis
not to speak about Davis's potential responsibility for the horrors of
Andersonville, insisting that "the only question that we deem open to
discussion" is "whether, like more than half of all illustrious heroes
and patriots of ancient or modern story, he has committed [what] the
victor in civil war ... calls treason."[36]

O'Conor steadfastly allayed the Davises' fears throughout the summer and fall of 1865 with his repeated insistence that the likelihood of
a military trial was remote.[37] Davis himself blanched at the swiftness
of military justice for Surratt and the other Lincoln assassins, finding
that "President Johnson is very quick on the trigger."[38] In O'Conor's
judgment, however, the "Bureau of Military *In*justice" would not have

---

[34] Charles O'Conor to Jeremiah Black, September 29, 1865, Reel 22, Jeremiah Black
Papers, LC [microfilm edition]. See also Colin McRae to Charles O'Conor, September
9, 1865, and Charles O'Conor to James M. Mason, October 9, 1865, vol. 8, James
Mason Papers, LC; Charles O'Conor to Varina Davis, September 13, 1865, Box 24,
Jefferson Davis Papers, MC. Despite this, O'Conor and Davis's other associates did
carry on some correspondence with Louis Schade, Wirz's attorney, and Frederick
A. Aiken, attorney for Mary Surratt. See Frederick Aiken to George Shea, September
5 and 10, 1865, Box 24, ibid. O'Conor also characterized Mary Surratt's execution as
a "tragedy." Charles O'Conor to James M. Mason, September 6, 1865, vol. 8, James
Mason Papers, LC.

[35] Glenn, *Between North and South*, 247.

[36] Charles O'Conor to Varina Davis, October 7, 1865, Jefferson Davis Papers, MC.

[37] O'Conor assured Varina Davis on this point, telling her that "I am thoroughly convinced that if he should ever have any trial it will be in a civil Court and in all
probability it will be a fair one." He insisted that he did not soften his views out of
a kindly meant but misguided regard for her feminine sensibilities, as "I have such
confidence in your firmness that I would send you bad news unhesitatingly if I had
any. So if I give you hopes you may rely upon it that they are founded on my convictions." Charles O'Conor to Varina Howell Davis, July 1, September 13, 1865, Box
24, Jefferson Davis Papers, MC.

[38] General Nelson A. Miles to E. D. Townsend, July 20, 1865, in U.S. War Department,
War of the Rebellion, ser. 2, 8: 710.

its way, as "the faction of cruelty and crime is probably too weak to accomplish its objects."[39]

Jeremiah Black was less sanguine about this threat. He prepared for an all-out fight against military jurisdiction, arguing that "it is not Davis alone but civil and constitutional liberty that is on trial."[40] At their New York meeting, Black and O'Conor contemplated a brief that would attack the use of military commissions. On returning home to Pennsylvania, Black drafted such a brief on Clay's behalf, arguing that the Constitution, as well as natural law, required that all criminal trials (except impeachment and those arising in the naval and land forces) be held before civil tribunals. The Bill of Rights, Black asserted, "has guarded this subject well. It is most emphatically guaranteed [in the Fifth Amendment] that trial shall always be by jury. If this language does not express the determination that trial by jury shall be the exclusive mode of ascertaining guilt or innocence in criminal cases, what other English words would have had that effect?" The guarantee of jury trial, Black continued, could not be suspended, even in time of war. Otherwise, a foreign invader "can shatter our constitution without striking a blow or bringing a gun to bear upon us. A simple declaration of hostilities is 'more terrible than an army with banners.' "[41]

O'Conor agreed with Black's argument, but not with his judgment. To his mind, the brief clearly established that military tribunals were "most odious as wholly without the sanction of law and mere devices of arbitrary power, for the purpose of coloring the murders with a false show of justice. If [the brief] could be improved it must be by some abler hand than mine." He nonetheless cautioned Black against circulating it before the government had actually decided to try Davis and Clay before a military commission. If publicized prematurely, the brief might backfire, O'Conor feared, and provoke an otherwise indecisive president and attorney general to demand an immediate trial.

39 Charles O'Conor to Jeremiah Black, September 29, 1865, Reel 22, Jeremiah Black Papers, LC [microfilm edition]. See also Charles O'Conor to Jeremiah Black, June 7, August 10, and September 25, 1865, ibid.

40 T. W. Pierce to Jeremiah Black, June 21, 1865, Reel 22, Jeremiah Black Papers, LC [microfilm edition]. Thomas W. Pierce was a close relative of Franklin Pierce. Ben H. Procter, *Not without Honor: The Life of John H. Reagan* (Austin: University of Texas Press, 1962), 174.

41 Brief on behalf of Clement Clay, n.d. (first page missing), 11, 12, Legal Cases File, Jeremiah Black Papers, LC.

At the very least, it would kindle resentment against his client. "In the President's place or that of the Attorney General, I could not read the paper with steady nerves," O'Conor wrote. The "experiment on the temper of these gentlemen" was too risky.[42] At any rate, the Clay brief did not go to waste. Black later recycled it, in some places verbatim, in his winning oral argument in *Ex parte Milligan*, which established that military commissions could not be used to try civilians where there were no active hostilities and the courts were open.[43]

O'Conor was focused instead on secession's instrumental value in the treason trial. He was convinced that it could win Davis his freedom. For O'Conor, deploying the secession argument was something like the nuclear deterrence theory of constitutional law: he raised the troubling prospect of its potential vindication in order to avoid confrontation entirely. By hinting at the possibility that Davis's case might bring the issue of secession squarely before the courts, and suggesting that a judge or jury might decide that secession had been legally undertaken, O'Conor hoped to induce the prosecution to drop the case against Davis.

To do this, O'Conor dealt directly with the Johnson administration. He tipped off the president that he planned to argue the constitutionality of secession at Davis's trial and that he considered it likely that the argument would succeed. In September 1865, O'Conor dispatched associate counsel George Shea to visit Johnson adviser Francis Preston Blair at his home in Silver Spring, Maryland. During their conversation, Shea told Blair in no uncertain terms that Davis would argue the legitimacy of secession at his trial. Shea underscored the defense's confidence by insisting that O'Conor desired the case to go before the Supreme Court to resolve the secession question in the nation's highest legal forum. Indeed, O'Conor would acquiesce in a plan to facilitate such an appeal through the enactment of new legislation to

[42] Charles O'Conor to Jeremiah Black, September 25, 1865, Reel 22, Jeremiah Black Papers, LC [microfilm edition].

[43] Oral Argument of Jeremiah Black, Ex parte Milligan, 71 U.S. 2, in Philip B. Kurland and Gerhard Casper, eds., *Landmark Briefs and Arguments of the Supreme Court of the United States: Constitutional Law*, 100 vols. (Washington, DC: University Publications of America, 1978), 4: 301–27, particularly 313, 318.

allow a writ of error in the case.[44] An appeal might not even be needed, Shea maintained, because there was good reason to believe that Chief Justice Salmon P. Chase (who was set to preside over Davis's trial in the circuit court) might well pronounce in favor of secession's legitimacy and direct Davis's acquittal. Chase's states' rights principles might induce him to endorse secession, Shea pointed out, and even if Chase could be counted on to decry secession from the bench, the possibility of an adverse jury verdict remained. Shea told Blair that he had met previously with the chief justice, who had indicated his willingness to free Davis.

Shaken by Shea's revelations, Blair duly reported back to President Johnson about the conversation. Blair evidently thought there was a chance that Shea could be right about Chase's potential secessionist leanings, telling Johnson that while he was sure the Supreme Court would decide against the right of secession, Chase "might decide otherwise, as he holds the states out of the Union & so mere belligerents."[45]

As the government well understood, Shea's threat was potent. There were two distinct but somewhat related grounds on which Davis could win an acquittal, and both seemed like real possibilities. Davis's defense could contend that secession was constitutionally permissible, and since his state had left the Union in 1861, Davis was no longer an American citizen who owed a duty of loyalty to the United States. He was thus incapable of committing treason against the nation.[46]

Alternatively, Davis could argue that the U.S. government's recognition of Confederate belligerency during the war precluded the postwar application of the law of treason to individuals who had acted on behalf on the Confederacy. In the *Prize Cases* (1863), the Supreme

---

[44] Lathrop, "The Bailing of Jefferson Davis," 640. Lathrop's account, as narrated by Shea, is a conflation of two different meetings Shea held with Blair and with Chief Justice Chase, in 1865 and 1868, respectively.

[45] Francis Preston Blair Sr. to Andrew Johnson, September 6, 1865, in Johnson, *Papers of Andrew Johnson*, 9: 32–33. See also William Ernest Smith, *The Francis Preston Blair Family in Politics*, 2 vols. (New York: Macmillan, 1933), 2: 325.

[46] The Crimes Act of 1790 specified that a treason defendant had to "owe allegiance to the United States," but the 1862 Confiscation Act did not. In either case, the government could merely allege that Davis owed allegiance to the United States, and indeed,

Court had decided that the United States could employ the international law of war in its contest with the Confederacy. Thus, despite its illegality, secession had effectively carried the Confederate states out of the Union. Under the law of war, the Confederacy was a separate entity – a belligerent power.[47] Throughout the war and its aftermath, the United States maintained that the Confederacy possessed a dual legal character as both belligerent (under international law) and criminal insurgency (under domestic law). But the Court had not clarified the collateral consequences of Confederate belligerency. It was possible, Davis's lawyers ventured, that because waging war was legal under international law, the government would not be permitted to charge individual Confederates for the same actions under the domestic law of treason.[48]

In an 1863 circuit court opinion, *U.S. v. Greathouse*, Justice Stephen Field had rejected the argument that the recognition of Confederate belligerency exempted individuals from treason prosecutions.[49] He had directed a verdict against certain Confederate seamen charged with treason, telling the jury in no uncertain terms that the domestic law of treason remained unaffected by the Supreme Court's ruling in the *Prize Cases*.

But in late 1865 there could be no assurance that Salmon Chase would reach the same conclusion. Chief Justice Chase was well known to be a devotee of states' rights, and it was unclear whether that philosophy would induce him to excuse Davis's behavior and endorse secession. His views on the reach of belligerent status were similarly opaque. Given the logical connection between belligerent status and secession, as belligerency depended in some sense on the effectiveness,

---

the prosecution's indictment offered no facts to prove Davis's citizenship. O'Conor could rebut the charge by establishing the constitutionality of secession, which would in turn show that Davis had not been a citizen at the time he levied war on the United States. Whether the trial would turn on the constitutionality of secession was thus his decision. He could, for instance, have argued instead that the statute of limitations barred the prosecution or, more promisingly, that the recognition of Confederate belligerency prevented the postwar prosecution of treason, as will be discussed later.

[47] That is, it was a quasi-legitimate entity with the capability of exercising military might through an organized army, to which the laws of war applied. This was, in some sense, a recognition of Confederate separateness from the United States, even if granted for certain limited purposes.

[48] These issues will be explored further in Chapters 10 and 12.

[49] U.S. v. Greathouse, 26 F. Cas. 18 (C.C.N.D.Cal. 1863) (No. 15,254).

if not necessarily the legality, of secession, it was impossible to know where Chase would come down on the issue.[50]

The unpredictability of a federal judge's views on the reach of Confederate belligerency became readily apparent to the government. Three days after Shea's meeting with Blair, William Annesley, the U.S. attorney for Ohio, wrote Attorney General James Speed about the difficulties the issue presented in securing treason convictions. Annesley told Speed that in a case he was currently prosecuting, *U.S. v. Burleigh*, the court had instructed the jury to recognize the de facto existence of the Confederate government. Burleigh, a Confederate operative, had been charged with piracy and robbery for taking part in a raid on a Union ship located on Lake Erie in 1864. As Annesley reported to Speed, the judge had told the jurors that if the prisoner had indeed engaged in the raid as charged in the indictment, "he was not guilty of the charge of Robbery … but was entitled to all the immunities of a prisoner of war … and if guilty of any infringement of the rules of war was amenable to a military but not a civil tribunal."[51] The jury eventually deadlocked, and when he was awaiting a new trial Burleigh escaped custody and made his way back to his native Scotland.[52]

So O'Conor's threat was not an idle one. The uncertainty of jury trial was a constant source of worry for both the administration and the nation. As O'Conor developed his bluff, he was assisted in his efforts by the public discussion of the Davis case and its relation to the results of the war. As newspaper reports revealed, Americans continually speculated about the outcome in Davis's case and what it might signify about the right of secession.

---

[50] Chase eventually held, in *Shortridge v. Macon*, 22 F. Cas. 20 (C.C.D.N.C. 1867) (No. 12,812), that belligerent status did not extend to after the war. For more on *Shortridge*, see Chapter 10.

[51] William Annesley to James Speed, September 9, 1865, Attorney General's Papers, Ohio Letters Received, Record Group 60, NA-CP. The case is unreported.

[52] See David Gardner Chadavoyne, *The United States District Court for the Eastern District of Michigan: People, Law, and Politics* (Detroit: Wayne State University Press, 2012), 82–84.

Most Northern papers were confident in 1865 that Davis would be convicted. The *Philadelphia Inquirer* insisted that the trial would necessarily "render traitors infamous, and ... have it judicially settled that Secession is illegal."[53] The case would act to cement the results of the war. The *New York Herald* believed that the trial would allow the courts to decide "whether carrying on war against the government of the United States is a crime that that government can punish. ... Certainly the people have decided by the war that the many States are one nation. Jeff Davis can be found guilty of this crime if any man can; and if he is convicted the question is settled."[54]

Others were unsure about the necessity of conducting a trial, given that the war had already rendered a verdict on the illegitimacy of secession. Why give the courts a second bite at the apple when a jury's determination was unpredictable? Some newspapers were deeply troubled by the idea that a mere court of law could undermine the outcome of a struggle that had consumed so many American lives. The *Chicago Tribune* insisted that that sacrifice could not be rendered meaningless because of a court's decision. According to the *Tribune*, the federal courts should be precluded from entertaining the notion of secession's constitutionality in Davis's case because to do so would undercut their own authority. If they did, they would be questioning "whether the entire fabric of our Government ... is ... a nullity." It was pointless to allow argumentation on this issue because no judicial pronouncement could unsettle the verdict of the war, the editors argued. Given that so many men had died, "in the trial of Jeff. Davis, we believe it will be *assumed* that a State has no right to secede." The trial should begin and end with the simple question of whether or not Davis had levied war against the United States, and was thus best suited to a hearing before a military tribunal, where Davis's conviction would be a certainty.[55]

[53] "Jeff. Davis and Other Criminals," *Philadelphia Inquirer*, December 7, 1865.
[54] "The Fate of Jeff. Davis," *New York Herald*, October 15, 1865.
[55] "Object of Jeff. Davis' Trial," *Chicago Tribune*, November 14, 1865. See also "A Queer Demand," *Chicago Tribune*, May 20, 1865.

These battles in the press over the possible outcomes – and significance – of Davis's trial provided the necessary backdrop for Charles O'Conor's strategy of negotiation and misdirection with Davis's prosecutors. By highlighting how much the government would lose in the event of an acquittal and how little there was to gain with a conviction, O'Conor hoped to stall his opponents. The world was watching the trial – and the world would interpret Davis's acquittal as a repudiation of the verdict that Union victory had rendered against secession. In representing Davis, O'Conor "t[ook] ground against the war itself," according to one of his political admirers.[56] He was challenging the idea that the answer to the secession question had already "been sealed by the blood of half a million men."[57]

[56] William Barclay Napton, *The Union on Trial: The Political Journals of Judge William Barclay Napton, 1829–1883*, ed. Christopher Phillips and Jason L. Pendleton (Columbia: University of Missouri Press, 2005), 298.
[57] "Object of Jeff. Davis' Trial," *Chicago Tribune*, November 14, 1865.

4

The Civil War as a Trial by Battle

Like many other Americans, Charles O'Conor wrestled with the difficult task of reconciling the war with the law. He recognized that the Civil War had functioned as an unorthodox legal forum – a "trial by battle" – and given a practical answer to the secession question, but he questioned the legitimacy of resolving the issue in such a brutal fashion. On principle, O'Conor was appalled that his countrymen had turned to violence to settle their society's most contentious legal dispute. They had, he remarked with disgust, submitted the question to "that sharp and summary instrument of moral reform, the sword."[1]

O'Conor had harbored "a horror" of war from an early age, his friend Charles P. Daly reported. This stemmed, Daly surmised, from "the shock" O'Conor had experienced as a young boy when, after meeting the adventurer Zebulon Pike, he subsequently learned of Pike's death in an American attack on Toronto during the War of 1812.[2] The Civil War had resulted in the loss of life on a massive scale, and many Americans who lived through it sought to ensure that all "this death be given meaning."[3] But O'Conor's disaffection with war went far beyond a sense of loss when confronted with the staggering

[1] Charles O'Conor to Gerrit Smith, November 10, 1873, Reel 14, Gerrit Smith Papers, LC [microfilm edition].
[2] Charles P. Daly, "Charles O'Conor: His Professional Life and Character," *Magazine of American History* 13 (June 1885): 516.
[3] Drew G. Faust, *This Republic of Suffering: Death and the American Civil War* (New York: Knopf, 2008), 170.

body count of the 1860s. In his opinion, the Civil War had corroded the legal system and had detached Americans from their deeply held convictions about the importance of the rule of law. During the war, O'Conor had been highly critical of the Lincoln administration's suppression of civil liberties and suspension of habeas corpus, and of the American public's complacency in the face of such irregularities. He complained that Lincoln's "far-reaching strides toward absolutism" were undertaken "with the full approval of the 20,000,000 victims who are to be enthralled to its establishment."[4] More to the point, he believed that the war had sapped Americans of their commitment to maintaining liberty through regularized legal adjudication of difficult questions, and caused them to substitute brute force for law. In 1867 O'Conor wrote that "bayonets have made such sad work with principles that it seems idle to appeal to them." In the postbellum world, he lamented, "force … is now the sole agency of government among us."[5] O'Conor was disheartened by the realization that Americans had become inured to the moral decay that trial by battle represented.

This disillusionment was tempered by a recognition of the instrumental value of viewing Union victory as determinative of the secession question. O'Conor conceded that the war itself had already provided an answer to the secession question, even if it was in a forum that resembled the medieval trial by battle. Legitimate or not, the war had rendered a verdict, and O'Conor sought to persuade Davis's prosecutors that they should let it stand undisturbed. In spite of its moral ambiguity as a means of legal adjudication, the Union's military triumph could spare his client the ordeal of a trial.

This chapter departs from the story of Davis's trial to explore in greater depth the ways in which the Civil War's survivors thought about the legitimacy of war as a method of lawmaking. O'Conor was not alone in conceiving of the war as a trial by battle through which the illegality of secession and the permanency of the Union had been decided

---

[4] Charles O'Conor to Samuel L. M. Barlow, August 10, 1861, Samuel Barlow Papers, HEHL.

[5] O'Conor to R. McKinley Ormsby, October 7, 1867, Charles O'Conor Papers, HU. See also Charles O'Conor to Joseph M. Finotti, March 16, 1876, Joseph Maria Finotti Papers, Georgetown University Special Collections Library, Washington, DC; Charles O'Conor to John Randolph Tucker, December 26, 1868, Tucker Family Papers, SHC.

in the Union's favor. Many Americans, both Northern and Southern, Republican and Democrat, reconstructed and unreconstructed, employed this metaphor as a way of making sense of the demise of the principle of state secession through the convulsion of the Civil War.[6] In the years immediately following Appomattox, both Northern Unionists and former Confederates struggled mightily to come to terms with the idea that a war could resolve a constitutional question that had ignited furious controversy throughout the antebellum period.

When they analogized the Civil War to the medieval trial by battle, the war's survivors sought to harmonize, albeit imperfectly, the seemingly incompatible imperatives of law and violence. The Civil War was deeply troubling to the worldview of nineteenth-century Americans, who took adherence to the rule of law very seriously.[7] Rather than turning to the legal process to determine the legitimacy of the ultimate expression of state sovereignty – the right of secession – Americans had instead engaged in a massive armed conflict in which 700,000 men died. The nation had to find a way to come to terms with the notion that a violent conflict could decide a fundamental disagreement over constitutional interpretation. The metaphor of trial by battle consoled defeated Confederates with the knowledge that the logical rationale for the right of secession had not been repudiated, even though the war had made exercise of that right impossible.

At the same time, triumphant Unionists likened the Civil War to a trial by battle to give the war's resolution of secession a legal and popular legitimacy beyond the strength of arms. But Americans also

---

[6] A similar argument to the one made throughout this chapter with respect to the right of secession could, I suspect, be applied to the destruction of slavery in the Confederate states. Comparing Northerners' and Southerners' thoughts about the end of slavery and that of secession might also prove a fruitful topic of inquiry, but it is not one that will be explored here. This is not to say that the death of slavery after the Civil War is somehow of less moment than the eradication of secession arguments, but simply that it is beyond the scope of this project.

[7] See Arthur Bestor, "The American Civil War as a Constitutional Crisis," *American Historical Review* 49 (1963): 327; Phillip S. Paludan, "The American Civil War Considered as a Crisis in Law and Order," *American Historical Review* 77 (October 1972). See Christopher L. Tomlins, *Law, Labor, and Ideology in the Early American Republic* (Cambridge: Cambridge University Press, 1993), chapter 1, for a discussion of the emergent centrality of legal discourse in nineteenth-century America. On the conflict between law and war in a modern context, see David Kennedy, *Of War and Law* (Princeton: Princeton University Press, 2006).

faced the uncomfortable realization that their society, which prided itself on its enlightened rationalism and adherence to the rule of law, had revived a repudiated medieval superstition to confront secession. They were forced to ask themselves whether they had become barbarians in the upheaval of the war. For many introspective Americans, the answer was an uncomfortable "yes."

Trial by battle had been a common method of proof prior to the advent of the jury trial in medieval Europe. In a trial by battle, two combatants engaged in a physical contest to decide the outcome of a legal dispute. Combatants placed their fate in God's hands, trusting that He would deliver victory to the righteous party. Trial by battle was a form of the medieval judicial ordeal, designed to determine a party's guilt or innocence, just like being burned with a hot poker or being submerged in a pool of water.

Trial by battle – otherwise known as wager of battle or judicial combat – almost certainly arrived in England along with the Normans in 1066, as there exists no earlier historical record of the wager of battle in the British Isles. The common law permitted trial by battle as a method of proof in both real actions (commenced by writ of right) and criminal cases initiated by private parties (appeals of felony). In such cases, a battle ensued when the criminal defendant or the tenant in a real action invoked his right to prove the truth of his assertions by wager of battle rather than an alternative method of proof.[8] Other forms of the ordeal fell into disuse after the Fourth Lateran Council in 1215, when Pope Innocent III condemned the participation of the clergy in judicial ordeals. Trial by battle survived, however, probably because it did not necessarily require the sanction of the clergy. Over time, trial by battle faded into disuse as jury trial became the preferred method of discerning the truthfulness of litigants and witnesses. Nonetheless, trial by battle remained a technically valid form of proof in England until 1819, when Parliament abolished it after a defendant, who had already been

---

[8] The history of trial by battle in English common law and the gradual advent of trial by jury is a complex and fascinating story. For more information, see Frederick Pollock and Frederic William Maitland, *History of English Law before the Time of Edward I*, 2 vols. (Washington, DC: Lawyers' Literary Club, 1959), 2: 600; Theodore F. T. Plucknett, *Concise History of the Common Law* (Boston: Little, Brown, 1956), 116–21; Robert Bartlett, *Trial by Fire and Water: The Medieval Judicial Ordeal* (Oxford: Clarendon Press, 1986), 103–26; John W. Baldwin, "The Intellectual Preparation for the Canon of 1215 against Ordeals," *Speculum* 36 (1961): 613–36.

acquitted by a jury, threatened to wage battle against his accuser in a subsequent appeal of felony.[9]

The terminology of trial by battle was also used to describe wars between nation-states.[10] Under the international law of the nineteenth century, war was always legal – and it was viewed explicitly as a means of lawmaking. Henry Wheaton, author of the definitive American international law treatise of the day, stated that "the independent societies of men, called States, acknowledge no common arbiter or judge.... Every state has therefore a right to resort to force, as the only means of redress for injuries inflicted upon it by others, in the same manner as individuals would be entitled to that remedy were they not subject to the laws of civil society."[11] Until the twentieth century, legal contests between nations had no common arbiter apart from a recourse to arms.[12]

Nineteenth-century legal thinkers routinely compared international contests of force to trial by battle. "A person is a separate individuality. A Nation is an aggregate individuality," the *Chambers' Edinburgh Journal* declared, and "as the judicial combat was a contest between

---

[9] This case was Ashford v. Thornton, 106 Eng. Rep. 149 (1818). As late as 1774, on the eve of the American Revolution, several members of Parliament protested vehemently against a proposal that would have abolished the appeal of felony and the right to defend one's innocence through trial by battle in Massachusetts as a way to crack down on the unruly colonists. MP John Dunning, later Lord Ashburton, insisted that even surly Americans could not be denied "that great pillar of the Constitution, the Appeal for Murder," for fear that such a statute would create a dangerous precedent and eventually cause Englishmen to lose this right as well. See Henry Charles Lea's *Superstition and Force* (1870; repr., New York: Greenwood Press, 1968),197–98; William Renwick Riddell, "Appeal of Death and Its Abolition," *Michigan Law Review* 24 (1925–26): 804.

[10] The line between individual combat and the wars of organized states could sometimes be fuzzy. For instance, in 1340, during the Hundred Years' War, King Edward III of England challenged King Philip VI of France to single combat or to a staged battle between 100 champions to settle their disputed claim to the throne of France. The French king declined. See Jonathan Sumption, *The Hundred Years War: Trial by Battle* (Philadelphia: University of Pennsylvania Press, 1999), 348–49.

[11] Henry Wheaton, *Elements of International Law*, ed. Richard Henry Dana (Boston: Little, Brown, 1866), 368.

[12] War was declared illegal in the Kellogg-Briand Pact, and in the twentieth century the League of Nations and later the United Nations were to be the only bodies that could legally wage a nondefensive war. Treaty Providing for the Renunciation of War as an Instrument of National Policy, 46 Stat. 2343 (1928) (popularly known as the Kellogg-Briand Pact); League of Nations Covenant, preamble; UN Charter, art. 1, 2. See also Stephen Neff, *War and the Law of Nations: A General History* (New York: Cambridge University Press, 2005), chapters 5, 8.

the individuality of two persons, so also is a war between the individuality of two nations."[13] Charles Sumner, who had been a professor of
international law at Harvard before entering the U.S. Senate, likened
war to a duel. "War as conducted under international law," he wrote,
"between two organized nations, is in all respects a duel, according
to the just signification of this word, differing from that between two
individuals only in the number of the combatants." Sumner pointed
out that the trial by battle had been rendered obsolete in every legal
arena other than the international one. Only in the future would
human society witness "the substitution of some peaceful tribunal for
the existing trial by battle" between nations.[14]

Why would nineteenth-century Americans repeatedly invoke a medieval legal concept in coming to terms with their civil war? Antebellum
Americans were steeped in a cultural revival of medieval romanticism,
and medieval ideas were freely available to the Civil War generation. In
the late eighteenth and nineteenth centuries, an interest in medieval customs flourished in both England and the United States. Great Britain
witnessed a surge in popularity in all things medieval. Nineteenth-
century castles were built in the medieval tradition, noblemen held
tournaments (complete with jousts, knights, banners, and well-born
ladies), and chivalry reemerged as an important social virtue. Arthurian
tales became popular both in printed form and on the stage. Alfred,
Lord Tennyson, published numerous epic poems with Arthurian heroes
and heroines, and Lady Charlotte Guest translated and published *The
Mabinogian*, a medieval Welsh collection of Arthurian legends.[15]

   In the United States, and particularly in the American South, this
medieval revival was marked by a strong interest in the writings of

[13] "Judicial Combats and the Wars of Nations," *Chambers' Edinburgh Journal* 190
(1847): 126.
[14] "Sumner on the War," *New York Times*, October 27, 1870. See also Charles Sumner,
*The True Grandeur of Nations: An Oration Delivered before the Authorities of the
City of Boston, July 4, 1845* (Boston: William D. Ticknor, 1845), preface. Sumner,
interestingly, never discussed the American Civil War in the context of international
contests of force.
[15] Mark Girouard, *The Return to Camelot: Chivalry and the English Gentleman* (New
Haven: Yale University Press, 1981); R. R. Agrawal, *The Medieval Revival and Its
Influence on the Romantic Movement* (New Delhi: Abhinav Publications, 1990), 94;
Stephanie Barczewski, *Myth and National Identity in Nineteenth-Century Britain*
(Oxford: Oxford University Press, 2000).

Sir Walter Scott, whose work embodied medieval romanticism. Scott's famous *Ivanhoe* featured a trial by battle, apparently inspired by Britain's abolition of the practice in 1819.[16] *The Fair Maid of Perth, or St. Valentine's Day*, one of his lesser-known works, chronicled a trial by combat between two individuals to settle a larger dynastic dispute (or civil war) between Scottish clans in lieu of a full-scale battle. Southerners devoured Walter Scott's writings. Mary Chesnut's Civil War memoir, for instance, is replete with allusions to many of Scott's works. Varina Davis wrote Chesnut in late 1864 to express her disgust with "old Torquil" of *The Fair Maid of Perth*, who sent his eight sons to their deaths in the trial by combat, "call[ing] so cheerily, 'Another for [his chieftain].'"[17] Scott's American audience extended far beyond the South. Scott and Lord Byron were the only nonreligious writers that the stern Congregationalist preacher Lyman Beecher allowed his daughter Harriet Beecher Stowe to read as a child. Oliver Wendell Holmes loved Scott's novels and their portrayal of a bygone, chivalrous era, in which the "sword and the gentleman" held sway. In Louisa May Alcott's *Little Women*, Meg devours *Ivanhoe*, and Jo longs to purchase Friedrich de la Motte Fouqué's medieval romances *Undine* and *Sintram* for Christmas.[18]

More specifically, American lawyers would have been vaguely familiar with – and critical of – the historical practice of trial by battle, but not its particulars. William Blackstone's *Commentaries on the Laws of England* devoted a scant three pages to a discussion of the wager of battle, characterizing the practice as one "of great antiquity, but much disused." Blackstone described trial by battle as resulting from "the military spirit of our ancestors, joined to a superstitious frame of mind: it being in the nature of an appeal to Providence, under an apprehension and hope (however presumptuous

---

[16] P. D. Garside, "Scott, the Romantic Past and the Nineteenth Century," *Review of English Studies* 23 (May 1972): 147–61; Hamilton Eckenrode, "Sir Walter Scott and the South," *North American Review* 206 (October 1917): 595–603; Michael O'Brien, *Conjectures of Order: Intellectual Life and the American South, 1810–1860*, 2 vols. (Chapel Hill: University of North Carolina Press, 2004).

[17] Mary Chesnut, *Mary Chesnut's Civil War*, ed. C. Vann Woodward (New Haven: Yale University Press, 1981), 666; Walter Scott, *The Fair Maid of Perth* (Edinburgh: T. and A. Constable, 1903), chapter 34.

[18] See Edmund Wilson, *Patriotic Gore: Studies in the Literature of the American Civil War* (New York: Oxford University Press, 1962), 51; G. Edward White, *Justice Oliver Wendell Holmes: Law and the Inner Self* (New York: Oxford University Press, 1993), 33; Louisa May Alcott, *Little Women* (Boston: Little, Brown, 1916), 8, 55.

and unwarrantable) that heaven would give victory to him who had the right."[19] Blackstone's distaste for the wager of battle was echoed by nineteenth-century legal treatise writers, who condemned the practice as "absurd and barbarous" and therefore "inconsistent with our advanced civilization."[20]

Still, referring to the war as a trial by battle called to mind a particular idea that held great resonance for nineteenth-century Americans, even though the analogy remained only a loose one. Like their own war, the medieval trial by battle intertwined three seemingly incompatible elements: divine Providence, the violence and irrationality of physical combat, and the reasonable and deliberative processes of law.[21] The prevailing understanding of the technicalities of trial by

---

[19] William Blackstone, *Commentaries on the Laws of England*, ed. Edward Christian, 4 vols. (Philadelphia: R. H. Small, 1825), 3: 335–38.

[20] Thomas L. Smith, *Elements of the Law, or, Outlines of the System of Civil and Criminal Laws in Force in the United States, and in the Several States of the Union* (Philadelphia: Lippincott, Grambo, 1853), 194; Henry Nicoll, *An Address Delivered before the Graduating Class of the Law School at Columbia College* (New York: Trow & Smith, 1869), 8. One writer briefly commented that because wager of battle did "not prevail in this country, I will not waste time describing [it]." Timothy Walker, *Introduction to American Law: Designed as a First Book for Students* (Cincinnati: Derby, Bradley, 1846), 525.

[21] Although the concept of trial by battle was undeniably a legal one, it also had deep resonance as a religious idea. Many nineteenth-century Americans clearly believed that God had a hand in the war, and that He had ordained the suffering occasioned by the war. This sentiment was perhaps most famously expressed by Abraham Lincoln in his Second Inaugural Address, in which he spoke of American slavery as "one of those offenses which, in the providence of God, must needs come, but which, having continued through His appointed time, He now wills to remove, and that He gives to both North and South this terrible war as the woe due to those by whom the offense came." Abraham Lincoln, "Second Inaugural Address," March 4, 1865, in Abraham Lincoln, *This Fiery Trial: The Speeches and Writings of Abraham Lincoln*, ed. William E. Gienapp (New York: Oxford University Press, 2002), 221. Religious leaders as well as political ones analogized the war to a trial by battle. For example, in late 1865, the Southern Presbyterian theologian John Adger referred to the Confederate war effort as "the cause [Confederates] were maintaining against a radical infidelity in humble prayer to [God's] wise, and sovereign, and merciful arbitrament." John Adger, "Northern and Southern Views of the Province of the Church," *Southern Presbyterian Review* 16 (March 1866): 397, 398. See Mark A. Noll, "'Both ... Pray to the Same God': The Singularity of Lincoln's Faith in the Era of the Civil War," *Journal of the Abraham Lincoln Association* 18 (Winter 1997): 1; Mark A. Noll, *The Civil War as a Theological Crisis* (Chapel Hill: University of North Carolina Press, 2006); Eugene Genovese, *A Consuming Fire: The Fall of the Confederacy in the Mind of the White Christian South* (Athens: University of Georgia Press, 1998); David Chesebrough, ed., *"God Ordained This War": Sermons on the*

battle was extremely vague even among the elite, and they invoked the concept for its larger rhetorical value. Nineteenth-century Americans adopted this language because it was uniquely useful for explaining their predicament in the post-war world. This idea allowed them to think about war as a means of legal adjudication.

The concept of trial by battle also proved remarkably malleable. Its frequent invocation betrayed Americans' profound ambivalence about the legitimacy of using violent means to dispose of the question of secession. Northerners who celebrated Union victory analogized the Civil War to a medieval trial by battle as a way of conferring the legitimacy of a *legal* proceeding – however obsolete – on the chaos of war. The trial by battle metaphor operated on two levels for Northerners. Its use permitted them to maintain their devotion to the rule of law by viewing the war as a binding and quasi-legal mode of adjudication. And it also betrayed their uneasiness with the very idea of using violence to achieve a legal resolution, as many Northerners exhibited intense discomfort with the concept of trial by battle as applied to the Civil War.

The analogy of trial by battle proved similarly pliable in the hands of ex-Confederate thinkers, who revealed their deep confusion about whether they could and would accept that the war had proved secession's unconstitutionality. Many former Confederates, particularly those who sought to make peace with the realization that their cause had failed, likened the war to a trial by battle to acknowledge the triumph of the nationalist conception of the Union while still clinging to the constitutional logic undergirding secession. Others who exhibited more defiance also likened the war to trial by battle as a way to criticize the idea that the outcome of a violent conflict could render a legitimate verdict on the legitimacy of secession.

Moreover, trial by battle inevitably conjured images of the medieval past, with both negative and positive, but not necessarily factually grounded, associations. Former Confederates frequently characterized the notion of using war to settle human disputes as "medieval," as a way of criticizing the "barbarism" of triumphant Northerners who blithely accepted the results of the trial by battle. But viewing trial by

Sectional Crisis, 1830–1865 (Columbia: University of South Carolina Press, 1991); James H. Moorhead, *American Apocalypse: Yankee Protestants and the Civil War, 1860–1869* (New Haven: Yale University Press, 1978).

battle as a relic of barbarism and a repudiated superstition did not prevent nineteenth-century Americans from simultaneously romanticizing the idea of judicial combat and consequently envisioning themselves as honorable participants in a chivalric and noble struggle.[22] The metaphor of trial by battle proved compelling to so many in post–Civil War America precisely because it remained remarkably supple.

The language of trial by battle resonated particularly forcefully with defeated Confederates, who drew heavily on the idea in their postwar amnesty petitions. As part of his notoriously lenient Reconstruction policy, President Johnson determined not to seek retribution against the vast majority of former Confederates. Instead, he welcomed them to return to the national fold as quickly as possible. Issued on May 29, 1865, Johnson's Amnesty Proclamation offered free and full pardon to those who had participated in the rebellion upon their swearing an oath to "defend the Constitution of the United States and the union of the States thereunder."[23] The proclamation exempted fourteen classes of persons from its largesse, including those who had held high civil or military office in the Confederacy and those who owned more than $20,000 worth of property. Anyone who fell within an exempted group could file a special application for pardon with the president. Johnson received at least 15,000 such applications in the two years following the Civil War and eventually granted more than 13,500 individual pardons.[24]

Drafting a petition for amnesty offered former Confederates an opportunity to set down their thoughts on the right of secession and

---

[22] Ex-Confederates were more prone to this romanticization than their Northern counterparts, both because of the culture of honor in the American South and because their defeat made them more prone than Northerners to a maudlin view of the war. See Bertram Wyatt Brown, *Southern Honor: Ethics and Behavior in the Old South* (New York: Oxford University Press, 1982); Edward L. Ayers, *Vengeance and Justice: Crime and Punishment in the 19th-Century American South* (New York: Oxford University Press, 1984), 30–33; Richard Hamm, *Murder, Honor, and Law: Four Virginia Homicides from Reconstruction to the Great Depression* (Charlottesville: University of Virginia Press, 2003).

[23] For a discussion of how pardoning formed the basis of Johnson's lenient Reconstruction policy, see Eric L. McKitrick, *Andrew Johnson and Reconstruction* (Chicago: University of Chicago Press, 1960), 142–52.

[24] Amnesty Proclamation, May 29, 1865, in Andrew Johnson, *The Papers of Andrew Johnson*, ed. Paul Bergeron, 16 vols. (Knoxville: University of Tennessee Press, 1967–69), 8: 128–30; Jonathan T. Dorris, *Pardon and Amnesty under Lincoln and Johnson* (Chapel Hill: University of North Carolina, 1953), 135.

their rekindled loyalty to the United States. Although Johnson's proclamation did not explicitly require former Confederates to renounce a
belief in secession, many amnesty applicants took it upon themselves
to explain their willingness to take such an oath in light of their prior
loyalty to the Confederacy. In so doing, many former Confederates
seized on the language and terminology of trial by battle, explaining
that their genuinely held belief in the legality of secession was overcome by the result of the trial by battle.

The phrasing of the allusions to trial by battle differed markedly
from petition to petition. The persistence of the language was thus
a reflection of each petitioner's distinct thought process rather than
the product of a few pardon brokers' boilerplate insertions.[25] Former
Confederate naval secretary Stephen R. Mallory admitted that he had
placed loyalty to his state above his duty as a citizen of the United
States during the Civil War. He had "regarded the commands of my
state as decisive of my path of duty; and I followed where she led."
Nonetheless, Mallory said that he now understood that secession had
been illegitimate, calling the Civil War a "trial by battle." Mallory
never specifically denied secession's constitutionality; instead, he told
Johnson that because he "recognize[ed] the death [of the Confederacy]
as the will of Almighty God, I regard and accept His dispensation
as decisive of the questions of slavery and secession."[26] Former
Confederate soldier Alpheus Baker of Eufaula, Alabama, "had been
taught ... that the Union was a revocable compact, & Secession a constitutional right." Baker explicitly compared the war to a legal trial,
and now that the contest had resulted in Union victory, he declared: "I
submit with resignation to the inevitable result. I regard the issue as
having been fully tried, & finally determined, and I would oppose all

---

[25] See Dorris, *Pardon and Amnesty*, 144–51, on the business of pardon brokering.

[26] Stephen R. Mallory to Andrew Johnson, June 21, 1865, in Johnson, *Papers of
Andrew Johnson*, 8: 268. Mallory did not claim to acquiesce in the results of the
war merely to wheedle a pardon out of President Johnson. He wrote privately in his
diary while imprisoned after the war that "the South acquiesces in the results of the
battle field; acquiesces in good faith and will conform in good faith to the theory
of the 'National Government' instead of the 'Federal Government,' and never again
attempt secession." Stephen Mallory diary entry, December 6, 1865, quoted in Joseph
Durkin, *Stephen R. Mallory: Confederate Navy Chief* (Chapel Hill: University of
North Carolina Press, 1954), 374.

effort to disturb the verdict, which has been rendered in the tremendous, world watched Trial."[27]

Former Confederate commissary general Lucius B. Northrop emphasized that he had always believed in the paramount sovereignty of the states. Still, he said that had recently taken the loyalty oath to the United States because he believed that "state rights and slavery – the two points involved [in the war] had finally been settled by a resort to arms." Former Confederate general P. G. T. Beauregard explained his actions during the war by professing, "I was defending the constitutional rights of the South." However, the war had established the illegitimacy of secession through a trial by battle. "Having appealed to the arbitration of the Sword, which has gone against us," Beauregard maintained, "I accept the decision as settling finally the questions of secession and slavery."[28]

While appearing to signal their acceptance of the war's outcome, former Confederates' invocation of trial by battle also offered a subtle critique of the fruits of Northern victory by suggesting that they had been obtained in a less than civilized manner. They could acknowledge that the war had annihilated the practical assertion of a right of secession without undermining the logical force of the pro-secession argument. But they did not dare to follow the concept of trial by battle to its logical conclusion. Had they done so, they would have discovered that the analogy between the Civil War and medieval trial by battle could prove hazardous to the Lost Cause worldview – the idea that the Confederate struggle had been brave and righteous.[29] The trial-by-battle metaphor was attractive to many former Confederates precisely because it permitted them to come to terms with the results of the war while still maintaining that their advocacy of secession had been valid. But because a trial by battle was supposed to reveal God's will, and not simply to favor the stronger combatant, defeat would necessarily

---

[27] Alpheus Baker Petition, Case Files of Applications from Former Confederates for Presidential Pardons, "Amnesty Papers," 1865–1867, Alabama Petitions, Reel 1, Record Group 94, NA-DC.

[28] Lucius Northrop to Andrew Johnson, July 11, 1865, in Johnson, *Papers of Andrew Johnson*, 8: 388–89; P. G. T. Beauregard to Andrew Johnson, September 16, 1865, in Johnson, *Papers of Andrew Johnson*, 9: 83.

[29] See Caroline E. Janney, *Remembering the Civil War* (Chapel Hill: University of North Carolina Press, 2013), and David W. Blight, *Race and Reunion: The Civil War in American Memory* (Cambridge, MA: Harvard University Press, 2001).

mean that God had ruled against the loser. Former Confederates who likened the Civil War to a trial by battle did not accept this logic, and their petitions revealed more anger than contrition. The verdict of Appomattox may have caused former Confederates to wonder how they had incurred God's wrath, but they did not number advocacy of secession among their sins.

In his amnesty petition to President Johnson, Clement C. Clay candidly admitted that the Union triumph had *not* caused him to alter his opinion about the constitutionality of secession. "I still think the States did not surrender that right [to withdraw from the Union] in adopting the U.S. Constitution," he wrote. Nevertheless, he grudgingly acknowledged that "the subordination of the States & supremacy of the General Government has been established in the Court of last resort – the field of battle – & its judgment is conclusive and final. The established theory now is, that the citizen owes his highest & first allegiance to the Genl. Govt. Such is the fact & none should dispute it."[30]

The type of defiance Clay exhibited was not conducive to continuing a political career after the war. Former Confederate postmaster John H. Reagan, who did remain involved in national politics during Reconstruction, publicly urged ex-Confederates "to recognize the supreme authority of the Government of the United States ... and its right to protect itself against disintegration by the secession of the states." In Reagan's view, Americans had chosen war as the ultimate legal tribunal to decide the rightfulness of secession precisely because no other forum could possibly have settled the momentous issues dividing North and South.[31] Confederates had freely entered into the

---

[30] Clement C. Clay Jr. to Andrew Johnson, November 23, 1865, in Johnson, *Papers of Andrew Johnson*, 9: 421; Clement C. Clay Jr. to Virginia Clay, August 11, 1865, Box 7, Clement Clay Papers, DU.

[31] Although after the war many Americans believed that no civil court's ruling on secession would have been considered definitive, it is worth exploring whether the question could have received adequate treatment in a court of law prior to the war. After resigning his Senate seat in response to Mississippi's secession in January 1861, Jefferson Davis remained in Washington for a week, hoping to be arrested in order to test the legality of secession. See Varina Davis, *Jefferson Davis, Ex-President of the Confederate States: A Memoir*, 2 vols. (New York: Belford, 1890), 2: 3. It is highly doubtful that the government could have proven that Davis had committed treason based on the bare fact of the Southern states' secession from the Union, without a war to enforce that purported right, because of the requirement of actual force or violence to prove that a defendant had "levied war" within the constitutional definition of treason. See Ex parte Bollman, 8 U.S. 75, 128 (1807). Still, even if a treason

wager of battle and could no longer appeal to some "law" outside of the contest of the war to relieve them from their duty to accept the rules laid down by the victorious North. For Reagan, the verdict of arms was final and binding:

The questions as to which party to the contest was right or wrong, or as to whether both were partly right and partly wrong, and as to whether we did right or wrong in staking all on the fate of battle, were discussed before the war was commenced, and were decided by each party for itself, and, failing to agree, they made their appeal to the dread arbitrament of arms. It was precisely because the parties could not agree as to the issues between them that they went to war, to settle them in that way. Why should we now think of reopening the discussion of these questions? What good would come of doing so? Wisdom requires us to accept the decision of battle upon the issues involved, and to be thankful that no more has been demanded by the conquerors.[32]

Other former Confederates who accepted the conditions of Reconstruction echoed Reagan's language. In a public letter to the editor of the *New Orleans Times* in 1867, former general James Longstreet, who became a social outcast in the South following the war because he joined the Republican Party, bluntly insisted that "the surrender of the Confederate armies in 1865 involved [first and foremost] ... the surrender of *the claim* to the right of secession." Former Confederates would not be able to move on with their lives, let alone become reintegrated into the United States, until they ended their insistence on the logic of secession, rather than simply repudiating the right to exercise it. The only solution, according to Longstreet, was to let

charge would have been difficult to sustain during the secession winter, it is possible that the right of secession could have been tested in another type of case – such as nonpayment of federal tariffs in the "seceded" states. Regardless, the larger question remains as to whether a pronouncement by a regularly constituted court – even the Supreme Court – on the legality of secession would have been considered legitimate. Given the controversy that erupted after the Supreme Court's 1857 decision in *Dred Scott*, it seems highly unlikely that a decision on the topic of secession rendered by a "mere" court would have been considered authoritative by the losing party. See Don E. Fehrenbacher, *The Dred Scott Case: Its Significance in American Law and Politics* (New York: Oxford University Press, 1978).

[32] John H. Reagan to "The People of Texas," August 11, 1865, reprinted in John H. Reagan, *Memoirs: With Special Reference to Secession and the Civil War*, ed. Walter F. McCaleb (New York: Neale Publishing, 1906), 287, 289. The editor of Reagan's memoir noted that the advice in his letter proved "distasteful" to the people of Texas. Ibid., 19. See also Ben H. Procter, *Not without Honor: The Life of John H. Reagan* (Austin: University of Texas Press, 1962), 171–73.

"these issues [expire] upon the fields last occupied by the Confederate armies. There they should have been buried."[33]

In Longstreet's view, might had substituted for right, and now that naked power was the law of the land, secession could not be vindicated in any court of law. "It is too late," he wrote, "to go back to look after our rights under the law and the Constitution. It is of no practical importance for us to know whether we have been deprived of these rights by lawful or unlawful process." What was more, he recognized, Confederates could no longer look to the law as a bulwark against naked aggression. In the post–Civil War South, it made no sense to revere the legal process as the only way to settle thorny questions. The constitutional right to secede from the Union and the legal right to hold slaves, Longstreet said, "are gone, and the only available law is martial law, and the only right, power. The more we seek for law, when there is no law, the greater will be our confusion."[34]

Comparing the Civil War to a trial by battle led many Americans to ask whether the war had transformed their society into a quasi-military state in which force of arms would triumph over the rule of law. Some Confederate sympathizers condemned the degeneracy of the American legal system in the aftermath of the war. Charles O'Conor compared civil war to the "deadly heat of fever, which consumes, without remedy, the vitals of the Constitution. I do not think opinions

[33] James Longstreet, letter to the editor, New Orleans Times, April 6, 1867, reprinted in the *New York Times*, April 13, 1867.

[34] Longstreet, letter to the editor. Former U.S. Supreme Court justice John A. Campbell agreed with Longstreet's dismal assessment of the utility of the law in the Reconstruction-era South. Campbell insisted that the experience of war had subjected the Southern states to "an ordeal of fire," and that the law and even the Constitution itself could no longer protect ex-Confederates from the illegal encroachments of the Reconstruction Congress on their rights. John A. Campbell to James Longstreet, April 5, 1867, in the *New York Times*, April 13, 1867. Campbell had been imprisoned for several months following the war, and after his release, according to his biographer, he revitalized his law practice by advocating expanded national authority. See Robert Saunders Jr., *John Archibald Campbell* (Tuscaloosa: University of Alabama Press, 1997), 210–14. Longstreet and Campbell's correspondence was reproduced (and praised) by many Northern papers, while ex-Confederates and Northern Democrats branded Longstreet a traitor. See *Washington National Intelligencer*, April 13, 1867; *Boston Daily Advertiser*, April 15, 1867; *Milwaukee Daily Sentinel*, April 17, 1867. See also William Garrett Piston, *Lee's Tarnished Lieutenant: James Longstreet and His Place in Southern History* (Athens: University of Georgia Press, 1987), 105, for a discussion of the reaction to Longstreet's letter.

of a judicial nature concerning the law or Constitution of any consequence." The republic had, in his view, "perished on the day that McDowell moved on to Richmond."[35]

Missouri Supreme Court judge William B. Napton, who supported O'Conor's presidential candidacy in 1872, quoted O'Conor's words about the war's consequences admiringly.[36] He agreed with O'Conor's assessment of the war's corrosive effect on the rule of law, and insisted that the battlefield's resolution of the secession issue was illegitimate. "A Union such as we had under the old Constitution could never be created or preserved or restored by force," he wrote. "There might be territorial unity – there might be conquest – but there could be no Union, in the old sense of the term." Napton believed that determining the legality of secession through military might was incompatible with the rule of law. "The right to [exercise the right of secession] was disputed and the rebellion was put down by force. So much for paper assertions and declarations. The right is settled by the might," Napton lamented.[37]

To many critics of Reconstruction policy, it seemed as though the postbellum courts, cowed by the experience of trial by battle, now lacked the fortitude to check the transgressions of the other branches of government. Georgia governor Charles Jenkins, defeated in his suit challenging the constitutionality of military Reconstruction in *Georgia v. Stanton*, complained to his lawyer Jeremiah Black about the Supreme Court's refusal to intervene in volatile controversies.[38] For Jenkins, the case was emblematic of a larger problem the war had engendered: the courts were now unwilling to override illegal policies because they recognized that their decisions could not possibly contend with the "law" as declared by a triumphant army. This was a direct result of recognizing the validity of secession's trial by

35 Charles O'Conor to Samuel Chester Reid Jr., November 29, 1876, Box 4, Samuel Chester Reid Papers, LC. This letter was also reprinted in the *New York Times*, December 6, 1876.
36 William Barclay Napton, *The Union on Trial: The Political Journals of Judge William Barclay Naptonn, 1829–1883*, ed. Christopher Phillips and Jason L. Pendleton (Columbia: University of Missouri Press, 2005), 523–24; see 508 for his views on O'Conor as a presidential candidate.
37 Napton, *The Union on Trial*, 312–13, 530.
38 Georgia v. Stanton, 73 U.S. 50 (1867).

battle. Wrote Jenkins, "The sword has decided against the right of secession[,] and it is not to be supposed that [the courts] will again ... assert [it]."[39]

Unionist thinkers predictably cast the triumph of their army in a different light, arguing that the war was a form of direct democracy through which the people had made law outside of the formal legal process. They insisted that victory on the field of battle constituted a valid – if not the most valid – form of adjudication. War was, in today's parlance, a form of "higher lawmaking" and popular constitutionalism.[40] Following Appomattox, General William T. Sherman insisted that Confederates had implicitly consented to abide by the decree of battle by waging war in 1861. The Confederates had *themselves* resorted to force to resolve the constitutionality of secession, he said, and the "government accepted their wager of battle." Upon defeat, "even their lives and personal liberty, thrown *by them* into the issue, were theirs only by our forbearance and clemency."[41] Lieutenant General Ulysses S. Grant was optimistic about ex-Confederates' acceptance of Union victory as binding law. He believed that the vanquished would recognize that "the right of a State to secede from the Union ... [had] been settled forever, by the highest tribunal, arms, that man can resort to."[42]

Some Confederates, by contrast, were sure that the verdict of the battlefield would not offer the last word on the secession question. Confederate vice president Alexander H. Stephens toyed briefly with the possibility of daring the federal government to try him for treason and thereby test the legality of secession in a court of law. Ultimately he thought better of this plan and proffered an amnesty petition to President Johnson.[43] Emboldened on his release, Stephens grew more defiant

---

[39] Charles Jenkins to Jeremiah Black, May 8, 1867, Reel 23, Jeremiah Black Papers, LC [microfilm edition].

[40] See Larry D. Kramer, *The People Themselves: Popular Constitutionalism and Judicial Review* (Oxford: Oxford University Press, 2004); Bruce Ackerman, *We the People: Transformations*, 2 vols. (Cambridge, MA: Belknap Press of Harvard University Press, 1998).

[41] "The Right of Conquest," *New Hampshire Statesman*, September 15, 1865.

[42] Ulysses S. Grant to Andrew Johnson, December 18, 1865, in Ulysses S. Grant, *The Papers of Ulysses S. Grant*, ed. John Y. Simon, 28 vols. to date (Carbondale: Southern Illinois University Press, 1967), 15: 434.

[43] Alexander H. Stephens, *Recollections of Alexander H. Stephens*, ed. Myrta Lockett Avary (New York: Doubleday, Page, 1910), 201.

and began writing a book designed to prove the constitutionality of secession. In the resulting tome, *A Constitutional View of the Late War between the States,* he maintained that secession still lived, even if Union victory made its exercise impossible. The right of secession survived outside of the field of battle, according to Stephens, in "other arenas – to those of Thought, of Public Discussions, Council Chambers, and Courts of Justice." The right of secession could not die in the crucible of the Civil War, simply because "it involves questions that cannot be settled by arms."[44]

No war could refute the logic of the secessionist position; military might simply could not overcome the force of reason, logic, and law. Virginia attorney and Lost Cause enthusiast Jubal A. Early concurred with Stephens's assessment of the invincibility of secession. Although Northerners argued that Confederate defeat had settled the questions of the war, Early would not admit that such matters could be resolved "with the sword." For Early, the war proved that "truth does not always prevail and that might is often more powerful than right." The war could not settle any dispute over states' rights, "any more than the traveller on the highway submits his money to the arbitrament of arms between himself and the robber."[45]

The illegitimacy of the "verdict" rendered by the Union army was a frequent topic of discussion in the Copperhead New York monthly the *Old Guard.* Edited by C. Chauncey Burr, the paper specialized in spirited defenses of slavery and secession during the war years, paired with ringing criticisms of the Lincoln government. After the war, the paper insisted that law, by its very nature, could not yield to the force of arms: "In the nature of things, wars 'settle' nothing beyond physical results. They are an exercise of force, and do not, and cannot,

---

[44] Alexander H. Stephens, *A Constitutional View of the Late War between the States,* 2 vols. (Philadelphia: National Publishing, 1868, 1870), 2: 658–59. Stephens believed that the right of secession might have a fair hearing in "judicial tribunals" when former Confederates were tried for treason. But by submitting his own amnesty petition, Stephens ensured that his case would not be among them. Stephens intimated that he believed the federal government shied away from trying Jefferson Davis for treason because his secessionist principles would achieve vindication in a court of law. Ibid., 2: 664.

[45] Jubal A. Early, *The Heritage of the South* (Lynchburg, VA: Press of Brown-Morrison, 1915), 116–18. Early's book was published in 1915 by his niece, but it was written by Early immediately after the Civil War, probably sometime in 1865. Ibid., 1.

hold reason and conscience, and just law and righteous government, amenable to the tribunal of blood and violence." Burr's highly formalistic interpretation of the law rested on a claim that the war could not change immutable legal principles, which remained firmly in place despite the convulsions of society. The war, for Burr, "did not repeal the laws of nature, nor change the position of the poles; nor blot out the stars; but the foundations of the earth and fixtures of the firmament remained."[46] "Your great, your sure remedy," the paper intoned, "is law. Law and justice are not always very swift, but with a brave and virtuous people, they are sure to break the power of the sword, and to whip the licentious force of arms at last." The spirit of the Constitution would somehow prevail. Burr believed that long-standing constitutional principles would demolish even formal written amendments to the Constitution, because those new amendments only served to ratify "sordid" principles forged in the chaos of civil war.[47]

Other secessionist writers were less certain of the law's ability to overturn the results of a military victory. Georgia lawyer and former Confederate congressman Jabez L. M. Curry believed that secession, whatever its constitutional merits, was a casualty of war: "How far the *ratio regium* [sic], the wager of battle, the avoir-dupois [sic] of numbers, can determine a question of conscience or law, need not now be discussed. Secession is now as dead as slavery."[48]

Albert Bledsoe, a lawyer and former mathematics professor who had published a treatise in 1865 detailing the constitutional and historical argument for secession, began publishing the *Southern Review* following the war.[49] In the *Review*, Bledsoe expressed no confidence that the law would eventually triumph over the forces of brutality

---

[46] "What the War Settled," *Old Guard* 7 (August 1869): 628–30. For information about Burr and his newspaper, see Frank Luther Mott, *A History of American Magazines, 1850–1865* (Cambridge, MA: Belknap Press of Harvard University Press, 1957), 544–46; Wood Gray, *The Hidden Civil War: The Story of the Copperheads* (New York: Viking Press, 1964), 214, referring to Burr as a "specialist in extremism."

[47] "State Sovereignty Not Dead," *Old Guard* 4 (May 1866): 257.

[48] J. L. M. Curry, "Did General Lee Violate His Oath in Siding with the Confederacy?" *Southern Historical Society Papers* 6 (August 1878): 54.

[49] Albert T. Bledsoe, *Is Davis a Traitor?* (Baltimore: Innes, 1866). See Chapter 7 for further discussion of Bledsoe's book.

and unreason and reassert its authority. The law was implemented by men, who had lived through the Civil War and would therefore be incapable of allowing the neutral principles of law to trump the reality of events. Although he refused to repudiate secessionist logic, Bledsoe acknowledged that "the wager [of battle] has long since been won, and the Supreme Court, with the rest of the winners, has possession of the bloody stakes. To imagine that the judges of that tribunal could now hold otherwise than that the 'right' in dispute had been 'decided,' would be sheer fatuity."[50]

The most prominent use of the trial by battle analogy occurred in the *Prize Cases*, an 1863 Supreme Court decision validating President Lincoln's blockade of Confederate ports. (This ruling – and the Court's decision in *Texas v. White* – are discussed in more depth in Chapter 10 and the Epilogue.) The claimants challenged Lincoln's action on the grounds that a blockade was an instrument of international law, which was unavailable to a parent government in a domestic insurrection. Was the Confederate struggle an international contest or a domestic rebellion? Writing for the majority, Justice Robert Grier explained that the United States could treat the Confederacy as a belligerent power under international law (thus sanctioning the use of the blockade), without conceding the legitimacy of secession under constitutional law. In the course of his opinion, Grier compared the Civil War to a trial by battle. He insisted that a court of law could not ultimately decide whether the secession of the Southern states was unconstitutional; this issue could only be settled in the crucible of war. Grier acknowledged that the seceded states had "combined to form a new confederacy, claiming to be acknowledged by the world as a sovereign State. Their right to do so is now being decided by wager of battle."[51]

The implications of Grier's description of the Civil War as a trial by battle became clear six years later in his dissent in the 1869 case *Texas v. White*. In that case, Texas had invoked the original jurisdiction of the

---

[50] Albert Bledsoe, "Review: *Prison Life of Jefferson Davis*," *Southern Review* 1 (January 1867): 233, 244–45.

[51] The Prize Cases, 67 U.S. 635, 673 (1862).

Supreme Court to compel the return of U.S. government bonds that the state had given in payment for rebel war materiel in early 1865.[52] The Court held that Texas, despite its purported secession from the Union in 1861, remained a state and could thus invoke the Supreme Court's jurisdiction. Chief Justice Salmon P. Chase, writing for the majority, took the opportunity to set forth a definitive pronouncement on the unconstitutionality of secession. Chase found the issue an easy one to decide, so much so that he found it "needless to discuss, at length, the question whether the right of a State to withdraw from the Union for any cause ... is consistent with the Constitution." According to Chase, secession had always been illegal; the ordinances of secession by the eleven Confederate states "were utterly without operation in law" and had effected no change in their status. For Chase, the "more perfect Union" created by the ratification of the Constitution had created "an indestructible Union, composed of indestructible states."[53]

Drawing on the "trial by battle" language of his *Prize Cases* opinion in his forceful dissent, Grier argued that Texas was *not* one of the United States and thus could not file suit in the Supreme Court. Grier insisted that the court should view the question of whether or not Texas was a state "as a *political fact*, not as a *legal fiction*." In other words, the court should defer to Congress's determination of the political status of the former Confederate states. Congress had chosen to hold and govern Texas "as a conquered province by military force," and Grier declared himself "not disposed to join in any essay to prove Texas to be a State of the Union, when Congress have decided she is not.... Politically, Texas is not *a State in this Union*." Grier maintained that the political branches of government could treat

---

[52] Article III, § 2, of the Constitution grants original jurisdiction to the Supreme Court in any suit in "which a state shall be a party." At issue in the suit was the ability of certain bondholders to receive payment on U.S. bonds given to Texas as part of the Compromise of 1850. Texas had sold some of the bonds to the defendants in the midst of the Civil War pursuant to a state act to "provide funds for military purposes," in exchange for supplies. Texas sued the defendants after the war for recovery of the bonds, arguing that the state, while in rebellion, was unauthorized to sell bonds for the "purpose of aiding the overthrow of the Federal government." White defended the suit on the grounds that, among other things, Texas was not presently one of the United States and could not therefore file suits invoking the original jurisdiction of the Supreme Court. The Court ultimately decided that Texas was entitled to restitution.

[53] Texas v. White, 74 U.S. 700, 725 (1868).

the defeated Confederate states in any manner they deemed proper because the Union army had conquered the Confederacy and the "seceded" states had become conquered territory. Texas, along with the other Confederate states, had put the right of secession to the test, Grier insisted, and the war had established that "the verdict on the trial of this question, 'by battle,' as to her right to secede, has been against her." Thus, the Confederate states' defeat had established the illegality of secession and reduced Texas to a conquered province.[54]

Grier's argument suggests that, unlike Chase, he did not believe that secession had always been illegitimate. For Grier, the legitimacy of secession had remained an open question for the duration of the Civil War. Because of its strength of arms, the Confederacy had enjoyed a temporary and limited status under international law as a belligerent (and foreign) power. While the action in the trial by battle was pending – that is, during the war – secession had enjoyed a shadowy kind of viability. Secession had *become* definitively unconstitutional only with the triumph of the Union army in 1865.

Grier's opinions in the *Prize Cases* and in *Texas v. White* make clear the logical correlation between "trial by battle" and the "conquered provinces" theory of Reconstruction, as famously articulated by Pennsylvania congressman Thaddeus Stevens. Stevens, a Radical Republican who believed strongly in racial egalitarianism, hoped to use the power of the federal government to effect massive social and political changes in the former Confederate states. In this way, he believed, Southern freedmen would not be "left to the legislation of their late masters." This newfound exercise of virtually limitless federal power, Stevens insisted, was justified by the fact that Southern states were no longer part of the Union. Instead, they had been conquered by United States forces in precisely the same way that a foreign nation might be overrun by an invading army.[55]

---

[54] Texas v. White, 74 U.S. at 737, 739–40 (Grier, J., dissenting).

[55] Stevens's views on secession and Reconstruction are often linked with those of Massachusetts senator Charles Sumner. Sumner endorsed the "state suicide" theory of the Union, which postulated that the states, in attempting to secede, had essentially self-destructed and reverted to territorial status by attempting this illegal act. Although Sumner's theory of "state suicide" is often mentioned in the same breath as Stevens's conquered province theory, the two differed mightily with respect to the view of secession implicit in each theory. The conquered province theory tacitly endorsed the legitimacy of secession while it was being tested during the war, but the state

Stevens protested against the more mainstream idea – which Chase later championed in *Texas v. White* – that the Southern states had always remained in the Union because they possessed no legal right to secede. Stevens mocked this theory. It was "a good deal less ingenious and respectable than the metaphysics of [George] Berkeley, which proved that neither the world nor any human being was in existence." For Stevens, the result of the trial by battle had rendered secession unconstitutional, and this defeat had given the victorious party the authority to govern – and remake – the conquered South. Stevens quoted Grier's "wager of battle" language to make this argument, and expanded on the logic of Grier's view. The Union and the Confederacy had "mutually prepared to settle the question [of Confederate independence] by force of arms," Stevens insisted. "On the result of the war depended the fate and ulterior condition of the contending parties." Congress's Joint Committee on Reconstruction, on which Stevens served, linked the conquered province theory to trial by battle. According to the committee's report, the two sides "chose the tribunal of arms wherein to decide whether or not [secession] should be legalized, and [the Confederate states] were defeated." As a result of military defeat, "the conquered rebels were at the mercy of the conquerors."[56]

Justice Grier's description of the Civil War as a trial by battle generated similar analyses in lower courts around the country. Some courts simply quoted Grier's *Prize Cases* "wager of battle" language verbatim, but others expanded on Grier's formulation in grappling with the many legal questions that grew out of the Civil War.[57] Many attorneys and judges invoked the language of trial by battle to give the legitimacy of

suicide theory was premised on the notion that secession had been illegal in 1861, and that the states that attempted secession immediately ceased to exist as states.

[56] Thaddeus Stevens, "'Reconstruction,' September 6, 1865, in Lancaster," and "'Reconstruction,' December 18, 1865, in Congress," in Thaddeus Stevens, *The Selected Papers of Thaddeus Stevens*, ed. Beverly Wilson Palmer and Holly Byers Ochoa, 2 vols. (Pittsburgh: University of Pittsburgh Press, 1997), 2: 24, 46; *Congressional Globe*, 39th Cong., 2d sess., January 3, 1867, 251; *Report of the Joint Committee on Reconstruction* (Washington, DC: Government Printing Office, 1866), viii, xi. For a discussion of Stevens's conquest theory, see McKitrick, *Andrew Johnson and Reconstruction*, 99–101; Hans L. Trefousse, *Thaddeus Stevens: Nineteenth-Century Egalitarian* (Chapel Hill: University of North Carolina Press, 1997), 217–18. Stevens died in 1868 and thus did not weigh in on Grier's *Texas v. White* dissent.

[57] See Pennywit v. Kellogg, 13 Ohio Dec. Repr. 389, 391 (1870); Smith v. Brazelton, 48 Tenn. 44, 47 (1870); Hall v. Keese, 31 Tex. 504, 529 (1868); Scheible v. Bacho, 41 Ala. 423, 431 (1868); Mayer v. George W. Reed & Co., 37 Ga. 482, 486 (1867); Hill v. Boyland, 40 Miss. 618, 626 (1866), all quoting Grier.

a legal action to the war's violent method of settling the secession question. In 1870, the West Virginia Supreme Court of Appeals characterized trial by battle as the only possible and acceptable means by which two nations could settle a legal dispute. With respect to two nations, the court insisted, "the right to enforce their supposed demands or grievances against each other by the wager of battle, is as clear as the right of the citizen to enforce by suit his demands against individuals." Judge Richard Moncure of the Virginia Supreme Court of Appeals amplified this conclusion by declaring that a Confederate victory in the Civil War would have indisputably established the validity of secession. Moncure insisted that if "the decision by this wager of battle had been different from what it was," Unionists could not have "said that the Confederate government was not a government."[58] Trial by battle was wholly dispositive, in his view.

The legitimacy of trial by battle was a topic that consumed nineteenth-century historians as well as lawyers. In 1866 *Superstition and Force*, a book chronicling the "primitive" legal customs of medieval society, first appeared. Its author, Philadelphia historian Henry Charles Lea, devoted a chapter to the historical practice of trial by battle. For Lea, the best way to gain insight into the character of any society was to investigate its legal customs. Lea saw wager of battle as an outdated custom mired in barbarism and viewed the history of European civilization as a teleological progression from primitive customs such as wager of law, battle, and the ordeal to the enlightened rationality of trial by jury. From the superior vantage point of nineteenth-century America, he observed contentedly that "wise in our generation, we laugh at the inconsistencies of our forefathers."[59]

Lea was not alone in viewing the trial by battle as a terrible medieval superstition, particularly in contrast to the modern and supposedly morally superior trial by jury. For instance, the *Albany Law Journal* called the concept of trial by ordeal "foolishly absurd." "The

---

[58] Caperton v. Martin, 4 W.Va. 138, 152 (1870); Walker v. Christian, 62 Va. 291, 296 (1871). See also "Charge to the Grand Jury at Richmond," *Washington National Intelligencer*, November 10, 1865. Other Reconstruction-era cases discussing the Civil War as a trial by battle include Keppel v. Petersburg R. Co., 14 F. Cas. 357 (C.C.D. Va. 1868) (No. 7,722); McCafferty v. Guyer, 59 Pa. 109 (1868); Green v. Sizer, 40 Miss. 530 (1866); Billgerry v. Branch & Sons, 60 Va. 393 (1869).

[59] Lea, *Superstition and Force*, 1, 73.

superstitions of our ancestors appear almost incredible to the enlightened spirit of the nineteenth century," the journal declared.⁶⁰ The
idea of importing such an uncivilized and backward practice into the
modern era would have been disquieting to many Americans.⁶¹ Law,
according to the prevailing understanding among nineteenth-century
legal scholars and historians, had progressed along the same lines as
other aspects of civilized culture, and a modern society's adherence to
the rule of law, rather than the prospect of violence, marked its distance from the barbaric customs of the past.⁶²

   Lea, who later gained renown as the first great American medievalist, first published the germ of his idea before in the war, in an 1859
article in the *North American Review*.⁶³ Lea completed his treatise in

⁶⁰ "Trial by Ordeal," *Albany Law Journal* 1 (1870): 305. See also "An Interesting
   Scrap of Legal History," *Milwaukee Daily Sentinel*, May 15, 1867; "Trial by Battle,"
   Cornhill Magazine 22 (1870): 715; "The Marriage Laws – No. II," *Upper Canada
   Law Journal* 3 (1867).
⁶¹ See George Stocking, *Victorian Anthropology* (New York: Free Press, 1987),
   esp. 117–28, for his discussion of the work of Sir Henry Maine. See also Norbert
   Elias, *The Civilizing Process: The History of Manners*, 2 vols. (New York: Urizen
   Books, 1939). On the subject of Victorians' obsession with manners and the civili-
   zation, see generally Karen Haltunnen, *Confidence Men and Painted Women* (New
   Haven: Yale University Press, 1982), esp. 92–123; Gail Bederman, *Manliness and
   Civilization* (Chicago: University of Chicago Press, 1995), 23–31; Daniel Walker
   Howe, "Victorian Culture in America," in *Victorian America*, ed. Geoffrey Blodgett
   (Philadelphia: University of Pennsylvania Press, 1976), 3–28; Stow Persons, *The
   Decline of American Gentility* (New York: Columbia University Press, 1973),
   1–129; Steven Mintz, *A Prison of Expectations: The Family in Victorian Culture*
   (New York: New York University Press, 1983), 80–81; John F. Kasson, *Rudeness
   and Civility: Manners in Nineteenth-Century Urban America* (New York: Hill and
   Wang, 1990).
⁶² See Paludan, "The American Civil War Considered as a Crisis in Law and Order,"
   and Phillip S. Paludan, *A Covenant with Death: The Constitution, Law, and
   Equality in the Civil War Era* (Urbana: University of Illinois Press, 1975); Bestor,
   "The American Civil War as a Constitutional Crisis," and James Q. Whitman, *The
   Verdict of Battle: The Law of Victory and the Making of Modern War* (Cambridge,
   MA: Harvard University Press, 2012).
⁶³ One historian referred to Lea as "America's most prominent medievalist of the nine-
   teenth century, while another called him "the greatest historian in nineteenth-century
   America and the most accomplished American historian of medieval Europe before
   [early twentieth-century historian] Charles Homer Haskins." John M. O'Brien,
   "Henry Charles Lea: The Historian as Reformer," *American Quarterly* 19 [1967]:
   104; Edward Peters, "Henry Charles Lea, 1825–1909," in *Medieval Scholarship:
   Biographical Studies on the Formation of a Discipline*, ed. Helen Damico and Joseph
   B. Zavadil, 3 vols. (New York: Garland Publishing, 1995), 1: 89. During the war,
   Lea engaged in organizational efforts on behalf of the Union. As a member of the
   Union League of Philadelphia, Lea raised money to recruit and equip black troops

the midst of the Civil War, but the first edition of the book did not comment directly on the parallels between his own country's recent experience and medieval trial by battle. Lea's private correspondence, however, does show that he connected trial by battle to the present. Indeed, it seems he saw the language as entirely commensurate with the occasion. In an 1861 letter to John Bell, who had run for president in 1860 on a platform that promised to keep the Union together, Lea declared that "the result of this contest is in the hands of the God of Battles, but whatever it may be, we are resolved that the right of secession shall no more be heard of in public law of the United States; or even if it should remain theoretically unsettled, that practically the ordeal through which the seceders must pass shall put an end to the day dreams of ambitious aspirants for a country to come."[64] Confronted with the exigencies of the Civil War, Lea reflexively applied the concept of trial by battle to the conflict.

Even if Lea resisted the conclusion that the United States had reverted to primitive legal customs during the Civil War, the book's audience made the connection. In reviewing Lea's first edition of *Superstition and Force*, the *Nation* reflected on the similarity between the "barbarous" custom of trial by battle among medieval Europeans and the experience of the Civil War. Trial by battle was the only legal forum available in international law to settle disputes. "After all," the magazine editorialized, "is not war itself – war, we will say, between sovereign states, which admit no arbiter – is this not a remnant both of superstition and impiety, the wager of battle on a frightful scale?"[65] Although the paper acknowledged the necessity of trial by battle, it also exhibited a certain squeamishness about its implications. Trial by battle remained the law in the international arena not because it was

---

and authored a number of pamphlets strongly supportive of the Union war effort. Edward Sculley Bradley, *Henry Charles Lea: A Biography* (Philadelphia: University of Pennsylvania Press, 1931), 77–122. For his early article, see [Henry Charles Lea], "Canonical Compurgation and the Wager of Battle," *North American Review* 88 (January 1859): 1–51 (although not identified within the article, Lea's authorship is confirmed in the preface of Lea, *Superstition and Force*).

[64] Henry C. Lea to John Bell, n.d., 1861, Box 3, Henry C. Lea Papers, University of Pennsylvania Special Collections Library, Philadelphia (repository hereafter cited as UPenn).

[65] "The Way Out of Barbarism," *Nation*, September 13, 1866, 208–9. Lea saved a clipping of this review in his personal papers, Box 158, Henry C. Lea Papers, UPenn.

desirable, but because there was no alternative when two nations could not resolve weighty legal questions.

The applicability of trial by battle to American shores also did not escape the notice of the new *American Law Review*, edited by the young Boston lawyers John Codman Ropes and John Chipman Gray.[66] Ropes and Gray, friends from their Harvard days who had opened a joint law practice on Gray's return from serving in the Union army, praised Lea's book for its accurate research. But they argued that it ignored the persistence of wager of law, trial by battle, and other "barbarous customs" in the history of "this country."[67] Recognizing that ancient practices such as trial by battle were not mere relics of the unenlightened European past, the review mentioned several instances in which these seemingly obsolete customs had crept into American law. John Chipman Gray, who had actually fought in the war, was far more sanguine than Lea about the idea that Americans had resorted to trial by battle in fighting the Civil War. For Gray, only a war could have settled the constitutional dispute between North and South over the legality of secession. Gray wrote his father in the spring of 1865 that "it does not seem to me that such a rebellion as this even after it has been put down can be treated like an ordinary violation of the laws of society." Because "the question of the right of secession and of State Rights generally was one with two sides and which honest men might well differ, war was the only tribunal to which it could be referred."[68]

Lea evidently took the review to heart and came around to the idea that the barbarous customs of the English past had made their way onto American soil. In March 1867 he wrote Gray to ask for more details about American cases involving "medieval" legal customs, which he then included in a section on wager of battle in America in the second edition of his book. Gray referred him to an appeal of felony case from colonial Maryland, as well as several more informal instances of judicial ordeals in America, and pointed out that several

[66] Roland Gray, *John Chipman Gray* (Boston: Massachusetts Historical Society, 1916), 14. For more details about Gray's life and his law partnership with John C. Ropes, see Albert Borden, *Ropes-Gray, 1865–1940* (Boston: Lincoln and Smith Press, 1942).

[67] "Superstition and Force, by Henry C. Lea," *American Law Review* 1 (1867): 378. See also John C. Gray to Henry C. Lea, July 27, 1866, Box 9, Henry C. Lea Papers, UPenn.

[68] John C. Gray Jr. to John C. Gray Sr., May 14, 1865, in John Chipman Gray and John Codman Ropes, *War Letters, 1862–1865* (Boston: Riverside Press, 1927), 484–85.

states maintained the option of wager of battle into the nineteenth century.[69] Reflecting on the fact that trial by battle had indeed crossed the Atlantic and infiltrated American society, Lea expressed disappointment that "America, inheriting the blessings of English law, inherited also its defects."[70]

Whatever their views on the legitimacy of trial by battle, many Unionists worried that the settlement achieved at Appomattox remained troublingly uncertain. Their concerns took two distinct forms. First, they doubted that secession's proponents would ever really accept the war's outcome, such that secession's illegality would never truly be established. Second, they worried that the results of the war would be difficult to contain, and that the demise of the secession would lead inexorably to the demise of federalism in the United States. The war might have unforeseen consequences: it might result in the complete eradication of state sovereignty and the birth of "consolidation" – the creation of a unitary system of national government.

A full ten years after the war had ended, Congressman (and future president) James Garfield remained uncertain about whether former Confederates had really accepted that the Civil War had "disproved" the constitutional theory undergirding secession. To Garfield's mind, former Confederates had believed so deeply in their pro-secession ideology that no war could produce a genuine change of heart. What was more, former Confederates could still wrest a victory for secession from the North if they convinced future generations of Americans of the merits of their viewpoint. Northerners had to remember, Garfield said, "that after the battle of arms comes the battle of history. The cause that triumphs in the field does not always triumph in history." Northerners thus could "never safely relax their vigilance until the ideas for which they have fought have become embodied in the enduring forms of individual and national life."[71] The victors had to divine

---

[69] John Chipman Gray to Henry C. Lea, March 15, 1867, Box 9, Henry C. Lea Papers, UPenn.

[70] Lea, *Superstition and Force*, 199. Lea's second edition (1870) still did not discuss the Civil War in the context of trial by battle.

[71] *Congressional Record* 4 (August 4, 1876): 5180. See also John Quincy Adams II, *Massachusetts and South Carolina* (Boston: J. E. Farwell, 1868), 11–13.

a way to change the hearts of the unreconstructed if their triumph was to last.[72]

Vermont chief justice Isaac Redfield did not share Garfield's concerns. The war would accomplish the aim of destroying secession. For him, a war "may fairly be considered an action pending in the only tribunal having full jurisdiction of questions between nations or fragments of nations – the tribunal of force – *ultima ratio regum*." The outcome of the war accordingly carried the same weight, if not more, than any court proceeding, and "may be, not inaptly, considered under the figure of a judgment, in an action in a court of justice; for such in fact is war more than anything else."[73]

However, because secession had succumbed to arms rather than logic, Redfield worried that the results might prove difficult to contain. The war had rightfully ensured the subordinate position of the states within the Union, but Redfield feared that the end of secession might well portend the destruction of the states entirely. Because the unnatural and inorganic experience of war and not the deliberative processes of government had made "the nation supreme and the states subordinate," there might be no way to prevent the growth of federal power at the expense of the states, threatening the survival of the very structure of American federalism. Only vigilance could prevent this extreme form of federal power from taking hold. Redfield called on

[72] Garfield exhibited much more certainty about the completeness of Union victory on taking the presidential oath of office almost five years later. In his inaugural address, Garfield insisted that "the supremacy of the nation and its laws should no longer be a subject of debate. That discussion, which for half a century threatened the existence of the Union, was closed at last in the high court of war by a decree from which there was no appeal – that the Constitution, and the laws made in pursuance thereof, are and shall continue to be the supreme law of the land, binding alike upon the States and the people." James Garfield, "Inaugural Address," March 4, 1881, in James D. Richardson, ed., *A Compilation of the Messages and Papers of the Presidents*, 11 vols., (Washington, DC: Bureau of National Literature, 1909), 8: 6.

[73] Redfield's letter was published in pamphlet form. Isaac Redfield, *Judge Redfield's Letter to Senator Foot* (New York: Hurd and Houghton, 1865), 7–8. Redfield's (and others') insistence on the legitimacy of war to settle the question of secession is somewhat at odds with the premises of international law, which sought to substitute legal rules for the Hobbesian state of nature in which nations related to one another. See Wheaton, *Elements of International Law*, ed. Richard Henry Dana (1866), §§1–15 (short citations to this treatise will identify the editor and the date of publication because Chapter 12 discusses important differences between various editions of the Wheaton treatise).

"the nation [to] exercise the utmost circumspection not to claim more of the States than its own indispensable necessities demand."[74]

Speaking to a New York audience on the nature of the American Union in 1875, attorney George Ticknor Curtis was bothered by the notion that the brutal process of war had resolved the question of secession. Curtis told his fellow New Yorkers that until 1861, secession's legality had remained an open question, with defensible positions on both sides of the issue. Curtis acknowledged that his own "northern" views on the question had taken shape during the course of his legal studies at Harvard, where he "sat at the feet of more than one great teacher of constitutional law, as it was held and taught in New England. Of course, I imbibed the doctrines of a school which found its grand expression in the speeches of [Daniel] Webster and the commentaries of [Joseph] Story. How could I help it?" Curtis realized that his experience had been repeated all over the North, while in the South "any young man who was being educated at the time in a Southern college and under Southern influences" would have learned the opposing principles. Raised on the state sovereignty ideology set forth by John C. Calhoun and other Southern constitutional theorists, ex-Confederates held their beliefs just as strongly as Curtis's Northern compatriots did. Each position, according to Curtis, "was, in its respective section, held with equal firmness and equal sincerity."

Despite the reasonableness of the pro-secession argument, Curtis insisted, "state secession from the Union, as a constitutional right, is as dead as are the thousands of brave men who were slain in asserting and defending it."[75] The bloodshed gave Curtis pause; he acknowledged that "all the intellectual elements of the controversy remain, of course, just what they were." "It might seem, in the abstract," he admitted uncomfortably, "somewhat paradoxical to suppose that such a question could be definitively settled by fighting." In fact, Curtis said he was troubled by the prospect of explaining this painful matter to future generations of American children, but he "consoled" himself

---

[74] Redfield, *Letter to Senator Foot*, 9.
[75] Curtis also believed, along with Judge Redfield, that Northern victory could lead down the slippery slope toward complete consolidation of the federal Union, and he urged his fellow Northerners to guard against this. George Ticknor Curtis, *A Discourse on the Nature of the American Union, as the Principal Controversy Involved in the Late Civil War* (New York: E. P. Dutton, 1875), 30–31.

with the notion that children should learn the harsh ways of the world
sooner rather than later.[76]

Oliver Wendell Holmes Jr. learned the lesson only too well. After his
youthful exuberance for the Union cause faded as a result of his injuries
at Ball's Bluff, he adopted a detached cynicism about the role of law in
human society. The war had taught him that law could always be supplanted by force. Despite the fact that Holmes celebrated the Union's
triumph over the Confederacy, he told his friend and fellow jurist Sir
Frederick Pollack that he "loathe[d] war." It had seared onto his consciousness the fragility of law and the expendability of human life. The
war had convinced Holmes that "force, mitigated so far as may be supplanted by good manners, is the ultima ratio, and between two groups
that want to make inconsistent kinds of world[s] I see no remedy except
force."[77] The war changed Holmes forever, and as Louis Menand put it,
he spent the rest of his life convinced that "certitude leads to violence."[78]
Because of the vast scale of the suffering, Holmes and others of the
Civil War generation rejected much of their youthful devotion to particular causes in favor of institutions (churches, charities, legislatures) that
could mediate individuals' passions and prevent war.[79]

One Northerner who proved that the war could indeed alter opinions about the validity of secession was Orestes Brownson. Since
the 1820s, Brownson, a New England newspaper editor and public intellectual, had avowed his allegiance to the states' rights doctrines of John C. Calhoun, even while staunchly denouncing slavery
as immoral. In his articles in the *Boston Quarterly Review*, he had
insisted that federal authority "needs a check, a counterbalancing
power ... [to ensure there is] no danger that the state will swallow up

[76] Curtis, *A Discourse on the Nature of the American Union*, 24–26, 28, 31. Curtis
expressed the same sentiments about the war twenty years later in his *Constitutional
History of the United States*, 2 vols. (New York: Harper's, 1895–96), 2: 293,
294, 300.

[77] Oliver Wendell Holmes to Frederick Pollack, February 1, 1920, in Oliver Wendell
Holmes and Frederick Pollack, *Holmes and Pollack: The Correspondence of Mr.
Justice Holmes and Sir Frederick Pollack, 1874–1932*, ed. Mark DeWolfe Howe,
2 vols. (Cambridge, MA: Harvard University Press, 1942), 2: 6.

[78] Louis Menand, *The Metaphysical Club* (New York: Farrar, Straus and Giroux,
2001), 61.

[79] See Wilson, *Patriotic Gore*, and George M. Fredrickson, *The Inner Civil War: Northern
Intellectuals and the Crisis of the Union* (New York: Harper and Row, 1965) for
more on Holmes.

the individual."[80] For Brownson, the war had transformed the Union. In the opening pages of his *American Republic*, which appeared in late 1865, Brownson announced: "I reject the doctrine of State sovereignty, which I held and defended from 1828 to 1861."[81] Former Confederates could never again hope to raise the specter of secession, Brownson wrote; it had died with the Confederacy: "The judgment of the court of last resort has been rendered, and rendered against the [Confederacy]. The cause is finished, the controversy closed, never to be re-opened." Like Isaac Redfield and George T. Curtis, Brownson worried that the eradication of state secession in the strife and violence of the Civil War might portend the end of states themselves. "In suppressing by armed force the doctrine that the States are severally sovereign, what barrier is left against consolidation?" Brownson queried. It remained the duty of public intellectuals such as Brownson himself to grapple with the consequences of the war and to prevent the enlarged power of the federal government from completely eclipsing the states.

But some Northerners – even those who had condemned slavery – denied that trial by battle was a legitimate means of binding a free people to the outcome of a war. Radical Massachusetts abolitionist Lysander Spooner unabashedly condemned the concept of trial by battle. Spooner believed that holding the Confederate states within the Union through force constituted a form of "political slavery," which differed from the chattel slavery practiced in the South only in degree but not in kind.[82] In his lengthy 1867 pamphlet *No*

[80] Orestes A. Brownson, "Slavery – Abolitionism," *Boston Quarterly Review* 1 (April 1838): 238, 257.

[81] Orestes A. Brownson, *The American Republic* (New York: P. O'Shea, 1865), xi. See also Arthur Schlesinger Jr., *A Pilgrim's Progress: Orestes A. Brownson* (Boston: Little, Brown, 1966), 259–60. One Confederate who admitted that his opinion on secession's constitutionality changed as a result of the war was David Levy Yulee, a former U.S. senator from Florida who had been arrested and held at Fort Pulaski following the war. Yulee told President Johnson in his amnesty petition, "I frankly own that events have seriously shaken the foundations of my opinions, and to much extent affected my views," but he declined to elaborate further, fearing that his present posture as a penitent prisoner might call the veracity of his statement into question. David L. Yulee to Andrew Johnson, June 24, 1865, in U.S. War Department, *The War of the Rebellion: A Compilation of the Official Records of the Union and Confederate Armies*, 128 vols. (Washington, DC: Government Printing Office, 1880–1901), ser. 2, vol. 8: 670.

[82] Spooner intimated that he might have been more friendly toward a war waged to liberate Southern slaves, but insisted that Northerners had not fought the Civil War

Treason, which was published in various newspapers, Spooner insisted that no truly democratic government could compel an individual's loyalty through military conquest. "The late war," wrote Spooner, "has practically demonstrated that our government rests upon force." Such a settlement of the political differences between North and South could never be permanent, Spooner insisted, because "a contest – however bloody – can, in the nature of things, never be finally closed, so long as man refuses to be a slave."[83] In a Union held together by force, the possibility of another Southern revolution would always linger. Spooner was something of an iconoclast, but his fears about the impermanence of a settlement through trial by battle resonated throughout the North. It was imperative that ex-Confederates be persuaded rather than compelled to renew their attachment to the United States.

At the end of 1865, the *Advocate of Peace*, the organ of the Boston-based American Peace Society, reproved Northerners for endorsing the notion that "the right of secession was 'submitted to the arbitrament of war,' and was settled by the conquest and surrender of the secessionists." The paper argued that a violent contest could settle nothing, quoting Charles Sumner's 1854 declaration about the inability of the Kansas-Nebraska Act to put the issue of slavery's expansion to rest: "Nothing is settled which is not right."[84] Because Confederates had genuinely believed in the constitutionality of secession throughout the Civil War, "they yet believe they were in the right, though defeated in the struggle for it." Former Confederates could not be swayed from their convictions merely because they had suffered defeat, and the paper predicted that the old question would someday come back to haunt the nation. The paper hoped that when secession's legality arose again, it would not be resolved "by the bloodstained sword, but by the peaceful arbitrament of judicial or political

---

with this purpose in mind. Because no higher purpose had animated the Northern war effort, he said, there was no justification for forcing the recalcitrant South to remain in the Union.

[83] Lysander Spooner, *No Treason, No. 1* (Boston: published by the author, 1867), 5, 9, available at www.lysanderspooner.org/notreason.htm (accessed November 1, 2016). See also Helen Knowles, "Seeing the Light: Lysander Spooner's Increasingly Popular Constitutionalism," *Law and History Review* 31 (August 2013): 531.

[84] Charles Sumner, "Speech of the Honorable Charles Sumner," February 21, 1854, in Stephen Douglas et al., *The Nebraska Question: Comprising Speeches in the United States Senate* (New York: Redfield, 1854), 117.

action." The *Philadelphia Christian Recorder*, published by the African Methodist Episcopal Church, expressed complete agreement with the Boston pacifists. Even after the conclusion of the war, the paper's editors maintained, the nation required an ordinary judicial trial to effect a true settlement of secession's legal status. Otherwise, they argued, "the question is left at issue, and may be again discussed amid the thunder of artillery and the flash of musketry on the bloody field of fratricidal war."[85]

Others held that only reasoned argument and historical inquiry into America's founding could definitively establish the permanence of the Union. Legal scholar John Codman Hurd's extensive treatise on federal-state relations in the United States, *The Theory of Our National Existence*, published in 1881, also revealed a deep discomfort with the use of violence to settle the question of secession's constitutionality. Hurd adopted a pose of studied neutrality from which he sought to discover the true locus of sovereignty through unbiased historical inquiry into the nature of the Union, divorced from contemporary political wranglings. The book began with an emphatic declaration that one could not simply rely on the results of the Civil War to demonstrate the fallacy of the pro-secession viewpoint and the compact theory of the Union.[86]

Hurd insisted that "military success and defeat cannot, in themselves, however decisive strategically, indicate any political supremacy

---

[85] J. P. B., "Settlement by War," *Advocate of Peace* (November/December 1865): 366; *Christian Recorder* (Philadelphia), May 18, 1867.

[86] John Codman Hurd, *The Theory of Our National Existence* (Boston: Little, Brown, 1881). Hurd's book drew on ideas he first articulated in a Reconstruction-era law review article. See John Codman Hurd, "Theories of Reconstruction," *American Law Review* 1 (1867): 238. Although Hurd's "Theories of Reconstruction" and his 1890 book *The Union-State* demonstrated a strongly Republican point of view on the Civil War, *The Theory of Our National Existence* did not take any position on the legitimacy of secession. Hurd in fact acknowledged that many Americans (before 1861), including a number of the founders, quite rationally believed the states to be the ultimate sovereign and the Union merely their creature. See Hurd, *The Theory of Our National Existence*, 101–3, 285–86. Reviewers of Hurd's book complained about his refusal to take a definitive stand. See "Constitutions of the New World and Old," *Law Magazine and Review Quarterly* 7 (1881–82): 178; "Review of *The Theory of Our National Existence*, by John Codman Hurd," *American Law Review* 16 (1882): 389. Hurd also received a letter from historian George Bancroft about his book's argument, which Bancroft confessed he had not "been able to get the key to." George Bancroft to John Codman Hurd, October 7, 1881, folder 150, Box 3, Ellis Gray Loring Papers, Schlesinger Library, Harvard University, Cambridge, MA.

for the affirmance or denial of which the victor and the vanquished
may respectively have taken up arms." To think about Union triumph
as decisive of any legal question was tantamount to acknowledging
that "the courts [would] have held," in the event of Confederate victory, "against the old 'overwhelming argument' that the doctrine of a
State's right of peaceable secession had been established, for the states
remaining in the Union." The war might have been akin to an international contest, but for Hurd, that removed it from the legal realm.
Attacking Isaac Redfield, Hurd denied that any parallel could exist
between "a war, the nature of which excludes the idea of a legal determination, and an action at law between two private parties." In a private action, a third party – a court – would decide the ruling and
the extent of victory, whereas the proponents of trial by battle "arro-
gated to [themselves] individually the right to settle, after the supposed
trial of the action, the issues which were to be judged." This type of
"settlement" was fleeting at best, Hurd argued. Without convincing
former Confederates of the merits of the perpetual Union, Northerners
could expect that unrepentant Southerners would eventually attempt
another secession.[87]

James Q. Whitman argues that the trial by battle between two
nations had been seen throughout human history as a legitimate means
of dispute resolution. A pitched battle was, ironically, a way to limit violence by channeling it into one specific venue over which the monarch
had control, rather than allowing it to spill over into society in other
ways. But the 1860s and 1870s marked a sea change in the legal history
of warfare. Wars became more savage. Single battles no longer settled
disputes definitively; war spilled off the battlefield and onto the home
front as lone battles became wars of attrition and exhaustion. Whitman
attributes this change to the greater stakes of war in the modern world.
Once contests erupted between republics with competing visions of
popular democratic ideals, wars became messier. The outcomes of wars
now mattered more to ordinary people, and the casualties of war grew
apace. Men were willing to risk more because the verdict of war carried
the judgment of God. In the millenialist conception of the 1860s, the
verdict of war represented the verdict of history.[88]

---

[87] Hurd, *The Theory of Our National Existence*, 1, 89, 449, 480.
[88] Whitman, *The Verdict of Battle*, chapter 6.

As trial by battle grew bloodier and war lost some of its legitimacy as a method of settling disputes, the romance of trial by battle also waned. Some worried that its price was too high. Drew Faust has argued that Americans struggled to come to terms with the vast scale of death the Civil War engendered.[89] Trial by battle in the nineteenth century was not the stylized chivalric encounter that eager combatants imagined in 1861. It was now uncontainable, disrupting the home front and thirstily consuming the lives of many hundreds of thousands of young men over the course of many battles. To paraphrase Robert E. Lee, war was so terrible that it prevented an introspective man from becoming too fond of it.[90]

Nineteenth-century Americans recognized that the war had effected monumental constitutional change through extraordinary and extra-constitutional means. Putting one's life on the line for a particular view of the Constitution was the most direct form of democracy that could exist. As Bruce Ackerman and Larry Kramer have recognized, profound constitutional change happens outside the formalized processes the law has designated, radiating up from the American people directly. But the laudatory spirit with which Ackerman and Kramer detail popular constitutionalism would have been alien to most nineteenth-century Americans. Looking at history, and having suffered in the Civil War, Oliver Wendell Holmes concluded gloomily that the determination of legal and moral truths in "every society rests on the death of men."[91] The vast scale of human sacrifice in the war gave Union victory a lawmaking power that "mere" paper decrees did not possess, but remaking the Constitution on the battlefield was frightening – and deadly – for the Civil War's combatants. For them, trial by battle was law, but it was also antithetical to law. It involved the people in direct democracy in the most tangible of ways, but it also bypassed the legal institutions that made ordered liberty possible in a democratic system.

Contrary to what many historians and constitutional scholars have assumed, accepting the fact that the Union had achieved victory on the

---

[89] Faust, *This Republic of Suffering.*
[90] John Esten Cooke, *A Life of General Robert E. Lee* (New York: D. Appleton, 1876), 184. See also Gary W. Gallagher, *Lee and His Army in Confederate History* (Chapel Hill: University of North Carolina Press, 2001), 80 n. 40.
[91] Oliver Wendell Holmes to Frederick Pollack, February 1, 1920, in Holmes and Pollack, *Holmes and Pollack*, 2: 36.

battlefield rather than in the courtroom was neither easy nor automatic for many Americans. In the post–Civil War era, Americans struggled to come to grips with the notion that a constitutional issue that had engendered such vigorous debate prior to 1861 could be definitively resolved in the crucible of war. To bolster the claim that war had long had such adjudicatory power, they likened their internecine conflict to the medieval practice of trial by battle. And as the wager of battle had relied on otherworldly intervention in a physical combat between two litigants, the Civil War had similarly pitted two mighty armies against one another in a military contest as a method of adjudicating a particularly thorny legal issue.

The widespread use of the metaphor of trial by battle – employed by people who held divergent opinions on the desirability of Union victory and the validity of the right of secession – highlights a deep uneasiness among nineteenth-century Americans about the relationship between the rule of law and the chaos of war. Although Civil War–era Americans prided themselves on their commitment to reason, they recognized that their civil war deviated monstrously from that ideal. The experience of armed conflict on such a massive scale forced Americans to confront the harsh reality that they had resorted to violence to settle the most contentious issue of their time.

The participants in Jefferson Davis's case operated against an understanding that the Civil War had functioned as a trial by battle. Not only had it provided an answer to – although perhaps not the last word on – the secession question, it had also destabilized the rule of law in the United States. The war had demonstrated that Americans' commitment to the legal system was troublingly thin, particularly in difficult circumstances. Testing secession in court was one way to neutralize this development. James Speed, the U.S. attorney general, considered it his job as the chief law officer of the United States to restore the rule of law in the aftermath of the Civil War. Throughout his term as attorney general, Speed sought to counteract the disruptive tendencies of the war by insisting that the government conduct the Davis prosecution in strict compliance with the letter of the law.

5

The Return of the Rule of Law

From the very beginning, Attorney General James Speed approached the Davis case with extreme caution. Speed's was the most important voice in the cabinet, with its members deadlocked and the president unable to decide on a definite course of action. His caution superseded calls by Secretary of State William Seward and, for a time, Secretary of War Edwin Stanton to try Davis in a way that would ensure his conviction and thereby reinforce the results of the war. Speed resisted that impulse, convinced that his primary duty was to return the legal system to its normal operation and to oppose what he saw as the country's dangerous postbellum slide toward lawlessness. His first priority was to conduct the case with due regard for the prisoner's rights, rather than to convict Davis at all costs.

A case as delicate as Davis's had to be handled with punctiliousness, Speed believed, so that the judicial determination of Davis's fate – and the larger issues for which it stood – could not be called into question. For this reason, Speed opposed charging Davis with war crimes and trying the former Confederate president before a military commission. For Speed, those options were too irregular to deploy in such volatile times. Prominent Boston attorney Horatio Woodman agreed with Speed. He told Edwin Stanton that although he believed that the Lincoln conspirators should be tried before a military commission, Jefferson Davis should not meet the same fate. To try Davis in any other way but "for *treason*, and by a *Jury*" would flout the rules of the legal system. Woodman maintained that Davis's trial was "vastly

more important, in all historical aspects, than any other trial of modern times, and [it would be] better for the nation and for history that
he be acquitted than that he be tried otherwise than by a jury."[1]

Former attorney general Edward Bates, who had served
under President Lincoln, worried that the chaotic atmosphere of
Reconstruction might lead Speed to sacrifice adherence to the law
for political expediency. Bates was disappointed that Speed had
given an "opinion that the persons charged with the murder of
the President can rightfully be tried in a military court." Bates felt
Speed had compromised himself and said he was "pained to be led
to believe that my successor, Atty Genl. Speed, has been wheedled
out of an opinion, to the effect that such a trial is lawful." It was the
attorney general's duty to lead the country's legal system back to its
normal operation, and Bates worried that Speed's endorsement of a
military trial for Lincoln's assassins pointed in the wrong direction.
It would give people the impression that force would substitute for
the rule of law in postwar America. Such a trial "denies the great,
fundamental principle, that ours is a government of Law, and that
the law is strong enough, to rule the people wisely and well: and if
the offenders be done to death by that tribunal, however truly guilty,
they will pass for martyrs with half the world." Bates also worried
that "great efforts are making to force the trial of Jeff Davis, in the
same illegal manner."[2]

Speed was closer to his predecessor Bates on these issues than Bates
would have predicted. Perhaps the attorney general's office attracted
men who prized the conservatism of the rule of law, or perhaps the
office molded its occupant. Although he had sanctioned a military proceeding for the Lincoln assassins, Speed wanted to ensure that Davis
would receive a fair trial that would not be regarded as a mere rubber
stamp. He acted with a great deal of caution in prosecuting Davis.
As a staunch Kentucky Unionist, Speed found Davis's actions to be
reprehensible and he harbored no doubt that Davis had committed
treason. In other countries, he argued, revolting against the government might be legitimate because their legal systems did not permit
any method of lawful constitutional change. But in the United States,

[1] Horatio Woodman to Edwin Stanton, May 22, 1865, Reel 10, Edwin M. Stanton
   Papers, LC [microfilm edition].
[2] Edward Bates, *The Diary of Edward Bates, 1859–1866*, ed. Howard K. Beale
   (Washington, DC: Government Printing Office, 1933), 483–84, 532.

rebellion was unjustifiable because the framers had "recognize[d] this right of revolution and ha[d] endeavored to make it peaceful" through the process of constitutional amendment. Thus, in Speed's opinion, "the man ... who seeks to overthrow this government by force, without having appealed to the peaceful mode of revolution provided, is certainly more guilty than traitors in any other part of the world. ... It seems to me, the fact that a peaceful mode of revolution was accessible to Davis adds very greatly to his guilt."[3]

But Speed did not let his conviction that Davis was guilty overwhelm all else. On the contrary, he counseled caution with regard to Davis's case. "Our war is over," he told Francis Lieber, "but the questions growing out of it have to be settled." In fact, he "dreaded the settlement of questions resulting from the war more than ... the war itself."[4] If not handled carefully and with due regard for the normalized operation of the law, they could disrupt the country permanently. Speed wanted to ensure that Davis's trial would be conducted with procedural regularity and fairness. He therefore opted not to move forward with the trial until the political situation in the nation, and particularly in the Southern states, had stabilized. "It seems to me," Speed reflected, "that a trial for high treason should not be presided over by bayonets; that it should be had in & by a community in which the laws are peacefully executed.... Some time must elapse before such a state of things can come."[5] Even more important than the return of legal stability was the appearance of even-handedness. Speed clearly believed that the American public, and indeed, the wider world, would perceive Davis's prosecution as unfair if it took place before a military commission.

Speed recognized that this conservative posture might entail sacrifice. If regularly constituted civil juries within former Confederate territory (and even outside of it) would not convict treason defendants, Speed would not rig the trials in the government's favor. He was willing to let traitors walk free, although he was unwilling to risk acquittals in treason cases. He thus instructed various U.S. attorneys struggling with such cases to drop prosecutions if the suits seemed

[3] James Speed to Charles Sumner, June 17, 1865, James Speed Papers, SHC; copy also in Reel 33, Charles Sumner Papers, HU. See also House Committee on the Judiciary, *Assassination of Lincoln*, 39th Cong., 1st sess., July 1866, H. Rep. 104, 1.

[4] Joshua Speed to James Speed, September 15, 1865, in James Speed, *James Speed: A Personality* (Louisville: John P. Morton, 1914), 67.

[5] James Speed to Francis Lieber, May 26, 1866, and June 27, 1865, Box 62, Lieber Papers, HEHL.

politically infeasible. In 1866 he authorized B. H. Bristow, U.S. attorney for Louisville, "to dismiss any indictment pending in your court against any person for a political offence, if, in your judgment, from the facts, & the present condition of the country, it is right and proper to do so." Speed similarly allowed J. M. Root, U.S. attorney from Cleveland, to abandon a case against a treason defendant: dropping the case would be permissible, he told Root, "if you are of the opinion, as your letter would seem to indicate, that it is inexpedient or impolitic to continue the prosecution, under all the circumstances of the case."[6] Speed certainly did not want to lose such cases, but he was willing to let defendants go unprosecuted rather than sully the legal process by altering the rules to make such defendants easier to convict. As he told Judge Underwood, who presided over the Davis case, "It is the earnest wish of the President, as of all loyal men, that the laws should be peacefully executed and offenders brought to justice. This cannot be done, however, with the dignity and calmness that becomes judicial proceedings, whilst confusion reigns and until by the harsh hand of war, the rebellious spirit now rampant shall be subdued and quieted."[7]

Speed's caution served Jefferson Davis's defense team well. O'Conor was jockeying for time. A quick, cursory trial, like those of the Lincoln assassins and the Andersonville defendants, carried out in a spirit of palpable public rage, was to be avoided at all costs. If he could delay the prosecution long enough, O'Conor judged that public anger would dissipate to the point where it would become impossible for the government to hang Davis. In his opinion, the worst thing Davis's attorneys could do would be to spur the prosecutors into action. O'Conor feigned "respectful and obedient acquiescence in the goodwill and pleasure of the powers that be so long as that course has any tendency to mitigate suffering and save life." Indeed, he would pursue an antagonistic line of action only if "a military commission is formed for the purpose of" implicating Davis in Lincoln's assassination.[8] As Horace Greeley told Varina Davis, "Delay is not unfavorable to Mr.

---

[6] James Speed to B. H. Bristow, May 31, 1866, and James Speed to J. M. Root, May 9, 1866, Letters Sent, 1865–1870, Attorney General's Records, Record Group 60, NA-CP.

[7] James Speed to John Underwood, April 24, 1865, Letterbook D, 272, Microfilm M 699, Attorney General's Records, Record Group 60, NA-CP.

[8] Charles O'Conor to George Shea, August 12, 1865, Box 24, Jefferson Davis Papers, MC.

Davis – ... passions are cooling, new interests arising, and ... the jury excited by President Lincolns' death must be obliged before Mr. Davis can safely go to trial."[9] To augment Speed's cautious approach, O'Conor sought to delay the trial through a process of negotiation with the Johnson administration, orchestrating and then readily accepting postponements on the part of the prosecution.

By late 1865, it was clear that the government's slow pace in conducting the Davis prosecution was becoming politically risky for Andrew Johnson. The president and the attorney general had to weigh the political fallout from delay against the risks of premature prosecution – namely, Davis's possible acquittal (signaling secession's legal victory) and the erosion of the rule of law in the United States. Indiana governor Oliver Morton sought to press Johnson to try Davis, telling the president that his duty was only to prosecute; he would avoid public censure merely by moving forward. Johnson should prosecute regardless of the potential for Davis's vindication, and let the court figure out the rest. Morton pointed out that the public was calling for Davis's punishment, "and if you promptly put Davis on his trial for treason your popular triumph will be complete. If he is acquitted let the Court and Jury take the responsibility." Morton advised: "If you stand firm by the doctrine that rebellion is treason, that treason is a crime, that a state cannot secede or be carried out of the Union by rebels in arms ... I tell you that even the Supreme Court cannot prevail against you with the Nation."[10]

Johnson and his advisers did not agree. Fearing a public vindication rather than a condemnation of secession in the federal circuit court, Speed and the rest of the administration found the case too risky to try – and too politically volatile to drop. Speed's lack of zeal in the Davis case earned him the frustration of many Unionists, including Francis Lieber. In Lieber's estimation, the Civil War presented the ultimate opportunity to cement the United States as a unified nation rather than simply a loose aggregation of distinct states, the former of which Lieber believed to be the ultimate form of political organization. Lieber wrote and spoke unceasingly on this topic following the

---

[9] Horace Greeley to Varina Davis, June 27, 1865, Box 24, Jefferson Davis Papers, MC.

[10] Oliver Morton to Andrew Johnson, November 6, 1865, in Andrew Johnson, *The Papers of Andrew Johnson*, ed. Paul Bergeron, 16 vols. (Knoxville: University of Tennessee Press, 1967–69), 9: 351–52.

war, and in his estimation, punishing Davis for treason would play a crucial part in establishing the permanency of the Union.

Lieber lamented that victorious Northerners were far too inclined toward leniency, complaining to family friend Richard Henry Dana that "the North somehow lacks true feeling of resentment, even just and righteous resentment. This goes through our whole history. I do not indeed deprecate the noble mindedness of the North but I do regret its lack of manly resentment."[11] Lieber blamed Attorney General Speed for the delays in the Davis trial. In 1866, he told his friend and fellow international law theorist Henry Halleck that Speed's excess of caution and insistence on a fully restored legal process in 1865 had caused too much time to elapse in trying Davis.[12] This delay Lieber regarded as fatal. "The trial of Jeff. Davis will be a terrible thing," he told Halleck. "Volumes, a library of the most infernal treason will be belched forth – Davis will not be found guilty and we shall stand there as completely beaten. The time was lost, and can never be recovered."[13]

Speed certainly did pursue a cautious course with regard to Davis's prosecution and hoped that a solution to the government's predicament would present itself in the course of time. Speed described his doubt and uncertainty to Charles Sumner, telling him that he hoped Davis would apply for a pardon and thus spare the government the trouble of trying him. Unfortunately, Davis's pardon depended very much on the prisoner's own temperament. The president could not offer to pardon Davis "without knowing whether it would be accepted or scornfully rejected." Speed also alluded to the doubtfulness of conviction, noting that "for his conviction, the Government is not responsible – the government is only responsible that he be tried." In light of all the uncertainty, Speed insisted that "the time has not come to determine what course the Government is to pursue" with respect

---

[11] Francis Lieber to Richard Henry Dana, December 29, 1867, Box 17, Dana Family Papers, MHS.

[12] Halleck served as general in chief of the Union army during the war, and he had written a major treatise on international law in 1861. He and Lieber became friends in the course of Lieber's preparation of his code of war, which the U.S. army adopted in 1863. See Frank Friedel, *Francis Lieber: Nineteenth-Century Liberal* (Baton Rouge: Louisiana State University Press, 1947), 324, 33; John Fabian Witt, *Lincoln's Code: The Laws of War in American History* (New York: Free Press, 2012).

[13] Francis Lieber to Henry Halleck, May 23, 19, 1866, Box 28, Francis Lieber Papers, HEHL.

to Davis.[14] After he resigned his office in 1866, he admitted, insight-fully, that "I was, on those grounds [of caution], the principal cause of the non-trial of Jefferson Davis."[15]

Careful calculation was not the sole reason for the slow prog-ress, however. William Evarts and John Clifford, hired to direct the Davis prosecution in August 1865, did not approach the case with any urgency. They convened at the Astor House hotel in New York on September 1, 1865, but after that initial meeting, the case began to fall by the wayside. The two attorneys half-heartedly exchanged a number of letters, but both were busy with other professional commit-ments and could not find an acceptable time to discuss the case further. Evarts and Clifford let time slip by without doing any preliminary preparations for trial.

Evarts reported to Clifford that it seemed as though the adminis-tration had settled into complacency, and he could not wrangle any definite directions out of the president or the attorney general. In his opinion, Davis would probably eventually be pardoned. As he told Clifford in November, "I was in Washington last week and spoke with the Atty Genl, on the subject of the trial of Davis. He said that the President was less restive under the delays than he had been, and I inferred that nothing would be done until peace was proclaimed. In the meantime all things tend towards pardon and oblivion of all misdeeds and it is difficult for me to feel as if we should ever actually figure in [a trial]."[16]

In the face of such indifference, Evarts's own attention waned. Although he and Clifford attempted to set up a meeting to discuss the case, either in New York or at Clifford's office in New Bedford, more than six months went by before the two of them could find a mutu-ally agreeable time to confer. In the meantime, Evarts was very busy in his law practice. As he explained to Clifford about one missed Davis

[14] James Speed to Charles Sumner, June 17, 1865, James Speed Papers, SHC; copy also in Reel 33, Charles Sumner Papers, HU.

[15] *Impeachment Investigation: Testimony Taken before the Judiciary Committee of the House of Representatives in the Investigation of the Charges against Andrew Johnson* (Washington, DC: Government Printing Office, 1867), 799 (testimony of James Speed).

[16] Robert C. Winthrop, *Memoir of the Hon. John H. Clifford* (Boston: John Wilson and Son, 1877); William Evarts to John Clifford, November 11, December 29, 1865, Papers August–December 1865, John Clifford Papers, MHS.

colloquy, "I am at present shut up in the trial of the 'Meteor,' but what time it may take I cannot say."[17] He also resisted the idea of taking time away from his more lucrative cases to work on a case that seemed to be going nowhere and that the government had all but indicated it had no intention of trying. After returning to New York from a business trip, Evarts reported that Speed had not been in touch with him and he had accordingly "not felt inclined to devote time to our matter unless I should find that something depended on it."[18]

In fact, rather than discussing their possible plan of action with regard to the Davis case, Evarts and Clifford proved more interested in far more mundane matters. On several occasions, Evarts boasted of the superior performance of his cows and horses at the county fair in Windsor, Vermont, where Evarts kept a country house. The distinguished lawyer even enclosed a clipping from the local newspaper with one letter, proudly marking where the paper had described his stock as "very superior animals."[19] Evarts recalled more than twenty-five years later that he had been retained in the Davis case only in 1867, rather than in 1865, after a series of "delay[s] to which I need not avert." Certainly the passage of time had dulled Evarts's memory, but his lack of true involvement in the case until two years after his retainer (and his possible embarrassment about his inattention to it) may have contributed to his faulty recollection.[20]

---

[17] William Evarts to John Clifford, April 7, 1866, Papers January–May 1866, John Clifford Papers, MHS. The case was The Meteor, 17 F. Cas. 178 (S.D.N.Y. 1866) (No. 9,498), reversed by United States v. The Meteor, 26 F. Cas. 1241 (C.C.S.D.N.Y. 1868) (No. 15,760), about a vessel several New York businessmen had attempted to sell to Chile following the Civil War. Chile was at war with Spain, and the Spanish minister had protested that the sale violated a neutrality treaty between Spain and the United States. Evarts, along with his law partner Joseph Choate, represented the ship's sellers. Evarts's biographer calls the case "by far the most significant of Evarts' post-war litigations." See Chester L. Barrows, *William M. Evarts: Lawyer, Diplomat, Statesman* (Chapel Hill: University of North Carolina Press, 1941), 134–35; *New York Times*, March 31, 1866.

[18] William Evarts to John Clifford, April 12, 1866, Papers January–May 1866, John Clifford Papers, MHS.

[19] William Evarts to John H. Clifford, November 11, 1865 (including newspaper clipping), and September 18, 1865, Papers August–December 1865, John Clifford Papers, MHS.

[20] William Evarts to Theodore Dwight, August 26, 1890, Evarts Letterbook, Box 8, Evarts Family Papers, Yale.

Delays in the case displeased congressional Republicans. Congress convened for the first time since the end of the war in December of 1865, and one of its first orders of business was addressing the lack of progress in Davis's case. In fact, Johnson's failure to act boldly in the Davis case became a partisan issue as well as a major source of tension between the president and Congress over the next several years.[21] On December 14, 1865, Representative James Henderson of Oregon introduced a resolution calling for treason against the United States to be punished, which passed the House unanimously.[22] In the Senate a week later, Senator Jacob Howard sought to spur the administration into action. Howard introduced a resolution pointing out that "several months have elapsed since Jefferson Davis ... was captured and confined for acts notoriously done by him. He requested that the president "inform the Senate upon what charges or for what reasons said Jefferson Davis is still held in confinement, and why he has not been put upon his trial."[23]

As a body, Congress rejected Speed's meticulous efforts to adhere to the rule of law in trying Davis. Although individual congressmen shared Speed's concerns about America's potential to slide into despotism in the aftermath of a violent war, Congress's primary goal was to facilitate Davis's trial by any means necessary and to engineer a conviction. No wonder Speed was so worried. Rather than scrupulously maintaining normal legal proceedings in the aftermath of the national crisis of the Civil War, many congressmen were willing to change the law in order to get a desirable verdict.

Congress wanted to ensure that the secession question could go before the Supreme Court instead of getting its final hearing before a Virginia jury. As the *New York Herald* pointed out, Davis's case would "decide, once and for all, that the Union is not a league of states, each possessing the sovereign right of secession, but that it is a sovereign nationality." This question was of monumental importance, which made the disposition of Davis's personal fate pale in comparison. The paper urged Congress to increase the original

---

[21] This became an issue in Johnson's impeachment investigation. See Chapter 12 for more.

[22] *Congressional Globe*, 39th Cong., 1st sess., December 14, 1865, 50.

[23] *Congressional Globe*, 39th Cong., 1st sess., December 21, 1865, 108.

jurisdiction of the Supreme Court, so that the case could be tried there. Such a plan was clearly infeasible, however, without a constitutional amendment to overturn *Marbury v. Madison*, which Congress never considered.[24] What seemed more likely was creating appellate jurisdiction for the Court to hear the case.

Facilitating an appeal was also tricky. If Davis were acquitted by the jury, the Constitution itself barred an appeal.[25] The Supreme Court could not, in general, even affirm a criminal conviction or hear an appeal from a nonfinal ruling on a question of law in a criminal case. At this time, no statute permitted the appeal of criminal cases to the U.S. Supreme Court.[26] Chief Justice Roger Taney had affirmed this principle as recently as 1862, when the Supreme Court had rejected an appeal by a criminal defendant. Taney noted that "in criminal cases, the proceedings and judgment of the Circuit Court cannot be revised & controlled here, in any form of proceeding, either by writ of error or prohibition, and consequently, we have no authority to examine them by a certiorari."[27] In the 1860s, the only mechanism for appellate review was a disagreement between the two circuit court judges on a point of law, which would then be certified to the Supreme Court for resolution.[28] This was unlikely but not impossible, given that Chief Justice Chase was known for his states' rights viewpoints – as O'Conor had pointed out to the prosecution. The federal circuit courts at this time consisted of two judges – the district judge and a member of the Supreme Court assigned to each circuit. But Chase was refusing to preside in Virginia altogether (as will be discussed in more detail in Chapter 9), which left the case in the hands of District Judge John C. Underwood. In the absence of the

---

[24] The *Herald's* plan would have been unconstitutional, as Congress cannot increase the original jurisdiction of the Supreme Court. See Marbury v. Madison, 5 U.S. 137 (1803). However, Charles Fairman notes that in deciding to hear the habeas corpus petition of Dr. Samuel Mudd in 1868, who was tried for his involvement in Lincoln's assassination (he was the doctor who set John Wilkes Booth's leg, broken in his fall from the balcony at Ford's Theatre) and imprisoned in the Dry Tortugas in Florida, the Court at least contemplated the possibility of overruling *Marbury* on this point. See Charles Fairman, *Reconstruction and Reunion*, 2 vols. (New York: Macmillan, 1971), 1: 488–92, for a discussion of Mudd's case.

[25] U.S. Const. amend. V.

[26] Judiciary Act of 1789, 1 Stat. 73 (1789), §§ 11, 22.

[27] Ex parte Gordon, 66 U.S. 503, 504–05 (1861).

[28] Judiciary Act of 1802, 2 Stat. 156 (1802), § 6. This was permissible even in a criminal case.

chief justice, O'Conor complained, "Mr. Davis will be tried ... before Underwood alone – th[us] rendering any review impossible."[29]

To ensure that Davis's case could reach the Supreme Court, Senator James Doolittle proposed a bill in late 1865 that would have established a review process in federal criminal cases. The bill allowed for a writ of error to the Supreme Court from a district or circuit court for any criminal offense punishable by death "within sixty days after the entry of the final judgment in such case in the courts below."[30] More controversially, Doolittle's bill also sought to manipulate the qualifications of jurors to ensure that the jury selected in Davis's case could be counted on to convict him.

This provision was extraordinary, and it highlighted Doolittle's philosophical distance from Attorney General Speed. Doolittle was willing to stretch the neutral principles of American law to convict Davis, which was precisely the impulse Speed hoped to check. The bill would have permitted federal judges to impanel jurors who declared that they had already formed an opinion as to the guilt of the accused prior to hearing the case. Under the proposed bill, judges could seat such jurors so long as they were otherwise qualified and genuinely believed that they

---

[29] Charles O'Conor to Thomas F. Bayard, October 19, 1867, in *Tyler's Quarterly Magazine* 29 (October 1947): 182. See also Fairman, *Reconstruction and Reunion*, 1: 86, 176.

[30] *Congressional Globe*, 39th Cong., 1st sess., January 22, 1866, 338. The bill did not pass in 1866, and when reintroduced in 1868, it did not contain this jurisdictional provision. The jurisdictional provision of the bill was not discussed in Congress and probably did not pass for the same reason the juror qualification provision ultimately did not: it did not seem valid to secure Davis's conviction through a manipulation of the legal process already in place. *Congressional Globe*, 40th Cong., 2d sess., April 8, 1868, 2275–77. Another problem loomed in the background of the proposed legislation to permit a right of appeal in Davis's case. It seems unlikely that O'Conor would have wanted to appeal a guilty verdict to the Supreme Court on the theory that the Court would reverse Davis's conviction on account of the constitutionality of secession. An appeal would likely only accomplish an affirmation of the perpetuity of the Union. He probably would have sought a pardon instead. Doolittle's proposed bill probably would have permitted only the defendant, not the prosecution, a right to appeal in the event of a disposition on the law in the Davis case, although further legislation could have remedied that problem. This is what occurred when federal criminal appeals were permitted in 1889. Judiciary Act of 1889, 25 Stat. 655 (1889), § 6; Judiciary Act of 1891, 26 Stat. 826 (1891), § 5. United States v. Sanges, 144 U.S. 310 (1892). See also Lester B. Orfield, "Federal Criminal Appeals," *Yale Law Journal* 45 (1936): 1223; Jack Friedenthal, "Government Appeals in Federal Criminal Cases," *Stanford Law Review* 12 (1959): 71.

could "impartially try the accused upon the crime charged in the indictment," despite their previous declarations.[31] As Doolittle explained,
the bill "provides for obtaining jurors in those cases of great publicity
where it is now almost impossible under the rulings of the courts to
obtain a jury." Because courts traditionally tried to prevent jurors who
already knew something about the case in question from being impaneled, Doolittle asserted, "the most intelligent persons are often excluded
from sitting on a jury." Doolittle later confirmed that he had proposed
the measure to facilitate Davis's trial, telling Andrew Johnson that "if
Congress will not pass such a law the responsibility of his trial will rest
with Congress."[32]

Doolittle's bill was controversial because of its willingness to sacrifice long-standing legal principles in the service of an immediate –
if supremely important – goal. It also created some strange alliances.
Charles Sumner, one of the most radical of the Radical Republicans
in Congress, emerged as one of the most doctrinaire defenders of the
regularized legal process. He objected to Doolittle's bill because it
sought to construct an entirely new set of legal procedures specifically
to convict Davis. As a committed nationalist and Radical Republican,
Sumner decried secessionist theory, arguing that "State Rights, in all the
denationalizing pretensions, must be trampled out forever, to the end
that we may be in reality as in name, a Nation."[33] He recognized that
Doolittle's bill was designed "to meet an actual case of unprecedented
historical importance; it is to pave the way for the trial of that grandest
criminal in the history of the world who is now in the custody of this
Government." But he staunchly maintained that the government could
not rewrite the law in order to convict Davis. Davis's case had to "be
approached carefully, most discreetly, and … with absolute reference to
the existing law of the land," according to Sumner. Kentucky Senator
Garrett Davis, a conservative, found himself somewhat bewildered to
be in agreement with Sumner on this point. "I feel no sympathy with
Jefferson Davis," Garrett Davis said, but "a proposition to change
the law in relation to the qualification of jurors in criminal cases is a
very grave one, and I think that the Senator from Massachusetts has

---

[31] *Congressional Globe*, 39th Cong., 1st sess., December 18, 1865, 67.
[32] James Doolittle to Andrew Johnson, September 23, 1865, in Johnson, *Papers of
     Andrew Johnson*, 9: 118.
[33] Charles Sumner, *Are We a Nation?* (New York: Young Men's Republican Union,
     1867), 3.

entered a very proper and just *caveat* against changing that law with a view to any individual case."[34]

Congress also sought to toll the statute of limitations on treason indefinitely to ensure that Davis could not avoid the death penalty. Under the Crimes Act of 1790, treason carried the certain penalty of death, but the act specified that prosecutions had to be brought within three years. In 1862, Congress had passed another treason act (the Second Confiscation Act) which permitted the imposition of a prison term and a fine instead of the death penalty, at the court's discretion. Somewhat puzzlingly, it also specified a lesser crime of "incit[ing] ... or engag[ing] ... in rebellion or insurrection" against the United States, which carried no threat of the death penalty.[35] The 1862 act did not supersede the earlier statute, as it permitted prosecutions for early (1861 or 1862) acts of treason under the 1790 act if a defendant had not previously been convicted of treason under the 1862 statute.[36] To many of Davis's foes in Congress, charging Davis under the 1790 act seemed like the better option, both because it took away the judge's discretion to impose a lesser penalty, and because a lower court had interpreted the 1862 act to prohibit the death penalty altogether for the crime of *domestic* treason.[37] Because Davis had levied

---

[34] *Congressional Globe*, 39th Cong., 1st sess., 338, January 22 and April 11, 1866, 1882–83.

[35] See Confiscation Act of 1862, 12 Stat. 589, §§ 1, 2 (1862). See also William Blair, "Friend or Foe: Treason and the Second Confiscation Act," in *Wars within a War: Controversy and Conflict over the American Civil War*, ed. Gary W. Gallagher and Joan Waugh (Chapel Hill: University of North Carolina Press, 2009), 27–50. The Confiscation Act was poorly drafted, the result of its sponsors' decision to stick several proposed bills together. See John Syrett, *The Civil War Confiscation Acts: Failing to Reconstruct the South* (New York: Fordham University Press, 2005), and James Oakes, *Freedom National: The Destruction of Slavery in the United States, 1861–1865* (New York: W. W. Norton, 2013). Oakes treats the act as fairly coherent, which it is not.

[36] See Confiscation Act of 1862, 12 Stat. 589, § 4 (1862). See Jonathan W. White, "The Trial of Jefferson Davis and the Americanization of Treason Law," in *Constitutionalism in the Approach and Aftermath of the Civil War*, ed. Paul D. Moreno and Johnathan O'Neill (New York: Fordham University Press, 2013). White argues that the specificity with which treason was pleaded in Davis's case reflected heightened standards of coherence and proof in the nineteenth century, but some of this was due to the statutory confusion caused by the poor drafting of the 1862 law.

[37] This was Justice Field in *U.S. v. Greathouse*, 26 F. Cas. 18 (C.C.N.D. Cal. 1868) (No. 15,254). Field was attempting to reconcile Sections 1 and 2 of the act. It was an improbable reading of the statute, but it worried Judge John Underwood and Congressman George Boutwell enough to correspond about it, fearing that it might

war against his own country rather than "aid[ing] and comfort[ing]" its foreign enemies, he might be guilty of a lesser form of treason and thus be exempt from the death penalty.

This meant that Congress had to work with the three-year statute of limitations of the 1790 act if the goal was execution. A tolling statute, passed in 1864, prevented the three-year limitations period from running while the Confederates remained beyond the practical reach of the law.[38] Nonetheless, it was unclear whether the government could charge Davis for his early treason, committed before the passage of the tolling statute, unless the prosecution could successfully contend that treason was a continuous offense that began in 1861 and ceased only with the end of the war in 1865. Three postwar years also did not seem like enough time. Considering the extent of Confederate sympathy that still lingered in the South, it was doubtful that treason prosecutions could be successfully conducted within three years of Appomattox.

In response to this problem, Representative William Lawrence of Ohio introduced a bill in Congress that would have completely eliminated a limitations period for federal crimes that carried the death penalty, including the crime of treason as defined by the Statute of 1790. Lawrence was quite explicit about his reasons for doing so: the law was aimed directly at Jefferson Davis. Allowing the criminal penalty for treason to expire in three years would ensure that "all the early treason of Jeff. Davis and those who cooperated with him will be entirely exempt from punishment." Lawrence's solution was potentially unconstitutional, as eliminating the limitations period might run afoul of the prohibition on ex post facto laws. In response to this criticism, Lawrence argued that the provision did not *create* a new crime but merely extended the state's time to prosecute the offense. This was analogous, according to Lawrence, to the distinction between a right and a remedy in contract law. Since Congress could constitutionally alter a contractual remedy without violating the Contracts Clause, it could also tinker with the statute of limitations in a criminal case. Lawrence was untroubled by the potential constitutional violation. In his opinion,

---

have purchase with Chief Justice Chase or with the Supreme Court as a whole. Boutwell's position was that Section 2 punished a lesser offense, which was not actually treason as the Constitution defined it. See George Boutwell to John Underwood, October 30, 1866, Box 1, John Underwood Papers, LC.

[38] Act of June 11, 1864, 13 Stat. 123 (1864).

the niceties of constitutional interpretation should not stand in the way of the supremely important task of ensuring that treason did not go unpunished. Lawrence accordingly declared himself "willing to go to the very verge of the Constitution for the purpose of reaching the early treasonable acts which inaugurated the late rebellion."[39]

Lawrence placed Davis's conviction above the restoration of the rule of law in the postwar United States, but other congressmen resisted this impulse. These included Radical Republican Thaddeus Stevens and one of the most conservative of Democrats, Andrew Jackson Rogers. Rogers and Stevens were united in opposition to Lawrence's proposed bill and his apparent willingness to flout constitutional standards to ensure the "right" outcome in Davis's case. Stevens characterized Lawrence's bill as one "evidently brought forward for the purpose of ascertaining how we can convict men whom we cannot convict under laws existing when the crimes were committed." He worried that the proposal would set a dangerous precedent, as it would alter the basic fabric of American law in order to make one man's conviction more certain. In his opinion, "any law which professes to change [the requirements of a criminal trial] looks to me so much like an attempt to commit judicial murder that I have always been afraid to attempt it."[40]

Some of Stevens's more moderate opponents accused him of hypocrisy and insincerity in opposing Lawrence's bill, but New Jersey congressman Andrew Rogers clearly thought he had found a kindred spirit.[41] It was "refreshing," according to Rogers, that he and

---

[39] *Congressional Globe*, 39th Cong., 2d sess., December 11 and 12, 1866, 68–69, 86–90. There was no settled law on this point. As it turns out, Lawrence's bill would go past the "verge" of the Constitution today. In *Stogner v. California*, the Supreme Court decided that reviving a criminal offense after the statute of limitations would have barred its prosecution was a violation of the ex post facto clause. The Court even cited debate over Lawrence's bill in support of this proposition. See Stogner v. California, 539 U.S. 607 (2003), 616–17.

[40] *Congressional Globe*, 39th Cong., 2d sess., December 11, 1866, 68–69.

[41] Stevens had previously argued that Davis should be tried under the laws of war by military commission, on the theory that the United States was still in a state of war, but that if his trial proceeded in a civil court, it had to be done in accordance with existing law. See Thaddeus Stevens, *The Selected Papers of Thaddeus Stevens*, ed. Beverly Wilson Palmer and Holly Byers Ochoa, 2 vols. (Pittsburgh: University of Pittsburgh Press, 1997), 2: 318, 15. Stevens's opponents speculated that he and other Radicals hoped to use Davis's case to establish the legality of secession in order to further the Radical Republican agenda for Reconstruction. Stevens intended to argue that secession had carried the Southern states out of the Union, but then the states

Stevens could stand together to ensure that Davis's trial would be conducted according to neutral principles of law. In Rogers's estimation, Lawrence's proposal was unconstitutional. Rogers argued that "there are serious objections to the passage of a law of this kind, not only upon grounds of policy but of legal import. If the passage of such a law be not strictly and technically within the meaning of the Constitution an ex post facto law, it is certainly a retroactive law." Furthermore, Lawrence's bill was anathema to the idea of an America grounded in the rule of law. "It will be a law against the genius of this Republic," Rogers stated – "against the spirit of our institutions."[42]

Lawrence's bill did not pass, but where President Johnson and Attorney General Speed hesitated, Congress sought to act. Hesitation, as Charles O'Conor had recognized, might prove fatal to the prosecution. Congress therefore tried to force the administration to carry out its duty to prosecute Davis for his crimes and vindicate the Union cause. In the meantime, Senator Howard's insistent call for information about the administration's lack of progress in the case could not go unanswered. The president ordered Speed to provide the administration's response to Howard's Christmastime inquiry. In January, Speed would have to provide his critics with an explanation for his inaction.

became "conquered territory" during the Civil War, which permitted the federal government to govern them directly and to remake laws and social institutions in the South. See Chapter 8 for a fuller explication of these ideas.

[42] *Congressional Globe*, 39th Cong., 2d sess., December 12, 1866, 86–90.

6

Speed Issues an Opinion

In response to Congress's inquiry about the administration's progress, Attorney General James Speed issued an official opinion on the Davis case in early January 1866. The opinion made it abundantly clear that Speed's priorities as attorney general did not align with those of the Republicans in Congress. Congress was bold; Speed was timid. Congress was inventive, willing to rewrite the rules and reconfigure the federal judiciary to secure a single, all-important conviction. Speed was pedantic and unwilling to depart from established precedent, despite the high stakes.

The opinion first addressed Davis's military custody. Military authority still superseded the civil in Virginia, Speed acknowledged, and the federal courts had not resumed their normal operation within Virginia and the other states of the former Confederacy. But Davis's military custody was to be only temporary, an anomalous result of the fact that the South was still under some degree of military control, and when the civil courts reopened, Speed expected that Davis would be transferred into civil custody.[1] Unlike the trials of Lincoln's assassins,

---

[1] See Gregory Downs, *After Appomattox* (Cambridge, MA: Harvard University Press, 2015), and John W. Burgess, *Reconstruction and the Constitution, 1866–1876* (New York: Scribner's, 1905), on military rule in Virginia as part of presidential Reconstruction.

Davis's prosecution was not to take place before a military tribunal.[2] Davis was to be charged with treason – a civil crime, specified in the U.S. Constitution, rather than a violation of the law of war – and according to Speed, "the civil courts alone have jurisdiction of that crime."

Having concluded that Davis could be tried only in the civil courts, Speed's opinion next tackled the question of where such a civil trial could be held. Speed insisted that the government would have to bring Davis to trial in Virginia – in "the state where [his] said crimes shall have been committed" – as required by Article III of the Constitution. He rejected the argument that Davis had been "constructively present" anywhere the Confederate army had marched during the war, doubting its constitutional validity. "Carried out to its logical consequences," Speed asserted, that doctrine "would make all who had been connected with the rebel armies liable to trial in any State and district into which any portion of those armies had made the slightest incursion."[3]

In reaching his conclusion, Speed drew on Chief Justice John Marshall's somewhat murky opinion in *Burr's Case*. As a circuit court judge in Virginia, Marshall had presided over Aaron Burr's treason trial in 1807, concerning Burr's involvement in an attempt to establish a breakaway western confederacy. The former vice president had been indicted for acts of treason that had occurred on Blennerhasset Island, then in the state of Virginia, even though it was clearly established that he had not been present in the state when the activities had occurred. In *Burr's Case*, Marshall had found the indictment against Burr to be faulty on two interrelated grounds, concerning the difficulties in proving an individual's participation in a conspiracy or general scheme to commit a group act of treason.

---

[2] Speed's opinion about the Lincoln assassins read in full: "I am of the opinion that the persons charged with the murder of the President of the United States can be rightfully tried in a military court." James Speed, "Murder of the President," *Opinions of the Attorney General* 11 (1865): 215. Francis Lieber's Code designated assassination as a violation of the law of war. See Francis Lieber, *Instructions for the Government of Armies of the United States in the Field: Originally Issued as General Orders No. 100, Adjutant General's Office, 1863* (Washington, DC: Government Printing Office, 1898), art. 148.

[3] James Speed, "Case of Jefferson Davis," *Opinions of the Attorney General* 11 (1866): 411–13.

Marshall first rejected the indictment for its failure to set forth any specific overt acts of treason that Burr had participated in while present in Virginia, of which the defendant would need to be informed in order to mount a proper defense. Neither could the doctrine of constructive presence legally place a treason defendant in a district where he had not actually been present, the opinion went on to state.[4] Marshall conceded the point that, under English criminal law as incorporated into American common law, all men were considered principals rather than accessories in treason. This made a defendant legally responsible for acts committed by co-conspirators – and presumably for acts committed in a different state – "but it is nowhere suggested that he is by construction to be considered present when in point of fact he was absent." Adherence to the letter of the Constitution and the basic guarantee of fairness to which a criminal defendant was entitled required that a person "may [only] be tried and convicted on his own acts in the state where those acts were committed, not on the acts of others in the state where those others acted."[5]

In supporting the theory that every perpetrator was a principal and not an accessory to the crime of treason, while rejecting the doctrine of constructive presence, Marshall's opinion was susceptible to two interpretations. When it came to charging individuals involved in a conspiracy to commit treason, in one interpretation a defendant could be tried only in the place where he had committed overt acts of treason (and these had to be violent acts). In the other, a defendant could be charged in a place where an act of treason had occurred, even if he had not been present, if the indictment charged him with specific overt acts he had actually undertaken (wherever they occurred), so long as those activities contributed to the general scheme of committing treason. These two divergent readings of Marshall's opinion were crucially important in the context of the Davis case. They determined whether Davis could be tried for his actions in ordering others to levy

---

[4] On the doctrine of constructive presence, see John Bouvier and Robert Kelham, *A Law Dictionary, Adapted to the Constitution and Laws of the United States of America, and of the Several States of the American Union* … (Philadelphia: G. W. Childs, 1862), 372.
[5] United States v. Burr, 25 F. Cas. 55, 171, 179 (C.C.D. Va. 1807) (No. 14,693). See also Peter Charles Hoffer, *The Treason Trials of Aaron Burr* (Lawrence: University Press of Kansas, 2008).

war against the United States at battles that were far removed from the Confederate capital. Davis's main instruments of war had been the pen and the telegraph. In endorsing the first reading of Marshall's *Burr* opinion, Attorney General Speed embraced the theory that Davis could only be liable where he wielded his pen – rather than everywhere Confederate soldiers had wielded the sword. As he had done privately in the cabinet in 1865, Speed again refused to interpret rules broadly to facilitate treason convictions.

Speed's opinion also considered whether Davis could be tried in Washington, DC, where an indictment had been found against him, based on his actual presence in the capital in 1861 as a United States senator.[6] But the mere paper declaration of a state's secession from the Union and Davis's decision to follow his state amounted to a very dubious case for treason. As the constitutional definition of treason requires a "levying of war," it strongly implies that an act of violence is necessary to commit treason.[7] In *Burr's Case* and *Ex parte Bollman and Swartwout* – both cases arising out of the conspiracy to form a western confederacy in 1807 – Chief Justice John Marshall had considered what kind of violent act would be necessary to prove a levying of war. The Marshall Court endorsed Judge Samuel Chase's ruling in *Fries's Case*, which required that "some actual force or violence must be used in pursuance of such design to levy war."[8]

Drawing on this doctrine, Attorney General Speed maintained that Davis could not be tried for treason in Washington, DC, based on his actions in resigning his seat in the Senate. Despite Davis's "actual presence" in the capital, which made him susceptible to a treason prosecution there, Speed "did not think he was in arms in the District of Columbia" when he was actually present there. There was no violent act in Washington. Thus, according to Speed's logic, the act of

---

[6] The indictment was found May 26, 1865. Indictment, U.S. v. Jefferson Davis, U.S. District Court, Washington, DC, May 26, 1865, copy at VHS. The indictment was not based on Davis's actions (or inactions) in Washington in 1861, but instead on the testimony of Francis Preston Blair and others about the attack on Fort Stevens in July 1864.

[7] See Jonathan W. White, "The Trial of Jefferson Davis and the Americanization of Treason Law," in *Constitutionalism in the Approach and Aftermath of the Civil War*, ed. Paul D. Moreno and Johnathan O'Neill (New York: Fordham University Press, 2013), on how American courts had come around to a stringent definition of overt acts of levying war by the time of the Civil War.

[8] Ex parte Bollman, 8 U.S. 75, 128 (1807).

secession was not treason in itself. Had the Southern states peaceably seceded from the Union without a war, there would have been no means by which to convict Confederates of treason. In the abstract, then, the bare fact of secession without a military follow-up did not constitute "levying war against the United States."[9] Because Speed insisted both on actual presence and an overt act of violence, most of the possible locations for trying Davis were ruled out. Accordingly, although federal courts in Washington, DC, Kentucky, and Tennessee had returned indictments against Davis, and the cabinet debated putting Davis on trial in Ohio, Indiana, or Pennsylvania, based on the Confederate military presence in those states, Speed staunchly insisted that Davis had to be put on trial where he had committed his crime. The uncomfortable fact remained that Davis had ordered his armies to levy war against the United States while sitting at his presidential desk in the Confederate capital of Richmond, Virginia.[10]

The opinion was thus laced with caution, focusing on the importance of returning the legal system to normal and restoring the American people's adherence to the rule of law. This was Speed's paramount concern, more important to him than ensuring that the outcome of Davis's case aligned with the battlefield's results. It would be "a direful calamity, if many whom the sword has spared the law should spare also," Speed wrote. "But I would deem it a more direful calamity still, if the Executive, in performing his constitutional duty of bringing those persons before the bar of justice to answer for their crimes, should violate the plain meaning of the Constitution, or infringe, in the least particular, the living spirit of that instrument."[11] Speed did not conceive of law as a tool to be used creatively to achieve desired ends. It constrained, rather than expanded, the government's options.

---

[9] *Impeachment Investigation: Testimony Taken before the Judiciary Committee of the House of Representatives in the Investigation of the Charges against Andrew Johnson* (Washington, DC: Government Printing Office, 1867), 799 (testimony of James Speed).

[10] *Impeachment Investigation*, 799 (testimony of James Speed). For more on the other indictments against Davis, see John Palmer to Andrew Johnson, July 19, 1865; Crawford W. Hall to James Speed, August 12, 1865; attached presentment *United States v. Jefferson Davis*, Sixth Circuit and District of East Tennessee; and C. W. Hall to James Speed, April 30, 1866, in Jefferson Davis Case File, NA-CP; see also Indictment, U.S. v. Jefferson Davis, U.S. District Court, Washington, DC, May 26, 1865, copy at VHS.

[11] Speed, "Case of Jefferson Davis," 411–13.

When Speed's opinion was read and discussed in the cabinet in 1866, he was able to convince his fellow cabinet members of his views. Secretary of War Edwin Stanton, despite his preference for a military trial, had already privately endorsed Speed's reading of Marshall's opinion in *Burr's Case*.[12] After a careful perusal of the opinion, Stanton concluded that Marshall had condemned the idea of constructive presence in a treason trial. "I think it is clear," Stanton wrote, "that Chief Justice Marshall was of the opinion that a party could not be convicted of treason, except within the District in which the overt act was committed and that the party charged must have been personally present, [in order] to be able to participate in, and aid by his presence, the particular overt act charged." Stanton acknowledged that Marshall's opinion was not perfectly lucid on this point and could be interpreted as a condemnation of a faulty indictment drawn against Burr rather than a wholesale rejection of the doctrine of constructive presence. It would be possible, in his judgment, to find a federal judge outside of Virginia who would read the opinion narrowly and hear the case. But, he queried, "can the Government afford to have a local and subordinate Court overrule the decisions of Judge Marshall in such a case as this?" Stanton would not endorse such a course of action, he said, as "that there is a strong public feeling against convictions by constructive presence and ... if the Government uses the local subordinate courts of the District [of Columbia] to procure such convictions ... its course will be very sharply criticized."[13]

These same concerns motivated Stanton to come around to Speed's views on the undesirability of trying Davis before a military commission. Stanton was persuaded that the most important thing was to conduct Davis's trial with due regard for existing legal norms. The process had to be as unassailable as possible. As he put it, "Davis ought not to be tried before any tribunal whose jurisdiction was seriously questioned or disputed, but that he should be tried in such a manner as should be most satisfactory to the national sense of justice."[14] In Stanton's opinion, "the trial of Jefferson Davis for treason will be a marked event in the judicial history of the country. It is of

[12] See Chapter 1 for more on individual cabinet members' views on military trial.
[13] Edwin Stanton to Joseph Holt, June 7, 1865, vol. 92, Joseph Holt Papers, LC.
[14] *Impeachment Investigation*, 397 (testimony of Edwin Stanton).

[great] importance that it should be conducted in such a manner as to meet the approval of the American Bar."[15]

To be sure, there were countervailing considerations. Many legal commentators wholeheartedly disagreed with Speed's view that Davis could not be tried outside of Virginia. Senator Jacob Howard, who had initially demanded the explanation for the government's delays, was clearly unsatisfied with Speed's overly legalistic reasoning. The precedents were less clear than Speed had suggested, Howard insisted in a long speech in the Senate criticizing Speed's opinion. Rather than assailing the internal logic of the opinion, Howard emphasized instead the terrible consequences that would follow therefrom. The Confederate troops had roamed far beyond Richmond, Howard pointed out, and since Davis had ordered their actions, he should be amenable to prosecution anywhere his armies had reached. If Speed's opinion were correct, Howard maintained, "then some very singular and most inconvenient consequences must flow from it." Speed's insistence on a Virginia trial was "ridiculous," he said, because Davis simply could not be convicted by a jury impaneled in the former capital of the Confederacy. Howard "regard[ed] it as wholly out of the question to try and convict Davis or any other rebel leader of the crime of treason in any rebel state, for the plain reason that no impartial jury can be there found to try him." Adhering to Speed's interpretation would ensure that treason would go unpunished after the Civil War.[16]

Attorney J. J. Coombs, who edited and published a condensed version of *Burr's Case* in the midst of the war, wrote an extended essay on the applicability of Marshall's opinion in *Burr* to the Civil War and reached far different conclusions from Speed. Coombs disagreed with Speed's assessment of the legal significance of the bare act of secession, arguing that bare secession (or purported secession) amounted to a constructive act of violence on the part of the Southern states. Under Coombs's theory, Davis could have been prosecuted prior to the beginning of the war. Coombs also read Marshall's opinion in *Burr's Case* very differently than Speed did. According to Coombs, the opinion had established only the inadequacy of the particular indictment found against Burr, which had charged him with acts of war committed in

---

[15] Edwin Stanton to Joseph Holt, June 7, 1865, vol. 92, Joseph Holt Papers, LC.
[16] *Congressional Globe*, 39th Cong., 1st sess., February 1, 1866, 566–69.

Virginia. Burr had not actually been in Virginia when those acts of violence had taken place, but he had participated in planning the general
scheme of treason from his base in Kentucky. His presence in Virginia
was only "constructive," but perhaps the indictment would have survived scrutiny if it had charged him with his own actual treasonous
acts in Kentucky. In Coombs's opinion, if those activities had played
"a *part* in the war prosecuted on Blennerhasset's Island, [Virginia,]" he
could still have been legally prosecuted in Virginia.[17]

Coombs insisted that this interpretation of Marshall's opinion was
the only possible one that would result in a sensible outcome in treason prosecutions arising out of the Civil War. If a treason indictment
could be found only in the district where the defendant's acts had taken
place, then the chief civilian architects of the Civil War could be held
liable only in Virginia, even if the armies they commanded had ranged
far and wide. Coombs considered this an unthinkable and absurd outcome. Coombs's "proper," broader reading of the Marshall opinion
would instead allow for the civilian leaders of the Confederacy to be
tried for treason outside of formerly Confederate territory.[18]

Indiana governor Oliver Morton endorsed Coombs's view and
volunteered to try Davis in his state. As he told President Johnson,
"There will be no difficulty in getting a jury that will do justice to
the Government and to Davis" in Indiana. Morton also believed that
jurisdiction would not be a problem in Indiana, reminding the president that Confederate forces of about 5,000 men under the command
of Brigadier General John H. Morgan had raided the state during the
war. Johnson responded noncommittally but let Morton know that
the issue was on his mind, remarking that "jurisdiction is one of the
problems that has been much in our way."[19]

In pressing this view of Marshall's opinion, Coombs drew on several
authorities. An anonymous article that appeared in Boston's *Monthly
Law Reporter* in 1851 underscored Coombs's conclusions. The author,

[17] J. J. Coombs, *The Trial of Aaron Burr for High Treason* (Washington, DC: W. H. &
     O. H. Morrison, 1864), 360.
[18] U.S. v. Burr, 25 F. Cas. 55, 138 (C.C.D. Va. 1807) (No. 14,693), at 238; Coombs, *The
     Trial of Aaron Burr*.
[19] Oliver Morton to Andrew Johnson, Andrew Johnson to Oliver Morton, November
     14, 1865, in U.S. War Department, *The War of the Rebellion: A Compilation of
     the Official Records of the Union and Confederate Armies*, 128 vols. (Washington,
     DC: Government Printing Office, 1880–1901), ser. 2, vol. 8: 798.

who was probably Harvard law professor Simon Greenleaf, argued that a person could be guilty of committing treason if he had conspired in the planning of an overt act but was not physically present when his co-conspirators carried out the act of levying war. The author argued that "all those who perform the various and essential military parts of prosecuting [a] war, which must be assigned to different persons, may justly be said to levy war." In his view, "All that is essential to implicate them is, that they be leagued in the conspiracy, and perform a part which will furnish the overt act."[20]

Greenleaf's influential treatise on the law of evidence underscored this point. In the treatise, Greenleaf maintained that "it is not necessary to prove that the prisoner was actually present at the perpetration of the overt act charged; it being sufficient to prove that he was constructively present on that occasion." *U.S. v. Hanway*, a treason prosecution arising out of a violation of the Fugitive Slave Act in 1851, also seemingly endorsed the notion that a person could be constructively present in a treason case. In the course of charging the jury, Justice Robert Grier had asserted: "An abettor in murder, in order to be held liable as a principal in the felony, must be present at the transaction; if absent he may be an accessory. But in treason all are principals, and a man may be guilty of aiding and abetting, though not present."[21]

Some members of Davis's defense team sought to turn the doctrine of constructive presence to their client's advantage, although Charles O'Conor ultimately rejected the idea. Davis's Mississippi lawyers, Giles M. Hillyer and Robert Lowry, concocted a plan to release Davis on bail by filing a writ of habeas corpus in the federal court in eastern Tennessee. Although Davis had been indicted in Tennessee, it was clear to the Davis defense team that his prosecutors seriously contemplated trying him only in Virginia. But Hillyer thought he could circumvent the administration's plans and get Davis released from prison; he was "perfectly certain that [Tennessee federal] Judge Trigg will bail him."[22]

[20] S. G., "On the Law of Treason," *Monthly Law Reporter* 14 (December 1851): 409, 416.
[21] Simon Greenleaf, *A Treatise on the Law of Evidence* (Boston: Little, Brown, 1860), § 243; United States v. Hanway, 26 F. Cas. 105, 125 (C.C.E.D. Pa. 1851) (No. 15,299).
[22] Connally F. Trigg was a Tennessee Unionist who had been appointed to the U.S. District Court for Tennessee in 1864 and became notorious for dismissing treason indictments out of hand. Parson William Brownlow complained to then-Governor Andrew Johnson that Trigg's court was "a complete farce": "The worst rebels and

When Hillyer and Lowry traveled to New York to float their idea past O'Conor, he instantly and emphatically condemned it, growing "petulant" when Hillyer pressed the issue. First, O'Conor argued, if Davis's lawyers attempted to proceed with the case in Tennessee, they would implicitly concede the claim made by some of Davis's most dogged opponents, that Davis had been "constructively" present anywhere the Confederate army had been during the war. This would make Davis vulnerable to prosecution outside of Virginia, where his best chance for acquittal lay. O'Conor also did not trust Trigg to release Davis. Most important, O'Conor insisted that Davis's attorneys must not alienate President Johnson or force his hand: "The case must not be robbed in anywise of its dignity, that is to say, that no devices, or what lawyers term 'sharp practice' must be resorted to," as such tactics "would injure, instead of help the cause."[23]

Many of the administration's critics would have agreed wholeheartedly with O'Conor's assessment of the utility of the prosecution's refusal to manipulate the law – for Davis's team. In the 1865 edition of his influential treatise on criminal law, Joel P. Bishop insisted that Davis should not be tried before a jury in Richmond. It would be nonsensical for the government do such a thing, he believed. Any man who could not swear that he had been loyal to the United States throughout the war would be barred from serving on the jury. And yet, if the jury consisted of men who could legitimately swear the oath of loyalty to the United States, Bishop proclaimed that the trial would be "a farce." He added, "The case could not go into a civil court and be there submitted to a jury, without

traitors, against whom indictments have been found, are all turned loose.... I have no idea that any one man will be convicted – all are expected to come clear." William G. Brownlow to Andrew Johnson, December 29, 1864, in Andrew Johnson, *The Papers of Andrew Johnson*, ed. Paul Bergeron, 16 vols. (Knoxville: University of Tennessee Press, 1967–69), 7: 323. Trigg also held the test oath to be unconstitutional, and the Supreme Court upheld his opinion in Ex parte Garland, 71 U.S. 333 (1866). For a discussion of Trigg in the context of Tennessee's divided loyalties in the Civil War, see Patricia E. Brake, *Justice in the Valley: A Bicentennial Perspective of the United States District Court of the Eastern District of Tennessee* (Franklin, TN: Hillsboro Press, 1998), 36–56.

23 Giles M. Hillyer to William B. Reed, November 22, 1866, and Robert Lowry to William B. Reed, December 14, 1866, in Jefferson Davis, *Jefferson Davis, Constitutionalist: His Letters, Papers, and Speeches*, ed. Dunbar Rowland, 10 vols. (Jackson: Mississippi Department of Archives and Records, 1923), 7: 82, 83; Robert Lowry to Varina Howell Davis, December 5, 1866, Box 24, Jefferson Davis Papers, MC; Robert Lowry to Burton Harrison, December 14, 1866, Box 6, Burton Harrison Papers, LC.

bringing the whole system of trial by jury into contempt." Bishop could not even bring himself to contemplate what might happen if Davis were acquitted. He wrote, "If the government is to be found in the wrong, then _____," leaving the rest of the sentence blank. Bishop sympathized with the predicament of the government prosecutors as they faced these dilemmas with the eyes of the nation trained on their every move. "I know, that, at a time such as this, it is very embarrassing for the government to do right," he wrote. "Should Mr. Davis be tried before a military court, all the demagogues in the country would raise the cry, that the constitution was violated, and our civil rights were in jeopardy; because thus they would suppose they could win the favor of the people. In like manner, all the haters of our country abroad would denounce the act, and they would claim that there is less liberty in our republic than in the monarchies of Europe." Bishop ultimately recommended that Davis be tried before a military commission, and that the government take pains to explain the fairness of this decision to the watching world.[24]

Bishop reacted to Speed's controversial opinion in his correspondence with Radical Republican senator Charles Sumner during the summer of 1866. Speed, Bishop charged, was far too wedded to stilted and formalistic analyses of the law in a time when imaginative reinterpretations would have served him better. Bishop conceded that his treatise could have used more elaboration on the topic of Davis's trial, but remained firm in his conviction that Davis should be tried before a military court, even on a treason charge. Treason could be punished in a military commission if prosecutors creatively redefined it as a violation of the law of war: that is, "the military offence of using the power of war to subvert the government, contrary to the duty of allegiance."[25] This was the moment for legal creativity.

The problem of entrusting the secession question to a court – and to the judgment of twelve jurors – was also a constant source of worry

---

[24] Joel Prentiss Bishop, *Commentaries on the Criminal Law*, 2 vols. (Boston: Little, Brown, 1865), 2: 653–54 nn. 4–6. Subsequent editions retained the notes relating to the Davis case. Charles Sumner cited Bishop's notations on the Davis case approvingly. See Charles Sumner to James G. Blaine, September 6, 1865, in Charles Sumner, *Selected Letters of Charles Sumner*, ed. Beverly Wilson Palmer, 2 vols. (Boston: Northeastern University Press, 1990), 2: 331.

[25] Joel P. Bishop to Charles Sumner, January 4, 5, and June 5, 1866, Reel 35, 36, Charles Sumner Papers, HU.

for Davis's prosecutors.²⁶ Would jurors believe that the law had to be
judged independently of the results of the field of battle? Or would
they be motivated by politics? During the war, Congress had required
all federal jurors to take the ironclad oath, swearing not only their
present fidelity to the United States government but also that they had
never aided the rebellion in the past. As Kentucky congressman Garrett
Davis had put it, the oath was intended to counteract the concern that
"traitors [would not] execute the law of treason against traitors."²⁷
But the ironclad oath was not foolproof. It was impossible to ensure
that every juror took his oath in good faith and that no clandestine
Confederate sympathizers would slip through the cracks and seize the
opportunity to acquit Davis.²⁸

The public discussion over the desirability of trying Davis before a
Virginia jury and risking an unthinkable outcome mirrored the ways
in which Davis's prosecutors thought about these issues. John Clifford
worried about the disastrous consequences of Davis's possible acquittal and began collecting newspaper clippings about the difficulties
of trying Davis. Visiting Virginia in March 1866, Clifford had a talk
with U.S. Attorney Lucius Chandler about the prospects of convicting

---

²⁶ The nineteenth century marked a change from earlier ideas about the jury's power
   to decide questions of law as well as questions of fact. Jury nullification was generally considered to be outside of the legitimate province of jurors by this time. See
   Akhil R. Amar, *The Bill of Rights: Creation and Reconstruction* (New Haven: Yale
   University Press, 1998), 98, and Larry D. Kramer, *The People Themselves: Popular
   Constitutionalism and Judicial Review* (Oxford: Oxford University Press, 2004),
   70, 135.
²⁷ See Harold M. Hyman, *The Era of the Oath: Northern Loyalty Tests during the
   Civil War and Reconstruction* (Philadelphia: University of Pennsylvania Press, 1954),
   21–23, 157–58.
²⁸ See also William Whiting, *The War Powers under the Constitution of the United
   States* (Boston: Little, Brown, 1864), 126. This problem was compounded after the
   Supreme Court's 1867 decision in *Ex parte Garland*, which did not allow federal
   courts to exclude ex-rebel lawyers who had received presidential pardons from arguing before the federal courts. This ruling clearly extended beyond attorneys, but
   it remained unclear whether repentant jurors were included. The issue was never
   resolved in the courts, and it was not a major concern among the attorneys who
   worked on the Davis case, although Evarts's notes reveal that he did spend some time
   contemplating the implications of the Supreme Court's test oath cases. See Cummings
   v. Missouri folder 2, Box 2, William Evarts Papers, Harvard Law School, Special
   Collections Library, Cambridge, MA. See also Hyman, *Era of the Oath*, 115–20, for
   a discussion of uncertainty as to the reach of the Garland opinion. As Hyman found,
   "The courts never decided upon the legality of jurors' test oaths." Hyman, *Era of the
   Oath*, 116.

Davis. Chandler told him that "it will be impossible to empanel a jury of Virginians with any chance of conviction, & that a packed jury of recent residents w[oul]d be worse than an acquittal for its moral effect."[29] A few weeks later Clifford conferred with Benjamin Butler, who informed him that Chief Justice Chase could not be counted on to preside over the trial, and that he (Butler) was prepared to chair a military commission to try Davis.

Clifford returned home disgruntled about the lack of direction from the president and the attorney general, the dire prospects for Davis's conviction, and the professional embarrassment that would likely result if Davis and his cause were exonerated by a Virginia jury. He was inclined to agree with Chandler's grim assessment of the prospects of Davis's conviction in civil court, but was equally discomfited by the possibility of trying Davis before a military commission. The only option left was to save his own reputation by withdrawing from the case, and he told Speed of his desire to exit in May 1866, when faced with the responsibility of making a court appearance the following month. He would not, he emphasized, assist the attorney general in "fir[ing] off a *brutum fulmen*."[30]

Clifford's desire to extricate himself from the hopeless business of seeking to convict Davis only strengthened as time went on. He implored Evarts to join with him in urging the president to abandon the prosecution.[31] Evarts advised Clifford that they should hold off, citing the government's lack of decisive action as a reason why they did not have to make any bold moves.[32] Clifford agreed, but he seized his chance to act when James Speed resigned as attorney general in July 1866, owing to his growing distaste for Johnson's Reconstruction policies, and was replaced by Ohio attorney Henry Stanbery.[33] Evarts and Clifford informed

---

[29] John Clifford diary, March 19, 1866, 1866 Diary, John Clifford Papers, MHS.

[30] John Clifford diary, May 18, 1866, 1866 Diary, John Clifford Papers, MHS. A brutum fulmen, according to *Black's Law Dictionary*, is "an empty noise or an empty threat … [a] judgment void on its face; one that is, in legal effect, no judgment at all." Bryan A. Garner, ed., *Black's Law Dictionary*, 8th ed (St. Paul: Thomson/West, 2004), s.v. "brutum fulmen."

[31] John Clifford diary, May 28, 1866, 1866 Diary, John Clifford Papers, MHS.

[32] William Evarts to Clifford, May 26, 1866, Papers January–May 1866, John Clifford Papers, MHS.

[33] In a public letter to Senator Doolittle, republished in the *New York Herald*, Speed stated that he left his post because of his disagreement with President Johnson's overly lenient Reconstruction policy and Johnson's opposition to the Fourteenth

Stanbery that since he had just assumed office and was newly confronted with the "grave responsibility" of deciding what to do in Davis's case, he should feel "entirely free to dispense with associate counsel, or to select from the profession of the country such as, in your own choice, should seem most suitable to the public interests in your charge."[34]

This gave Clifford the opening he needed, telling Stanbery that "if it is the purpose of the Government to proceed with the trial of Jefferson Davis upon the indictment pending against him, in Virginia, I do not feel that any public or professional duty would require me to take a part in the proceeding." He bluntly informed the new attorney general that the trial would likely vindicate the cause of secession in a court of law. "I can see no reasonable probability," he wrote, "of any other result of such a trial, than the re-opening of a question which has already been solemnly determined by the highest tribunal to which it can ever be submitted, with almost certain impunity to the prisoner, and the consequent humiliation of the Government and the country."[35] When Stanbery asked Clifford to make abundantly clear whether or not he meant to withdraw from the obligation of prosecuting Davis, Clifford carefully requested "permission to withdraw, entirely, from the relation of counsel for the Government" in the matter.[36] Stanbery accordingly released Clifford from his obligations.

In fact, Stanbery adopted Speed's cautious wait-and-see stance. If anything, Stanbery's trepidation was greater than Speed's, and he sought to distance himself from responsibility for Davis's fate. Stanbery later stated that he believed that trying Davis (or anyone else) on a charge of treason was a mistake. It would merely unsettle what trial by battle had already decided in the government's favor. In Stanbery's opinion, Davis's case presented the worst possible forum

---

Amendment. See James Speed to James R. Doolittle, July 14, 1866, reproduced in James Speed, *James Speed: A Personality* (Louisville: John P. Morton, 1914), 96–101.

[34] William Evarts and John Clifford to Henry Stanbery, August 14, 1866, Jefferson Davis Case File, NA-CP; copies also in Papers June–August 1866, John Clifford Papers, MHS, Box 1, and William M. Evarts Papers, LC.

[35] William Evarts and John Clifford to Henry Stanbery, August 14, 1866, Jefferson Davis Case File, NA-CP.

[36] Henry Stanbery to John Clifford, August 22, 1866, and John Clifford to Henry Stanbery, August 27, 1866, Papers June–August 1866, John Clifford Papers, MHS. See also John Clifford diary, August 25, 27, 1866, 1866 Diary, John Clifford Papers, MHS.

in which to resolve the legitimacy of secession, an issue that needed no further resolution beyond the verdict of the war. To try Davis was to incur a terrible risk. The issue, once again, was the necessity of proving secession's illegality to a jury. Stanbery considered it "a very dangerous matter to call upon juries to settle that question for us."[37]

Although Attorney General Speed had intended to argue the case himself if Davis ever saw the inside of a courtroom, Stanbery made it clear that he did not plan to take a similarly active role in the trial. A "sharp debate ensued" within the cabinet when Stanbery announced that he did not desire "to give the subject his personal attention, see to framing the indictment, preparing the case, etc." The president did not order the new attorney general to supervise the case more directly, so responsibility for it passed to Evarts and the other outside counsel.[38]

Neither Stanbery nor Evarts wanted to direct the Davis prosecution. Although Stanbery had informed the cabinet about the limited role he intended to have in the trial, he did not communicate this decision very clearly to Evarts. Evarts had initially understood his role as a limited one because the primary responsibility for a case as important as Davis's lay with the attorney general. "I had always assumed that whenever the trial should take place, the Attorney General would represent the government," Evarts said. "I had never had any other expectation than that. I expected to be associated with him. I was not retained to take the place of the Attorney General." Evarts had known when Stanbery took office in 1866 that the new attorney general did not consider it his duty to try cases in the circuit courts personally, "but I insisted that there was a reasonable public expectation, in case of the trial of Mr. Davis for treason, that the Attorney General would take the lead for the government."[39]

Stanbery must have made his intentions clearer to his associate counsel some time before the fall of 1867, when he reminded Evarts that he did "not expect to be present at this prosecution. My official duties, as provided by law, require me to be here, and in attendance

---

[37] *Impeachment Investigation*, 561 (testimony of Henry Stanbery). Charles O'Conor characterized Stanbery as a highly honorable gentleman and able lawyer. See Charles O'Conor to Judge John W. Edmonds, November 20, 1868, vol. 6, James Roberts Gilmore Papers, Johns Hopkins University Library, Baltimore.

[38] Welles, *Diary of Gideon Welles*, 2: 614.

[39] *Impeachment Investigation*, 647, 657 (testimony of William Evarts).

upon the Supreme Court of the United States for the preparation & argument of the cases of the Government pending in that court." Stanbery instructed Evarts to take the lead, although he promised to "be ready at all times to meet the counsel of the Government for consultation here."[40] Despite his personal feelings that Stanbery should participate more fully, Evarts confirmed that he understood that he could not expect the personal oversight of the attorney general in the case.[41]

Putting aside the question of Stanbery's involvement in the case, confusion reigned about the administration's strategy more generally. Evarts had accepted the government's retainer initially with the expectation that he would try all treason cases in the civil courts, but he could not gain any concrete understanding about how even this first case was to be conducted. As time wore on, he could not discern any definite policy on the part of the government; he could not even discover whether the government intended to proceed at all in the Davis case. U.S. Attorney Lucius Chandler was also frustrated with the lack of definite policy. "I felt, and have felt all along, that it was quite important that I should know what the views of the administration were in reference to the trial of Mr. Davis," he said. "I came here [to Washington] on two, and perhaps, three occasions ... to ascertain whether it was wished that the trial should be had. ... I called upon the President and introduced the subject, but I never could get from him anything other than that the Attorney General had the whole matter in his charge."[42] But as it turned out, it seemed no one had the matter in his charge. This deadlock eventually led the public to take notice of the lack of progress in the Davis case.

[40] Henry Stanbery to William M. Evarts, October 25, 1867, Letterbook G, Microfilm M 699, Attorney General's Records, Record Group 60, NA-CP.

[41] William Evarts to Henry Stanbery, November 2, 1867, Attorney General Letterbook G, Microfilm M 699, Attorney General's Records, Record Group 60, NA-CP.

[42] *Impeachment Investigation*, 503, 505 (testimony of Lucius Chandler).

7

Public Opinion and Its Uses

By 1866, many Northern newspapers that had initially called for Davis's trial and execution shifted their focus from Davis's treason to the government's delay in trying him. A couple of themes emerged from the newspaper coverage. First, the press could not agree on whom to blame for the failure to prosecute. This issue followed partisan lines: Republican papers condemned President Johnson, and Democratic ones condemned the Republican Congress and Republican judges. Second, a growing segment of the Northern public was calling for mercy toward Davis. The anger that had permeated Northern press coverage of Davis's treason prosecution in 1865 had dissipated, as had the feeling that Davis's conviction was a certainty. The tide had begun to turn in Davis's favor.

James Gordon Bennett's gossipy *New York Herald*, the most widely read newspaper in the United States, had called angrily for Davis's trial and execution soon after his arrest in May 1865.[1] A year and a half later, Bennett's paper saved its harshest criticism for the unending delays in Davis's prosecution. After reviewing the actions of the judges, the administration, and the prosecuting attorneys, the *Herald* concluded that "it is clear now that the President is not to blame, and we think it is equally clear that the Chief Justice is, for thus violating

---

[1] The *Herald* proclaimed on its editorial page that it was the nation's most widely read newspaper. Its circulation, as it boasted at the top of its pages, was 84,000 copies a day. See Carl Sandburg, *Abraham Lincoln: The Prairie Years and the War Years*, ed. Edward C. Goodman (New York: Sterling, 2007), 124, on the paper's reach.

the constitution, which guarantees every man a speedy and impartial trial." The paper recommended that "this disgraceful state of things ... be brought to an end either by the trial of the prisoner or by his release."[2] The *New York World*, published by the conservative Manton Marble, agreed with the *Herald*'s assessment of the situation. Incensed at "the gross illegality of detaining [Davis] in custody nineteen months without putting him on trial or confronting him with the witnesses expected to testify to his guilt," by November 1866 the paper was recommending that the government discharge the prisoner without delay. The *World* excused Johnson for the lack of progress, insisting that the president had found himself mired in an impossible political situation manufactured by the Radical Republicans and the chief justice (also a Radical Republican). Instead, the paper denounced the Radicals: "Chief Justice Chase and his sycophant, Judge Underwood, shrink from trying Mr. Davis lest his acquittal should expose them to the obloquy of the Radicals who thirst for his blood, and lest Chief-Justice Chase's chances of the Radical nomination should be diminished."[3] According to the *World*, the Radicals had created Johnson's dilemma and had sought to "postpone and prevent a trial, and put the odium on the President."[4]

By contrast, the Republican magazine the *Nation* was convinced that the stagnation in the Davis case was the result of Johnson's calculation, although the paper was no less convinced that the government had missed its window of opportunity to try Davis. In June 1866 the *Nation* accused Johnson of purposely delaying Davis's trial to allow public furor to die down. The paper insisted that trying Davis would never result in conviction, predicting that the trial, "if it ever comes off, will be a farce, and that, so far from helping to 'make treason odious,' it will surround the very existence of such a crime with a fog." The paper argued that "the one great object of the long postponement of the trial [on Johnson's part] was to give time for the growth of such an indifference in the public mind as would render this result possible."[5]

---

[2] *New York Herald*, October 15, 1866.
[3] *New York World*, November 13, 1866. See the following chapter for more on the judges' Radical Republican views and their role in the Davis trial.
[4] *New York World*, November 13, 1866.
[5] *Nation*, June 14, 1866.

Northern papers from across the political spectrum also highlighted the troubling possibility of Davis's acquittal. The *New York World* could not see why the government would risk such an outcome. "To submit the secession question to a court is to imply that it is still open to doubt!" the paper declared. Even if a court did "decide that secession is a constitutional right," Unionists would not "yield [their] convictions on this subject." Because the people of the United States would accept only one outcome in the trial and would repudiate any contrary decision, the *World* pronounced "the trial of Mr. Davis" to be "little better than a judicial farce."[6] *Harper's Weekly* also delved into the uncertainty of jury trial, noting that an acquittal would be devastating for Americans, because it would mean that the government had "waged [war] against those whom the [courts] would have justified in their action." There was no reason to undercut the results of the trial by battle, particularly because the courts were not particularly trustworthy. "Is the race of Taneys extinct?" the editors queried, hearkening back to Chief Justice Roger Taney's politically unpopular decision in *Dred Scott*. The decision was simply too important to be entrusted to a not entirely trustworthy Supreme Court. "Does any body mean to assert that the right of this Government to exist is a question for a court to decide?"[7]

Both the *Philadelphia Inquirer* and the Radical Republican *Chicago Tribune* railed against the declining national commitment to convicting Davis. The *Inquirer* considered the delays (which it attributed to President Johnson) to be "cruel to the country and without reasonable excuse." Punishing treason was necessary to cement American nationhood. Without a conviction against Davis and a consequent vindication of the Union cause, the editors declared, "we may as well stop talking about treason, and expunge the word at once from our dictionaries." In fact, the *Inquirer* asserted, if the government did not make an example of Davis and ensure his punishment, the nation would again be coping with the calamity of disintegration and civil war as soon as the South could again muster the resources to combat the North.[8] The *Chicago Tribune* urged its readers to recall the terrible deeds committed by

---

[6] *New York World*, May 16, 1866.

[7] "A Superfluous Jury," *Harper's Weekly*, May 26, 1866; "Is Ours a Valid Government?" *Harper's Weekly*, July 14, 1866. See also "Object of Jeff. Davis' Trial," *Chicago Tribune*, November 14, 1865; "A Queer Demand," *Chicago Tribune*, May 20, 1865; "The Trial of Davis," *Harper's Weekly*, November 25, 1867.

[8] *Philadelphia Inquirer*, April 2, 1866.

Davis and demand his trial. As it had since Davis's arrest, the *Tribune* recommended that he be tried before a military commission. If he were tried before a jury in Virginia, the editors wrote, "the chances are one thousand to one that they would not only acquit Jeff Davis but would put upon record a verdict that he had a perfect right to institute a rebellion, that Virginia had a right to secede, and that the Government of the United States had no right to coerce the seceded states."[9]

The African American abolitionist Frederick Douglass echoed some of these critiques but also urged the president to spare Davis. In March 1866 he told a crowd that "Davis would never be punished, simply because Mr. Johnson had determined to have him tried in the one way that he could not be tried, and had determined not to have him tried in the only way he could be tried." On the other hand, Douglass did not hold a grudge against former Confederates and had "no objection to raise against the mitigation of [Davis's] punishment."[10] The country might well be better off if it healed old wounds by sparing Davis, he thought. Douglass's calls for mercy resonated with Maine senator William Pitt Fessenden, who believed that any real acceptance of defeat in the South required forbearance from the North. According to Fessenden, Davis's release – or fair prosecution in accordance with the regular protections afforded a criminal defendant – would "be the precursor of a better state of feeling" in the South that would hasten the Reconstruction process.[11]

Southern papers picked up on the shift in Northern public opinion. They began to predict hopefully that Davis would eventually go free because the North lacked the determination to convict him at all costs. In Davis's home state of Mississippi, the *Natchez Courier* expected that the government would eventually release Davis, because "it would be impossible to convict him before any court, except, indeed, a military commission." According to the *Courier*, it was impossible that the secession question, "for the arbitrament of which thousands have willingly laid down their lives ... is now to be settled by a few pettifogging

[9] *Chicago Tribune*, January 12, 1866; see also February 1 and November 13, 1866; May 21, 1867.
[10] Frederick Douglass, "The Issues of the Day: An Address Delivered in Washington, DC," March 10, 1866, in Frederick Douglass, *The Frederick Douglass Papers*, ed. John Blassingame, 5 vols. (New Haven: Yale University Press, 1979), 4: 122.
[11] Kenneth Rayner to William Pitt Fessenden, April 23, 1867, and William Pitt Fessenden to Kenneth Rayner, May 9, 1867, Kenneth Rayner Papers, NYHS.

attornies in a district Court." A conviction could be ensured only
through packing a jury, the *Courier* argued, and a large proportion
of the American public would condemn such an effort.[12] The *New
Orleans Crescent* concurred, predicting that the government would not
risk entrusting Davis's fate to a jury because of the danger of reopening
the secession debate. The Unionist position "cannot safely be trusted to
the arbitrament of reason and law," the paper claimed. The government
was well aware that "the discussions which would arise on the trial of
Mr. Davis would only weaken the results [of the war]."[13]

The turnabout in public sentiment worked to Davis's great advantage,
as Charles O'Conor recognized – and had predicted. With the political
tide turning in Davis's favor, O'Conor sought to elicit public sympathy for his client by assisting in the production of three propaganda
pieces about him. The most influential of them was *The Prison Life of
Jefferson Davis*, published in 1866 and ostensibly written by Davis's
first physician at Fort Monroe, Dr. John Craven. In fact, the book was
ghostwritten by a New York Democrat named Charles G. Halpine,
whose "object [was] to put the whole present plea of the South in
the mouth of Mr. Davis, interpolating political matters from southern sources in his real conversations with Dr. Craven."[14] Halpine, an
Irish American journalist known for writing humorous stories about
his war experiences (published under the pseudonym Miles O'Reilly),
highlighted and embellished the cruelty of Davis's treatment in prison.
Halpine regarded the book as a powerful piece of Democratic propaganda. He recommended it to President Johnson as "the most powerful campaign document ever issued in this country – a document that
could not but abate the fanaticism of the radicals ... & strengthen
& rally the conservative opinions of the country to your increased
support."[15] *The Prison Life* did indeed arouse public sympathy for
Davis. Historian Edward Eckert wrote that it successfully changed

---

[12] *Natchez Courier*, May 24, 1866.
[13] "The Trial of Jefferson Davis," *New Orleans Crescent*, October 3, 1866.
[14] Charles Halpine to Samuel L. M. Barlow, April 23, 1866, Box 62, Samuel Barlow
Papers, HEHL.
[15] Charles Halpine to Andrew Johnson, March 20, 1866, quoted in Edward Eckert,
"Fiction Distorting Fact": The Prison Life, Annotated by Jefferson Davis (Macon,
GA: Mercer University Press, 1987), xlii. Halpine later reported that Johnson was in

"the defeated leader of an unsuccessful rebellion into a martyr" for the Lost Cause.[16]

Davis himself gave *The Prison Life* a mixed review. Although he certainly appreciated the public sympathy the work aroused, he was outraged by his own ridiculous and vaguely effeminate characterization. In probably the book's most inspired fabrication, he was described feeding crumbs to a pet mouse, "the only living thing he now had power to benefit," a tidbit that prompted him to inscribe a dismissive "pshaw" in the margin of his personal copy.[17]

The Prison Life was partly O'Conor's handiwork. Before the book's publication, Richard O'Gorman, another New York Democrat and a crony of Halpine's, wrote to O'Conor to ask for his guidance in producing an effective work. O'Gorman reported that Davis's physician, Craven, "has a defective memory and it needs jogging. He is willing that it should be jogged by any one friendly to Davis. Do you remember anything that Mr. Davis would have said or would be likely to have said about his own condition, or that of this Republic? If so, I am pretty sure the physician will remember it, too." O'Conor undoubtedly provided useful hints for transmission to Craven.[18]

O'Conor also made use of the pro-secession argument to strengthen Davis's political position, thus heightening the government's fear that a jury would accept it. He encouraged secessionist treatise writers to publish works detailing the legal and historical basis of the pro-secession argument, in order to stimulate public awareness of the legal and historical grounding of secessionist constitutional theory. His goal was to focus attention on whether the war's resolution of the secession

---

favor of the project. Charles Halpine to Samuel L. M. Barlow, April 23, 1866, Box 62, Samuel Barlow Papers, HEHL. My discussion of Halpine's role in ghostwriting the book is taken from Eckert, *"Fiction Distorting Fact,"* and William B. Hanchett, "Reconstruction and the Rehabilitation of Jefferson Davis: Charles G. Halpine's *Prison Life*," *Journal of American History* 56 (1969): 282, although neither mentions O'Conor's involvement in the production of the book.

[16] Eckert, *"Fiction Distorting Fact,"* xvi.

[17] Eckert, *"Fiction Distorting Fact,"* 86.

[18] "History Made to Order," *New York Independent*, June 5, 1905, 1378. O'Gorman's letter was found approximately thirty years after O'Conor's death, in his personal copy of *The Prison Life*. O'Conor later ended up prosecuting O'Gorman for public fraud as part of his busting of the Tweed Ring in the 1870s. O'Conor's extensive law library was auctioned off after his death. Charles O'Conor, *Catalogue of the Law Library of the Late Charles O'Conor* (New York: Geo. A. Leavitt & Co., Auctioneers, 1885).

question had been just, and whether the issue could be revisited in a court of law. By highlighting the constitutional claims underlying the secession argument, O'Conor wished to raise implicitly the possibility that a court might endorse secessionist logic. B. J. Sage, a New Orleans attorney and committed secessionist, attracted O'Conor's attention with a pamphlet he had published under the pseudonym P. C. Centz (Plain Common Sense) in late 1865, entitled *Davis and Lee: A Protest against the Attempt of the Yankee Radicals to Have Them and the Other Confederate Chiefs Murdered*. Sage later expanded the pamphlet into a full-length book entitled *The Republic of Republics*. The purpose of both versions was to "keep up the battle for State sovereignty" and the constitutionality of secession, and thereby "prevent trials of Davis and Lee."[19]

Sage later bragged that O'Conor held his work in high regard. Indeed, O'Conor recommended Sage to his friend Samuel Tilden as "a democrat of unswerving fidelity" and "a gentleman of great intelligence and extensive political knowledge."[20] According to Sage, O'Conor had characterized his work as "an admirably prepared and overwhelmingly conclusive brief for Davis's defence."[21] O'Conor hoped that Sage's book would spark public debate about the legitimacy of secession and persuade Johnson not to use Davis's case to cement the principle of the perpetuity of the Union in a court of law.

For O'Conor, the pamphlet was purely instrumental, much to Sage's chagrin. O'Conor never divulged his plans to avoid trial to Sage, who complained bitterly about the fact that he was never able to defend secession's constitutionality in Davis's case. Indeed, Sage reported to Jefferson Davis that O'Conor had "acquiesced" in the government's decision when he should have insisted on a public trial of secession, unaware that O'Conor had contrived the whole thing. Sage stridently

---

[19] B. J. Sage to Jeremiah Morton, November 10, 1868, Box 3, Morton-Halsey Papers, Small Special Collections Library, University of Virginia, Charlottesville (repository hereafter cited as UVA).

[20] Charles O'Conor to Samuel J. Tilden, May 28, 1868, Box 5, Samuel J. Tilden Papers, NYPL.

[21] B. J. Sage, "Some Great Constitutional Questions," *Southern Historical Society Papers* 12 (1884): 484, 488; B. J. Sage, *The Republic of Republics*, 3rd ed. (Philadelphia: William W. Harding, 1878), frontispiece. See also B. J. Sage, *The Republic of Republics*, 4th ed. (Boston: Little, Brown, 1881), vi (the third and fourth editions of the book differed markedly); B. J. Sage to Jeremiah Morton, May 17, 1868, Box 3, Morton-Halsey Papers, UVA.

viewed the case as a great opportunity to defend the Confederate cause. In his opinion, "If Jefferson Davis had managed his own case he would have been tried (or at all events he would not have helped to evade it) and constitutional liberty would have had a vindication as decisive historical and grand as [the Magna Carta] and the Confederate cause would have been understood and approved by the whole English-speaking world." But Sage did ultimately acknowledge that "we can never tell how long [Davis] might have been troubled but for the actual course of things. Perhaps what was, was right."[22]

Albert Bledsoe, who had been a classmate of Davis's at West Point and later a mathematics professor at the University of Virginia, also wrote a book defending secession. Bledsoe's *Is Davis a Traitor? Or Was Secession a Constitutional Right Previous to the War of 1861?* focused on the adoption of the Constitution and the views of the founding fathers. The book's "sole object" was "to discuss the right of secession with reference to the past; in order to ... wipe off the charges of treason and rebellion from the names and memories of ... all who have fought or suffered in the great war of coercion." Bledsoe acknowledged that debates over secession were primarily theoretical at this late date, but he maintained that the public discourse was vital, because "this is the great issue on which the whole Southern people, the dead as well as the living, is about to be tried in the person of their illustrious chief, Jefferson Davis."[23]

The book did not otherwise discuss Davis's pending trial, but Bledsoe corresponded with Davis's lawyers and certainly hoped that his work would establish the legitimacy of the Confederacy. Bledsoe recorded in his diary that he had received several letters from O'Conor and William B. Reed that praised his book.[24] "When Davis begged me to publish the book, just before the time set for the trial," Bledsoe wrote, "he knew that no one would analyze and discuss the subject as I had done." In Bledsoe's rather immodest recounting, Reed and O'Conor, "the two most eminent of [Davis's] counsel, admitted that

[22] B. J. Sage to Jefferson Davis, February 8, 1874, and August 3, 1874, Box 19, Jefferson Davis Papers, MC. See also B. J. Sage to Jefferson Davis, August 24, 1867, and May 2, 1868, Box 24, ibid.

[23] Albert T. Bledsoe, *Is Davis a Traitor?* (Baltimore: Innes, 1866), v, 5.

[24] None of Bledsoe's correspondence survives, but he recorded the gist of letters he received in his diary.

I opened and cleared up the great theme to their minds."[25] Like Sage, Bledsoe mistakenly believed that O'Conor intended to make use of his argument in court. But O'Conor used the book as a propaganda piece instead. To ensure that *Is Davis a Traitor?* found a wide popular audience, O'Conor hired a literary agent to promote the book.[26]

O'Conor's campaign to exert political pressure on the Johnson administration also included the collection of signatures from well-known abolitionists for a "memorial," or petition, that the Davis defense team planned to send to President Johnson, members of his cabinet, Chief Justice Chase, and congressional Republicans. At O'Conor's direction, George Shea met with Republicans in New York, Boston, Philadelphia, and Washington, and eventually recruited Horace Greeley, the wealthy abolitionist Gerrit Smith (who had funded John Brown's raid on Harpers Ferry), Cornelius Vanderbilt, Senator Henry Wilson, and others either to sign the memorial or contribute funds for Davis's bail.[27] Thereafter, Senator Wilson, a long-time opponent of slavery and the Southern "Slave Power," introduced a joint resolution in Congress criticizing the administration for depriving Davis of his Sixth Amendment right to a speedy trial.[28]

---

[25] Albert T. Bledsoe diary, Entry 44, Albert T. Bledsoe Papers, UVA. See also Mrs. S. Bledsoe Herrick, "Personal Recollections of My Father and Mr. Lincoln and Mr. Davis," *Methodist Review*, 3rd ser., 41 (April 1915): 666, 673.

[26] As O'Conor told Davis's former private secretary Burton Harrison, "Mr. Bledsoe has written a book concerning the great southern question and expects some aid from you and me in funding an agent for him. I would like to see you about it." Charles O'Conor to Burton Harrison, December 31, 1866, Box 6, Burton Harrison Papers, LC.

[27] Greeley had in fact convinced Shea to serve on the Davis defense team; see Horace Greeley, *Recollections of a Busy Life* (New York: J. B. Ford, 1869), 414; Theron G. Strong, *Landmarks of a Lawyer's Lifetime* (New York: Dodd, Mead, 1914), 124–26. Gerrit Smith once compared Jefferson Davis to John Brown, implying that Brown's hanging had resulted in his martyrdom and that Davis did not deserve the same exalted legacy; see Gerrit Smith, *Gerrit Smith on the Bailing of Jefferson Davis*, July 10, 1867, broadside, HU. Charles O'Conor to George Shea, March 25, 1867, Box 1, Bryan Family Papers, Manuscripts Division, Library of Virginia, Richmond (repository hereafter cited as LVA).

[28] *Congressional Globe*, 40th Cong., 1st sess., March 22, 1867, 267–68. Richard H. Abbott, *Cobbler in Congress: The Life of Henry Wilson, 1812–1875* (Lexington: University Press of Kentucky, 1972), 162–63. Antebellum Northerners often opposed slavery on the grounds that it concentrated economic and political power in the hands of elite white Southerners, whom they denominated the "Slave Power."

Shea reported that he had almost persuaded Wendell Phillips, William Lloyd Garrison, Henry Ward Beecher, and John Andrew to lend their support. He also planned to "call upon [House Republican] Henry J. Raymond, Senators Dixon and Doolittle" to discuss the memorial. O'Conor thought that the memorial might convince congressional Republicans that their efforts to secure Davis's conviction would earn them the enmity of prominent men in their party.[29]

Horace Greeley and Gerrit Smith emerged as the two most vocal Republican Davis supporters. They pressed Davis's cause in speeches, in open letters to President Johnson and Chief Justice Chase, and, in Greeley's case, in the *New York Tribune*. They emphasized mercy – and the importance of reuniting the country. Greeley believed that trying Davis for treason would undercut the goal of putting the Union back together. He acknowledged that the Confederate cause had been unjust, both because it had never commanded the loyalty of a majority of Southerners and also because it was based on the immorality of slavery. In spite of the iniquity of the Confederate cause, however, Greeley was concerned that visiting the punishment for a nation's revolt on a single individual might cast the American Revolution itself in a bad light. For Greeley, it was a "general American doctrine, that, after a revolt has levied a regular army, and fought therewith a pitched battle, its champions, even though utterly defeated, cannot be tried and convicted as traitors." Greeley further claimed that the Southern states might even be justified in throwing off the governance of their Northern counterparts, telling Salmon P. Chase that "it is not necessary nor wise to maintain that Twelve Millions of people in the Southern states have no right to be governed otherwise than as Twenty Millions in other States may see fit." Perhaps most important, Greeley called Jefferson Davis an honorable man who had waged war against the United States in a fair contest. Therefore, the government's insistence

29 S. H. Gay to Wendell Phillips, December 29, 1865, and Charles O'Conor to George Shea, March 25, 1867, Box 1, Bryan Family Papers, LVA; George Shea to Charles O'Conor, August 13, 14, 20, 1866, and Gerrit Smith to George Shea, October 21, 1867, Box 24, Jefferson Davis Papers, MC; George Shea to Gerrit Smith, October 27, 1867, Reel 16, Gerrit Smith Papers, LC [microfilm edition]; George Parsons Lathrop, "The Bailing of Jefferson Davis," *Century Magazine* 33 (February 1887): 637–38, 640.

on a treason trial "did not impress [him] as statesmanlike, nor even sagacious."[30]

Gerrit Smith also invoked the founders, claiming that "since no small share of the statesmen of the North and a large majority of the statesmen of the South, including even Jefferson and Madison, have believed that they saw this doctrine in the constitution," it was impossible to argue that secession was clearly foreclosed by the Constitution. Smith, intriguingly, called into question whether the trial by battle had indeed settled the secession issue. Perhaps the question was still an open one, he said, because no court of law had pronounced against it. He suggested to Salmon P. Chase that the best way to resolve the question to everyone's satisfaction was to amend the Constitution to declare secession's illegality unequivocally.[31] Davis's powerful and

[30] Horace Greeley to George William Blunt, John Alexander Kennedy, and John O. Stone, May 23, 1867 (privately published, 1867), broadside, NYHS; Greeley, *Recollections of a Busy Life*, 413, 414; *New York Tribune*, June 24, 1867. For Chase's response, see Salmon P. Chase to Horace Greeley, June 25, 1867, and Horace Greeley to Salmon P. Chase, May 31, 1866, in Salmon P. Chase, *The Salmon P. Chase Papers*, ed. John Niven, 5 vols. (Kent: Kent State University Press, 1993), 5: 159, 99. See also William A. Blair, *With Malice toward Some: Treason and Loyalty in the Civil War Era* (Chapel Hill: University of North Carolina Press, 2014), and David W. Blight, *Race and Reunion: The Civil War in American Memory* (Cambridge, MA: Harvard University Press, 2001), for more on the strange alliance between Davis and his postwar supporters in the North.

[31] Gerrit Smith to Salmon P. Chase, May 28, 1866, broadside, NYHS. See also Gerrit Smith to William Lloyd Garrison, March 20, 1867, Box 24, Jefferson Davis Papers, MC. Smith's point about the necessity of a constitutional amendment to declare the permanency of the Union is an interesting one. *Harper's Weekly* also claimed that the Constitution had been ambiguous about the possibility of legal secession, and suggested that "the only thing that would strengthen the resolution of the war would be a constitutional amendment declaring secession to be void, and in the absence of this, no Supreme Court ruling on the point would suffice." "Is Ours a Valid Government?" *Harper's Weekly*, July 14, 1866. Davis attorney B. J. Sage made a similar point in his polemic on the right of secession, *The Republic of Republics,* arguing that if the U.S. government had really wanted to establish secession's illegality, Congress would have ratified a constitutional amendment to that effect, just as it had done with slavery in the Thirteenth Amendment. Sage, *The Republic of Republics*, 4th ed., 426. Such an amendment was proposed, but Congress never acted on it. See Herman V. Ames, *The Proposed Amendments to the Constitution of the United States during the First Century of Its History* (Washington, DC: Government Printing Office, 1897), 380. In fact, enacting a postwar constitutional amendment could have caused a major constitutional problem, because it would have essentially admitted the ambiguity of the Constitution on this point and perhaps provided an excuse for Confederate secession. Instead Chase, in his opinion in *Texas v. White*, firmly insisted that secession had always been unconstitutional and had not *become* so as a result of the war. See Epilogue for more.

vocal Northern allies helped turn the tide of public opinion against retribution.

Not everyone agreed that Davis's case should be abandoned, however. Frustrated with government foot-dragging in the Davis case, in May 1866 Judge John C. Underwood of the federal district court sought to force the trial to go forward in Virginia. The government had not yet presented an indictment in federal court in Virginia, and the prosecutors had intended to seek an indictment before the circuit court when it met, rather than in the district court. The government deemed the circuit court a far more appropriate forum for Davis's case, both because the circuit court had jurisdiction over "major" federal crimes and because Chief Justice Chase would preside alongside Underwood.[32] With two judges on the bench, the possibility of appeal to the Supreme Court would be preserved. Nonetheless, U.S. Attorney Lucius Chandler felt compelled to comply when, on the last day of the district court's term, Underwood directed him to prepare an indictment, and then informed him that the work had to be completed by early afternoon because the judge had to leave town by three o'clock. Chandler later admitted that he had "but two or three hours to prepare the indictment" and that the document he had "very hurriedly prepared" was, by his own estimation, not adequate for conducting a prosecution against Jefferson Davis.

The 1866 indictment, a scant four pages long, alleged a lone count against Davis and failed to specify under which treason statute he was charged. More important, the indictment did not provide a factual basis for convicting Davis of any overt act of treason. In formalized language, the indictment alleged the legal conclusion that Davis, on May 15, 1864, "did compass, imagine, and intend to raise, levy and carry on war insurrection and rebellion, against the United States of America," but provided no specific facts about any behavior that might amount to levying war.[33] The indictment was found on the testimony of four men with no discernible connection to Davis, who testified to such commonplace recollections as "[I] heard Jeff Davis make his

---

[32] Judiciary Act of 1789, 1 Stat. 73 (1789), §§ 9, 11.

[33] May 15, 1864 was the day the Battle of New Market took place, but the indictment did not mention a specific incident. See E. B. Long, *The Civil War Day by Day* (Garden City, NY: Doubleday, 1971). None of the witnesses mentioned any actions taken by Davis in May 1864.

Inaugural Address at Richmond in 1862 influencing the People to take up arms against the U.S. Govt," and "I [once] had a personal interview on official business with Jefferson Davis myself, and acknowledged him to be the President of the Confederate States in 1862 and in 1863."[34] In fact, the witnesses' inability to provide any meaningful information about Davis, let alone provide a solid factual basis for the indictment, invites the conclusion that Chandler found them randomly on the street in the course of his frantic rush to prepare the indictment. Despite the thinness of the testimony presented by Chandler, the grand jury at Norfolk returned the indictment against Jefferson Davis.[35]

The grand jury consisted of members of the African American community, recently arrived transplanted Northerners, and some local white Virginians who had remained loyal to the Union.[36] The Copperhead *New York Daily News* sneeringly characterized the grand jurors as criminals and men with questionable "moral attributes." The paper contended that four of the men had been "held by the Confederate authorities as prisoners of State, at Richmond, under suspicion of their correspondence with the enemy," with the clear implication that such Unionist leanings were to be condemned rather than lauded. The *Daily News* protested that the court and the prosecution had rigged the proceedings against Davis by selecting a grand jury predisposed against him.[37]

In charging the grand jury, Underwood took the opportunity to deliver a lengthy tirade against white Virginians, whom he condemned for "the subjection of women of the [dark] complexion to the wild

---

[34] *Impeachment Investigation: Testimony Taken before the Judiciary Committee of the House of Representatives in the Investigation of the Charges against Andrew Johnson* (Washington, DC: Government Printing Office, 1867), 503 (testimony of Lucius Chandler); Jefferson Davis Treason indictment, May 10, 1866, U.S. District Court, District of Virginia, copy at LVA; Notes on witnesses' testimony for May 10, 1866, indictment (probably taken by Chandler) (J. F. Milligan, Judge G. P. Scarbourg, John Goode Jr., and J. Hardy Hendon), Jefferson Davis Trial Papers, University of Chicago Library, Chicago (repository hereafter cited as UChi).

[35] See Jonathan W. White, "The Trial of Jefferson Davis and the Americanization of Treason Law," in *Constitutionalism in the Approach and Aftermath of the Civil War*, ed. Paul D. Moreno and Johnathan O'Neill (New York: Fordham University Press, 2013), for more on heightened pleading standards in treason prosecutions by the time of the Civil War.

[36] See Chapter 13 for more on the grand jurors and the requirement that federal jurors take the ironclad loyalty oath.

[37] *New York Daily News*, May 12, 1866.

fury of unbridled licentiousness." Underwood also made it clear to the grand jurors that he thought that Davis was guilty. He told them that "treason [was] the greatest of all crimes and ought to be signally punished." He also instructed the jurors that "the leaders in the late rebellion, may be treated either as traitors or public enemies, as they undoubtedly were both by the law of nations."[38]

Underwood's comments provoked his audience. One courtroom observer reported that Underwood had made "the most intense fool of himself – and [had] caus[ed] us to see that if he and his packed jury of ferrets and Yankees were to be permitted to have anything to do with Mr. Davis he would have but a slim chance for justice." The *Richmond Dispatch* condemned Underwood for partiality in declaring in advance "that Mr. Davis is guilty of treason, the greatest of crimes, and should be hung! And this man is called a judge!" O'Conor informed the Davises that "our amiable and virtuous jury-packing Judge" was so biased that "neither the government nor Mr. Davis would be willing to trust Judge Underwood alone."[39]

Chandler and his superiors recognized immediately that the hastily drawn district court indictment, as it was drafted, could by no means withstand an attack by defense counsel. The single allegation was simply too general; rather than asserting a specific act of violence that amounted to treason, the indictment made broad conclusory statements that Davis had committed treason. Attorney General Speed acknowledged "that the existing indictment is not good and valid in law," and Davis himself wrote that, "in the [prosecutors'] hot haste to get in their work, the indictment was drawn with the fatal omission of an overt act."[40] The poor quality of the indictment ensured that the government would have to draw up a new one, preferably in circuit court, in the event that the prosecution against Davis ever went forward.

[38] *New York Times*, May 12, 1866.
[39] David Lee Powell to Elizabeth Lewis Dabney Saunders, June 8, 1866, section 40, Saunders Family Papers, VHS; *Richmond Dispatch*, May 11, 1866; Charles O'Conor to Jefferson Davis, May 27, 1868, and Charles O'Conor to Varina Howell Davis, October 18, 1866, Box 24, Jefferson Davis Papers, MC.
[40] Edwin Stanton, "Advice in the Matter of Jefferson Davis, in Cabinet," Reel 11, Edwin M. Stanton Papers, LC [microfilm edition]; Jefferson Davis, "Robert E. Lee," *North American Review* 150 (January 1890): 55, 65.

More fundamentally, the indictment was unworkable because the government remained unwilling to try Davis in the absence of the chief justice, which precluded a trial in district court, where Underwood would preside alone. In the circuit court it was possible, in the absence of the Supreme Court justice assigned to circuit duty, to hold court before the district judge alone, but in light of Underwood's poor reputation for objectivity and fairness, the lawyers insisted on Chase's presence at any trial that might take place. It also seemed appropriate, given the importance of the case, to require the presence of the chief justice of the United States and not just that of a controversial district court judge. Furthermore, the rules of appellate jurisdiction did not allow appeals in federal criminal cases. This effectively ensured that the only method of review in the Davis case would be a split judicial decision: if the district and Supreme Court justice disagreed, the case would receive an automatic appeal to the Supreme Court.

Barring new legislation to ensure the review of criminal decisions, the Davis case – with its possible supremely important pronouncement on the legality of secession – simply could not reach the Supreme Court without Chase's presence. The cabinet discussed the possibility of trying the case in the absence of the chief justice. Seward urged a trial before Underwood alone rather than a further delay, but Browning, McCulloch, and Stanbery balked, on the grounds that "it would be a farce and disreputable to the Government to try such a case before Underwood."[41] Prosecutor Evarts agreed that he could "not expect to proceed with the case in the absence of the Ch. J."[42]

O'Conor was willing, however, to seize on the indictment to secure Davis's release on bail. The new indictment had, if nothing else, ostensibly established that Davis was now within the jurisdiction of the federal civil courts, although a formal copy of the indictment had not been served on Davis personally, as required by law.[43] *Ex parte Milligan*,

---

[41] Orville Hickman Browning, *Diary of Orville Hickman Browning*, ed. James G. Randall (Springfield: Illinois State Historical Library, 1925), 165.

[42] William Evarts to Richard Henry Dana, November 15, 1867, Box 17, Dana Family Papers, MHS.

[43] Under the Crimes Act of 1790, "any person who shall be accused and indicted of treason, shall have a copy of the indictment ... delivered unto him." Crimes Act of 1790, 1 Stat. 112, § 29, (1790). Davis's lawyer James Brady confirmed Davis had not received one. Case of Davis, *Reports of Cases Decided by Chief Justice Chase*, ed. Bradley Johnson (New York: Diossy, 1876), 24 (hereafter cited as *Chase's Reports*). The official citation to the Davis case is 24 7 F. Cas. 63, 1 Chase 1 (C.C.D. Va.

decided a few months earlier, had confirmed the federal courts' ability to issue writs of habeas corpus freeing prisoners from military custody.[44] On June 5, 1866, Davis's lawyers James Brady, James Lyons, William B. Reed, and Robert Ould, acting on O'Conor's instructions, appeared before Judge Underwood and demanded that Davis either be tried immediately or released on bail. In spite of their indignant protestations about the violation of Davis's Sixth Amendment right to a speedy trial, Davis's lawyers were well aware that the government was not prepared to proceed: they were looking only to free Davis from Fort Monroe. To Underwood, they emphasized Davis's ill health, telling the judge that Davis's sickly condition was growing worse in the summer heat. Unmoved, Underwood rejected the bail application, staying the trial until the prosecution was ready and until Chief Justice Salmon Chase was able to attend court, most likely in October.

Unsatisfied, O'Conor and co-counsel Thomas Pratt appeared in Chief Justice Chase's chambers in Washington three days later – on June 8, a Friday – to request that Chase, as circuit judge, bail Davis himself.[45] Chase denied their petition, citing the shakiness of federal civil court authority in the unreconstructed states of the former Confederacy. Martial law had not ended in Virginia, and Chase

1867–1871) (No. 3,621a), but references to the official report will hereafter be to the original report in *Chase's Reports*, rather than the version in the *Federal Reporter*, as the report was abridged when reprinted.

44 Ex parte Milligan, 71 U.S. 2 (1866). It was unclear whether Milligan's reach extended to former Confederate territory, as the opinion emphasized that Milligan himself applied for habeas in Indiana, and "Martial rule can never exist where the courts are open and in the proper and unobstructed exercise of their jurisdiction. It is also confined to the locality of actual war." *Milligan*, 71 U.S. at 127. In 1866 there was some debate about whether a state of war still existed in the states of the former Confederacy. See Andrew Johnson, Proclamation 157, August 20, 1866, in Andrew Johnson, *The Papers of Andrew Johnson*, ed. Paul Bergeron, 16 vols. (Knoxville: University of Tennessee Press, 1967–69), 11: 100; Gregory Downs, *After Appomattox* (Cambridge, MA: Harvard University Press, 2015).

45 Bail was permitted under the Judiciary Act of 1789, §33(b), 1 Stat. 73. Anticipating that Chase might object to granting bail in potentially capital treason cases, O'Conor set his co-counsel to work researching cases in which Chase had bailed (or continued bail for) treason defendants in Maryland, beginning with an investigation of lawyer and former Confederate general Bradley Johnson, who had been under indictment for treason before serving as Chase's official reporter of decisions in the circuit court. See Charles O'Conor to William Wilkins Glenn, June 5, 1866, Box 3, John Glenn Papers, MdHS; "Chief Justice at Chambers in re proposed application to release Jefferson Davis on bail," June 7, 1866, "Correspondence, 1864–1874," Box 3, Bradley T. Johnson Papers, DU.

declared himself unwilling to preside over a court that "must act in a quasi-military character, subject to such control by the President and by Congress as might be deemed essential to complete pacification and restoration." Chase refused to issue rulings that could be peremptorily overruled by the military.[46] He did, however, suggest that as a district judge, Underwood was not subject to the same constraints. As the chief justice of the United States, and "exercising, as I did, the highest judicial authority of the nation," Chase was, in his own estimation, required to act with more circumspection than other federal judges. He thus urged O'Conor and Pratt to renew their application to Judge Underwood – immediately.[47]

O'Conor left Chase's office on June 8 convinced that the chief justice had quietly but directly instructed Underwood to grant bail. Indeed, O'Conor had received a tip from an inside source to that effect. By delegating the task to Underwood, Chase could stand on ceremony but still rid himself of a troublesome case. Accordingly, on the following Monday, O'Conor appeared in Richmond again before Judge Underwood and renewed the application for Davis's bail before the district court. O'Conor was shocked to discover that Underwood's opinion had not changed over the course of the weekend: Davis's bail was again denied.

O'Conor quickly pieced the story together. On Friday Underwood had been set to grant bail, but he had been dissuaded by the events of the intervening weekend. Davis's staunchly Republican opponents in Congress, led by George Boutwell of the House Judiciary Committee, had opposed the movement afoot to release Davis on bail. In response to that effort, the committee had hurriedly introduced a resolution, later followed up by a report, indicating that Davis had been heavily involved in planning the Lincoln assassination. On Monday, Boutwell had introduced the resolution implicating Davis in Lincoln's murder, over the objections of Democrat and fellow committee member Andrew Jackson Rogers, whose protests of Davis's innocence had

---

[46] This state of affairs was, as Chase intimated, at odds with the spirit if not the letter of *Ex parte Milligan*, 71 U.S. 2 (1866), which proclaimed the civil authority superior to the power of military justice.

[47] Case of Davis, *Chase's Reports*, 26–29; Bradley Johnson, "Chief Justice at Chambers in re proposed application to release Jefferson Davis on bail," folder marked "Correspondence, 1864–68," Box 3, Bradley T. Johnson Papers, DU.

been shouted down on the House floor. In the face of such a reaction, Underwood could not afford to free Davis. O'Conor surmised that "the Radicals in the House managed to terrify Underwood into refusing to bail the Chief."[48]

The demonstrated strength of the Radicals' opposition to Davis's release also terrified O'Conor, who abandoned his requests for Davis's release from military custody. Throughout the summer of 1866, O'Conor petitioned the president to move Davis from Fort Monroe to Fort Warren in Boston or, better yet, to Fort Lafayette in New York, where O'Conor could consult with him regularly. Military prison, as O'Conor now realized, was preferable to some other alternatives. If the president were to free Davis from military imprisonment, it was entirely possible that, on his release, "the [Radicals would] manage to have him arrested and cast into a common jail as a criminal under indictment by a civil court." O'Conor appealed to Johnson's political instincts, reminding the president that Davis's death on his watch would be an exceedingly unattractive prospect and that "there [was a] great danger that, under any course of treatment, [Davis] may not survive the summer."[49] O'Conor's pleas to move Davis fell on deaf ears. Davis's continued incarceration at Fort Monroe, unpleasant though it was, kept him out of the control of the Radicals as the attorney general prepared to try a case "which deeply concerns the national Justice."[50]

Although Davis was still imprisoned at Fort Monroe at the end of 1866, O'Conor's strategy of avoidance and delay had maneuvered the government into a much more difficult position than it was in just after the war, in May 1865. Certain options that were available in 1865 were now infeasible in the more cautious climate of 1866. Thanks to the efforts of Attorney General Speed and others concerned about the

---

[48] Francis Burton Harrison, ed., *Aris Sonis Focisque: Being a Memoir of an American Family, the Harrisons of Skimino, and Particularly of Jesse Burton Harrison and Burton Norvell Harrison* (New York: De Vinne Press, 1910), 196–97. See also *New York Herald*, June 12, 1866.

[49] Charles O'Conor to Thomas G. Pratt, July 12, 1866, Box 247, Jefferson Davis Amnesty Papers, NA-DC; Charles O'Conor to Edwards Pierrepont, August 7, 1866, and Charles O'Conor to Henry Stanbery, August 17, 1866, Jefferson Davis Case File, NA-CP.

[50] Edwin Stanton, "Advice in the Matter of Jefferson Davis, in Cabinet," Reel 11, Edwin Stanton Papers, LC.

war's corrosive effect on the rule of law, the Constitution seemed less pliable in 1866 than it had a year and half earlier. It no longer seemed that the law would inexorably ratify the results of the war.[51] Davis had also managed to recruit allies from across the political spectrum, some of whom supported him for the unlikeliest of reasons.

---

[51] For instance, when John Surratt returned to the United States in 1867 to face trial for the Lincoln assassination, he was tried before a federal civil court, in contrast to the hastily convened military commission his mother had faced in May 1865. While Mary Surratt had been convicted and hanged, the civil jury trying her son for murder two years later failed to reach a verdict. On John Surratt's trial, see Elizabeth D. Leonard, *Lincoln's Avengers: Justice, Revenge, and Reunion after the Civil War* (New York: W. W. Norton, 2004), 229–63; Andrew C. A. Jampoler, *The Last Lincoln Conspirator* (Annapolis, MD: Naval Institute Press, 2008).

8

Thaddeus Stevens, Secession, and Radical Reconstruction

In 1866, Pennsylvania congressman Thaddeus Stevens, one of the most radical of the Radical Republicans, sought to forge an alliance with Jefferson Davis. This would have surprised outsiders, to say the least, because Stevens was a staunch racial egalitarian whose political views were diametrically opposed to Davis's. There was also no personal connection between Davis and Stevens, although the two had held national office at the same time. While Davis was in prison, however, Stevens sent two letters to Fort Monroe tendering an offer to represent Davis in his treason trial.[1] Like O'Conor, Stevens was interested in Davis's connection with secession. But unlike O'Conor, who genuinely wanted to save Davis's life, Stevens's interest in the case was purely instrumental. As Stevens (and Davis) recognized, proving the constitutionality of secession at this late date could, ironically, further the Radical Republican agenda for Reconstruction.

---

[1] Thaddeus Stevens to R. J. Haldeman, January 8, 1866, Box 6, Clement Clay Papers, DU. Davis's counsel William B. Reed also confirmed Stevens's offer to represent Davis, telling Edward McPherson, who collected Stevens's papers for a possible biography, that "Mr. Stevens was willing and anxious to take part in the defence of Mr. Davis the President of the late Confederate States. I was a recipient of a message to that effect." William B. Reed to Edward McPherson, January 20, 1869, Box 50, Edward McPherson Papers, LC. See also William B. Reed to Edward McPherson, January 13, 1869, cited in Fawn Brodie, *Thaddeus Stevens: Scourge of the South* (New York: W. W. Norton, 1959), 399 n. 27 (original not found at Library of Congress); R. J. Haldeman to Virginia Clay, June 28, July 24, 1865, Box 5, Clement Clay Papers, DU.

During Reconstruction, the federal government retained ultimate control over the former Confederate states, placing troops in the states, removing state governors and appointing new ones, mandating that the states rewrite state constitutions to outlaw slavery, requiring the states to ratify new constitutional amendments, insisting that the states repeal the secession ordinances of 1860–61, and, ultimately, determining how and when these states would be readmitted as full members of the Union. As no explicit constitutional basis for plenary federal control over states existed, Republican politicians and constitutional theorists advanced various justifications for this unprecedented degree of federal control over the Southern states.[2]

Several of these theories were premised on the idea that the states of the former Confederacy were not full members of the federal Union following Confederate defeat. Stevens, a longtime champion of African American rights, became the primary expositor of the "conquered province" theory of Reconstruction. According to this interpretation, the seceding Southern states had effectively written themselves out of the Union during the Civil War and had become part of a separate nation. Stevens was a realist when it came to secession. Just because secession was illegitimate did not mean that the states had never exercised the right. Everyone knew that the Confederate states had not been part of the Union during the war.[3] Secession had

---

[2] These included Richard Henry Dana's "Grasp of War" theory, which premised extraordinary federal power on the grounds that a state of war still existed in the ex-Confederate states; Charles Sumner's state suicide theory, which posited that by attempting secession – an illegal act – the Southern states had reverted to territorial status; Samuel Shellabarger's theory, which relied on the Constitution's guaranty of a republican form of government to each of the states in order to justify federal intervention in the former Confederate states; and Thaddeus Stevens's conquered province theory, discussed in this chapter. See Eric L. McKitrick, *Andrew Johnson and Reconstruction* (Chicago: University of Chicago Press, 1960), 99–119, and John W. Burgess, *Reconstruction and the Constitution, 1866–1876* (New York: Scribner's, 1905). See also Gregory Downs, *After Appomattox* (Cambridge, MA: Harvard University Press, 2015), although Downs does not emphasize the theoretical grounding of these policies.

[3] *Congressional Globe*, 39th Cong., 1st sess., December 18, 1865, 73. See Burgess, *Reconstruction and the Constitution*, 59; William A. Dunning, "The Constitution of the United States in Reconstruction," in William A. Dunning, *Essays on the Civil War and Reconstruction* (New York: Macmillan, 1898), 109; Eric Foner, *Reconstruction: America's Unfinished Revolution, 1863–1877* (New York: Harper and Row, 1988), 232.

not been illegal in 1861, in this theory; only Union victory in 1865 had made it so.

Union victory over the Confederacy meant that the conquering sovereign (the U.S. government) had complete dominion over the vanquished Southern states. For as long as the federal government wished, it could exercise full authority over the Southern "states" by virtue of the right of conquest. Although he never articulated its legal basis, Stevens's conquered province theory drew on the doctrine of conquest as it had developed in England in the seventeenth century. First announced in 1608 in *Calvin's Case* by Lord Edward Coke, and later expounded in William Blackstone's *Commentaries*, the doctrine of conquest permitted the English crown to gain legal title to land by force and also to make law in conquered territory, according to prescribed rules.[4] Territory acquired by war fell into two categories, the first consisting of empty or uncultivated lands "discovered" by the English, and the second consisting of occupied territories acquired by conquest or ceded by treaty. To the "empty" lands such as the North American colonies, inhabited only by "savage" indigenous peoples, English settlers took English law, the birthright of every English subject, which immediately went into force in those areas. In conquered territory already populated by civilized peoples who had their own laws, the English king was permitted to alter and change local law at will, but until he did so the ancient laws of that country remained in place.

The U.S. Supreme Court formally incorporated the English doctrine of conquest in *Johnson v. McIntosh*. *McIntosh*, the foundational case in American Indian law, articulated the legal theory that permitted plenary federal control over – and ultimate ownership of – Indian land in the United States. Writing for the Court, Chief Justice John Marshall announced that as the successor to the English crown, the federal government could revoke Indian land title at will, based on the

---

[4] Calvin's Case (1608), 77 Eng. Rep. 377 (KB); William Blackstone, *Commentaries on the Laws of England*, ed. Edward Christian, 4 vols. (Philadelphia: R. H. Small, 1825), 1: 104–5. See also Gavin Loughton, "Calvin's Case and the Origins of the Rule Governing 'Conquest' in English Law," *Australian Journal of Legal History* 8 (2004): 143. Loughton argues that although *Calvin's Case* intimates that the law of conquest developed in medieval times, dating back to the Angevin conquest of Ireland and the conquest of Wales in the twelfth and thirteenth centuries, the rule first came into being with the colonization of America in the early seventeenth century. See Loughton, "Calvin's Case," 160.

doctrine of the English "discovery" of the theoretically "unoccupied" North American continent. Marshall's opinion necessarily dealt primarily with the government's right to extinguish the property interests of "fierce savages, whose occupation was war" and whose "character and habits" justified their having "the rights ... wrested from them."

But Marshall also took the opportunity in *McIntosh* to expound on the type of authority that would be generated through conquest of "civilized" peoples (such as the defeated Confederates). "Conquest," Marshall wrote, "gives a title which the Courts of the conqueror cannot deny." Although Marshall's language betrayed some ambivalence about the Supreme Court's affirmation of the principle that legal rights can be created through sustained violence, he noted that American claims to Indian land "have been maintained and established ... by the sword." The courts were obliged to sustain the brutal policies that the political branches had undertaken. In language later echoed by Justice Robert Grier in the aftermath of the Civil War, Marshall acknowledged that a huge stretch of the continent was held by force, and "it is not for the Courts of this country to question the validity of this title, or to sustain one which is incompatible with it." Marshall softened the impact of his validation of absolute legal authority generated by the force of arms, noting that humanitarian impulses and public opinion would serve as an effective check on the baser instincts of the conqueror of a civilized people.[5]

Marshall's ideas – and his reliance on Lord Coke – came in handy half a century later. A postbellum ruling that the states of the former Confederacy had removed themselves from the Union through secession, and thus constituted a separate, conquered nation, would help to bolster the theoretical basis of the Radical Republican agenda in Congress. The doctrine of conquest would authorize the U.S. government to exercise plenary control over internal affairs in the Southern

---

[5] Johnson v. M'Intosh, 21 U.S. 543 (1823). For Grier's similar argument, see Chapter 4, discussing his dissent in Texas v. White, 74 U.S. 700 (1868). For more details, see Robert A. Williams Jr., *The American Indian in Western Legal Thought: The Discourses of Conquest* (New York: Oxford University Press, 1990), 199, 200, 312–17; David H. Getches, Charles F. Wilkinson, and Robert A. Williams Jr., *Cases and Materials on Federal Indian Law* (St. Paul: West Group, 1998), 63–72; Lindsay Robertson, *Conquest by Law* (New York: Oxford University Press, 2005).

states and to replace their laws at will – and Thaddeus Stevens was eager to make use of the theory. Richard Haldeman, a Pennsylvania Democrat and supporter of Clement Clay, first approached Stevens on Clay's behalf in July 1865. Stevens promptly informed Haldeman that he did not believe either Davis or Clay could be convicted of treason, because by conferring belligerent status on the Confederacy, the United States had implicitly consented to treat its combatants under international rather than domestic law. Stevens told Haldeman that "having acknowledged him [Clay] as a belligerent, I should treat him as such, and in no other light, unless he was in conspiracy to assassinate Mr. Lincoln, of which I have seen no evidence and do not believe."[6]

Stevens also stated on the floor of the House in 1866 that "he did not believe that Mr. Davis could be tried for treason, nor that he had been guilty of treason. His offence was that of a belligerent, not of a traitor."[7] In this, Stevens echoed Horace Greeley and Gerrit Smith in arguing that Davis could not be held individually liable for the actions of the Confederacy, which the U.S. government had treated as a separate, belligerent power during the war. Stevens reiterated that "the war was acknowledged by other nations as a public war between independent belligerents. The parties acknowledged each other as such, and claimed to be governed by the law of nations and the law of war in their treatment of each other." Davis lawyer William B. Reed recognized the congruity between Stevens's views and those of the Davis camp, characterizing Stevens's speech as "fearful ... in its temper, tho' in its doctrine is not so unfavorable to *our* case."[8]

After Stevens's death in late 1868, his friend and estate executor Edward McPherson, clerk of the House of Representatives, corresponded with Reed about Stevens's involvement in the Davis case. Reed assured McPherson that his deceased friend Stevens had indeed made a secret offer to participate in the Davis defense. McPherson was incredulous. Reed reiterated his claim, telling McPherson that "I think I am right and you are wrong about Mr. Davis' case. It was to

[6] Thaddeus Stevens to R. J. Haldeman, January 8, 1866, Box 6, Clement Clay Papers, DU.
[7] *Congressional Globe*, 39th Cong., 1st sess., December 11, 1866, 69.
[8] *Congressional Globe*, 39th Cong., 2d sess., January 3, 1867, 252; William B. Reed to Varina Davis, January 3, 1867, Box 24, Jefferson Davis Papers, MC.

the trial in court that he referred when he expressed a willingness to take part."[9]

Reed reported that Davis's attorneys respected Stevens's talents as an attorney but objected to his Radical agenda for Reconstruction. Davis had rejected Stevens's offer, Reed said, "for obvious reasons, none of them disparaging to Mr. Stevens. His doctrine was that the Southern States were fought and conquered as foreign enemies and therefore there was no treason."[10] As Davis himself stated much later, he chose to decline Stevens's offer, "not from any lack of confidence in his ability ... but I was aware what would be his line of argument. It would have been that the seceding states were conquered provinces, and were to all intents and purposes a foreign power which had been overthrown.... That would have been an excellent argument for me, but not for my people." Burton Harrison was less sanguine about Stevens's offer. "The wily old rascal has a purpose of his own to accomplish," he remarked in 1866. "He wants Mr. Davis tried for treason and acquitted, then he thinks his nice little political schemes will come along as a natural consequence."[11]

Stevens was not the only one who saw the logical alignment of Radical Reconstruction and the doctrine of secession. Attorney General Edward Bates had once confided his own fears about the consequences of Confederate belligerency to the prominent Boston lawyer Richard Henry Dana: "There is no escape ... in law or logic. If Virginia be *out* of the Union, it *must* be because her convention voted her out. And that ordinance, to produce that legal result, *must* be a lawful and valid act. And all who hold that doctrine *must* be secessionists."[12]

---

[9] William B. Reed to Edward McPherson, January 20, 1869, Box 50, Edward McPherson Papers, LC.

[10] William B. Reed to Edward McPherson, January 20, 1869, Box 50, Edward McPherson Papers, LC.

[11] Jefferson Davis interview, *Cincinnati Enquirer*, July 12, 1881; Burton Harrison to Mother, June 13, 1866, in James Elliot Walmsley, "Some Unpublished Letters of Burton N. Harrison," *Publications of the Mississippi Historical Society* 8 (1904): 81, 83.

[12] Edward Bates to Richard Henry Dana, December 28, 1863, Box 16, Dana Family Papers, MHS. A logical counter to this argument would be that an event need not be legal to effect legal consequences. For instance, if a man escaped from prison, the state would not be forced to pretend he was still in captivity just because his actions had not been legal in securing his freedom. See John Harrison, "The Lawfulness of the Reconstruction Amendments," *University of Chicago Law Review* 68

The *Richmond Dispatch* also noted this incongruent connection. The paper lambasted Stevens and his Radical Republican cronies for their desire to place the Confederate states under the control of the federal government. "If these States are out of the Union," the paper maintained, "his deductions are logical enough.... [T]he question is, how did they get out, for they certainly were in at one time." The *Dispatch* argued that Stevens must be endorsing the legality of secession, which should operate to exonerate Davis: "It must have been by Secession; and this, we believe, is a part of Thad's creed. If the States went out by secession, the war was against an independent power, and Jefferson Davis and his compeers, so far from being traitors ... are patriots." Only if the government endorsed President Johnson's theory that the Confederate states had never left the Union, the paper said, "can a case of treason be made out."[13]

At the same time, exploiting the connection between secession and Radical theories of Reconstruction earned Stevens the enmity of more moderate Republicans. As Gregory Downs argued in *After Appomattox*, the theoretical foundations of Reconstruction were not all that strongly connected to the on-the-ground activity in the postbellum South. Critics charged that Stevens was highly selective about when and where he decided to be doctrinaire. He deployed doctrine when it furthered his political goals and ignored it when it was convenient to do so. Stevens and fellow Radical Charles Sumner had, surprisingly, emerged as two of the foremost critics of the various proposals to engineer a civil jury that would be certain to convict Davis. They pushed for trial by military commission instead, "as belligerents, under the law of nations and the laws of war." If Davis were to be tried civilly, they believed that he had to be "tried, if any where, only in the Richmond District. The doctrine of constructive presence, and of constructive treason, will never, I hope, pollute our statutes, or judicial decisions." Stevens insisted on this point, even though, he acknowledged, "it is obvious that no conviction could ever be had."[14]

(2001): 442–43, on the legal effectiveness of actions undertaken by the illegal governments in the seceded states. Harrison focuses not on the legal effect of secession itself but on the Supreme Court's recognition of the governments' de facto status.

[13] *Richmond Dispatch*, December 25, 1865.

[14] Thaddeus Stevens, "'Reconstruction,' September 6, 1865, in Lancaster," and "'Reconstruction,' December 18, 1865, in Congress," in Thaddeus Stevens, *The*

Wisconsin senator James Doolittle – a moderate Republican – was outraged. Doolittle was the architect of the 1865 proposal to pack federal juries in order to achieve treason convictions, which Stevens and other Radicals had sanctimoniously opposed because it polluted the integrity of the Anglo-American jury trial. But Stevens and his allies, Doolittle surmised, only pretended concern about the constitutional rights of criminal defendants. The real motive behind his objection to the Doolittle bill was a desire to impede Davis's civil trial – and thus to preserve the secession argument in order to bolster the case for military Reconstruction. In Doolittle's estimation, the Radicals had pushed for a trial of prominent Confederates by military commission because they feared that a civil trial would expose their hypocrisy in advocating states' rights theories. Stevens's regard for the normal rules of criminal procedure and jury selection struck Doolittle as entirely disingenuous.

Doolittle blasted Stevens's unsavory motives in his private correspondence. A friend encouraged him to "press to a vote and make a speech on your bill to facilitate treason trials, and show up to the public why Chase, Sumner and Thad Stevens oppose a civil trial and support a military commission to escape an exposure of their secession dogmas about the fugitive slave law." The Radicals had deployed state sovereignty theories intermittently – most prominently in the 1850s with the passage of state personal liberty laws to thwart the enforcement of the federal Fugitive Slave Act. Now the argument was potentially useful again for propping up a plan for the wholesale reconstruction of the Southern states. Conveniently, this would also strengthen the Radicals' political position by making it impossible for the president to try Davis without endorsing this theory. In Doolittle's view, Stevens was a wily operator who sought to manipulate the law for his own political advantage. In response, his friend urged him to break the stalemate in Davis's case: "Strike boldly and show whose

---

Selected Papers of Thaddeus Stevens, ed. Beverly Wilson Palmer and Holly Byers Ochoa, 2 vols. (Pittsburgh: University of Pittsburgh Press, 1997), 2: 24. See William Wilkins Glenn, *Between North and South: A Maryland Journalist Views the Civil War*, ed. Bayly Ellen Marks and Mark Norton Schatz (Cranbury, NJ: Associated University Presses, 1976), 283; Varina Davis, *Jefferson Davis, Ex-President of the Confederate States: A Memoir*, 2 vols. (New York: Belford, 1890), 2: 782–86, for more information on Stevens's views.

fault it is why Davis is not tried for treason, and that the radicals by refusing legislation on the subject are embarrassing the President."[15]

Although Davis and his defense team did not accept Stevens's offer, the idea that the staunchest opponents of the white South – the Radical Republicans – might have something to gain by championing Davis's cause and the cause of secession encouraged Davis's team. The two judges assigned to preside over the case (Judge Underwood and Chief Justice Chase) were both well-known Radical Republicans, and Chase had come close to endorsing state sovereignty views in the past. O'Conor floated the possibility that Judge Underwood – despite being "a devoted courtier at the feet of Sambo," in O'Conor's biting terminology – might actually decide in Davis's favor to establish that secession was legal. This could further Underwood's Radical agenda by shoring up theoretical support for Reconstruction. Underwood was, as O'Conor reminded Davis, "a thorough Thad. Stevens radical. Of course he believes that the Seceding States read themselves out of the Union and have been conquered. He sees that these premises lead inevitably to your acquittal."[16]

---

[15] R. P. L. Baber to James R. Doolittle, February 28, 1866, and see also R. P. L. Baber to James Doolittle, March 29, 1866, Box 1, James R. Doolittle Papers, LC [microfilm edition]. For a discussion of the relationship between Baber and Doolittle, see Duane Mowry, "Richard Plantagenet Llewelyn Baber: A Sketch and Some of His Letters," *Ohio History* 19 (1910): 370. Most scholars who have looked at Stevens's position on postwar treason trials have highlighted only his advocacy of military punishment. Hans L. Trefousse, *Thaddeus Stevens: Nineteenth-Century Egalitarian* (Chapel Hill: University of North Carolina Press, 1997), 170–71; William A. Blair, *Why Didn't the North Hang Some Rebels?* (Milwaukee: Marquette University Press, 2004), 16; William A. Blair, *With Malice toward Some: Treason and Loyalty in the Civil War Era* (Chapel Hill: University of North Carolina Press, 2014), 249. On the one hand, Stevens advocated military trials for offenses under the law of nations, and on the other, he opposed conducting civil trials that dispensed with constitutional niceties, but his views were actually coherent. Fawn Brodie, who, among Stevens's biographers, paid the most attention to the duality in his thinking on this point, found his views to be inconsistent. She characterized his willingness to defend Davis as an "about-face" from his initial position that Davis should have been summarily shot when he was captured, or that he should have been tried before a military commission for war crimes. Brodie, *Thaddeus Stevens*, 399.

[16] Charles O'Conor to Varina Howell Davis, October 21, 1867, and Charles O'Conor to Jefferson Davis, October 2, 1867, Box 24, Jefferson Davis Papers, MC. In a letter to Charles Sumner, Underwood confirmed that he had been convinced, "very much against my will," by Sumner's writings on the view that the Confederate states should remain under the control of the federal government until they "submit[ted] to a genuine republican government." John C. Underwood to Charles Sumner, July 17, 1865, Reel 34, Charles Sumner Papers, HU.

The radicalism of both Chase and Underwood could, ironically, work to Davis's advantage. Both judges were unpredictable, and they clearly pursued their own agendas in presiding over Jefferson Davis's case. Chapter 9 turns to Chase and Underwood to explore their thinking in greater detail.

9

Underwood and Chase

John C. Underwood, the district judge, and Chief Justice Salmon P. Chase, assigned to circuit duty in Virginia, were known to be Radicals at a time when some Radical Republicans were nudging toward an endorsement of secession because of its connection with a sweeping program of Reconstruction in the South. Both also behaved questionably. In truth, if a jury would be unpredictable, the judges assigned to preside over the Davis case were equally erratic and worrisome. Underwood manifested open hostility toward former Confederates and appeared too eager to preside over the case, eschewing judicial evenhandedness. Chase, on the other hand, was too cautious, abandoning his duty to preside because of the trial's troublesome political considerations.

Underwood, in particular, was something of a renegade. Originally from upstate New York, he had moved to Virginia in the late 1840s when he married a Virginia woman, a cousin of Stonewall Jackson. A decade later, Underwood joined the nascent Republican Party. He was forced from his adopted home by a mob angry about his fiery antislavery tirades at the party's national convention. Underwood returned to New York, where he remained until he was appointed, in the midst of the Civil War, to serve on the federal court in loyal Virginia territory – primarily Alexandria and Norfolk (Figure 9.1).[1]

[1] See William W. Freehling, *The Road to Disunion: Secessionists Triumphant, 1854–1861*, 2 vols. (New York: Oxford University Press, 2008), 2: 236–40.

FIGURE 9.1 District Judge John C. Underwood. Library of Congress.

Underwood courted scandal during and after the war when he engaged in what seemed to be self-dealing in the administration of the Second Confiscation Act, by directing the confiscation and subsequent public sale of property belonging to the notorious rebel William McVeigh. When McVeigh stood accused of disloyalty to the U.S. government, Judge Underwood refused to allow him to answer the charges against him, on the theory that he was "a resident of the city of Richmond, within the Confederate lines, and a rebel."[2]

McVeigh's residence in Confederate territory disqualified him, in Underwood's opinion, from asserting his personal loyalty to the United

---

[2] McVeigh v. United States, 78 U.S. 259 (1870); Windsor v. McVeigh, 93 U.S. 274 (1876); Gregory v. McVeigh, 90 U.S. 294 (1874). See also Day v. Micou, 85 U.S. 156 (1873).

States, in spite of the fact that the Confiscation Act operated on individuals who had committed acts of treason, rather than on Confederate territory at large.[3] Having stricken McVeigh's answer, Underwood entered a default judgment against him and condemned the property. In the course of subsequent litigation, it was revealed that Underwood – along with his wife and business associates – had acted to buy up McVeigh's various properties in Richmond at drastically reduced prices. Underwood had also interpreted the Confiscation Act as destroying all previous interests in the property, rather than only those that belonged to the disloyal owner. This had the effect of defrauding McVeigh's (Northern) creditors. Underwood's decisions in the *McVeigh* case were subsequently overturned by the Supreme Court.[4]

Judge Underwood was becoming an embarrassment for the Virginia Republican Party, but he did not lack the zeal to convict Confederates. Charles O'Conor had predicted that Underwood would follow his idol Thaddeus Stevens in tying secession to the Radical vision of Reconstruction, and try to ensure Davis's acquittal to achieve real social change in the occupied South. But Underwood resisted Stevens's

---

[3] See 12 Stat. 589 (1863). By contrast, the Captured and Abandoned Property Act operated on Confederate territory, with an ex-post reclamation process for those who could prove individual loyalty to the Union. 12 Stat. 820, § 3 (1863). The Supreme Court confirmed this distinction in *Mrs. Alexander's Cotton*, 69 U.S. 404 (1864).

[4] See Charles Fairman, *Reconstruction and Reunion*, 2 vols. (New York: Macmillan, 1971), 823–28; John O. Peters, *From Marshall to Moussaoui: Federal Justice in the Eastern District of Virginia* (Petersburg, VA: Dietz Press, 2013), 63–67. The Supreme Court also checked Underwood in 1868 when he began releasing criminal defendants who applied to him for writs of habeas corpus. Section Three of the Fourteenth Amendment barred former Confederates from serving in state office, and Underwood interpreted this to mean that pro-Confederate state judges were disqualified from serving on the bench. According to Underwood, the amendment itself (without enabling legislation) immediately effected the removal of all state judges thus disqualified, rendering all of their decisions and convictions invalid. Under this theory, Underwood began vacating criminal convictions, an action that led state and federal judicial officials to panic; if unchecked, Underwood would wind up emptying Virginia's jails. Further complicating the issue was the fact that Underwood was presiding over the habeas petitions (as a circuit court judge) alone, without awaiting the presence of Chief Justice Chase, which meant there could be no appeal from his rulings. In response, the state of Virginia took the extraordinary measure of filing an original petition in the Supreme Court to seek a writ of prohibition that would prevent Underwood from releasing prisoners. The Court ruled in favor of Virginia, declaring that enforcement legislation by Congress was necessary to effect judicial removal under Section Three. Act of March 27, 1868, § 2, 15 Stat. 44 (1868); Habeas Corpus Act of 1867, 14 Stat. 385 (1867). See Fairman, *Reconstruction and Reunion*, 601–6.

influence in this area and remained committed to the task of punishing prominent Confederates for treason. As early as April 1865, Underwood notified the president that he was "encouraged by your recent declarations in favor of the punishment of the leading rebels," telling Johnson that he was ready to summon a grand jury to indict Confederates. He sought to assure Johnson of the pro-Union credentials of some of the Virginia court's personnel. In Underwood's opinion, it was imperative that treason trials go forward as soon as possible. The South could become a perilous place for loyal Union men if the government did not act decisively. "The returning rebels now swarming in our towns are so defiant in their conduct," Underwood reported, "that the condition of loyal men in this State will be not only uncomfortable but extremely unsafe unless the power of the Government to punish treason shall be fully demonstrated."[5]

Underwood did not imagine that this would be an easy task in Virginia. As he revealed to Attorney General James Speed, Underwood suspected U.S. Attorney Lucius Chandler of being a Confederate sympathizer. The judge had observed that "Chandler is constantly engaged with leading rebels in advising and preparing papers to aid them in procuring pardons from the President." While this in itself might have seemed innocuous enough, Underwood had heard from several sources that J. R. Anderson, who had formerly operated the Tredegar Iron Works during the war, and several of his friends, "have promised Mr. Chandler $200,000 if he shall succeed in procuring their pardons." This led Underwood to believe that Chandler was, "for some consideration ... neglecting his public duties."[6]

[5] John C. Underwood to Andrew Johnson, April 21, 1865, Attorney General Letters Received, Virginia, Attorney General's Records, Record Group 60, NA-CP. Underwood's court (sitting in Norfolk) secured indictments against a number of leading Confederates in May 1865, including Robert E. Lee and Jubal Early, but Davis was not among them. As Judge Underwood later explained, "Several members of the grand jury gave as a reason for not having indicted [Davis] that he had been already indicted in the District of Columbia and that it would be a work of supererogation to indict him over again." Indictments against Various Confederate Leaders, U.S. Circuit Court, Virginia District, Ended Cases, 1–68, Federal Records, U.S. v. Jefferson Davis, LVA; *Impeachment Investigation: Testimony Taken before the Judiciary Committee of the House of Representatives in the Investigation of the Charges against Andrew Johnson* (Washington, DC: Government Printing Office, 1867), 578–79 (testimony of John C. Underwood).

[6] John C. Underwood to James Speed, July 28, 1865, Jefferson Davis Case File, NA-CP. Davis's defense attorney Charles O'Conor also indicated that he believed Chandler

Even more problematic, from Underwood's perspective, was ensuring that a jury summoned from formerly Confederate Virginia would convict Davis. He was determined to do whatever he could to impanel a pro-Union jury, even going to the very limits of the law – or beyond – to do so. In January 1866 Underwood testified before the Joint Committee on Reconstruction about the intractable problem of the pro-Confederate jury pool in Virginia and baldly proposed the solution of packing juries to return guilty verdicts. Underwood confirmed that he did not believe that Davis or Robert E. Lee could be convicted otherwise. When pressed about whether he could so pack a jury to convict Davis, Underwood responded: "I think it would be very difficult, but it could be done; I could pack a jury to convict him: I know very earnest, ardent Union men in Virginia."[7]

Indeed, Underwood seemed to be too enthusiastic – and far too candid – about his efforts to secure a conviction against Davis. Others (such as O'Conor) did their own scheming behind the scenes, but Underwood's bluntness about government maneuvers in treason prosecutions, coupled with his self-serving behavior in the confiscation suits, ensured that many observers and participants in the Davis case viewed him warily. Even the ultra-Republican newspaper the *Nation* declared that "the cause both of justice and good government would

might be sympathetic to Davis, reporting to Davis's wife that Chandler "says he will try to get a white jury," against the distinct wishes of the more Radical Underwood. Charles O'Conor to Varina Davis, October 21, 1867, Box 24, Jefferson Davis Papers, MC. Chandler later resigned, probably at the request of William Evarts, in the summer of 1868, but Evarts's main difficulties with Chandler stemmed from his incompetence, rather than his rebel sympathies, as will be discussed in Chapter 11. Chandler committed suicide in 1876 by drowning himself in the Atlantic Ocean off the coast of Norfolk, where he had been employed as a pension agent. He had suffered a severe head injury, from which he never fully recovered, when the Virginia state capitol collapsed in 1870. *Norfolk Landmark*, April 18, 1876.

7 Report of the Joint Committee on Reconstruction, H.R. Rep. 39–30 pt. 2, at 10 (1866) (testimony of John C. Underwood). According to the reported decision in Davis's case, prepared ten years after the fact, Underwood initially hesitated before charging Confederates with treason. See Case of Davis, in *Reports of Cases Decided by Chief Justice Chase*, ed. Bradley Johnson (New York: Diossy, 1876), 8 (hereafter cited as *Chase's Reports*). But the case report was quite biased in Davis's favor; see discussion in Chapter 14. Underwood's own writings and statements at the time reveal that he was quite eager to see Davis convicted. A year after his statement to the Joint Committee, Underwood gave a more measured assessment of the need to pack a jury to convict Davis. According to Underwood, as of 1867, there would be "no difficulty in the world [to secure a jury that would convict Davis]; but a year ago very few men would have had the courage to serve upon a jury." *Impeachment Investigation*, 580 (testimony of John C. Underwood).

be served if the fountains of [Underwood's] eloquence could be sealed up," and the Radical *Chicago Tribune* called him a "disgrace to the bench and to the profession of law."[8]

Davis's supporters were, unsurprisingly, even more wary of Underwood. Paul Bagley, who had earlier sought unsuccessfully to broker a deal between Johnson and Davis for Davis's pardon, considered it imperative to remove Davis from Underwood's grasp. Bagley implored the president to ensure that Davis would have another judge, telling Johnson that Underwood had "stated to me that under existing instructions in regard to jurors that he was sure a jury could be impaneled that would convict Jefferson Davis ... and so far from making any secret of this plan advised me to suggest it to the country: to all of which I can testify." In Bagley's opinion, conducting Davis's trial before Underwood would amount to a certain miscarriage of justice. "It used to be fashionable to try a man before they hanged him," Bagley commented.[9]

Underwood's jaundiced attitude concerned Davis's lawyers as they renewed their bid to secure his release on bail in May 1867.[10] To combat Underwood's bias against their client, they had taken precautions to ensure a good outcome. What followed was an elaborately staged performance in the federal court in Richmond. O'Conor had arranged with the prosecuting lawyers that they would not object to the motion to bail Davis, because they were not ready for trial.[11]

---

[8] See Fairman, *Reconstruction and Reunion*, 1: 601–8; Roy F. Nichols, "United States vs. Jefferson Davis, 1865–1869," *American Historical Review* 31 (January 1926): 273; *Nation*, May 9, 1867; *Chicago Tribune*, May 11, 1867. See also *Chicago Tribune*, May 19, 1867.

[9] Paul Bagley to Andrew Johnson, November 21, 1867, Jefferson Davis Case File, NA-CP; Paul Bagley to Jefferson Davis, August 31, 1867, in Jefferson Davis, *Jefferson Davis, Constitutionalist: His Letters, Papers, and Speeches*, ed. Dunbar Rowland, 10 vols. (Jackson: Mississippi Department of Archives and Records, 1923), 7: 128.

[10] In March, O'Conor dispatched George Shea to apply to Chief Justice Chase directly for bail. Chase refused to entertain Shea's appeal, telling the defense lawyers that "the application must be made to Judge Underwood at the Court in Richmond.... The case is not in my jurisdiction." So O'Conor pressed on before the circuit court – presided over by Judge Underwood alone. George Shea's notes, May 1, 1867, Box 24, Jefferson Davis Papers, MC. O'Conor applied to Chase in March because Congress finally allotted the federal circuits in March 1867, which should have obviated Chase's objection to presiding over the case in Virginia. See further discussion in this chapter of Chase's dubious interpretation of the jurisdictional constraints on him.

[11] *Impeachment Investigation*, 578–79 (testimony of John C. Underwood).

Prominent northern Republicans, including Horace Greeley, were also dispatched to the courtroom in Richmond to act as sureties on Davis's bail and to show that the decision to free Davis enjoyed widespread support. Perhaps most important, the Johnson administration's acquiescence to the habeas petition and the bail application had already been assured. Railroad mogul and Johnson administration insider John W. Garrett had been moved by Varina Davis's personal pleas on her husband's behalf. Thus motivated, Garrett visited Secretary of War Edwin Stanton, then languishing on his sickbed, to importune him to release Davis without incident into the custody of the federal marshal.[12] Stanton was angry about the intrusion, but Garrett eventually convinced him that Davis's "death in prison would be most embarrassing to the United States," and Stanton agreed to direct the military officials at Fort Monroe to comply with the writ of habeas corpus.[13] When O'Conor appeared in court in May 1867 to secure Davis's release, he "had received every assurance from the Attorney-Gen'l and others that all would go well for us."[14]

The move was still risky, however, as O'Conor's co-counsel James Lyons pointed out. Lyons warned Davis that Underwood was unpredictable and urged him to veto O'Conor's decision to apply for bail. "This step will be fatal to you," Lyons predicted. The writ of habeas corpus would move Davis from military to civil custody, and once there the erratic judge could either immediately put him on trial "before a Jury composed of negro[e]s and the worst kind of white men," or simply refuse the application for bail and "commit [Davis] to the Jail of this City [Richmond], or the State Penitentiary" where conditions would be far worse than at Fort Monroe.[15]

---

[12] See Varina Davis to John W. Garrett, September 8, 1865; April 10, [n.d., Friday morning]; May 1 and 30, 1867, Box 76, Robert Garrett Papers, LC. (My thanks to the Garrett family for allowing me use of the manuscript collection.)

[13] V. Davis, *Jefferson Davis, Ex-President of the Confederate States*, 2: 779–80. See also William Wilkins Glenn, *Between North and South: A Maryland Journalist Views the Civil War*, ed. Bayly Ellen Marks and Mark Norton Schatz (Cranbury, NJ: Associated University Presses, 1976), 283–86.

[14] Glenn, *Between North and South*, 287. See also Francis Burton Harrison, ed., *Aris Sonis Focisque: Being a Memoir of an American Family, the Harrisons of Skimino, and Particularly of Jesse Burton Harrison and Burton Norvell Harrison* (New York: De Vinne Press, 1910), 204–5.

[15] James Lyons to Jefferson Davis, May 5, 1867, Jefferson Davis Papers, Transylvania University, Lexington, KY.

But O'Conor's gamble paid off. After two years of steady rebuff, Davis was released from custody. On application by Davis's defense counsel, Underwood issued a writ of habeas corpus, which was served on Davis's jailer at Fort Monroe. With a huge crowd gathered in the courtroom on May 13, 1867, General H. S. Burton produced the body of Jefferson Davis in the circuit court. Knowing that the government was not prepared for trial, O'Conor challenged the prosecution to proceed. Prosecutor William Evarts stated that the government was unable to do so and did not object to bail.[16] In light of the prosecution's continued delays, Underwood released Davis on bail, despite the fact that he was charged with a potentially capital crime. As James Lyons had predicted, Underwood faced considerable criticism for granting Davis's bail application. An anonymous New Yorker angrily reminded the judge that "there are 100,000 graves of soldiers crying out for revenge and he a traitor is allowed to walk the streets on his own recognizance. Revenge. Revenge. Deep and complete. Will be carried out on [Davis's] d—d soul."[17]

Pandemonium erupted when Underwood released the prisoner (Figure 9.2). O'Conor recalled that Davis, "thin, wasted and careworn," was exhausted by the outpouring of emotion from the "strong men" who came to offer him their support.[18] The hysteria surrounding Davis continued in New York, where the former Confederate president stopped for a few days at O'Conor's home, on his way to Canada to be

---

[16] Sixteen men signed the bail bond, including Horace Greeley, Gerrit Smith, Cornelius Vanderbilt, and twelve Virginians. O'Conor reported to his wife that Davis's counsel had to agree to increase the amount of bail from $100,000 to $110,000 because so many Richmonders clamored to be put on the bond, telling her that "after the number was full one man burst into tears exclaiming that he would never see a happy hour again until he was let in; so we had to give more bail than the government had asked for." Augustus Schell and Horace Clark acted on behalf of Cornelius Vanderbilt. V. Davis, *Jefferson Davis, Ex-President of the Confederate States*, 2: 788; Charles O'Conor to Cornelia O'Conor, May 13, 1867, reproduced in Charles W. Sloane, "Charles O'Conor: Some Incidents of His Life, From His Private Papers, Parts I & II," *United States Catholic Historical Magazine* 4 (1891): 406–7.

[17] "A New Yorker" to John C. Underwood, May 14, 1867, Box 1, John Underwood Papers, LC. See also "Resolutions of the Grand Army of the Republic – Post No. 102," *Chicago Tribune*, May 25, 1867. At the same time, a Virginian who railed against Underwood's "tyrannical views" and termed him an "infernal damn scoundrel" recommended that he leave the state immediately. John C. Underwood scrapbook, entry 104, John Underwood Papers, LC.

[18] Charles O'Conor to Cornelia O'Conor, May 13, 1867, in Sloane, "Charles O'Conor," 406–7.

FIGURE 9.2 Jefferson Davis, free after his bail hearing in May 1867. Notice the pro-Davis tone of this image, which appeared in a Northern paper. *Harper's Weekly*, June 1, 1867.

reunited with his elder children. Displaced ex-Confederates and their New York allies came to see him in droves, prompting the Republican New Yorker and diarist George Templeton Strong to remark disgust-edly: "Why doesn't the Common Council offer him the Governor's room in the City Hall to receive his friends in?" (Figure 9.3).[19]

---

[19] Burton Harrison to Mother, May 18, 1867, in James Elliot Walmsley, "Some Unpublished Letters of Burton N. Harrison," *Publications of the Mississippi Historical Society* 8 (1904): 82; George Templeton Strong, *Diary of George Templeton Strong*, ed. Allan Nevins and Milton Halsey Thomas, 4 vols. (New York: Macmillan, 1952), 4: 136. See also Don C. Seitz, *The James Gordon Bennetts: Father and Son*

FIGURE 9.3 Jefferson and Varina Davis in Montreal in 1867, after Davis's release from Fort Monroe. Courtesy of the Archives and Records Services Division, Mississippi Department of Archives and History.

O'Conor was jubilant. In his opinion, Davis's release signaled that the administration recognized the country's softened attitude toward

(Indianapolis: Bobbs-Merrill, 1928), 205–6, for details about Davis's brief sojourn at O'Conor's home in New York.

the former Confederate president. He was confident that his cautious wait-and-see strategy had paid off. "The business is finished," O'Conor boasted. "Mr. Davis will never be called upon to appear for trial." Southern papers agreed. The *Charleston Mercury* wrote that the "bigots of consolidation and centralism ... shrink from trying Mr. Davis under the constitution.... He will never be tried." The *Georgia Weekly Telegraph* interpreted the bail hearing as "equivalent to the abandonment of the prosecution and a final discharge of Mr. Davis."[20]

The *Christian Recorder*, an African American newspaper in Philadelphia, worried that the pro-Davis press was right. Because the stakes of the case were so high, the government was faced with a difficult dilemma. "Refuse to try him," the editors warned, "and the [secession] question is left at issue, and may again be discussed amid the thunder of artillery and the flash of musketry on the bloody field of fratricidal war. Acquit him, and the right of secession is acknowledged, and, therefore, can be again repeated with impunity."[21]

Despite the predictions of his supporters following his release on bail in May 1867, Jefferson Davis's prosecution did not end there. He remained under a treason indictment for the next two years.

Chief Justice Chase refused to participate in any of the initial proceedings in Davis's case (Figure 9.4). Chase's reluctance to involve himself with the Davis matter had become apparent early on. In the summer of 1865, President Johnson had requested a meeting with the chief justice about the Davis matter, but Chase refused to consult on the topic. He decried the impropriety of such a conversation between the heads of the executive and judicial branches.[22] Chase told the president that Davis's trial remained "a matter exclusively for the consideration of the executive department of the government, about which I, as the head of the judicial department, did not wish to express any opinion; that when I held a court, I should try anybody who came before me, but did not desire to express an opinion

---

[20] *Charleston Mercury*, May 15, 1867; *Georgia Weekly Telegraph*, May 17, 1867.

[21] *Philadelphia Christian Recorder*, May 18, 1867.

[22] Salmon P. Chase to Charles Sumner, August 20, 1865, in Salmon P. Chase, *The Salmon P. Chase Papers*, ed. John Niven, 5 vols. (Kent, OH: Kent State University Press, 1993), 5: 64–65.

FIGURE 9.4 Salmon P. Chase, chief justice of the United States. Library of Congress.

in reference to persons to be tried, or time or place or mode of trial." The chief justice's frustrating communications with the president signaled to Johnson that Chase might be dragging his feet to make Johnson look like a Confederate sympathizer. Johnson's confidante John S. Brien raised the question: was Chase "to get clear of trying

[Davis]? Or is it for the purpus [*sic*] of continuing, the charges against you of preventing the trial?"[23]

Gideon Welles criticized Chase for standing on ceremony, noting that the chief justice had been willing to advise the administration on other judicial matters. Welles also noted that Chase's haughtiness had irked the president, who now saw the chief justice as "cowardly and arrogant, shirking and presumptuous, forward and evasive, an indifferent lawyer, a poor judge, an ambitious politician, possessed of mental resources yet afraid to use them, irresolute and aspiring and ambitious, intriguing, selfish, cold, grasping, and wholly unreliable when he fancies his personal advancement is concerned." Welles viewed Chase's careful insistence on judicial integrity as a sham that masked, poorly, the fact that "there was no desire on the part of the Chief Justice to preside at the trial of Davis."[24]

According to Charles O'Conor, Chase's reluctance to work on the case stemmed from his political ambitions: specifically, his longstanding and never fully dormant desire for the presidency. In fact, O'Conor believed that Evarts would aid Chase in this quest, as he desired to take Chase's place on the Supreme Court. In late 1867 O'Conor told Davis, "Chase is an eager candidate for the Presidency and is quite anxious to get rid of the case. Forcing it on before Underwood seems good policy for him. Evarts desires to help him in the hope of being selected for the judicial seat which his translation would leave vacant."[25] The prosecutors agreed with O'Conor about Chase (although not about Evarts's complicity in the scheme), as it seemed apparent that the chief justice feared that presiding over the Davis trial could only thwart his ultimate political goal.[26]

Although Chase never admitted, either publicly or privately, that he sought to avoid presiding over Davis's trial, his actions proved that

[23] John S. Brien to Andrew Johnson, October 18, 1866, in Andrew Johnson, *The Papers of Andrew Johnson*, ed. Paul Bergeron, 16 vols. (Knoxville: University of Tennessee Press, 1967–69), 11: 363.
[24] Gideon Welles, *Diary of Gideon Welles*, ed. Edgar Thaddeus Welles, 3 vols. (Boston: Houghton Mifflin, 1911), 2: 316.
[25] Charles O'Conor to Jefferson Davis, October 2, 1867, Box 24, Jefferson Davis Papers, MC.
[26] See John Bigelow, *Retrospections of a Busy Life*, 5 vols. (New York: Baker & Taylor, 1909), 4: 125–26.

this was his motive. A consummate politician, Chase jockeyed for the Democratic presidential nomination in 1868, despite having run as a Republican for the same office in 1860 and in 1864. The disposition of the Davis case was bound to be a difficult issue for Chase, no matter which way it turned out. Acquitting Davis would raise the ire of loyal Northerners, and convicting Davis would alienate ex-Confederates and their Northern allies. From a political standpoint, it was safest to avoid any association with it at all.

At first, Chase objected to sitting on the federal bench in the formerly Confederate South because of the military presence in Virginia, which he believed would force the civil courts to operate under military restraint.[27] The chief justice – as "head of one of the coordinate Departments of the Government" – bore a special responsibility to resist the incursion of military rule. As he had initially told Charles O'Conor in the course of Davis's bail application, Chase considered it beneath his dignity to hold court in a military district, where his decisions could potentially be undermined by a military commander or the president. It was acceptable, if not precisely desirable, for district judges to remain under the ultimate control of the military, but "members of the highest tribunal of the United States should not be subjected to that supervision."[28]

Chase also worried that holding court in Virginia while martial law still prevailed would impair his judicial integrity. In his estimation, President Johnson had already exhibited his willingness to allow the military to override the regular judicial process. He had done so when he released treason defendants who had received a military parole from confinement without a trial. A case in point hit close to home for Chase. A federal grand jury in Maryland had indicted former Confederate general Bradley Johnson for treason. Johnson, according to Chase (who later selected him to serve as his official reporter of circuit court decisions), was a "double traitor" to both Unionist Maryland and the country.[29]

[27] Ex parte Milligan, 71 U.S. at 2.
[28] Salmon P. Chase to Jacob Schuckers, September 24, 1866, in Chase, *Salmon P. Chase Papers*, 5: 124.
[29] Salmon P. Chase to Jacob Schuckers, September 24, 1866, in Chase, *Salmon P. Chase Papers*, 5: 126.

Bradley Johnson caught a lucky break when General Ulysses S. Grant interceded with the president on his behalf. Grant had urged the president to treat the parole Grant had offered to Robert E. Lee's army at Appomattox as a general amnesty for all Confederate officers who had surrendered on the battlefield.[30] The question of whether a military parole should extend this far was a judicial one, pending before Maryland district judge William Giles in Bradley Johnson's case, but the president had decided it summarily by releasing Johnson from prison and honoring Grant's expansive interpretation of the parole. Chase refused to participate in treason trials under such conditions.[31] Bradley Johnson's case demonstrated to Chase that the judicial authority of the United States could be abrogated by the president, and the chief justice stood on principle in refusing to participate in treason trials under such circumstances.

Chase sought to bolster his position by pointing out that former chief justice Roger Taney – whose politics had assuredly not aligned with Chase's – had similarly refused to preside over the Maryland circuit court alongside Judge Giles when the state was "substantially and practically under martial law."[32] Chase's ceremonious invocation of Taney angered Davis defense lawyer and former Baltimore mayor George William Brown, who had been arrested and imprisoned for fifteen months when Lincoln acted to prevent Maryland from seceding

---

[30] See Ulysses S. Grant to Robert E. Lee, April 9, 1865, in U.S. War Department, *The War of the Rebellion: A Compilation of the Official Records of the Union and Confederate Armies*, 128 vols. (Washington, DC: Government Printing Office, 1880–1901), ser. 1, vol. 34, pt. 1: 56. See also William A. Blair, *With Malice toward Some: Treason and Loyalty in the Civil War Era* (Chapel Hill: University of North Carolina Press, 2014), 236–37.

[31] After Judge Giles released Bradley Johnson on bail and the president decided to honor the terms of the military parole, the U.S. attorney for Maryland dropped the indictment against Johnson; it was to be refiled only on specific instructions from the attorney general. William Giles to Reverdy Johnson, January 22, 1867, and Ulysses S. Grant to Andrew Johnson, April 2, 1866, Box 2, Bradley T. Johnson Papers, UVA. President Johnson's generous interpretation of the terms of the military parole carried great consequences, as it meant that only Confederate civilians, such as Davis, could be tried for treason.

[32] *Impeachment Investigation*, 547–49 (testimony of Salmon P. Chase); George William Brown to Franklin Pierce, July 14, 1866, Reel 3, Franklin Pierce Papers, LC [microfilm edition].

in 1861.[33] Taney had never declared his unwillingness to preside over the circuit court in Maryland after hearing the controversial *Ex parte Merryman* case in 1861, although he had consistently claimed that illness prevented him from joining Judge Giles on circuit prior to the chief justice's death in 1864. What was more, when Chase succeeded to Taney's seat at the end of 1864, he had served on the Maryland circuit court without objection, despite studiously avoiding several treason cases that had come before the Maryland federal court.[34]

Chase's recitation of his qualms about sitting on the court in Virginia thus rang false to Brown. No doubt recalling his own time spent in federal custody, Brown commented bitterly that Chase "professes to object to sitting where martial law exists, but he had no difficulty in holding court here [in Maryland] when martial law prevailed." In Brown's opinion, Chase's objection to presiding in Virginia stemmed not so much from his distaste for military justice in the abstract as from his determination to bolster a harsh program of Reconstruction. Chase opposed the president's more lenient Reconstruction plans and wanted to prevent "the implied recognition of Virginia as a member of the Union that holding court there would convey."[35]

Chase also deemed President Johnson's April 1866 proclamation declaring the insurrection at an end and removing the sanction of military tribunals and martial law an insufficient basis for resuming his responsibilities on the bench in Virginia. Despite Johnson's efforts, Chase maintained that the proclamation had been ignored in the South, noting he had "observed that military commissions

---

[33] See James M. McPherson, *Battle Cry of Freedom* (New York: Oxford University Press, 1988), 289–90. McPherson called Brown a "[victim] of the obsessive quest for security that arises in time of war, especially civil war." Ibid., 290.

[34] See Jonathan W. White, *Abraham Lincoln and Treason in the Civil War: The Trials of John Merryman* (Baton Rouge: Louisiana State University Press, 2011), 51.

[35] George William Brown to Franklin Pierce, July 14, 1866, Reel 3, Franklin Pierce Papers, LC [microfilm edition]. Chase was only appointed to the Supreme Court in 1864, but martial law prevailed throughout the war in Maryland. See James G. Randall, *Constitutional Problems under Lincoln* (1926; repr., Urbana: University of Illinois Press, 1964), 170–73; George William Brown to Franklin Pierce, July 14, 1866, Reel 3, Franklin Pierce Papers, LC [microfilm edition]. For information on Brown's imprisonment, see George William Brown, *Baltimore and the 19th of April, 1861* (Baltimore: Johns Hopkins University Press, 1887), 97–112; George William Brown Letters, Box 6, Brune-Randall Papers, MdHS.

were [still] being held" in contravention of the proclamation, and he declined once again to hold court in Virginia. Chase conferred with the president on the matter, and although Johnson insisted that the proclamation had done away with his objections, Chase remained unconvinced throughout the summer of 1866. He sought to persuade the president to issue a new proclamation specifically enjoining military and naval officers from interfering with any of the duties of federal courts.[36]

In response to these entreaties, Johnson did issue a new proclamation on August 20, 1866. This time, Chase deemed it "fair to conclude that martial law & Military government are permanently abrogated," so that he was now free to participate in a trial in the circuit court in Virginia when the court next met, in November. But Chase had identified a new problem: Congress had passed the Judicial Circuits Act in July, which had reduced the number of federal circuits from ten to nine, and had accordingly altered the geographical boundaries of all but two of them. In passing the act, however, Congress had failed to specify how Supreme Court justices would be assigned to circuit duty. Chase's old circuit – the fourth – had added the districts of West Virginia and South Carolina and subtracted that of Delaware, but the districts of Maryland, Virginia, and North Carolina remained intact.[37] Although Virginia's circuit allocation remained unaltered, Chase was inclined not to preside there without an official assignment and sought confirmation of this decision.

After corresponding with his fellow Supreme Court justices about the matter, Chase concluded that the justices should refuse to carry out circuit duty until Congress acted to remedy the faulty legislation.[38] As Chase informed Congress, he feared that circuit court rulings could

---

[36] Salmon P. Chase to Jacob W. Schuckers, September 24, 1866, in Chase, *Salmon P. Chase Papers*, 5: 124.

[37] Act of July 23, 1866, 14 Stat. 209 (1866) (changing the number of federal circuits); Act of July 15, 1862, 12 Stat. 576 (1862) (allocating the federal circuits).

[38] Salmon P. Chase to Noah Swayne, September 29, 1866, and Salmon P. Chase to David Davis, October 4, 1866, in Chase, *Salmon P. Chase Papers*, 5: 129, 131. Salmon P. Chase to Members of the Supreme Court, October 5, 1866; Chase to Nathan Clifford, October 6, 1866; and Samuel Miller to Salmon Chase, October 11, 1866, Reel 36, Salmon Chase, *The Salmon P. Chase Papers*, ed. John Niven (Frederick, MD: University Publications of America, 1987) [microfilm edition], (hereafter cited as *Chase Papers* [microfilm edition]).

be reversed on appeal if Supreme Court justices presided without an official circuit allotment by statute.[39] Justices Grier, Nelson, and Miller agreed with Chase's views on the insufficiency of the act, although Justices Clifford and Davis maintained that there was no barrier to holding court, at least in the states whose circuit assignment had not changed.[40]

The justices formed their opinions about the appropriateness of Chase's presence on the bench in the newly reconstituted Fourth Circuit with Jefferson Davis – and Chase's feelings about his case – firmly in mind.[41] It was not lost on them that Chase was looking for a way out, despite his vehement denials. Chase told his secretary and friend Jacob Schuckers that "it is quite certain" that it was improper for him to "exercise jurisdiction in any Circuit except by allotment or assignment under an act of Congress." In explaining himself, Chase disclaimed any responsibility for the consequent inability of the government to obtain a legal judgment declaring the Confederate war effort to be treasonous. He steadfastly maintained that he "neither s[ought] nor shun[ned] the responsibility of trying Jeff. Davis or any other man."[42] Chase remained either oblivious to or willfully ignorant of the public scrutiny focused on Davis's case.

The president tried to meet Chase's new objections. In October 1866 he asked Attorney General Stanbery to determine whether there was any additional step he could take to remove the barriers to jurisdiction. Stanbery's response indicated that he had tired of the chief justice's excuses. He pointed out that Congress had acted to ensure the proper working of the federal courts, and Johnson's proclamations had ensured that the military authorities in Virginia would remain subordinate to their civilian counterparts. Stanbery did acknowledge that Congress's failure to reallocate the federal circuits had caused some confusion, but insisted that the president's hands were tied in terms of

[39] *Impeachment Investigation*, 545 (testimony of Salmon P. Chase).
[40] See Chase, *Salmon P. Chase Papers*, 5: 135–36 n. 10. Nathan Clifford to Salmon P. Chase, October 13, 1866; David Davis to Salmon P. Chase, October 22, 1866; Samuel Miller to Salmon P. Chase, October 11, 1866, Reel 36, *Chase Papers* [microfilm edition]. See also Fairman, *Reconstruction and Reunion*, 1: 172–77.
[41] See Fairman, *Reconstruction and Reunion*, 1: 175–76.
[42] Salmon P. Chase to Joseph Schuckers, September 24, 1866, in Chase, *Salmon P. Chase Papers*, 5: 126.

remedying the problem. In Stanbery's opinion, congressional careless-
ness in this matter could easily be overcome if the chief justice were
willing to take on the responsibility of hearing Davis's case. Either the
Congress or the Supreme Court *itself* could allot circuits.[43] Indeed,
in March 1867 Congress finally responded to Chase's concerns and
ordered the Court to allot the circuits itself.[44]

Once his formal objections to presiding expired, Chase found new
reasons for avoiding his circuit duty in Virginia whenever the Davis
case came near the docket. Chase worried about his personal safety
while in Richmond, he said, prompting the governor to reassure him
that he would not be molested in the city. He decried the awkwardness of staying at the same hotel as Davis, which required that new
arrangements be made for the chief justice's lodgings. When these
problems were addressed, Chase simply found himself too busy in
Washington to make the trip.[45] In November 1867, for example,
prosecutor Richard Henry Dana awaited Chase's promised arrival in
Richmond on the 2:30 train, but "the train came without him, & a
telegram came to the District Judge from him, saying that he sent
papers, etc. by mail, wh. would arrive by morning."[46] Despite his difficulties in making it to Richmond, Chase's other duties did not, however, prevent him from attending the circuit court in North Carolina
in the summer of 1867.[47]

Chase repeatedly insisted that he did not intend his absence from
the bench to obstruct the prosecution. Instead, he blamed the delays
in the trial on the prosecution's lack of preparation and the series of
continuances the government requested, rather than on his own lack
of involvement. After all, Chase maintained, the prosecution could certainly have chosen to proceed in his absence, "either by military commission ... or by a court held by the District Judge.[48] But Chase's bland

43 12 Op. Att'y Gen. 69 (1866). See also Case of Davis, *Chase's Reports*, 74.
44 Act of March 2, 1867, 14 Stat. 28 (1867).
45 J. A. Schofield to John Underwood, March 30, 1867; Salmon P. Chase to John
    C. Underwood, May 13, 1867, and November 23, 1867, Box 1, John Underwood
    Papers, LC.
46 Richard Henry Dana to Sarah W. Dana, November 25, 1867, Box 17, Dana Family
    Papers, MHS.
47 Salmon P. Chase, Address of the Chief Justice to the Gentlemen of the Bar of North
    Carolina, June Term, 1867, in *Chase's Reports*, 132 (1867).
48 Salmon P. Chase to Thomas W. Conway, January 1, 1868, printed in *New York
    Tribune*, September 19, 1870; reprinted in Chase, *Salmon P. Chase Papers*, 5: 183–84;

reassurances about the adequacy of a trial before Judge Underwood notwithstanding, he was well aware of the fact that the government attorneys – and the country – considered his presence to be essential.[49]

Historians have judged Chase's actions harshly, arguing that political considerations rather than jurisdictional barriers prevented Chase from attending court in Richmond. Harold Hyman concluded, for instance, that "Chase sought and found technical reasons to make all but impossible a treason trial for Jefferson Davis."[50] And Chase's contemporaries were no less critical, generally viewing his reasons for declining to sit on the bench as illusory and evasive. Many of them pointed out that Chase's difficulties in the Davis case stemmed not only from his lofty political ambitions but also from the awkwardness of his prewar state sovereignty views.[51] Although Chase had always deployed such arguments in the service of antislavery positions, his long-standing commitment to state sovereignty principles would make ruling against the constitutionality of secession an awkward proposition for him.

As an antislavery Democrat throughout the antebellum period, Chase had pursued abolitionist goals through the use of state sovereignty arguments. Chase believed that the national government had no legitimate role in regulating slavery, which was entrusted solely to the

---

also reprinted in *Albany Law Journal* 2 (1870–71): 233. See also Salmon P. Chase to Joseph Schuckers, September 24, 1866, in Chase, *Salmon P. Chase Papers*, 5: 126.

[49] See *Impeachment Investigation*, 545 (testimony of Salmon P. Chase).

[50] Harold Hyman, introduction to *Reports of Cases Decided by Chief Justice Chase in the Circuit Court of the United States Fourth Circuit, 1865–1869*, by Bradley T. Johnson (1876; repr., New York: DaCapo Press, 1974), xxi; John Niven, *Salmon P. Chase: A Biography* (New York: Oxford University Press, 1995), 409.

[51] Two of Davis's biographers, as well as numerous internet sites devoted to proving that Chase did not believe secession to be treason, have attributed the following quotation to Chase: "If you bring these leaders to trial, it will condemn the North, for by the Constitution secession is not rebellion." Robert McElroy, *Jefferson Davis: The Real and the Unreal*, 2 vols. (New York: Harper & Brothers, 1937), 2: 540; Hudson Strode, *Jefferson Davis*, 3 vols. (New York: Harcourt Brace, 1955), 3: 250. These two authors provide no source for this quotation other than a reference to Johnson's case report for *U.S. v. Davis*. The phrase does not appear in the case, and another somewhat similar quotation that McElroy attributed to Chase was actually uttered by Charles O'Conor. Case of Davis, *Chase's Reports*, 12. The source of the quotation is mysterious, but it seems to have first appeared in Mildred Rutherford, "The War Was Not a Civil War," *Miss Rutherford's Scrap Book* 1 (1923): 12. Unfortunately, it has been reproduced many times, now with the new twist that Chase uttered it to Secretary Stanton. In fact, Senator Mark Hatfield referred to the quotation on the floor of the Senate in 1976, when that body discussed restoring Jefferson Davis's

states and territories. Applying a states' rights philosophy as an anti-slavery attorney in Ohio, Chase had wanted to exclude slavery totally and completely from the state, in spite of the limited recognition of unfree status that the Fugitive Slave Clause of the U.S. Constitution mandated. On behalf of escaped slaves, Chase had argued for limits on Ohio's toleration of slave transit through the state and its recognition of slave status conferred in other states. In one case, Chase had even argued that a free state's sovereignty overrode the federal interest in returning escapees to bondage. When a slave crossed the border into Ohio, Chase insisted provocatively, he "was a man, under protection of the Constitution and the laws of Ohio, and beyond the reach of the fugitive slave law."[52]

Indeed, the *Natchez Courier* attributed the chief justice's evasive actions in avoiding the Davis case to embarrassment, because Chase had long espoused the same states' rights beliefs that Davis had. The paper mocked Chase's explanations for avoiding circuit duty. "Was [there] ever so flimsy a pretext; so illy-covered a deceit?" the paper queried. "Mr. Chase cannot instruct a jury that Jefferson Davis has been guilty of treason, without confessing himself equally guilty of misprision of treason," the *Courier* asserted. "He dare not try Jefferson Davis."[53] The *New Orleans Crescent* similarly rebuked Chase's series of "invent[ed]" objections, which imparted "a rather strong element of the farcical into public affairs."[54] Ohio congressman Lewis D. Campbell believed that Chase "knows that if he has to try Jeff. Davis he must either acquit him or back down from his former [state sovereignty] positions – either of which horns of the dilemma would greatly interfere with his [political] aspirations."[55]

As anger waxed against the government and waned against the prisoner in the Northern press, some of the animosity found its way to Chase. The *New York Herald* criticized Chase's "pretended

citizenship. See Robert Penn Warren, *Jefferson Davis Gets His Citizenship Back* (Lexington: University Press of Kentucky, 1980), 94.

[52] See Paul Finkelman, *An Imperfect Union: Slavery, Federalism, and Comity* (Chapel Hill: University of North Carolina Press, 1981), quotation on 169; see 155–80, for a discussion of Chase's antislavery advocacy.

[53] *Natchez Courier*, November 23, 1867.

[54] *New Orleans Crescent*, October 8, 1866.

[55] Lewis Campbell to Andrew Johnson, November 20, 1865, in Johnson, *Papers of Andrew Johnson*, 9: 406–8.

difficulty," the purpose of which, the paper surmised, was to "mak[e] political capital out of the victim and the administration."[56] The *Cincinnati Commercial* reported that Chase and other Radical Republicans did not want Davis to come to trial because "such a trial would make patent to the public the fact that in regard to the doctrine of State rights ... they stand, by their previous record and expressed opinions, on *identically the same platform*."[57] The *New York World* also commented on the "awkwardness of [Chase's] position in respect to the treason trials." After detailing Chase's states' rights pronouncements, the *World* concluded that "it is not surprising, therefore, that he has evinced so persistent a reluctance to preside at the trial of Jefferson Davis." Any charge Chase could give to the Virginia jury would be undercut by his own record on states' rights ideology.[58]

Chase's plight was not unsympathetic, given the inherent difficulties the Davis case presented. It made sense that Chase would want to avoid the Richmond circuit court at all costs and would reach for justifications that would excuse his absence from circuit duty in Virginia. But Chase himself never admitted, even in his private moments, that his reasons for avoiding the Davis case were anything less than valid. He offered the same procedural technicalities in explaining his behavior in private correspondence with his family that he did publicly. Chase told his daughter Nettie that "[he did] not intend to hold Courts in rebel states until the question whether Martial Law is to be continued in practical force is settled by its absolute & complete abrogation at least so far as the National courts are concerned."[59] In a letter to his son-in-law William Sprague, he indicated that he was well aware of the public pressure surrounding his inaction in the Davis case. Noting that the "papers [were] beginning to ask again about the trial of Davis," he steadfastly refused to abandon his judicial principles merely to appease the public. Chase insisted, again, that "the Circuit Court can be held at Richmond" in his absence, and that he would not "allow the

[56] *New York Herald*, October 15, 1866.
[57] *Cincinnati Commercial*, May 10, 1866 (emphasis in the original).
[58] *New York World*, May 17, 1866.
[59] Salmon P. Chase to Janet R. [Nettie] Chase, June 5, 1866, in Chase, *Salmon P. Chase Papers*, 5: 104.

fact that [a prominent person like] Jefferson Davis is a prisoner within
the District of Virginia to affect my action in any respect whatever."[60]

Chase's rectitude was selective, however. He decried the impropriety
of discussing the case with President Johnson, of meeting with Davis
when the two coincidentally found themselves on the same boat during Davis's transport to Fort Monroe, and of staying at the same hotel
with Davis while in Richmond for court hearings. But his caution did
not extend to several other potentially problematic activities. In the
midst of the Davis trial, Chase spent several days at prosecutor William
Evarts's country home in Windsor, Vermont, where, according to one
report, he romanced several local ladies.[61] Even more ethically dubious were Chase's later ex parte communications with defense counsel
in the summer and fall of 1868, in which he provided Davis's lawyers
with the argument that their client's treason prosecution was barred
by Section Three of the Fourteenth Amendment.[62] Unsurprisingly,
Charles O'Conor subsequently managed to convince Chase to dismiss
the indictment on that very basis. In spite of Chase's protestations to
the contrary, it was apparent that he was driven, above all, by a desire
to avoid the Davis case.

[60] Salmon P. Chase to William Sprague, September 24, 1866, Reel 36, *Chase Papers*
[microfilm edition]. The microfilm copy of this letter is mostly illegible; consult original at Pennsylvania Historical Society, Philadelphia.
[61] Salmon P. Chase diary, May 16, 1865; Salmon P. Chase to Andrew Johnson, May
17, 1865; and Salmon P. Chase to Charles Sumner, May 20, 1865, in Chase,
Salmon P. Chase Papers, 1: 550, 5: 54–55, 49. John C. Gray Jr. to Mother, May 17,
1865, in John Chipman Gray and John Codman Ropes, *War Letters, 1862–1865*
(Boston: Riverside Press, 1927), 488; Salmon P. Chase to John C. Underwood, May
13, 1867, Box 1, John Underwood Papers, LC; Helen Evarts to Charles B. Evarts,
August 1, 1866, Box 45, Evarts Family Papers, Yale. See also Salmon P. Chase to
William Sprague, July 25, 1866, in Chase, *Salmon P. Chase Papers*, 5: 122.
[62] See Chapter 14.

Secession and Belligerency in *Shortridge v. Macon*

Chase stayed away from Richmond and the volatile Davis case, but he had the opportunity to address secession in another circuit court case in 1867, this time in North Carolina. In *Shortridge v. Macon*, Chase confronted secession, Reconstruction, and the postwar consequences of the Union's recognition of the Confederacy's wartime status as a belligerent power. He took strongly Unionist positions on all three issues, despite his states' rights and Radical leanings, signaling to Davis's lawyers that he was not favorably inclined to their cause. The *Shortridge* case reveals Chase's analysis of the intersection of the domestic law of treason and the international law of war. The reach of the international law of war was the most difficult strictly legal question implicated in postwar treason cases. During the Civil War, the Union had treated the Confederacy as a separate nation (a belligerent power) under the law of war, and it seemed possible that wartime recognition of Confederate belligerency could have significant postwar effects – even potentially prohibiting treason prosecutions.

International law had traditionally been termed "the law of nations," and as such, it applied between nations, and only between nations.[1] It did not reach within states, because to do so would violate a state's sovereignty. A rebellious group was not the proper object of the law of nations unless and until it achieved independence, thereby becoming a member

---

[1] See Lassa Oppenheim, *Oppenheim's International Law*, 2 vols. (Oxford: Oxford University Press, 2008), 1: 1.

of the family of nations. Thus Grotius, writing in the early seventeenth century, did not treat civil war as a legitimate subject for the application of international law. In his seminal *De Jure Belli ac Pacis* (*On the Law of War and Peace*), he wrote that it was not "lawful for subjects to make war against their sovereign.... [If] any injury be done us by the will of our sovereign, we ought rather to bear it patiently, than to resist by force."[2] Grotius struggled to prevent the law of nations from attaching to revolutionary movements. He acknowledged that "in civil wars necessity does sometimes make way for right [under the law of nations]," but stressed that the internal affairs of states were to remain internal.[3] By implication, a nation only invited trouble by intervening in a neighbor's civil war.

International law began to take more cognizance of internal conflicts with the rise of revolutionary movements in Europe in the seventeenth and eighteenth centuries. Eminent eighteenth-century international law jurists Emer de Vattel and Cornelis van Bynkershoek moderated Grotius's hard-line stance and conceded the potential applicability of international law in cases of rebellions. For instance, Vattel believed that "when a party is formed in a state, which no longer obeys the sovereign, and is of strength sufficient to make head against him," the conflict could be termed a civil war. Legally speaking, "a civil war breaks the bands of society and government, or at least it suspends their force and effect; it produces in the nation two independent parties, considering each other as enemies, and acknowledging no common judge."[4]

The American Civil War was the seminal event that formalized the application of international law to a domestic conflict. Scholars have noted that the Civil War was a watershed moment in the history of international law. This is partly because of the rather exalted status modern scholars have accorded to Francis Lieber, who has been heralded as the progenitor of modern international humanitarian law, based on the code he drafted in the midst of the Civil War setting forth standards for the conduct of warfare.[5] Beyond this, Arnold McNair characterized the "American Civil

---

[2] Hugo Grotius, *The Rights of War and Peace*, 3 vols. (1625; repr., London: D. Brown, T. Ward, and W. Meares, 1715), 1: 178.

[3] Grotius, *The Rights of War and Peace*, 3: 403.

[4] Emer de Vattel, *The Law of Nations* (1758; repr., Northampton, MA: Simeon Butler, 1820), § 292–93. See also Cornelis van Bynkershoek, *A Treatise on the Law of War* (Philadelphia: Farrand & Nicholas, 1810), 14.

[5] See, e.g., John Fabian Witt, *Lincoln's Code: The Laws of War in American History* (New York: Free Press, 2012); Jordan Paust, "Dr. Francis Lieber and the Lieber Code,"

War as the decisive date when we perceived Recognition of Belligerency as a specific legal institution and fitted it out with a body of legal rights and duties."[6] The Civil War solidified the nascent understanding that the law of war could apply between a rebellious breakaway republic and its parent government.[7] Both could be treated as "belligerents," even if only the latter was a recognized state. Belligerency was a form of quasi-statehood, based on the rebel government's control over territory and its ability to command authority in the international arena, solely recognized for the purpose of conducting war.[8] Thus, belligerent status was not equivalent to full recognition as a state, but it denoted two significant legal consequences: the law of war would govern the conflict between belligerents (or between a state and a mere belligerent), and a belligerent power was an *entity* rather than a mere collection of individuals.[9]

On the eve of the Civil War, the state of the law of belligerency was muddled. It was not yet perfectly clear that the law of nations would govern the activities of the Union or the Confederacy in their dealings with each other or with other countries. Henry Halleck, an international law scholar, later became general in chief of the Union army, and his 1861 international law treatise was intended to provide

American Society of International Law Proceedings 95 (January 2001): 112–15; Jeremy Rabkin, "The Politics of the Geneva Conventions: Disturbing Background to the ICC Debate," *Virginia Journal of International Law* 44 (Fall 2003): 169–205; Laura Dickinson, "Military Lawyers on the Battlefield: An Empirical Account of International Law Compliance," *American Journal of International Law* 104 (January 2010): 1–28; Amalia Kessler, "Deciding against Conciliation: The Nineteenth-Century Rejection of a European Transplant and the Rise of a Distinctively American Ideal of Adversarial Adjudication," *Theoretical Inquiries in Law* 10 (July 2009): 423–83; Gabriella Blum, "The Fog of Victory," *European Journal of International Law* 24 (February 2013): 391–421.

[6] Arnold McNair, "The Law Relating to the Civil War in Spain," *Law Quarterly Review* 53 (1937): 484. See also Roscoe R. Ogelsby, *Internal War and the Search for Normative Order* (The Hague: Martinus Nijhoff, 1971), 33; Quincy Wright, "The American Civil War (1861–1865)," in *The International Law of Civil War*, ed. Richard A. Falk (Baltimore: Johns Hopkins Press, 1971), 30–109; Robert Gomulkiewicz, "International Law Governing Aid to Opposition Groups in Civil War: Resurrecting the Standards of Belligerency," *Washington Law Review* 63 (1988): 43, 47; Thomas H. Lee, "The Civil War in U.S. Foreign Relations Law: A Dress Rehearsal for Modern Transformations," *Saint Louis University Law Journal* 53 (2008–2009): 53, 54.

[7] See Doris A. Graber, *The Development of the Law of Belligerent Occupation, 1863–1914* (New York: Columbia University Press, 1949), 5, 14.

[8] See Oppenheim, *Oppenheim's International Law*, 1: 154–55, 164–65.

[9] See Stephen C. Neff, *Justice in Blue and Gray: A Legal History of the Civil War* (Cambridge, MA: Harvard University Press, 2010), 17–19.

legal support for the Union cause. The treatise argued that the attainment of a certain amount of military power would not automatically transform a faction in a civil war into a state. No amount of military success, he emphasized, could confer statehood. Furthermore, a parent government was not bound by the rules of international law in its dealings with a rebellious group. It could choose to apply domestic law only; its use of international law was solely a matter of largesse, not obligation. Halleck also warned foreign states against intervention in "the civil wars of [their] neighbors." They had to remain "passive spectator[s]," because to do otherwise "would be a direct violation of the rights of sovereignty and independence." Halleck's analysis was certainly a thinly veiled reference to the Confederacy's bid for foreign recognition. He went so far as to insist that any statements by Vattel or Henry Wheaton recognizing the belligerent status of rebellious groups under international law had been either incorrect or misinterpreted.[10]

Treating the Confederates solely under the domestic law of the United States would severely limit the U.S. government's policy options. Yet treating them under international law, while in many respects strategically advantageous, would tacitly recognize the separate existence of a Confederate nation, which would seemingly concede the validity of secession. It was a profound dilemma. Domestic law was simply inadequate in a crisis of this magnitude because it was aimed at disloyal individuals rather than at the Confederate entity as a whole. The Confederacy's military strength forced the Union to use the tools of international warfare (blockade, prize, regularized prisoner exchange) in conducting the war.[11] Additionally, applying the law of nations to the contest would prevent an international incident with Great Britain. Refusing to treat the Confederacy under the law of war made foreign diplomacy exceedingly difficult, as European powers like Great Britain and France would be bound to follow the unpredictable rules of U.S. domestic law in dealing with the Confederacy rather than a fixed set of standards that applied to all wars. From a European perspective, U.S. domestic law was slanted in favor of American interests and, perhaps more important, was subject to change on a whim.

---

[10] Henry W. Halleck, *International Law: or, Rules Governing the Intercourse of States in Peace and War* (San Francisco: Bancroft, 1861), 331–33, 73–76. See also Neff, *Justice in Blue and Gray*, 19, on Halleck's slanted take on earlier authorities.

[11] See Neff, *Justice in Blue and Gray*, and Witt, *Lincoln's Code*.

International law – with its generally agreed-upon content – offered a solution to the diplomatic problem.

Could Lincoln's government manage to avail itself of the advantages of international law without also necessarily accepting its liabilities? In the early months of the Civil War, Lincoln and his cabinet had wrestled with this very question. Lincoln wanted to declare a blockade of Confederate ports, but Attorney General Edward Bates balked. Rather than formally instituting a blockade, Bates recommended that Lincoln "clos[e] the ports of the insurgent states." Bates believed this terminology to be crucially important, as a "nation cannot blockade its own port, in its own possession – because blockade *is an act of war*, which a nation *cannot* commit agst. itself."[12] With the support of Secretary of State William Seward, Lincoln went ahead anyway and instituted a blockade.[13] By denying the separateness of the Confederacy while applying the rules of international law to the conflict, Lincoln was claiming the advantages of international law and rejecting its drawbacks. The war was thus of a "mixed" character. The Union's legal position, as advanced by war department solicitor William Whiting, was that "by war, the subject loses his rights, but does not escape his obligations."[14]

In crafting this policy, Lincoln and Seward were guided mostly by expediency, but in so doing, they hit upon a brilliant – but risky – strategy. They "stumbled into a distinctive way of thinking about the laws of war, one that would serve the nation well over the next four years and more."[15] For the two of them, law was a tool. The Union's legal policy would be guided by pragmatism and innovation rather than brittle adherence to doctrine. Their approach "was grounded not in … abstract principles … but in a practical idea about what the laws of war could accomplish for the Union war effort." But there

[12] Edward Bates, *The Diary of Edward Bates, 1859–1866*, ed. Howard K. Beale (Washington, DC: Government Printing Office, 1933), 182, 427.
[13] Abraham Lincoln, Proclamation of a Blockade April 19, 1861, in Lincoln, *Collected Works of Abraham Lincoln*, ed. Roy P. Basler, 8 vols. (New Brunswick, NJ: Rutgers University Press, 1953), 4: 338–39. .
[14] William Whiting, *The War Powers under the Constitution of the United States* (Boston: Little, Brown, 1864), 246–47. This book went through multiple editions (eight, by my count) with slightly different titles, published both during and after the war. See Witt, *Lincoln's Code*, 205.
[15] Witt, *Lincoln's Code*, 146.

was no guarantee that their perspective would win widespread acceptance. Plus, the law needed to be flexible while at least maintaining the
appearance of coherence and predictability. To be viewed as "law," it
had to be logically rigid enough not to collapse.[16]

In April of 1861 it was not clear whether Lincoln's precarious stance
on the Confederacy's legal status would be sustained by the Supreme
Court. The dual legal status of the Confederacy was of paramount
importance; indeed, it encapsulated "the grand theme of the legal history of the American Civil War."[17] Unionist legal thinkers wrestled
with its uncertain parameters and consequences for much of the war
and its aftermath. As historians have recognized, the issue cropped up
in innumerable contexts during the war – including the confiscation
of enemy property and slave emancipation – and pragmatic considerations guided the Lincoln administration's responses to difficult legal
questions. Because they were adapted in the midst of war to provide
justifications for Union objectives, those answers were not always perfectly coherent.[18]

Belligerency and secession came into conflict soon after the declaration of the blockade, with the capture in June 1861 of privateers
flying under a Confederate flag on the ship *Savannah*. The *Savannah*'s
crew, armed with letters of marque from the Confederate government,
maintained that they had acted in an officially recognized capacity in
running the blockade, and were thus entitled to be treated as belligerents under the law of war. The United States government determined
instead to try them as pirates – "the enemy of mankind" – under the
theory that they enjoyed no status conferred by any duly constituted
government.[19] After their capture, prominent Philadelphia attorney

---

[16] Witt, *Lincoln's Code*, 156; William A. Blair, *With Malice toward Some: Treason and Loyalty in the Civil War Era* (Chapel Hill: University of North Carolina Press, 2014), 4.

[17] Neff, *Justice in Blue and Gray*, 5.

[18] Neff, *Justice in Blue and Gray*, 28, 258–64. See also Blair, *With Malice toward Some*; Burrus Carnahan, *Act of Justice: Lincoln's Emancipation Proclamation and the Law of War* (Lexington: University Press of Kentucky, 2007); Mark Weitz, *The Confederacy on Trial: The Piracy and Sequestration Cases of 1861* (Lawrence: University Press of Kansas, 2005); Witt, *Lincoln's Code*; James G. Randall, *Constitutional Problems under Lincoln* (1926; repr., Urbana: University of Illinois Press, 1964).

[19] Charles P. Daly, *Are the Southern Privateersmen Pirates? Letter to the Hon. Ira Harris, United States Senator* (New York: James B. Kirker, 1862).

Sidney George Fisher confided his concerns about the prosecution to his diary:

A "Confederate" privateer out of Charleston has been captured and brought into New York. How will her crew be treated by our government, as prisoners of war or as pirates?[20] Under the theory that the Union is unbroken, they are by act of Congress pirates. On the other hand, this rebellion is of such large proportions that it is in fact a sectional war. Will the government treat it as a mere insurrection or accord to the South the rights of war? If so, privateers cannot be regarded as pirates. The question is not free from difficulty in principle or in policy. If these men are punished as pirates, measures of retaliation of a desperate character may be expected on the other side, passions would become more and more exasperated and frightful character of ferocity may be given to a contest which is deplorable at best.[21]

The *Savannah*'s crew were tried in federal court in New York, in a case argued by Davis prosecutor William Evarts. The case revealed that there was clearly pushback against the Union's theory that the government could disregard belligerent status and treat the Confederacy as nonexistent when it was advantageous to do so. The jury refused to convict, and the government declined to prosecute the case again, eventually exchanging the crew for Union prisoners of war. This was a reminder to the Lincoln government that not everyone viewed the law opportunistically. Some Americans, like the New York jurors, clearly believed that it was not infinitely malleable.

The Supreme Court confronted the problem of the Confederacy's belligerent status in the *Prize Cases* (1863). The Court split five to four on the question of whether the president needed congressional authorization to implement a blockade, which was tantamount to a declaration of a state of civil war. A bare majority affirmed Lincoln's ability to order the blockade without Congress's assent. But if the Court was divided about what measures under domestic law were necessary to set a blockade afoot, it was unanimous in endorsing the legitimacy of a blockade against the Confederate government. The Court embraced

---

[20] As Stephen Neff points out, privateering had fallen into disfavor in the international community by the 1860s, but the United States had declined to sign on to the Declaration of Paris, in which the European powers had banned privateering. Neff, *Justice in Blue and Gray*, 22–23. See also Daly, *Are the Southern Privateersmen Pirates?*

[21] Sidney George Fisher, *A Philadelphia Perspective: The Diary of Sidney George Fisher Covering the Years 1834–1871*, ed. Nicholas B. Wainright (Philadelphia: Historical

the Lincoln administration's theory that the blockade itself was permissible under international law and that the United States government was justified in treating the Confederacy as a belligerent power under the laws of war.[22] Under the Court's analysis, the attainment of belligerent status was *automatically conferred* by virtue of certain objective markers of success: a breakaway group became a belligerent once it had achieved a powerful enough military presence to compel the parent government to make war on the rebels as a group, rather than pursuing criminal prosecutions against individuals.[23]

The collateral consequences of the Confederacy's belligerent status remained unclear, however, after the *Prize Cases*. If the Union recognized the existence of the Confederacy for the limited purposes of the law of nations, where would that status end? Would it shield individuals from prosecution under domestic law if they had acted on behalf of the Confederacy in a manner that was consistent with the law of war? Charles O'Conor, among others, believed that the *Prize Cases'* holding precluded the option of trying Confederate officials for treason following the war. If the implications of the Confederacy's dual status might prove hard to contain, O'Conor would attempt to harness the possibility of its spill-over effects in the service of Davis's cause.

O'Conor had kept the Davis case out of court by design, but he had made tentative plans about what argument he might present if Davis were to be prosecuted. Davis's case presented a novel question, he believed. No circumstance in the United States had been remotely analogous to the Civil War: no mere rebellion had achieved anything like the Confederacy's level of success, which had forced the Union's hand in recognizing Confederate belligerency. In Davis's case, O'Conor would contend that by acknowledging Confederate belligerency in the *Prize Cases*, the United States had lost its ability to prosecute Confederate leaders for treason. International and domestic law were not an à la carte menu from which the Union could freely pick and choose. In

Society of Pennsylvania, 1967), 394. For more on the case of the *Savannah*, see Weitz, *The Confederacy on Trial*.

[22] The Prize Cases, 67 U.S. 635 (1862). The cases were argued in February 1863 and decided on March 10 of the same year.

[23] The Prize Cases, 67 U.S. at 673. See also Wyndham L. Walker, "Recognition of Belligerency and Grant of Belligerent Rights," *Transactions of the Grotius Society* 23 (1937): 177, 208.

choosing the law of nations during the war, the Union had accepted the collateral consequences of that decision, including forgoing the opportunity to charge the Confederate belligerents with treason.

Honor and policy, as well as the finer points of law, prevented the government from charging Davis with the crime of treason, O'Conor maintained. If the Union had summarily put down the rebellion, the government could have charged the rebels with treason. But this option was not available with respect to the defeated Confederates, whose military success had compelled "an institution and acceptance of the rules and usages which obtain in regular wars between independent nations."[24] War, in modern times, was governed by legal standards, so that it would not descend into abject brutality. A victorious parent state could choose to exact revenge on defeated belligerents, perhaps even to the extent of summary execution, but it could not try them for treason. "Trials for treason in the civil courts are not remedies adapted to the close of a great civil war," O'Conor argued. They were not appropriate once the parent state had recognized that the contest would be governed by the "rules and usages of war," which the United States had done in the *Prize Cases*. To substitute the law of treason would be "inexpressibly revolting and contemptible" because it would allow the government to act on a "small, mean scale which it actually feared to employ during the conflict."[25] Condemning Davis to die for treason would also dishonor none other than the American founders, because they, like Davis, had waged a war for independence against a stronger nation, and they, like Davis, could easily have been defeated.

Besides, trials were ill adapted to circumstances like Davis's, O'Conor believed. Everyone knew that he had engaged in a massive war against the United States government. What "facts" were there for a jury to find? Under such circumstances, "trial and judgment can only be regarded as a mockery." Courts were not appropriate vehicles in the voluble postwar world, because they "are instituted only for the normal state of society." They could not sort out right and wrong in the aftermath of a conflict as bloody as the Civil War. It was not so much

---

[24] O'Conor argued that no law "capable of being enforced" restrained the victorious party in a civil war, although the disapprobation of humanity might check a victor's worst impulses. Case of Davis, *Reports of Cases Decided by Chief Justice Chase*, ed. Bradley Johnson (New York: Diossy, 1876), 12 (hereafter cited as *Chase's Reports*).

[25] Case of Davis, *Chase's Reports*, 12–13.

law as the naked power of conquest that the Union should invoke in condemning Davis. "When battle is the recognized order of things," O'Conor claimed, "the crimes of vanquished combatants are to be condoned or punished according to the law that governs combats." The scale of the war, and the quasi-legitimacy the Confederacy had enjoyed as a result, meant that the Union could not punish treason as an individual crime, he said: "The law of nature forbids it."[26]

According to O'Conor, the text of the Constitution also forbade it. He focused on the language of the Treason Clause. What, precisely, did "levying war" against the United States entail? Davis, he reasoned, could "not be convicted unless it was for having *levied* war. The case then resolved itself into the inquiry whether in any just interpretation of that phrase [he] had *levied* war." For O'Conor, "levying" war was distinct from "waging" it. Only the former was treasonous; the latter term tracked the recognition of belligerency. "My position was," he told Davis, "that if you had [levied war against the United States], that act was merged in the war which was *waged* by both parties. It might be safely admitted that this merger could not have taken place without an acknowledgment by the United States government that a *public war* existed." O'Conor told Davis, "it is only in the original conspiracy and in adapting its means to the purposes of active resistance that war can be *levied*."[27] Treason was nullified and divested of any meaning once the U.S. government had engaged in the war and thus treated the Confederacy as a belligerent. In other words, the Constitution itself imported the concept of belligerency, excusing treason when it rose to the level of war. Under this theory, rebellion could constitute treason only if it were one-sided.

Was there really a difference between "levying" and "waging" war? Most of the legal treatises of the day did not endorse O'Conor's interpretation, finding the two terms to be self-evidently synonymous.[28] English lawyer Joseph Chitty's influential criminal law treatise, which O'Conor owned, provided a sample indictment for high treason,

---

[26] Case of Davis, *Chase's Reports*, 11–17. *Chase's Reports* was compiled not by Chase himself but by his reporter of decisions, Bradley Johnson. O'Conor acknowledged that he provided the statements directly to Johnson, both in the case report itself and in a letter to Jefferson Davis. See Charles O'Conor to Jefferson Davis, February 8, 1878, Jefferson Davis Papers, MC.

[27] Charles O'Conor to Jefferson Davis, February 8, 1878, Jefferson Davis Papers, MC.

[28] The modern version of *Black's Law Dictionary* equates "levying" war with "declar[ing] or wag[ing] (a war)." Bryan A. Garner, ed., *Black's Law Dictionary*, 8th ed. (St. Paul: Thomson/West, 2004), s.v. "levying."

charging a hypothetical defendant with "procuring and providing, arms and offensive weapons, (to wit) guns, muskets, pikes and axes, therewith to levy and wage war, insurrection and rebellion, against our said lord the king."[29] Nineteenth-century treatise writers did not parse the language of the Treason Clause closely. Instead, they devoted most of their attention to the particular problems that earlier American treason cases had presented, largely relating to questions of the defendant's specific intent: had he intended to overthrow the government, or merely to resist particular government acts?[30] Francis Wharton's criminal law treatise, which O'Conor also owned, did touch on the "levying" war language, and acknowledged that "taken most literally ... the words 'levying of war' are perhaps of the same import of the words raising or creating war." In Wharton's opinion, however, the clause also "comprehended making war, or carrying on war."[31]

But O'Conor's semantic point had some support. The *Oxford English Dictionary* defines the word *levy* as "to undertake, commence (or) make war." The word is derived from the French *lever*, meaning to raise. By contrast, *wage* means to "carry on (war, a contest)" and comes from the French *gager*, meaning to gage, or pledge.[32] Ironically, O'Conor's argument found the most support in War Department

---

[29] Charles O'Conor, *Catalogue of the Law Library of the Late Charles O'Conor* (New York: Geo. A. Leavitt & Co., Auctioneers, 1885). So far as possible, I have tried to cite the edition of the work found in O'Conor's library; if the edition in his library was published following the period when he worked on the Davis case, I have selected the latest edition prior to the Civil War. Joseph Chitty, *A Practical Treatise on the Criminal Law: Comprising the Practice, Pleadings, and Evidence, Which Occur in the Course of Criminal Prosecutions*, 3 vols. (Springfield, MA: G. and C. Merriam, 1836) 2: 78, 83.

[30] See, e.g., Joel Prentiss Bishop, *Commentaries on the Criminal Law*, 2 vols. (Boston: Little, Brown, 1865), 2: 654; Joseph Story, *Commentaries on the Constitution of the United States*, 3 vols. (Boston: Hilliard, Gray, 1833), 3: 670. An example of an early treason case in this vein is *Fries's Case*, which involved armed resistance to a tax. United States v. Fries, 9 F. Cas. 826 (C.C.D. Pa. 1799) (No. 5,126). See also Jonathan W. White, "The Trial of Jefferson Davis and the Americanization of Treason Law," in *Constitutionalism in the Approach and Aftermath of the Civil War*, ed. Paul D. Moreno and Johnathan O'Neill (New York: Fordham University Press, 2013); Blair, *With Malice toward Some*, chapter 1, on the early American law of treason.

[31] Francis Wharton, *A Treatise on the Criminal Law of the United States: Comprising a General View of the Civil Jurisprudence of the Common and the Civil Law* (Philadelphia: Kay & Bros., 1857), § 2720.

[32] *Oxford English Dictionary*, 2nd ed. (Oxford: Oxford University Press, 1989), s.v.v. "levy" and "wage."

solicitor William Whiting's treatise on the president's war powers, which O'Conor read in preparation for the Davis case. As William Blair has pointed out, Whiting's treatise sought to provide a justification for virtually unlimited governmental authority in times of crisis.[33] This purpose was wholly at odds with O'Conor's, although Whiting's textual analysis proved helpful. In providing a constitutional justification for the Second Confiscation Act, Whiting touched on the specific language of the Treason Clause. The Constitution punished "levying" war, which Whiting conceded covered "only rais[ing] or begin[ning] war." Clearly, according to Whiting, engaging in a long, ongoing "rebellion, involving millions in a fratricidal contest," was by far a worse (and distinct) crime. Congress could thus punish such behavior by statute even though it broadened the scope of the constitutional text.[34]

Where would Salmon Chase come down on this issue? Would he be a pragmatist and endorse Lincoln and Seward's position? Or would O'Conor's logic force his hand? Justice Stephen Field thought that his 1863 ruling in *U.S. v. Greathouse* might prove instructive to the chief justice. While riding circuit in California in 1863, Field had had the opportunity to confront the question of whether treason could in any way be excused by the U.S. government's recognition of the belligerent status of the Confederacy. In *Greathouse*, the defendants, Confederate seamen who had been granted letters of marque by Jefferson Davis, had sailed to San Francisco to seize U.S. vessels, which they then intended to use to transport merchandise to Mexico. Instead they were captured and held at Alcatraz, and when they were charged with treason, they argued that the Confederate government's sanction of their activities rendered them legal under the law of nations. The defendants claimed that the U.S. had conferred belligerent status by blockading Confederate ports and agreeing to regularized prisoner exchange with Confederate officials.

In charging the jury, Field had directed a verdict against the defendants, insisting that, despite the U.S. government's acknowledgment of Confederate belligerency, the Confederacy enjoyed no legal status

---

[33] Blair, *With Malice toward Some*, 97–99.
[34] Whiting, *War Powers under the Constitution*, 123. Whiting's interpretation is somewhat problematic, given that the Treason Clause limits the definition of treason "only" to levying war.

under the domestic law of the United States and that acting on its behalf did not excuse the treason of the defendants. Field rejected O'Conor's narrow reading of the Treason Clause and maintained that sanction from the Confederate government provided no immunity from a treason prosecution.[35] "The existence of civil war," he wrote, "and the application of the rules of war to particular cases, under special circumstances, do not imply the renunciation or waiver by the federal government of any of its municipal rights as sovereign toward the citizens of the seceded states."[36] Three years later, Field recognized that his legal reasoning in *Greathouse* might well prove instructive to Chase in dealing with the Davis debacle, and he recommended his opinion to the chief justice.[37]

Chase picked up Field's cue. In Chase's first circuit court session in formerly rebellious territory (North Carolina in June 1867), he took the opportunity to confront head-on the question of what legal recognition the Confederacy would receive in the postwar world. Chase put an immediate end to speculation that his states' rights principles would lead him to endorse secession. His opinion also laid bare his understanding that the law had to incorporate social reality and the results of the war.

Shortridge v. Macon was an action in assumpsit. A Pennsylvania plaintiff sued a North Carolina defendant to recover on a prewar promissory note. During the war the defendant had paid the amount due on the note to the Confederate government as required by the Confederate Sequestration Act. This law required the property of Unionists (including debts owed them) to be turned over to the Confederate government.[38] The defendant contended that compliance

---

[35] Field relied on early American and English precedent to argue that the term *wage* encompassed the "levying of war." Indeed, Field equated the two terms, using them interchangeably: "It is not, however, necessary that I should go into any close definition of the words 'levying war'; for it is not sought to apply them to any doubtful case. War has been levied against the United States. War of gigantic proportions is now waged against them, and the government is struggling with it for its life." U.S. v. Greathouse, 26 F. Cas. 18, 22 (C.C.N.D.Cal. 1863) (No. 15,254).

[36] U.S. v. Greathouse, 26 F. Cas. at 24.

[37] Stephen J. Field to Salmon P. Chase, June 30, 1866, in Salmon P. Chase, *The Salmon P. Chase Papers*, ed. John Niven, 5 vols. (Kent: Kent State University Press, 1993), 5: 116.

[38] The act confiscated all the property of alien enemies, i.e., Northerners, located in the Confederate states. Because debts owed by Southerners to Northerners were included

with the Confederate statute had discharged his debt. In making this argument, Macon's counsel relied on the *Prize Cases*, arguing that the U.S. government's recognition of the Confederacy's belligerent status accorded its actions a certain legitimacy that American courts were bound to respect. Chase rejected the defendant's contentions.[39]

Chase's opinion was wide-ranging. In the course of denying Macon's claim, Chase condemned secession as well as the argument that a state's secession would excuse an individual's treason, and repudiated the idea that Confederate belligerency had any collateral consequences in the postwar world. The opinion revealed the extent to which Chase considered himself bound by the decision of the battlefield. "Those who engage in rebellion must consider the consequences," Chase declared. "If they succeed, rebellion becomes revolution, and the new government will justify its founders." Otherwise, their military actions would be deemed illegal and could "originate no rights which can be recognized by the courts of the nation" against which they had rebelled.[40]

Chase flatly denied secession's constitutionality, relying on the results of the war to do much of the analytical work for him. "No elaborate discussion of the theoretical question seems now to be necessary. The question as a practical one is at rest, and is not likely to be revived." But, he maintained, the "answer which it has received [on the field of battle was the one that] construction of the constitution warrants and requires." Moreover, he held, secession was not a defense to treason. Treason was

in this definition of alien property, all Southern debtors were required to pay their debts to the Confederate government rather than to their initial "alien" creditor. See Daniel Hamilton, *The Limits of Sovereignty: Property Confiscation in the Union and the Confederacy during the Civil War* (Chicago: University of Chicago Press, 2007), and Weitz, *The Confederacy on Trial*, on the operation of the Confederate Sequestration Act.

39 A year later, in *Keppel v. Petersburg R. Co.*, Chase confronted the same question in a slightly different form in Virginia. Chase still insisted that no legal acts undertaken in hostility to the government would be recognized, but he conceded that regular legal "transactions between individuals," such as marriages and wills, could not be invalidated. Because many activities fell into a murky area between the two extremes, Chase acknowledged that the courts could not apply any general rule in sorting through the many legal transactions that had taken place in the former Confederacy. Keppel v. Petersburg R. Co., 14 F. Cas. 357 (C.C.D. Va. 1868) (No. 7,722). See also Ford v. Surget, 97 U.S. 594; Erwin Surrency, "The Legal Effects of the Civil War," *American Journal of Legal History* 5 (April 1961):145, 150–58; Charles Fairman, *Reconstruction and Reunion*, 2 vols. (New York: Macmillan, 1971).

40 Shortridge v. Macon, 22 F. Cas. 20, 23 (C.C.D.N.C 1867) (No. 12,812).

the levying of war, and war levied "under the pretended authority" of the Confederate government "was treason against the United States." North Carolina's secession ordinance did not "thereby [absolve] the people of the state from all obligations as citizens of the United States."[41]

Chase then addressed the Confederacy's belligerent status. It was illogical to contend that the sheer scope of the rebellion exempted its perpetrators from being charged with treason. It made no sense to punish a small-scale rebellion but to excuse war when "levied by ten thousand or ten hundred thousand." The Union had treated the Confederacy under the law of war to prevent atrocities and to ensure that other countries adhered to the rules of neutrality. But those concessions "established no rights except during the war." The Supreme Court had said no differently in the *Prize Cases*. The Court had "simply assented to the right of the United States to treat the insurgents as belligerents." This did not constitute a renunciation of sovereign control over Confederate territory, and the Court had never suggested that "by the act of rebellion, and by levying war against the nation, [the Confederate states] became foreign states, and their inhabitants alien enemies."[42]

Davis supporters and antislavery men Gerrit Smith and Horace Greeley immediately resisted Chase's announcement that the consequences of belligerency expired with the end of the war. In fact, the *Shortridge* opinion was targeted at them. Smith had spoken openly and often against trying Confederates for treason and had put up money for Davis's bail bond in May 1867.[43] He reasoned that according belligerent status to the Confederacy had signified a promise by the United States to treat the Confederacy only as a foreign enemy. The Civil War had been waged between two nation-states. Now, after its victory, the Union could not choose to regard Davis as having retained his duties as an American citizen during the war. The government could not renege on its pledge and subject the Confederates to any punishment other than the bitterness of defeat. As Smith put it, quoting Edmund Burke,

[41] Shortridge v. Macon, 22 F. Cas. at 21–22.
[42] Shortridge v. Macon, 22 F. Cas. at 22–23.
[43] Gerrit Smith, *No Treason in Civil War* (New York: American News Company, 1865); Gerrit Smith to Salmon P. Chase, May 28, 1866 (broadside), NYHS; Gerrit Smith to William Lloyd Garrison, March 20, 1867, Box 24, Jefferson Davis Papers, MC. These letters, printed as broadsides, enjoyed wide public circulation.

"I do know not the method of drawing up an indictment against a whole people."[44]

The government insisted that it *could* apply both the law of war against the Confederacy and the law of treason against individuals, but Smith denied that such a duality could be lawful or humane. To try Davis for treason after the implicit pledge of individual immunity that belligerency had promised "would be to call in question our victory, to outrage humanity, to violate the spirit of the Constitution.... It would sacrifice that hope of a restored Union which rests on impartial justice to all men."[45]

Smith's public letter explaining his reasons for providing bail for Jefferson Davis in early June 1867 caught Chase's attention. In his letter, Smith again urged leniency toward Davis and reiterated his view that the Confederate leaders could be punished only by "the law of war – of that law, which knows no treason."[46] Chase received Smith's letter while in Raleigh and had it in mind when writing the *Shortridge* opinion.[47] In a scarcely veiled allusion, the opinion criticized "some persons, distinguished by ability and virtue, who insist that when rebellion attains the proportions and assumes the character of civil war, it is purged of its treasonable character."[48]

The other target of Chase's barely concealed barb was Horace Greeley. Greeley's *New York Tribune* reacted immediately to Chase's pronouncement against any semblance of Confederate legitimacy in *Shortridge*. Greeley, in his rebuke, accused the chief justice of undermining the very foundations of democratic government, because the *Shortridge* opinion minimized the importance of the consent of the governed and undercut the right of revolution. The *Tribune* criticized the shaky logic of the decision, asserting that "in the view of this [*Shortridge*] doctrine, the more formidable the rebellion the greater the crime; so that to have four-fifths of the people in sympathy with

[44] Smith, *No Treason in Civil War*, 7.
[45] Gerrit Smith to Salmon P. Chase, May 28, 1866 (broadside), NYHS.
[46] Gerrit Smith, *On the Bailing of Jefferson Davis*, June 6, 1867 (broadside), HU.
[47] Chase to Gerrit Smith, June 25, 1867, in Chase, *Salmon P. Chase Papers*, 5: 161–62.
[48] Shortridge v. Macon, 22 F. Cas. at 21–22. See Fairman, *Reconstruction and Reunion*, 1: 641 n. 79. Fairman misconstrued Chase's language as a rebuke directed at Thaddeus Stevens rather than at Gerrit Smith; the two men's positions shared many similarities. See Smith, *No Treason in Civil War*, 20–21.

the rebels would only aggravate the wickedness of their outbreak. But, in a republic based on popular consent, the case is gravely altered."[49] In Greeley's opinion, punishing ex-Confederates for their loyalty to the Confederacy called into question the principles of the American Revolution and the notion that men could throw off a government they found oppressive.[50]

Chase did not mince words in his reply to Greeley. He lambasted the editor for his irresponsibility in defending the Confederacy. "How could you!" Chase wrote. "Don't [*sic*] the Constitution say, what shall constitute 'treason.' Isn't it 'Levying war'? Didn't the rebels 'levy war'? Didn't they, then, 'commit treason'? … There is the Constitution and it is so plain that it can't be made plainer."[51] Chase's tone with Smith was more restrained. In a polite letter to Smith soon after the opinion was announced, Chase confirmed that he had indeed aimed his *Shortridge* opinion at Smith and (to a lesser extent) Greeley. First and foremost, Chase stressed his belief that the Union should treat the Confederates with mercy and pardon them. But he said that decision lay with the president rather than the judiciary. The courts were bound to apply the rules of law. There "is no middle ground between Treason & *de facto* Government," Chase insisted. The choice was stark. Failing to condemn the Confederacy was tantamount to condemning the Union. "If the rebels levying war against the Government were not traitors," he maintained, "secession was a valid act, and our war was one of conquest."[52] Smith had the last word in the exchange, denying that the government could invoke the domestic law of treason in the aftermath of the war. The law of war alone governed Davis's actions, he insisted. "Try Mr. Davis, if you will, for assassinating President Lincoln or for starving prisoners," he wrote, "but we cannot try him for treason."[53]

---

[49] *New York Tribune*, June 24, 1867.

[50] See also Lysander Spooner, *No Treason, No. 1* (Boston: published by the author, 1867), available at www.lysanderspooner.org/notreason.htm (accessed November 1, 2016).

[51] *New York Tribune*, June 24, 1867; Salmon P. Chase to Horace Greeley, June 25, 1867, in Chase, *Salmon P. Chase Papers*, 5: 159.

[52] Salmon P. Chase to Gerrit Smith, June 25, 1867, in Chase, *Salmon P. Chase Papers*, 5: 161–62; 160–61 n. 7.

[53] Gerrit Smith, *Remarks of Gerrit Smith on the Words of the Chief Justice*, July 15, 1867 (broadside), HU.

In addition to Greeley and Smith, Chase intended his *Shortridge* opinion to reach the Davis defense team, so that they would be aware of his views. *Shortridge* would send the message that his states' rights positions would not lead him to endorse secession or the postwar reach of Confederate belligerency. Chase knew that both Greeley and Smith were in continuous contact with Davis's defense lawyers, particularly George Shea, and had reason to trust that his opinion would be passed on.[54]

Still, he was not taking any chances that his ideas would be missed. He also circulated the opinion widely, particularly to those in Davis's camp. Thomas F. Bayard, a prominent Delaware attorney and Peace Democrat who had assisted O'Conor with the Davis defense, literally stumbled across *Shortridge* when a large package containing fifty copies of the opinion arrived at his father's office.[55] Bayard deduced that Chase had intended *Shortridge* to be a shot across the bow. It was an unmistakably clear signal of his views on the postwar illegitimacy of secession.

Reading the opinion led Bayard to the ineluctable conclusion that Chase would not endorse Thaddeus Stevens's view, which aligned secession with Radical Reconstruction. The states had not removed themselves from the Union in 1861 and were not conquered foreign territory. "It is needless to say," Bayard wrote, "how entirely [*Shortridge*] conflicts with the deliverances of Stevens and Sumner &c – whose doctrine is that the southern people are *outside* the Constitution and laws not liable to privileges and penalties to be treated as conquered enemies subject to the *grace* of the Conquerors alone."[56] Chase had no

---

[54] I was unable to find explicit evidence in any extant letter that Greeley or Smith communicated Chase's sentiments directly to Shea, but Shea certainly discussed the details of the trial with Smith on a regular basis, as well as his personal views of Chase. See George Shea to Gerrit Smith, August 22, 1866; May 10, October 18, 23, November 11, 18, 23, 1867; April 27, May 23, June 14, July 9, December 9, 1868, Reel 16, Gerrit Smith Papers, LC [microfilm edition]. Also, Chase did not mark his letters to either Greeley or Smith as "private."

[55] Bayard complained once to his father about the weight of the responsibilities O'Conor placed on him, saying they took him away from his paying work despite the fact that he was "not *counsel* for Mr. Davis." Thomas F. Bayard to James A. Bayard, April 12, 1868, vol. 12, Bayard Family Papers, LC.

[56] Thomas F. Bayard to James A. Bayard, August 17, 1867, vol. 11, Bayard Family Papers, LC.

practical use for the secession argument in the postwar context, and felt free to deny its constitutional basis.

Because of *Shortridge*, some of Davis's lawyers changed their views of the case. Former Baltimore mayor George William Brown felt shaken after reading the opinion. "After reading the rulings of Judge Chase in a recent case in North Carolina," Brown told Davis, "I could not help feeling thankful that your trial did not take place before him. He held that the war gave to Southern people no rights and exonerated them from no responsibilities." The opinion, frankly, angered Brown. Chase had shown himself willing to tolerate glaring inconsistencies in the legal rules governing the Confederate states and their residents.[57] Brown was disappointed that Chase had shown himself to be a "creative" legal thinker, a pragmatist, who would be willing to shape the law to achieve crucial social objectives.

Several Davis supporters were not entirely persuaded that *Shortridge* truly encapsulated the chief justice's views, in spite of Chase's efforts to assure them. Former Confederate judge Alexander Clayton wrote Davis in January 1868 that the *Prize Cases*' recognition of belligerent status transformed individual acts of rebellion into collective war. "The whole communities are responsible as Governments," Clayton wrote. "The concession of belligerent rights, means this if it means any thing. This concession once made, and acted upon by both parties, cannot be retracted by either, but through a breach of faith." Clayton acknowledged that Chase's recent ruling in *Shortridge* gave him pause, as it was clear that the chief justice had publicly endorsed the opposite view. But Chase was not looking at things clearly, he said, and if the Supreme Court were given the chance to reconsider, Chase would have to concede that belligerents could not "be subjected to municipal law." The logic was just too powerful to be discounted: the Court simply could not "disregard [it] or set [it] aside." In spite of *Shortridge*, Clayton believed that a court could not "willingly countenance such an inconsistency."[58]

[57] George William Brown to Jefferson Davis, June 30, 1867, Box 24, Jefferson Davis Papers, MC.

[58] Alexander M. Clayton to Jefferson Davis, in Jefferson Davis, *Jefferson Davis, Constitutionalist: His Letters, Papers, and Speeches*, ed. Dunbar Rowland, 10 vols. (Jackson: Mississippi Department of Archives and Records, 1923), 8: 408.

Former Confederate diplomat James M. Mason agreed. *Shortridge* notwithstanding, Mason argued that Chase could not manipulate the law to this extent. Although Mason recognized that Chase's presidential ambitions tended to cloud his judgment, he insisted that Chase was bound to exonerate Davis on the grounds of Confederate belligerency. The law itself constrained him. "Whatever my opinion of the man, or of his complication with party, yet he stands at the head of the Judiciary, [and] is undoubtedly an able lawyer," Mason wrote. "I thus have relied, and yet rely, that on such a trial, with the world looking on, he cannot rule that to be law, which he knows, is *not* law."[59] Even in the face of powerful evidence to the contrary, Clayton and Mason adhered to a formalist belief in the inviolability of law, which would not stretch to accommodate politics.

Charles O'Conor knew better. Chase had effectively broadcast his views to the Davis camp, and he would not render a result in Davis's case that would conflict with the needs of the healing country. Any hope he might have entertained that Chase might be inclined to endorse secession had now evaporated, but O'Conor had never really believed that Chase could be counted on to exonerate Davis. In his view, the chief justice was too ruled by political ambition to feel constrained by the law or to act publicly in Davis's favor. Davis had been released from prison on bail in May 1867, a month before the *Shortridge* ruling. Davis was still at risk for prosecution, however, which had to be avoided at all costs – now more than ever, O'Conor realized.

This proved particularly true a few months after *Shortridge*, in late 1867, when the smart and savvy Boston lawyer Richard Henry Dana joined the government's team. It remained to be seen whether Dana's hiring signaled a new seriousness of purpose that would bear out the government's early promise to bring Davis to justice.

[59] James M. Mason to Jefferson Davis, April 22, 1868, in Davis, *Jefferson Davis, Constitutionalist*, 7: 237–41.

Richard Henry Dana Comes on Board

In the fall of 1867 William Evarts wanted to regroup. John Clifford had left the prosecution more than a year earlier, and Evarts prevailed on Attorney General Stanbery to replace him with his good friend Richard Henry Dana, a prominent Boston lawyer and author (Figure 11.1). In describing the position to Dana, Evarts only hinted at the problems that had plagued the case from the beginning. He told Dana that, "as Mr. Stanbery does not prefer to take part in the case, I am now alone with the Dist. Atty. of Virginia," but suggested that it seemed unlikely that the case would ever make it to trial.[1] As a friend, Evarts had kept Dana informally apprised of the Davis matter since he had taken the case. After he accepted his retainer from the government in 1865, Evarts had also asked for Dana's advice on the Davis prosecution. He invited Dana and his own cousin and fellow attorney Rockwood Hoar to his country home in Windsor, Vermont, saying, "I want to talk with him and you about several things, especially J. Davis and reconstruction."[2]

Dana was a good choice to assist in the Davis prosecution. Charles O'Conor once faintly praised him as Evarts's "only assistant who possesses any ability."[3] Dana had served as the U.S. attorney for

---

[1] William Evarts to Richard Henry Dana, October 17, 1867, Box 17, Dana Family Papers, MHS.
[2] William Evarts to Richard Henry Dana, September 4, 1865, William Evarts Papers, HEHL.
[3] Charles O'Conor to Jefferson Davis, April 18, 1868, Box 24, Jefferson Davis Papers, MC.

FIGURE 11.1 Prosecutor Richard Henry Dana. Harvard University Libraries.

Massachusetts for a number of years, and in that capacity he had developed an expertise in the law of prize that few other Americans could claim at the time.[4] During the war, as the U.S. attorney for Massachusetts, Dana was called on to defend the constitutional-ity of President Lincoln's blockade in prosecuting prize cases. He

[4] See John Raymond and Barbara Frischholz, "Lawyers Who Established International Law in the United States, 1774–1914," *American Journal of International Law* 76 (1982): 802.

had prosecuted the case of the *Amy Warwick* in the district court in Massachusetts, and when that case was consolidated with several others in the Supreme Court as the *Prize Cases*, Dana had argued it along with Evarts. Dana's expertise in prize law showed to great advantage in the Supreme Court, and it was his oral argument and brief (rather than Evarts's) that appeared in extended form in the reported decision. This was quite an honor for Dana, as his friend Evarts was by far the better-known attorney. In compiling the official report of the case, the Supreme Court reporter and former U.S. attorney general Jeremiah S. Black told Dana he had selected his argument because he believed that "you and Mr. C[arlisle, for the claimants] gave at once the fullest clearest and strongest expositions of the general doctrines you contended for."[5] Dana also produced an erudite edition of Henry Wheaton's influential international law treatise, *Elements of International Law*, which appeared in 1866.[6] He was thus extremely well versed in – and could claim some credit for crafting – the Union's legal policy toward Confederates during the Civil War.

Dana's affinity for the law of prize extended far back, as he had spent a formative part of his youth at sea. Like Evarts, Dana was the scion of an old New England family and could count some of the earliest settlers of Cambridge, Massachusetts, as his ancestors. Dana's ancestors had owned much of the land in Cambridgeport and had established a family mansion on "Dana Hill," just south of Central Square. Dana's grandfather Francis had been a delegate to the Continental Congress and a signer of the Articles of Confederation, but Dana's father, Richard Henry, was far less successful, eking out a living composing romantic poetry after a series of family financial losses that forced the Danas to sell their mansion. Still, when Richard Henry Jr. followed family tradition and entered Harvard College in 1831 (where he befriended Evarts, who was then studying at Harvard Law School), the Dana name still carried a great deal of weight in his native Cambridge. It would have seemed highly unlikely that Richard

---

[5] J. S. Black to R. H. Dana, August 17, 1863, Box 16, Dana Family Papers, MHS. Dana himself modestly explained that Evarts's argument went unreported because of his "absence from the country on public duty." Richard Henry Dana, *Speeches in Stirring Times and Letters to a Son*, ed. Richard Henry Dana III (Boston: Houghton Mifflin, 1910), 285.

[6] See Chapter 12 for more on the treatise.

Henry Dana, a Boston Brahmin, would forsake his elite existence as a Cambridge landlubber for the allure of the open sea, but Dana did precisely that, abandoning his studies for two years to sign on as a common sailor on a voyage around Cape Horn to California.

During Dana's third year at Harvard, his eyesight failed. Rather than remaining idle at home with his family while he recuperated, or depleting the family's meager finances by embarking on a grand tour of Europe, Dana signed on as an ordinary seaman on a brig headed for California, hoping that the respite from intensive reading would improve his health. On the journey, Dana's sight did improve, and he wrote a famous travelogue, *Two Years before the Mast*, about his adventure. Vivid with descriptions of his life as a sailor and his encounters with the ruggedness of California, *Two Years before the Mast* won Dana a level of fame as a man of letters that was never equaled in his later career as a lawyer. The book revealed the adventuresome spirit of young Dana, even if it did whitewash his experiences. In the book, Dana recounted in passing, for example, that the American Indian women he encountered had "but little virtue," but failed to discuss in more detail, as one of Dana's shipmates complained, "the beautiful Indian lasses, who so often frequented your humble abode."[7]

Dana returned to Harvard after his travels, and finished his undergraduate studies before enrolling in Harvard Law School. On graduating from law school, Dana married and entered the practice of law, eventually establishing a solid but not dazzlingly successful law practice in Boston. Dana's biographer James Hart describes Dana's placid existence in later life as a confining experience. Although he appreciated the comfort and prestige of being an important man in an important city, Dana felt that something was lacking in his life when he reminisced about his travels in California, and he longed for the freedom he had experienced at sea.[8] His decision to devote much of his practice to maritime law and to take on many seamen as clients

---

[7] Richard Henry Dana Jr., *Two Years before the Mast* (New York: Worthington, 1890), 162; B. G. Stinson to Richard Henry Dana, March 16, 1841, quoted in Samuel Shapiro, *Richard Henry Dana, Jr., 1815–1882* (East Lansing: Michigan State University Press, 1961), 9.

[8] James David Hart, "The Education of Richard Henry Dana, Jr.," *New England Quarterly* 9 (March 1936): 3, 22–25. See also James David Hart, "Richard Henry Dana, Jr.," PhD diss., Harvard University, 1936.

probably stemmed from his desire not to abandon wholly his rugged youth as he settled into a stable career.

In 1867, although Dana was, at fifty-two, a prominent and well-respected lawyer in Boston and Cambridge, having worked on the highly publicized defense of the fugitive slave Anthony Burns in the 1850s, he did not enjoy the national recognition that his friend Evarts did. Dana was famous enough that Charles Dickens sought him out when he visited the United States in the 1840s, but he remained best known as an author, rather than as a lawyer.[9] As a result, Dana's life was dominated by his ambition to increase his public profile and secure high public office, hopes that were met, more often than not, by disappointment.[10] Serving as a prosecutor in the Davis case – and securing a verdict against Davis and a pronouncement against the right of secession – would certainly raise his profile, Dana realized, especially as the case had languished for two years prior to his involvement. As O'Conor snarkily remarked to Davis, Dana had "adduced his retainer in the 'greatest case of modern times' as an official acknowledgment of his superiority" in his chosen profession.[11]

This is not to say that Dana was uninterested in establishing the illegality of secession in a court of law. In fact, in what became known as his famous "Grasp of War" speech, given at Boston's Faneuil Hall in June 1865, Dana had spoken about the demise of state sovereignty ideology in the United States. Dana's speech was intended to provide a theoretical foundation for Reconstruction in the South, and he told the crowd that the United States government possessed the ability to oversee the internal activities of the Confederate states because the Union still retained its war powers in dealing with the defeated Confederacy. Even though the hostilities had ended, the federal government was entitled to treat the Confederacy as within the "grasp of war." The Union could continue its dominion over the former Confederate states until the underlying problems that had caused the war had ceased – that is, until those states threw off the vestiges of the social and legal system that had nurtured slavery and disunion. "We have a right to

[9] Shapiro, *Richard Henry Dana, Jr.*, 12.
[10] Dana served in the Massachusetts legislature from 1867 to 1868 and ran for Congress in 1868.
[11] Charles O'Conor to Jefferson Davis, April 18, 1868, Box 24, Jefferson Davis Papers, MC.

require whatever the public safety and public faith make necessary,"
he declared. Holding the states within the grasp of war, Dana argued,
did not undermine the proper balance of authority in the federal system, because the measures were temporary and necessary.[12] Dana also
took the opportunity to set forth his views on the federal system. He
insisted on the importance of maintaining decentralization, because
"our system is a system of states, with central power; and in that system is our safety." Still, Dana emphasized that although states' rights
survived the war, "state sovereignty we have destroyed."[13]

In compiling Dana's speeches after his death, his son Richard Henry
III revealed that, in the days following Appomattox, his father had
worried about the difficulty of "preserv[ing] the fruits of the war without acknowledging the right of secession." Dana intended his Grasp of
War speech to counteract this tendency. The elder Dana's undelivered
notes on the speech reveal that he believed that the war had been
waged to destroy secession, and that without vigilance, Northerners
would unwittingly permit the hard-won results of the war to slip away.
"If the dogma of State Supremacy is not destroyed, for practice as well
as in theory, the war will have been in vain," Dana wrote.

The prosecution of treason was central to this endeavor because
it would establish the death of secession. Dana argued that no
state could absolve an individual of allegiance to the republic. He
denounced "the tenet that the United States is not a nation, a government, a sovereignty, – that the citizens owe to it no direct allegiance, – that they cannot commit against it the crime of treason, if
they carry with them into their treason the forms of state authority."
In his view, the fact that the United States had fought a "great war"
against the rebellious Confederates as an organized political entity (as

---

[12] See Michael Les Benedict, "The Conservative Basis of Radical Reconstruction,"
in *Preserving the Constitution: Essays on Politics and the Constitution in the
Reconstruction Era* (New York: Fordham University Press, 2006), and Gregory
Downs, *After Appomattox* (Cambridge, MA: Harvard University Press, 2015).
Benedict characterizes the "grasp of war" theory as "conservative" because of its temporary nature, but the theory in fact gave vast powers to the federal government to
remake Southern society, and depending on the scale of the "remaking," war powers
could linger for an extended period of time. One could argue, for instance, that the
social conditions of white supremacy that gave rise to the Civil War still exist today.

[13] Richard Henry Dana, "'Grasp of War' Speech," June 21, 1865, in Dana, *Speeches in
Stirring Times*, 252, 259, 240.

recognized in the *Prize Cases*) did not prohibit treason prosecutions against individuals. Treason prosecutions were an appropriate means of cementing the legal determinations of the battlefield. Now that the war had demanded such sacrifice on behalf of its combatants, Dana maintained, *"The right of this republic to be a sovereign, among the sovereignties of the earth, must be put beyond further dispute."*[14]

With his good friend Dana on board – and with Congress breathing down his neck about the lack of progress in the Davis case – Evarts began to tackle the prosecution's problems head-on. Evarts was acutely aware of Attorney General Stanbery's reluctance to become personally involved in the case and he warned Dana that "the whole thing legal and political will be upon *us*."[15]

Initially, at least, Dana brought an energy to the prosecution that had been missing for the previous year and a half. To bring himself up to speed on the issues in the Davis case, Dana compiled and read every treason case in U.S. history. Dana also worried about the prospects of convicting Davis in Richmond and groped for a solution to the problem of the pro-Confederate jury pool. James Speed's 1866 attorney general opinion rejecting the doctrine of constructive presence had limited the prosecutors to trying Davis in Virginia. In response, Dana seized on the idea of trying Davis in the newly created (and highly Unionist) state of West Virginia, based on the theory that West Virginia had been part of the state of Virginia throughout much of the Civil War.[16]

The U.S. Constitution provides that any federal criminal trial must be "held in the state where the said Crimes shall have been committed," and the Judiciary Act of 1789 had further specified that in cases carrying the death penalty, the defendant had to be tried in the county

---

[14] Richard Henry Dana III, "Introductory Sketch," in Dana, *Speeches in Stirring Times*, 5; Richard Henry Dana Jr., "The Faneuil Hall Address," in Dana, *Speeches in Stirring Times*, 262, emphasis in the original.

[15] William Evarts to Richard Henry Dana, October 28, 1867, Box 16, Dana Family Papers, MHS.

[16] See also U.S. Const. amend. VI. Dana was not alone in advocating that Davis be tried in West Virginia. Edwin Stanton asserted in June 1865 that if Davis were tried in Virginia, he could be tried in any number of cities. As he wrote to Joseph Holt concerning the proper venue for Davis's trial, "And why not in Wheeling! He committed treason enough to hang a legion of men before the State of West Virginia was organized." Edwin Stanton to Joseph Holt, June 7, 1865, vol. 92, Joseph Holt Papers, LC.

where he had committed his offense, or at least that his jurors had to be summoned from that county. Although this had been the law for more than eighty years, during the war Congress repealed the provision that required federal jurors to be summoned from a particular county.[17] Dana used this provision and the legal separation of West Virginia from Virginia during the war to mount an argument for trying Davis in West Virginia for his treasonous actions prior to the division of the state in 1863. In Dana's opinion, the states of Virginia and West Virginia were still entwined for the purposes of federal court jurisdiction.[18] Dana's plan to try Davis outside of Richmond never came to fruition, probably owing to the very imperatives that motivated the attorney general in making his recommendations with regard to the Davis case in the first place: the concern that Davis's trial be conducted with the utmost propriety to ensure the public's acceptance of the verdict.

Time was of the essence, and Evarts and Dana had to secure a new indictment in place of the faulty one hurriedly drawn by U.S. Attorney Lucius Chandler a year earlier. This had to be done before the limitations period expired the following spring. Evarts and Dana traveled to Richmond in November 1867, where they appeared in court to inform Judge Underwood that, yet again, the government was not ready to try the case, and to ask for a postponement. While in the city they took the opportunity to move forward with amassing evidence for the new indictment against Davis. Stopping in Washington on his way to Richmond, Dana met with Charles Sumner, Henry Wilson, George Boutwell, and Benjamin Butler to discuss the Davis case. Dana debunked the rumors circulating in the newspapers that the government intended to proceed to trial immediately. These men remained anxious to see Davis's trial commence, but Dana reported that he "was

---

[17] This was not because of a fear of disloyal jurors but resulted from concern about the excessive cost of transporting jurors from distant parts of a state. See *Congressional Globe*, 37th Cong., 2d sess., July 3, 1862, 3099. See also U.S. Const. art. III, § 2; Judiciary Act of 1789, § 29, 1 Stat. 73 (1789); Act of July 16, 1862, 12 Stat. 588 (1862) (relating to the competency of witnesses).

[18] Richard Henry Dana Jr., "Memorandum of Constitutional and Statutory Provisions in Reference to Treason," n.d., folder titled "Legal Notes Concerning the Civil War – Sedition and Treason," Box 40, Dana Family Papers, MHS. Based on internal references, Dana produced these notes between 1866 and 1870. The Supreme Court heard the boundary dispute with regard to several contested counties in State of Virginia v. State of West Virginia, 78 U.S. 39 (1870).

able to give them good reasons for the delay, & for not doing anything to hasten it."[19]

Evarts even used a bit of gallows humor to highlight the utter inadequacy of Chandler's 1866 indictment (based on the testimony of witnesses gathered at a moment's notice) and his lack of initiative in drawing a new one over the preceding year and a half. On reaching the hotel in Richmond, Evarts related, "I have arrived at the fact that J. D. used to wear a Confederate uniform on great occasions, and have *a* witness who can prove it, in the person of a colored waiter who came to me last evening to see whether he would do for my service." Questioning the man as to his former occupation, Evarts discovered that the waiter had served Davis in the Confederate White House. "So, you see," he concluded with heavy sarcasm, "I am ahead of Chandler on overt acts and witnesses to prove them."[20]

Evarts and Dana believed that the responsibility for drafting the indictment rightfully belonged to the local U.S. attorney rather than to senior counsel, but they were deeply concerned about Chandler's ineptitude and lack of initiative, so they spent their time in Richmond working on the new indictment more directly. Holed up in a room at the Spotswood Hotel, Evarts and Dana reviewed official Confederate documents, selecting the ones to present as evidence of Davis's treason to the grand jury (Figure 11.2).[21] Dana marveled in particular at Davis's audacity in a speech he gave at the African Church in Richmond in February 1865, when he promised to show Lincoln and Seward "what the South must teach them – that they were talking to their *masters*."[22]

[19] Richard Henry Dana to Sarah Dana, November 24, 1867, Box 17, Dana Family Papers, MHS.

[20] William M. Evarts to Richard Henry Dana Jr., November 15, 1867, Box 17, Dana Family Papers, MHS. As Jonathan White points out, by the time of the Civil War, the law of treason in the United States had matured to the point that it had stringent requirements for proof of overt acts. See Jonathan W. White, "The Trial of Jefferson Davis and the Americanization of Treason Law," in *Constitutionalism in the Approach and Aftermath of the Civil War*, ed. Paul D. Moreno and Johnathan O'Neill (New York: Fordham University Press, 2013).

[21] The particular Confederate documents Evarts and Dana drew on can be found in folders 626–35, Box 32, Evarts Family Papers, Yale. See also "Papers & Books to Be Used in the Case of U.S. v. Jefferson Davis," Jefferson Davis Case File, Record Group 60, NA-CP.

[22] Richard Henry Dana to wife, November 25, 1867, Box 17, Dana Family Papers, MHS. See Jefferson Davis, "African Church Speech," in Jefferson Davis, *The Papers of Jefferson Davis*, ed. Lynda L. Crist, 14 vols. (Baton Rouge: Louisiana State University Press, 1971–2014), 11: 383–86.

FIGURE 11.2 The Spotswood Hotel, Richmond, Virginia, where Evarts and Dana worked on the Davis indictment in the late fall of 1867. Library of Congress.

After conferring with Chandler on the preparation of the indictment, they left town with the understanding that he had its drafting well in hand and would complete it shortly. After all, Chandler had directly informed the attorney general earlier in the month that the "preparation of the indictment has been commenced" and promised he would "hand it to [him] this week."[23]

[23] Lucius H. Chandler to Henry Stanbery, November 6, 1867, Jefferson Davis Case File, Record Group 60, NA-CP.

Although Evarts and Dana had impressed on Chandler the importance of drafting the indictment in a timely manner, by January 1868 he had produced nothing. With a March deadline (the conclusion of the last session of the court before the statute of limitations was set to expire), Evarts began to panic. He complained to Dana that he had "not a word from Dist. Atty Chandler nor [his assistant] Genl. [H. H.] Wells nor have I any confidence that they have done or are doing anything." Even though he believed that the responsibility for the indictment properly lay with Chandler, the utter silence from that quarter led Evarts to contemplate a highly costly break from his business in New York and a trip to Boston to confer with Dana on the matter. But, Evarts grumped, he had not even received the necessary documents from Chandler and could not move forward.[24]

Evarts expressed his harsh disapproval to Chandler and heard nothing from him for ten days, at which point Chandler unexpectedly materialized in federal court in Brooklyn, "whither he had followed [Evarts]." As Evarts was busy trying a case, Chandler left. Evarts expected that he would see Chandler later that day in his office in Manhattan, but when Evarts arrived there, he "found a bushel of papers and a note from Chandler saying he had gone off. & finding he had brought his illegible original minutes of evidence before Gr. Jury, he had taken them back and would send me a copy!" On inspecting Chandler's documents, Evarts disgustedly perceived that they were "the same papers we looked over two months ago at Richmond and nothing else." In this state of unpreparedness, Evarts wondered whether he and Dana should write "a demonstration to the Atty Genl. against trying at all."[25]

While he and Dana contemplated whether they should urge the government to drop the case, Evarts attempted to spur Chandler into doing the necessary work on the indictment. Evarts bluntly demanded to know why Chandler had not acted, detailing his displeasure at Chandler's "hurried visit to New York" and the fact that "four weeks have now passed since your visit and I have not yet received any report

---

[24] William Evarts to Richard Henry Dana, January 7, 1868, Box 18, Dana Family Papers, MHS.
[25] William Evarts to Richard Henry Dana, January 22, 1868, Box 18, Dana Family Papers, MHS.

of the evidence before the grand jury." Time was slipping away. At the time of Evarts's last meeting with Chandler, all parties were aware that "the three years within which an indictment can be found is rapidly running out and will expire in April."[26] To underscore his seriousness, Evarts sent a copy of this rebuke to Attorney General Stanbery.[27]

Dana was even more frustrated than Evarts with Chandler's incompetence in drafting the new indictment and handling the Davis case. After reading Evarts's missive to the attorney general detailing his criticisms of Chandler's performance, Dana informed him that the letter did not put the case forcefully enough. "I am sorry to say," he wrote Evarts, "that your note does not satisfy me. We are in a bad position and must take steps at once." In Dana's opinion, Chandler's mismanagement of the case was so severe that "we cannot go on with Chandler as U.S. Attorney. He will bring the thing into disrepute and disgrace, which you and I will have to bear. He will bring the whole cause to grief, and us to mortification." Dana contemplated resigning his position as associate counsel because of the public embarrassment that would ensue, but hesitated because he did not want to abandon Evarts, who had gone to the trouble of recommending Dana for the case. As Dana bluntly put it, "I know your kindness to me in all this matter, and do not wish to desert you, but I am not willing to desert my post in the legislature, and receive the ridicule and sneers of the public at a mismanaged come-to-grief case, as this will be, since we must depend upon Chandler, and he is totally worthless."[28]

Dana recommended that he and Evarts should continue working on the case only if they explicitly informed their superiors in the Johnson administration that they believed the prosecution was doomed to defeat and that they proceeded against their better judgment. Dana's biographers have argued that Dana acted out of the noblest of impulses in persuading the government to drop the case – that he was sacrificing

---

[26] William Evarts to Lucius Chandler, February 18, 1868, Jefferson Davis Trial Papers, UChi; copies can also be found in Box 18, Dana Family Papers, MHS, and Box 1, William Evarts Papers, LC.

[27] William Evarts to Henry Stanbery, February 18, 1868, Box 1, William Evarts Papers, LC.

[28] Richard Henry Dana to William Evarts, January 25, February 14, 1868, Dana copybook, vol. 164, Dana Family Papers, MHS.

his professional ambitions, which would have been furthered by a conviction, to avoid an outcome that would be disastrous for the nation.[29]

A careful reading of Dana's private correspondence with his good friend Evarts contradicts such an uncritical conclusion. In fact, Dana's main concern was to ensure that in the event of spectacular failure, he and Evarts could appear personally blameless for the defeat. Dana contemplated the idea of going public with his preestablished doubts after an acquittal. "I want it to appear that we advised the Government, and advised it early, against prosecuting this trial," Dana told Evarts. "If it drags along and gives out, or if our jury disagrees, I do not wish to appear to talk afterthoughts. I wish it to appear that we made known our opinion to the government frankly and early."[30]

More hesitant than Dana, Evarts cautioned that their letter to the attorney general should not point to Chandler's incompetence as a reason for dropping the case. If they did so, they might expose their own lack of attention to the prosecution, Evarts reasoned. "We must be careful of our own position and avoid the imputation of having been too busy about our other affairs to attend to our obligation under this retainer," he told Dana. He also reminded Dana that anyone outside the case would scoff at the notion that assembling proof of overt acts of treason was difficult.[31] Evarts suggested that Dana draft a letter to the attorney general, which Evarts would also sign, explaining their recommendation that the case should be abandoned. Aside from the very significant problem of convicting Davis of treason before a jury in the former Confederate capital, Evarts reminded Dana, "of course the general fact of the progress of time which has put the trial out of date, from causes not controllable, will be an element in your letter."[32] Evarts judged that the letter would be more effective and bring less

[29] Shapiro, *Richard Henry Dana, Jr.*, 137; James Hart, "Richard Henry Dana, Jr.," 409–10; Charles Francis Adams Jr., *Richard Henry Dana*, 2 vols. (Cambridge, MA: Riverside Press, 1890), 2: 338. Richard Henry Dana's son, Richard Henry III, recognized that his father's reasons for dropping the case stemmed from more practical motives. See Richard Henry Dana III, "The Reasons for Not Prosecuting Jefferson Davis," *Proceedings of the Massachusetts Historical Society* 64 (1931): 201–9.

[30] Richard Henry Dana to William Evarts, March 14, 1868, Dana copybook, vol. 164, Dana Family Papers, MHS.

[31] William Evarts to Richard Henry Dana, February 18, 1868, Box 18, Dana Family Papers, MHS.

[32] William Evarts to Richard Henry Dana, February 16, 1868, Box 18, Dana Family Papers, MHS.

censure on himself with Dana as the primary author. Because Dana had worked on the case for only a short period of time, it would not appear that the lawyers' wariness had resulted from Evarts's laxity in attending to it in favor of more lucrative work.

In the meantime, Evarts's rebuke to Chandler finally provoked a response from Chandler's associate H. H. Wells. Wells informed Evarts that Chandler had been ill and unable to work on the indictment for that reason and promised that he and Chandler would confer on the matter immediately. They would act with "promptness and diligence." Evarts and Dana, in return, remained at the ready to look over Wells's and Chandler's work, "as soon as the materials are placed before us." While they were waiting, Dana produced (and reproduced, through many drafts) a letter to the attorney general that detailed their objections to proceeding against Davis.[33]

In the letter Dana admitted that he "was moved, from the first, by doubts of the expediency of trying [Jefferson Davis] at all." As his initial doubts had now "ripened into convictions," Dana professed himself compelled to spell out his objections to the attorney general. There was no question, Dana contended, that Davis had committed treason against the United States. Rather, Dana's reservations about bringing Davis to trial stemmed from his fear of jury nullification. "After the most serious reflection," he wrote, "I cannot see any good reason why the Government should make a question whether the late Civil War was treason, whether Jefferson Davis took any part in it, & submit these questions to the decision of a petit jury of the vicinage of Richmond."[34]

Dana entertained no personal doubts about the unconstitutionality of secession. It was abundantly clear to him that Mississippi's secession could not purge Davis of his United States citizenship. Given that "the Constitution in terms settles the fact that our republic is a state

---

[33] H. H. Wells to William Evarts, February 24, 1868, Box 1, William Evarts Papers, LC; William Evarts to Richard Henry Dana, February 26, 1868, draft, and Richard Henry Dana and William Evarts to Henry Stanbery, February 26, 1868, Box 18, Dana Family Papers, MHS.

[34] Richard Henry Dana and William Evarts to Henry Stanbery, February 26, 1868, and Richard Henry Dana to William Evarts, August 24, 1868, Box 18, Dana Family Papers, MHS. There are many drafts of this letter in Dana's papers. Quotations in the following paragraphs are also from this letter, initially drafted by Dana and Evarts to send to Stanbery in February, and eventually sent by Dana to Evarts in August.

against which treason may be committed," he wrote, "the only constitutional question attending the late war was whether a levying of
war against the United States, which would otherwise be treason, is
relieved of that character by the fact that it appeared in the form of
secession from the Union by State authority." Davis's actions in levying
war against the United States could be considered nontreasonous only
if "secession was a constitutional right making an act legal and obliga-
tory upon the [Confederate] nation which would otherwise have been
treason." According to Dana, the legal questions involved in the trial
had already been settled by the war itself, as well as by more traditional legal arbiters. Dana asserted unequivocally that the constitutional status of secession was no longer an open question: "This issue
I suppose to have been settled by the action of every department of the
government, by the action of the people itself, by those events which
are definitive in the affairs of men."

Dana also insisted that the Supreme Court had already declared
secession's illegitimacy as a matter of law in the *Prize Cases* in 1863.
According to Dana, the Court's decision established "that the acts of
the states, whether secession ordinances, or in whatever form cast,
could not be brought into the cases, as justifications for the war, &
have no legal effect on the character of the war, or on the political
status of territory or persons or their property."[35] Dana maintained
that this rule had been followed in the federal courts ever since the
Prize Cases ruling. The other branches of government had concurred
in the Court's "assessment of secession and war as treason, [as] a matter of history, as well as in the action of the people of this Republic,
by the highest sanction of war." Accordingly, Dana predicted, the federal judges would undoubtedly instruct the Davis jury "in conformity
with these decisions ... that the late attempt to establish & sustain by
war, an independent empire within the United States was treason,"
and the only question that could properly be submitted to the jury
was whether Davis had served as Confederate president and waged
war against the United States. In the nature of things, Dana asserted,

---

[35] Dana's assessment of the *Prize Cases* as definitively establishing the legal illegitimacy
of secession was, in the most generous interpretation, wildly optimistic, and could
rightfully be characterized as knowingly incorrect, as will be explored in the next
chapter.

Davis's notorious behavior during the war could hardly be open to interpretation.

It was thus a mistake to submit this case, with essentially no factual disputes, to a Richmond jury, Dana contended. Since the "fact" of Davis's activities during the Civil War was not seriously in question, asking a jury to determine his guilt seemed pointless and, more important, unnecessarily risky. Why would the government give this nonquestion "to a jury with the power to find in the negative or affirmative or to disagree?"

As Dana reminded the attorney general, the jury did not have to give a reason for its decision to convict or exonerate Davis, and its determinations could well be contrary to the facts and the law of the land. The legality of Confederate secession would be at issue in the trial whether the judge condemned it from the bench or not. It was simply too dangerous to put Davis on trial in Richmond, Dana believed. As he put it, "We know that these indictments are to be laid in what was enemy's territory for five years, not yet restored to the exercise of all its political functions & when the fires are not yet extinct. We know that it only requires one dissentient juror to defeat the Government & to give Jefferson Davis & his favorers a triumph." Despite the requirement that federal jurors take the ironclad oath confirming their past and present loyalty to the United States, a Confederate sympathizer could easily slip through the cracks in the former Confederate capital, refuse to convict Davis, and cause the trial to result in a hung jury. Additionally, as Dana pointed out, social pressure or fear of violent reprisal might induce even Richmond Unionists to exonerate Davis.

Like others before him, Dana judged a hung jury or an acquittal to be potentially catastrophic for the United States government, as either outcome would be interpreted as a backdoor vindication of the right of secession. The adequacy of the legal system would be called into doubt – as would the very legitimacy of the war effort against the Confederate states. While the potential negative consequences of trying Davis for treason were immense, the benefits to be gained by securing his conviction were minimal at best, since the war had already provided a satisfactory answer to the secession question. As Dana pointed out, the best possible outcome – Davis's conviction – would secure "only a reaffirmation ... of a rule of public law already settled for this country in every way in which such a matter can be settled. ... The risks of ... a great state trial are assumed for the sake of a verdict which if obtained will settle nothing in law or national practice not now settled, & nothing, in fact, which is not now history."

Finally, Dana pointed out the practical problems that would arise if Davis were convicted. Even if the government managed to secure a guilty verdict against Davis, thus vindicating the Unionist position in the war, the president would then face the problem of punishing him. Politically, from the vantage point of 1868 this prospect was exceedingly unattractive. It would be beneath the dignity of the government and incommensurate with the gravity of the crime to inflict a punishment less than death if Davis were convicted, Dana argued. But, he wrote, "after this lapse of time & all that has occurred in the interval, the people of the United States would not desire to see [a sentence of death] carried into effect." The passage of time since Davis's capture also meant that the government could now drop the case without incurring the wrath of indignant loyal citizens who wanted to see Davis come to justice, he said, because "the public interest in the trial has ceased, among the most earnest & loyal citizens." By laying out such a blistering case against the wisdom of taking Davis to trial, Dana hoped to convince the attorney general that the law had already condemned secession in the *Prize Cases* and the government had nothing to gain but humiliation in seeking to establish the matter again in such a perilous forum. But in point of fact, Dana's 1868 letter drastically oversold the *Prize Cases*. In asserting that the case had condemned the right of secession, Dana was contradicting his own earlier view on the matter. Five years earlier he had claimed that the case said absolutely nothing about the legality of secession. Dana's statements about the heft of the *Prize Cases* were part of a larger project among Unionist lawyers in the postwar period to minimize uncertainties and disagreements and to recast their tentative legal theories as settled rules of law. In 1863 the Court had declared international law to be available to the Union in its contest with the Confederacy in the *Prize Cases*, but beyond that, the consequences of the decision were unclear and, as yet, undeveloped. By reinterpreting the case in the context of postwar treason trials, Dana sought to stretch its meaning in the service of the government's needs.

12

The Reach of the *Prize Cases*

In writing to the attorney general about the *Prize Cases*, Richard Henry Dana was describing – and revising – his own legacy. Dana was certainly in a position to know about the *Prize Cases*: he and Evarts had argued it in the Supreme Court in early 1863, following Dana's successful turn as government counsel in the *Amy Warwick* case, one of several district court proceedings later consolidated into the *Prize Cases*. In the *Prize Cases*, the Court had ratified President Lincoln's action in declaring the blockade during the Civil War, and had incidentally sanctioned the Union's use of international law against the Confederacy. Justice Robert Grier's majority opinion drew heavily on Dana's argument, and Supreme Court reporter Jeremiah Black chose to highlight Dana's argument in the official report of the decision. The Court's opinion endorsed Dana's view that the existence of a state of war – and the Confederacy's consequent status as a belligerent – was a question of fact. The *law* of war attached to the *fact* of war, Dana convinced the Court.

But at the time the decision was handed down in 1863, there was a great deal of public confusion about the implications of the opinion: did recognition of the Confederacy as a "belligerent power" under international law carry the implication that the Confederate states constituted an independent nation?

Well-known international lawyer William Beach Lawrence of Rhode Island weighed in on the issue in the English *Law Magazine* in September 1863. Lawrence's article intimated that the *Prize Cases* had recognized the Confederacy as an independent state by acknowledging residents of Confederate territory to be alien enemies. Lawrence took the position that, in sanctioning the U.S. government's treatment of Confederate seamen as subjects of an adverse power rather than simply as disloyal citizens to be punished under domestic law, the Supreme Court had taken a bold step toward legitimating secession. The Court's ruling, he declared, "was somewhat at variance with the views of those who had hitherto denied the right of secession."[1]

Lawrence's daring argument immediately attracted Richard Henry Dana's attention. Dana knew that Lawrence's opinion carried a significant amount of weight. Lawrence had earned his reputation in international law circles by editing – and annotating, with extensive and meticulous footnotes – several editions of Henry Wheaton's famous treatise on international law, widely regarded as the definitive American treatment of the subject. Dana was angry and alarmed when he read Lawrence's article. In his opinion, Lawrence had perverted the meaning of the *Prize Cases*, and what was more, he had done so in completely irresponsible ways. Dana could not let the article go unchallenged, so he wrote a letter to the *Boston Daily Advertiser* to refute what he viewed as Lawrence's dangerous statements.

Dana's letter was reprinted in *Law Magazine*, and later that year he expanded his letter and published it himself in pamphlet form, which he sent to many friends and leading lawyers in the United States. In the pamphlet, Dana sought to correct Lawrence's "misapprehension" by showing that "the Court made no such recognition [of the right of secession], followed no such corollary, announced no such declaration, and arrived at no such result." Dana believed that Lawrence's misstatements about the supposedly pro-secession implications of the *Prize Cases* stemmed from Lawrence's personal advocacy of a "state right of secession," and he accordingly characterized Lawrence as an unrepentant Copperhead. But it worried Dana that many "prominent men, advocating far different doctrines, seem to have looked at the decision in the same light." Therefore he thought it important to correct what he viewed as a pernicious but widespread misunderstanding

[1] William Beach Lawrence, "International Law: Letter from the Hon. William Beach Lawrence," *Law Magazine* 138 (1863–64): 139, 140.

of the case – the idea that the Confederacy could only be regarded as enemy territory.[2]

It was *more* than enemy territory, Dana explained. The Confederacy was of dual legal character. It was enemy territory – under the control of a belligerent power – for purposes of the law of war, but that concession did not signify its existence under U.S. domestic law. The Court had specified that "the belligerent party who claims to be sovereign may exercise both belligerent and sovereign rights."[3] The availability of one body of law did not imply the loss of the other. Dana believed that this misapprehension had arisen because Americans, even those learned in law, were generally unfamiliar with the peculiarities and technicalities of prize law, in which Dana was an expert. By recognizing the Confederacy as a belligerent power under international law, the Supreme Court had made *no judgment whatsoever* about the legal status of secession under the United States Constitution.

Deeming the litigants' Richmond residence to be "enemy territory" implied no legal judgment about the status of that territory for the purposes of domestic law. Such a finding only reflected the undisputed *fact* that Richmond at that time lay beyond a "boundary marked by lines of bayonets, which can be crossed only by force." Any person living beyond this boundary in territory controlled by the Confederacy, regardless of his personal loyalty to the United States or lack thereof, was to be treated as an alien enemy. Dana confirmed that "the decision hath this extent, no farther."[4]

Dana was right to point out that the Court had addressed only one side of the equation, which was the Confederacy's existence for purposes of international law. The Court did not discuss the domestic side of the war. Grier's opinion had declared only that the use of

---

[2] Dana's son Richard Henry Dana III reiterated that his father had done a great service to the nation in seeking to correct this misinformation, as "many prominent persons" believed Lawrence's interpretation. Richard Henry Dana, *Speeches in Stirring Times and Letters to a Son*, ed. Richard Henry Dana III (Boston: Houghton Mifflin, 1910), 235.

[3] The Prize Cases, 67 U.S. at 673.

[4] Richard Henry Dana, "Enemy's Territory," *Law Magazine and Law Review* 16 (1863): 350, 353, 355; Richard Henry Dana, *Enemy's Territory and Alien Enemies* (Boston: Little, Brown, 1864), 8. See also *Mrs. Alexander's Cotton*, 69 U.S. 404 (1864), which confirmed Dana's views about the irrelevance of personal loyalty under the law of war..

international law did not affect the analysis of secession under the domestic Constitution. It did not purport to offer any view on the Confederacy's constitutional status. The district court opinion in the *Amy Warwick*, one of the *Prize Cases*, had been far clearer in laying out the distinction between the domestic and international aspects of the war. Judge Peleg Sprague had designated the Confederacy "a traitorous confederation" while still recognizing that, because of the widespread extent of the rebellion, it had achieved the status of a belligerent for purposes of international law. According to Sprague, Confederates could be punished under the domestic law of treason as well as under the law of war.

Sprague's opinion had laid out the theory in a way that was understandable to a less meticulous reader than Dana. The Confederates "are at the same time belligerents and traitors, and subject to the liabilities of both," the *Amy Warwick* opinion specified, "while the United States sustains the double character of a belligerent and a sovereign, and has the rights of both."[5] Unfortunately, Justice Grier did not model the Supreme Court's *Prize Cases* opinion on Sprague's lucid style. Nor did he adopt War Department solicitor William Whiting's plain statement, that acknowledging "the belligerent law of civil, territorial war" did not "admit the right of secession. It is not any vote or law of secession that makes an individual a public enemy."[6]

The *Prize Cases* were disturbingly silent on secession, aside from Grier's even more disturbing throwaway line about the issue, in which he admitted that its legality was "being decided by wager of battle."[7] Dana freely acknowledged in his 1863 article that the Court had not offered a definitive statement on the constitutionality of secession, nor on the status of the states or individual Confederates under U.S. domestic law. In fact, "the Court decided absolutely nothing as to the [legal] effect of the ... secession ordinances," he wrote.[8] Dana confirmed this reading of the opinion as late as 1866, when he told family friend and fellow international law specialist Charles Sumner that the

---

[5] The Amy Warwick, 1 F. Cas. 799, 803 (D. Mass. 1862) (No. 341).
[6] William Whiting, *War Powers of the President, Military Arrests, and Reconstruction of the Union* (Boston: John L. Shorey, 1864), 246–47.
[7] See Chapter 4. Grier's implication that the question had been open to debate did not originate in Dana's argument before the Court.
[8] Dana, *Enemy's Territory and Alien Enemies*, 4, 10.

Court's decision had not settled anything regarding the status of the Confederate states under U.S. law.

Dana felt that the Court had ruled in favor of the claimants (and vindicated the government's views) because his opposing counsel, Daniel Lord, had told the justices during oral argument that they would have to make a stark choice. If they intended to maintain the position that secession was illegal, Lord had argued, they would have to treat the Confederates solely as an illegal band of rebels and declare the blockade invalid, which was an exceedingly unattractive prospect. "That was the dilemma to which Daniel Lord & als. tried to force the Court," Dana told Sumner. In contrast, Dana said, he had "showed them a way out, which they followed." He had bifurcated the legal inquiry by advancing the theory of the Confederacy's dual legal status. This had permitted the Court to sanction the blockade while bypassing the secession issue entirely. As Dana reminded Sumner, recognizing the Confederacy as a belligerent was wholly unrelated to secession's constitutionality. "Assume any theory you please as to the political status of the rebel states and their inhabitants," he wrote, "the Prize Law, in a civil war, operates on property or persons within de facto firm possession of those warring against us."[9] There was nothing in the *Prize Cases* opinion that supported *any* particular position with regard to the legal status of the Confederate states: the decision was simply mute on that point.

Dana's 1863 pamphlet on the *Prize Cases* met with the general approbation of the most distinguished members of the legal community, to whom he distributed it widely. Justice Robert Grier, who had authored the *Prize Cases* opinion, wrote Dana two letters concerning the pamphlet, telling him that he thought Dana's restatement of the case to be entirely correct. Grier confirmed that the decision was indeed quite narrow and did not purport to pronounce on the legality of secession or the Confederacy's status under U.S. law: "We decided the questions before us and nothing more." The judge also puzzled over William Beach Lawrence's apparent inability to comprehend that the decision clearly bifurcated Confederate status. In a second note, Grier expressed his satisfaction that Dana's commentary would make

---

[9] Richard Henry Dana to Charles Sumner, February 5, 1866, Reel 35, Charles Sumner Papers, HU.

it impossible for the Court's opinion to be misconstrued: "I did not suppose that [the opinion in the case] contained anything (as Peter said of Pauls epistles) that was 'hard to be understood' and which 'the *unlearned and unstable*' could possibly '*wrest*' '*to their own destruction.*' But with your commentary no one can be so stupid as to misunderstand it, however willing he may be to pervert it."[10]

Grier's confidence in the lucidity of his opinion notwithstanding, the letters Dana received about his pamphlet revealed that his explication was indeed necessary, because it clarified that the Supreme Court had not pronounced on secession. Many people thought it had. The opinion was not well understood outside of the immediate circle of Lincoln administration insiders who had crafted the dual status theory. The American lay public – and the American bar – were mostly unfamiliar with the international law of blockade and prize, and the Court's opinion was subtle enough that some Northerners believed that the *Prize Cases* had tacitly endorsed the legitimacy of the Confederate government.[11] Attorney General Edward Bates, who had opposed the blockade when Lincoln first proposed it, told Dana that the public's misimpression about the case stemmed from "some newspaper reporters, and partisan hacks, who recklessly publish, without the slightest compunction for the falsehood, or even an emotion of shame, for its detection and exposure."[12]

Senator Henry Winter Davis confessed to Dana that he had personally "feared there would be some difficult[y] in reconciling [the *Prize Cases*] with the views which law and policy require should preside.... Your exposition of those cases has quite relieved me from all difficulty." T. J. Coffey, a lawyer in Bates's office, wrote Dana to thank him for producing the pamphlet, adding that "it will be effective to correct the misapprehension, so widely spread, as to what the Court did decide." The *Washington National Intelligencer* blamed the "strange misunderstanding of this decision" on "certain political theorists who supposed themselves to find in it some support for the doctrine which

---

[10] Robert Grier to Richard Henry Dana Jr., December 24, 1863, and January 15, 1864 (emphasis in the original), Box 16, Dana Family Papers, MHS.

[11] See John Raymond and Barbara Frischholz, "Lawyers Who Established International Law in the United States, 1774–1914," *American Journal of International Law* 76 (1982): 802.

[12] Edward Bates to Richard Henry Dana, December 28, 1863, Dana Family Papers, MHS.

teaches that the States in the insurgent territory have ceased to exist [on the theory that they seceded from the Union]." The paper sought to correct this misapprehension by quoting Dana at length on the proposition that the *Prize Cases* decided nothing as to the legal status of the Confederate states under domestic law. Rather unflatteringly, William Evarts attributed the public misunderstanding of the *Prize Cases* to the fact that Supreme Court reporter of decisions Jeremiah Black – who had skirted the edges of secessionist theory – had reported Dana's argument in the official report, instead of Evarts's.[13] Evarts believed that since his own argument had explicitly clarified the distinction Dana had recently highlighted in his pamphlet, Black – that "sad reporter" – had chosen to exclude it to provide some basis for the erroneous belief that the Court had recognized secession.[14]

Not unreasonably, William Beach Lawrence interpreted Dana's pamphlet as an impeachment of his loyalty to the Union. In a public letter to the *Boston Daily Advertiser*, Lawrence took issue with Dana's "gratuitous attack." Lawrence refuted Dana's insinuation "connecting me with State secession, by ascribing to me opinions in common with its advocates," and protested against "the utter fallacy of the accusation." Lawrence denied that he was a secessionist but said he did believe that the Supreme Court should address the constitutional issue directly, rather than leaving it to be decided on the battlefield. If the Union were ever to be restored, Lawrence insisted, "it will be through the instrumentality of the Supreme Court settling, according to judicial

---

[13] Black had crafted President James Buchanan's argument in 1860 that denied the states' ability to secede from the Union but also denied the federal government's ability to prevent their secession. Jeremiah Black, "Power of the President in Executing the Laws," *Opinions of the Attorney General* 9 (1860): 516. See William M. Evarts, *Arguments and Speeches of William Maxwell Evarts*, ed. Sherman Evarts, 3 vols. (New York: Macmillan, 1919), 1: 214, for Evarts's argument.

[14] Henry Winter Davis to Richard Henry Dana, n.d., 1863, and T. J. Coffey to Richard Henry Dana, December 24, 1863, Box 16, Dana Family Papers, MHS; *Washington National Intelligencer*, December 23, 1863; William Evarts to Richard Henry Dana, December 28, 1863, Box 16, Dana Family Papers, MHS. Dana received (and saved) letters of praise for his pamphlet from George Boutwell, David Davis, Edward Everett, Noah Swayne, Reverdy Johnson, William Seward, and Charles Francis Adams, among others. See Box 16, ibid. In point of fact, Evarts's argument on the distinction between the Confederacy's status for purposes of domestic law versus international law was not any clearer than Dana's. See Evarts, *Arguments and Speeches*, 1: 214–94, esp. 242–54.

forms, those mighty questions, which now seem destined to perpetuate the fratricidal struggle."[15]

In 1863, then, Dana and Lawrence were in agreement that the Court had not denied the constitutionality of secession in the *Prize Cases*. Five years later, in suggesting to the attorney general that the Supreme Court had already settled the question, Dana was inverting what he had said previously about the case. In 1863, he had tried to convince the world that the Court's silence on the Confederacy's constitutional status meant that the Court had not ratified secession. In 1868, he interpreted that same silence as confirmation that "secession and war [were] treason" under domestic law. Dana's 1868 letter elided the careful distinction he had elucidated in 1863. Enough time had passed for him to recast the *Prize Cases* as a definitive statement *against* secession. The Lincoln and Johnson administrations had insisted on secession's illegality and the lower courts had followed that determination, especially in light of Union military victory. "The rule in the *Prize Cases*" meant, according to Dana in 1868, that the Davis judges would "instruct the jury, in conformity with these decisions," that the war had been treasonous.[16]

Dana's dispute with William Beach Lawrence did not end with their flurry of public exchanges on the *Prize Cases*. Lawrence had edited the eminent Wheaton treatise on international law since 1855, until Wheaton's family, unimpressed by "the Calhounism" of Lawrence's 1863 edition of the volume, offered Dana the job instead.[17] Lawrence's wartime version of the treatise displeased the Lincoln administration, and Secretary Seward refused to correspond with the author, sending the book back when a copy arrived on his desk.[18] Gossip circulated among international law scholars in the United States and abroad that "Lawrence's Wheaton – [was] ... tainted and *sickened* by the views of the Copperhead." Its "editor was an ultra secessionist," Henry Halleck

---

[15] "Mr. Lawrence's Annotations of Wheaton," *Boston Daily Advertiser*, January 30, 1864. Dana kept a clipping of this article; see vol. 175.1, Dana Family Papers, MHS.

[16] Richard Henry Dana to William Evarts, August 24, 1868, Box 18, Dana Papers, MHS. See also Richard Henry Dana and William Evarts to Henry Stanbery, February 26, 1868, ibid. (an earlier draft of the same letter).

[17] Richard Henry Dana, "The Lawrence-Wheaton Controversy," unpublished pamphlet, 1. Copy in vol. 175.1, Dana Family Papers, MHS.

[18] William B. Lawrence, *The Treaty of Washington: Letters from the Hon. William B. Lawrence* (Providence: Hammond, Angell, 1871), 7.

declared.[19] In fairness, the 1863 treatise was not so much secessionist as it was perfectly neutral on the issue, which was itself a dangerous position to take in the midst of the war.

Dana reworked the 1863 volume and, in 1866, produced an emphatically pro-Union Wheaton treatise. One of Dana's goals was to remove Lawrence's implication that "the Supreme Court had sustained the doctrine of secession" in the *Prize Cases*. Dana did not spend much time on secession but simply equated it with the right of revolution and assumed it to be unconstitutional.[20] His Wheaton won the approval of Unionist legal theorists Henry Halleck and Francis Lieber. The book was "now a most excellent one," Halleck wrote Lieber, having been "purged of the rebellion character of Lawrence's notes."[21] But Lawrence was incensed, and he fired back against Dana with a plagiarism suit that turned acrimonious enough to last for twenty years.

Lawrence charged that Dana's Wheaton had been written with the express intention of rubber-stamping the muddled stance of the State Department on the Confederacy's existence. Whereas he himself had laid out both Unionist and Confederate legal arguments, Dana was a progovernment shill, Lawrence charged. In his opinion, the 1866 treatise was nothing more than a carefully constructed brief for Republican legal theories. Lawrence had been skeptical in 1863 about the logical coherence of the Lincoln administration's "mixed" theory of the war. His edition of Wheaton had stressed the conceptual problems with the government's "delicate position" on the dual legal status of the Confederacy, and Seward had retaliated.[22] Those wartime theories, Lawrence said,

---

[19] Francis Lieber to Richard Henry Dana, December 22, 1863, Box 16, Dana Family Papers, MHS; Henry Halleck to Francis Lieber, May 25, 1863, Box 9, Francis Lieber Papers, HEHL. See also Henry Halleck to Francis Lieber, February 22, 1864, ibid.

[20] Brief for Respondent at 185, Lawrence v. Dana, 15 F. Cas. 26 (C.C.D. Mass. 1869) (No. 8,136), copy in vol. 175.1, Dana Family Papers, MHS. Henry Wheaton, *Elements of International Law*, ed. Richard Henry Dana (Boston: Little, Brown, 1866), 84–85, 376–77.

[21] Henry Halleck to Francis Lieber, July 5, 1867, Box 10, Francis Lieber Papers, HEHL. See also Lieber to Johann Kaspar Bluntschli, August 23, 1867, Box 24, ibid.; Henry Halleck to Richard Henry Dana, February 16, 1867, Box 17, Dana Family Papers, MHS; Francis Lieber to R. H. Dana, October 26, 1864, Box 16, ibid.

[22] Lawrence, *The Treaty of Washington*, 7. See also William B. Lawrence to Charles Sumner, July 30, August 11, 1865, Reel 34, Charles Sumner Papers, HU; William B. Lawrence to William Henry Seward, December 29, 1861, and September 29, 1866, Reel 67, 96, William Seward Papers, LC.

spilled over into Reconstruction, which was premised on the "dangerous and wicked doctrine that the southern states are out of the Union, and can only re-enter it as conquered provinces."[23] But Dana's Wheaton endorsed all of those views, he claimed, because it was "got up entirely for Seward & in such a way as to command the largest subvention" for the Lincoln administration.[24] The book deliberately misrepresented the unsettled state of the law concerning the legal status of the Confederacy, Lawrence said. It presented these fraught issues with a false clarity because it selected one point of view and declared that view to be law.

Dana did recast the tentative, makeshift legal maneuvers and theories that had sustained the Union war effort as settled "law," just as Lawrence had charged. In this, he joined a number of pro-Union legal thinkers who wanted to manufacture certainty in the war's aftermath – and to whitewash any evidence that uncertainty had ever existed.[25] After the war's conclusion, the Unionists were the lawmakers – and the law's expositors – and they could erase the power that secessionist arguments had once had.

John Phillip Reid wrote that, "unwritten and without a judiciary to settle conflicts, the imperial constitution was whatever could be plausibly argued and forcibly maintained."[26] Legal historians of the Civil War have tended to treat the Civil War Constitution as similarly pliable. Constitutional interpretation, in most historians' accounts, automatically bent to the needs of American society. Law, under this theory, wholly lacked autonomy. It existed only to ratify the political process and to

[23] Lawrence v. Dana, 15 F. Cas. at 26, Closing Argument for the Complainant, 16, vol. 175.1, Dana Family Papers, MHS. Lawrence was alluding here to Dana's 1865 "Grasp of War" speech.

[24] William B. Lawrence to Charles Sumner, July 30, 1865, Reel 34, Charles Sumner Papers, HU. See also William Beach Lawrence to Charles Sumner, August 11, 1865, ibid. See also William Beach Lawrence to Charles Sumner, July 30, August 11, November 27, December 2, 1865; June 1, 1867, Reels 34, 39, Charles Sumner Papers, HU.

[25] Francis Lieber and William Whiting were also engaged to do this. See discussion of Lieber in this chapter. For more on Whiting, see Cynthia Nicoletti, "Writing the Social History of Legal Doctrine," *Buffalo Law Review* 64 (2016): 121, and Cynthia Nicoletti, "The Disputed Legality of the Emancipation Proclamation, 1862–1865" (manuscript on file with the author).

[26] John Phillip Reid, "In a Defensive Rage: The Uses of the Mob, the Justification in Law, and the Coming of the American Revolution," *New York University Law Review* 49 (1974): 1043, 1087.

gild it with the appearance of neutrality. Notably, John Fabian Witt and Stephen Neff have viewed the law on the dual status of the Confederacy through such a lens.[27] In declaring the blockade, Lincoln and Seward crafted a supple policy that was designed to facilitate the needs of the war effort, and the courts sustained their theories, messy though they were.

But this view fundamentally mischaracterizes the way Americans (even victorious Northerners) thought about the relationship between law and politics in the 1860s. It overstates the degree to which Americans were confident that the law would adapt to society's needs. Not everyone viewed the law so instrumentally as Lincoln and Seward.[28] For most nineteenth-century legal thinkers, the law was not infinitely malleable. In their view, law was formalistic; "it evolved in accordance with a[n internally] logical pattern," rather than changing in response to the political climate of the day.[29] Law constrained human behavior, and legal doctrine was not easily dismissed in favor of expediency. The Civil War challenged this view, but it did not destroy it.[30] The project of crafting treatises and legal documents that presented the Unionist point of view on the dual status of the Confederacy as settled and determinate was valuable for this reason. It was a process of law creation, but it was done under the cloak of legal formalism. As one of the

[27] John Fabian Witt, *Lincoln's Code: The Laws of War in American History* (New York: Free Press, 2012), and Stephen C. Neff, *Justice in Blue and Gray: A Legal History of the Civil War* (Cambridge, MA: Harvard University Press, 2010). Witt and Neff are not alone in this. Harold Hyman, for instance, argued that the Civil War saw the development of the theory of "adequate constitutionalism": the government possessed whatever power was necessary. See Harold M. Hyman, *A More Perfect Union: The Impact of the Civil War and Reconstruction on the Constitution* (Boston: Houghton Mifflin, 1975).

[28] William Blair has recently demonstrated that Americans were unsure about the legitimate uses of the law of treason throughout the war and in its aftermath. See William A. Blair, *With Malice toward Some: Treason and Loyalty in the Civil War Era* (Chapel Hill: University of North Carolina Press, 2014).

[29] Morton White, "The Revolt against Formalism in American Social Thought of the Twentieth Century," *Journal of the History of Ideas* 8 (1947): 131, 137. See also William Wiecek, *The Lost World of Classical Legal Thought: Law and Ideology in America, 1886–1937* (New York: Oxford University Press, 1998), 5; Morton Horwitz, *The Transformation of American Law, 1780–1860* (Cambridge, MA: Harvard University Press, 1977), esp. chapter 8.

[30] See Perry Miller, *The Life of the Mind in America: From the Revolution to the Civil War* (New York: Harcourt, Brace & World, 1965); George Frederickson, *The Inner Civil War: Northern Intellectuals and the Crisis of the Union* (New York: Harper Torchbooks, 1965).

administration's critics charged, it was "revolution ... disguise[d] ... under the pretense of constitutional authority."[31]

In the wake of the Civil War, American legal thinkers engaged in a nationwide debate about what legal doctrine permitted – and whether those limits would or should be sustained by judges. No one was certain that the Supreme Court's decision in the *Prize Cases* would be interpreted to preclude treason prosecutions. It seemed possible that formalism would win out over functionalism, particularly in light of Attorney General Speed's desire to stanch the upheaval the war had wrought in the United States. It was not immediately apparent to the war's survivors that the courts could be counted on to acquiesce in the government's views.

Davis's trial provoked a nationwide debate on the postwar reach of belligerent status and its intersection with the domestic law of treason. Much of the argument centered on the magnitude and scope of the treason. Those who argued against the idea that belligerency excused treason pointed out that under such a theory, only small acts of treason would be punishable. If the rebels were able to gather enough strength to require the U.S. government to strike back against them with the army, their treason would be excused. William Evarts, among others, pointed out that such a contention was simply untenable. In arguing the case of the *Savannah* privateers in federal court in New York in 1861, Evarts had denied that the blockade shielded Confederates from treason prosecutions under domestic law. For the court to find otherwise, Evarts argued, was nonsensical, because it would amount to a declaration that rebels could somehow transcend treason if only enough of them banded together. "How absurd to present for the recognition of a Government, in its Courts of Judicature, the proposition that there is no treason, from the number of the confederates in the treachery," Evarts asserted. "Your honors see at once that, the idea of setting up such a defence, on a trial for treason, against a private soldier, found in arms against the Government, is absurd."[32]

Although Evarts handily dismissed the idea that recognition of belligerency would preclude treason prosecutions, this problem occupied legal

---

[31] Joel Parker, *The War Powers of Congress, and of the President* (Cambridge, MA: H. O. Houghton, 1863), 8, 10.

[32] A. F. Warburton, *Trial of the Officers and Crew of the Schooner Savannah* (New York: Notable Trials Library, 1997), 199.

scholar Francis Lieber throughout the war and its aftermath. Lieber saw the recognition of the Confederacy as a belligerent power as a mistake. Dual status was inherently problematic, he believed. Lieber was the author of General Orders No. 100, a code of war that President Lincoln had issued to the Union army in 1863 to govern its conduct during the Civil War. The document ostensibly sought to codify rules already in place, but Lieber also struck out boldly in new directions.[33] In important ways, the code sought to lay out, in written form, rules that would redound to the benefit of the United States government in its contest with the Confederacy. It was, therefore, not so much a recapitulation of settled principles of international law as it was an argument for a particular position.

The last section of Lieber's code dealt with the rules of war as they applied to insurrections, rebellions, and civil wars. Here, Lieber deviated from the position on belligerency ventured by Lincoln and Seward in 1861 and later formalized by the Supreme Court in the *Prize Cases*. Lieber would not concede Confederate belligerency. He would avoid the legal term entirely.[34] An acknowledgment of belligerency, he recognized, was inherently problematic because of its potential spillover effects. For instance, it might be interpreted to shield individual Confederates from criminal liability for treason under domestic law. In the code, Lieber asserted that treating the Confederacy under the laws of war did not automatically render it a belligerent power. Nor did the law of war attach to the conflict simply because it was a war, Lieber said, as the Supreme Court had suggested in the *Prize Cases*. In the *Prize Cases*, the Court had, as Richard Henry Dana confirmed, treated the existence of a state of war as a question of fact (attained through an objective assessment of military success). The law of war applied as a matter of course.

Lieber rejected that formulation, insisting instead that the United States had extended the laws of war to the Confederate conflict as a policy decision, a matter of largesse, rather than legal obligation.

---

[33] See Witt, *Lincoln's Code*; Martti Koskenniemi, *Gentle Civilizer of Nations* (Cambridge: Cambridge University Press, 2001), esp. chapter 1.

[34] The long-standing conflict over the *name* of the war (rebellion, civil war, Northern aggression) was not just semantic but in fact had significant legal consequences. See John M. Coski, "The War between the Names," *North and South* 8 (January 2006): 62; David Armitage, *Civil Wars: A History in Ideas* (New York: Knopf, 2017), chapter 5.

Lieber argued that dealing with the Confederacy according to set rules of civilized warfare did not actually connote any recognition of the Confederacy "as a *public* [belligerent] *or sovereign power* [nation]."[35] It was no acknowledgment of legitimacy of any kind.

Lieber further clarified his thoughts on the matter in a letter to Charles Sumner. "Adopting the laws of war in a rebellion toward the rebels does not constitute them public enemies," he wrote. "I maintain – and have always done so – that the bold and noble ideas of the English regarding de facto and de jure governments (now adopted by all intelligent govern[men]ts), apply in great measure to large rebellions, but it does not constitute rebels full belligerents." Rebellions could have either positive or negative aims, Lieber argued, and the world could not simply adopt a uniform legal policy (based on objective markers) to deal with them. A rebellion could "be the beginning of revolutionizing an insupportable despotism," or "it may be a godless crew of a few arrogants against a people's government," Lieber wrote. Because the American Civil War had involved "a regular conspiracy of … men without honour or principle," the late rebellion could not be justified, he said, and the Confederacy should enjoy no legally sanctioned status.[36]

To guard against granting any such legitimacy, Lieber argued that achieving belligerent status required another step beyond the institution of a blockade or the initiation of prisoner exchange. As he explained, only *explicit recognition* by the parent nation or by other nations could create a legitimate belligerent.[37] The key, he wrote, "is acknowledgment. When two sovereigns fight they are belligerents in the sense of the law of the nations, not because they carry on war, but because they are sovereigns; and fights when people fight that are not sovereigns, they are not belligerents, until a sovereign declares: I treat you as belligerents." In Lieber's opinion, "de facto belligerency" could

---

[35] Francis Lieber, *Instructions for the Government of Armies of the United States in the Field: Originally Issued as General Orders No. 100, Adjutant General's Office, 1863* (Washington, DC: Government Printing Office, 1898), art. 153 (hereafter cited as Lieber Code).

[36] Francis Lieber to Charles Sumner, June 4, 1866, Reel 79, Charles Sumner Papers, HU.

[37] Under Lieber's rules, belligerency looked very much like full diplomatic recognition of a government. In fact, Lieber believed belligerency to be a step on the road to full statehood.

not exist, "simply because belligerency does not inhere in a fighting body, but in the acknowledgment ... by others."[38] Because the evil policies of slavery and the subversion of the political system had driven the formation of the Confederacy, it had not deserved any such acknowledgment. "The adoption of the rules of regular war toward rebels," he wrote, "does in no way whatever imply a partial or complete acknowledgment of their government, if they have set one up, or of them, as an independent or sovereign power." Only victory in the field could confer legitimacy on the Confederate government. Lieber refuted the notion that treating rebels under the rules of war would prevent a government from trying them for treason once the war had concluded. Regardless of the U.S. government's decision to deal with the Confederacy as a nation, "armed or unarmed resistance by citizens of the United States against the lawful movements of their troops is levying war against the United States, and is therefore treason."[39]

Still, Lieber was worried that his view would not take hold. After the war, he wanted to ensure that the Confederate leaders would be convicted and put to death. Judge Advocate General Joseph Holt hired Lieber in May 1865 to sift through the papers of the Confederate government and determine whether any evidence existed of high-level involvement in the Lincoln assassination.[40] In this capacity, Lieber had the time to reflect on Jefferson Davis's crimes and the possibility that he would escape punishment. In Lieber's view, treason trials were essential to kill the lingering spirit of secessionism in the United States. The American public was far too forgiving of the former Confederate leaders for Lieber's liking; he lamented that "the Americans are the least vindictive creatures that ever existed, so much so that their forgetfulness of wrong at times appears to me to amount to a lack of

[38] Francis Lieber to Charles Sumner, August 11, 1865, Reel 79, Charles Sumner Papers, HU.

[39] Lieber Code, art. 149–57. See also Francis Lieber to Charles P. Daly, January 16, 1862, Box 3, Charles P. Daly Papers, NYPL; Charles P. Daly, *Are the Southern Privateersmen Pirates? Letter to the Hon. Ira Harris, United States Senator* (New York: James B. Kirker, 1862).

[40] Robert Wolfe, "Francis Lieber's Role as Archivist of the Confederate Records," in *Francis Lieber and the Culture of the Mind*, ed. Charles R. Mack and Henry H. Lesesne (Columbia: University of South Carolina Press, 2005), 42–48. See also Dallas D. Irvine, "The Genesis of the Official Records," *Mississippi Valley Historical Review* 24 (September 1937): 221; Frank Friedel, *Francis Lieber: Nineteenth-Century Liberal* (Baton Rouge: Louisiana State University Press, 1947), 370–75.

earnestness." The United States could not afford to show mercy to the most notorious among the Confederates. If Davis were either pardoned by the president or acquitted in his treason trial, Lieber predicted, the former Confederate president would again enter public life, be elected to the Senate, "and be the democratic candidate for the next presidency." Lieber was shocked to learn that even Charles Sumner believed that Davis should receive a pardon. This was an untenable solution. "Death, for say the 10 of the worst [rebels] was necessary," as Lieber explained to Sumner, "not out of a desire for revenge," but in order to "stamp treason as treason."[41]

Lieber also pressed his views on belligerency and treason with the public. In his article "The Status of Rebel Prisoners of War," which appeared in the *Independent* in May 1865, Lieber argued the government should follow the approach outlined in his General Orders No. 100. It was true that prisoners of war were generally only answerable for violations of the law of war and not their captor's domestic law, but that rule applied only to contests fought between two sovereign nations. The United States had been obliged, for reasons of humanity, to apply the laws of war to the Confederates, but that did not constitute any obligation to forgo other penalties the rebels might face. In fact, said Lieber, it was patently absurd to apply such a rule to the Confederates. The laws of war were "made for the intercourse of warring parties who commit no crime by warring with one another," he argued, whereas the Confederates "prove that they commit a crime – i.e., treason or armed rebellion against their lawful government" when

[41] Francis Lieber to Charles Sumner, May 4, July 5, August 4, November 8, 1865, June 4, 1866, Reels 79–80, Charles Sumner Papers, HU. In the course of examining the Confederate records, Lieber began to express doubts about the earnestness of the Johnson government's desire to mount a case against Davis. Lieber hinted to both Sumner and Henry Halleck that he had uncovered documents that could prove that, at the very least, Davis's administration had tacitly approved a conspiracy to assassinate Lincoln, but he insisted that his evidence would be buried by the Southern-sympathizing Johnson administration and never see the light of day. However, when he turned over his report on the Confederate archives to Stanton, and ultimately to Congress in early 1866, he was unable to produce any direct evidence that Davis had taken part in such a conspiracy. See Francis Lieber to Henry Halleck, May 23, 1866, Box 28, Francis Lieber Papers, HEHL; Francis Lieber to Charles Sumner, July 2, August 16, 1866, Reel 80, Charles Sumner Papers, HU. See also Friedel, *Francis Lieber*, 374; Elizabeth D. Leonard, *Lincoln's Avengers: Justice, Revenge, and Reunion after the Civil War* (New York: Norton, 2004), 216.

they "call for the application of rules of war." Immunizing Confederates from treason prosecutions because of the application of the rules of war would only encourage brutality in civil wars. It made sense for a parent nation to follow the rules of international warfare in a domestic conflict only if there were "no consequences with reference to the legal and ultimate status of those who have risen in rebellion."[42]

Gerrit Smith reacted directly to Lieber's "Prisoners of War" article in an address delivered at New York's Cooper Institute in June 1865, titled "No Treason in Civil War." In conducting the war by the rules of international warfare, Smith argued, the Union had implicitly consented not to pursue any retribution against rebels once the war had concluded. Instituting the blockade "was our waiver of all right, our surrender of all claim, to punish the South for treason – [it] was, indeed, our virtual agreement not to punish her for it. This is so from the simple fact, that, under the law of war, there is no treason."[43] Smith singled out Francis Lieber for rebuke, as his General Orders No. 100 contained a brutal "hint ... that we should hold the finally vanquished to be guilty of treason," which stood in contrast to historical precedent and should not be followed, according to Smith. Francis Lieber's writings were not the law, Smith emphasized, however much Lieber insisted that they should be. "Order Number One Hundred," Smith asserted, was "but [an] *ex parte* [paper], and therefore can not repeal, or, in any wise or in any degree, modify the understanding between the belligerents to conduct the war according to the law of war."[44]

---

[42] Friedel, *Francis Lieber*, 362; Francis Lieber, "The Status of the Rebel Prisoners of War," in Lieber, *The Miscellaneous Writings of Francis Lieber: Reminiscences, Addresses, and Essays*, ed. Daniel C. Gilman, 2 vols. (Philadelphia: J. B. Lippincott, 1880), 2: 293–97. Lieber sent a copy of the piece to the attorney general. See Francis Lieber to James Speed, May 19, 1865, Attorney General Letters Received, New York, Attorney General's Records, Record Group 60, NA-CP.

[43] Gerrit Smith, *No Treason in Civil War* (New York: American News Company, 1865), 7.

[44] Smith, *No Treason in Civil War*, 7, 9. Smith strangely cited the entry on treason in the *New American Cyclopedia*, probably written just before the war, in support of his views, but attributed authorship of the anonymous article to Francis Lieber, perhaps hoping to catch Lieber in an inconsistency. Lieber confirmed in a letter to Charles Sumner that he had not written that piece. Francis Lieber to Charles Sumner, June 4, 1866, Reel 80, Charles Sumner Papers, HU. See "Treason," in George Ripley and Charles A. Dana, eds., *The New American Cyclopedia*, 16 vols. (New York: D. Appleton, 1862), 15: 581–84.

And indeed it was an ex parte paper. It bound the Union army by virtue of the president's order, but it did not embody widely agreed-upon, unexceptional principles of international law as it was customarily understood. The *Nation*, a Republican paper, claimed that Lieber's code "did not claim to have any international force or effect," and insofar "as it had any sanction at all and was more than a theory, [it was] a part of the municipal law of the land."[45] Although Lieber is seen today as the progenitor of the modern laws of war, he was far less important in his own day, much to his chagrin.[46]

In 1866 Lieber felt himself to be a voice in the wilderness, ignored in favor of those who would excuse Confederate treason on the basis of international law. His article in the *Independent* had met with deafening silence. The following year, Lieber sent the piece to Edward McPherson, clerk of the House of Representatives, and begged McPherson to publish it in his influential annual handbook of politics. Lieber insisted that his article provided a necessary corrective to the dangerous belief – "still all but universal in the South, and occasionally adhered to in the North – not to speak of all the Copperheads – that *introducing the laws of war in a rebellion is tantamount to acknowledging rebels as an independent power* and *uncriminate* them, if I can make a word. My article is so far as I know the only serious paper which takes the opposite ground."[47] Lieber intended to counter the view espoused by Gerrit Smith and others, that Davis could not be criminally punished for treason, calling that proposition a "fine syllogism," which held, as he outlined it to McPherson:

Rebels make war against their government.
Making war against us is treason.
But because making war [requires that] the laws of war are extended to
    them; because you cannot punish so many;
Therefore committing treason is not treason and you cannot punish it.[48]

---

[45] "Recent Works on International Law," *Nation*, November 23, 1871.
[46] See, e.g., Witt, *Lincoln's Code*, 3.
[47] Francis Lieber to Edward McPherson, June 15, 1866, vol. 6, Edward McPherson Papers, LC (emphasis in the original).
[48] Lieber to McPherson, June 15, 1866, vol. 6, Edward McPherson Papers, LC.

This was a ridiculous outcome, Lieber maintained, although he reluctantly conceded that the logic of it proceeded relentlessly from the dual-status theory. The problem was doctrinal, as Lieber explained to Charles Sumner. The United States Supreme Court (and members of the judiciary, such as Chief Justice Chase) should never have conceded that rules of war applied to the Confederacy as a matter of law. Adopting the government's theory that Confederate belligerency and Union sovereignty could exist at the same time – and denominating the Confederacy a full belligerent – had caused this problem. This view, "so far from solving the difficulty," he said, had led to "inextricable confusion." Most legal thinkers were wedded to doctrine, and immunity from treason seemed like the logical corollary of recognition of Confederate belligerency. Belligerency was difficult to quarantine, as Smith's speeches revealed. The better approach was the one Lieber had put forth in his General Orders: refusal to treat the Confederacy as a belligerent power altogether.[49]

Lieber, whom John Fabian Witt characterized as the consummate "functionalist," thus revealed himself to be worried about doctrine.[50] Lieber was well aware that doctrinal concessions could have consequences and that not everyone was as supple a legal thinker as the architects of the Union's legal policy. The categories were more porous and more interconnected than Lincoln and Seward wanted to admit. This was why Gideon Welles and Edward Bates had opposed Lincoln and Seward's decision to declare a blockade in 1861. As late as 1873, Welles complained that the blockade had made "the Confederate organization ... a quasi-government," which "inevitably [led] to embarrassments."[51] Charles Francis Adams III, whose grandfather had served as minister to Great Britain during the Civil War, contended that neither Lincoln nor Seward knew any international law, which was why they had instituted a blockade without recognizing what it signified. According to Adams, Seward's blasé attitude toward Confederate belligerency had caused numerous problems for Union diplomacy during

---

[49] Francis Lieber to Charles Sumner, June 4, 1866, Reel 80, Charles Sumner Papers, HU.
[50] Witt, *Lincoln's Code*, 195.
[51] Gideon Welles, "Mr. Lincoln and Mr. Seward: Remarks on the Memorial Address of Charles Francis Adams on the Life of William H. Seward," *Galaxy* 26 (December 1873): 793. See also Gideon Welles, *Diary of Gideon Welles*, ed. Edgar Thaddeus Welles, 3 vols. (Boston: Houghton Mifflin, 1911), 1: 173.

the war.[52] Welles's assessment was harsher: Seward "seems to have little idea of constitutional and legal restraints, but acts as if the ruler was omnipotent. Hence he has involved himself in constant difficulties."[53]

The specific issue of applying the law of treason after a large rebellion was one of those intractable "difficulties." Visiting criminal penalties on individuals after the Union had dealt with the Confederacy in its corporate capacity struck many as unjust and disproportionately harsh to an unlucky few. Richard Henry Dana and Francis Lieber unsurprisingly insisted that post–Civil War treason trials were appropriate.[54] William Beach Lawrence disagreed. For Lawrence, applying international law carried certain consequences, including forgoing the right to punish insurgents under domestic law once the legitimate government had reestablished control over rebellious territory. In the supplement to his 1863 edition of Wheaton, Lawrence argued that in recognizing Confederate belligerency, the United States had indicated that it would not try Confederates for treason in the event of Union victory. Although there was no crystal-clear ban on such actions, Lawrence argued, only "obsolete precedents, now universally repudiated by the civilized world" would allow "the Federal government to punish the leaders for rebellion" – and ordinary "private individuals have ever in modern times been deemed exempt from [such] penalties."[55]

In support of this position, Lawrence cited Spanish legal scholar Antonio Riquelme, who had written in the wake of the Revolutions of 1848. Riquelme believed that once a revolutionary force became "sufficiently strong to resist [the government's] action, and to constitute two parties of equally balanced forces, the existence of civil war is thenceforward determined." When an internal conflict reached that level, Riquelme insisted, "we treat of it in international law, since

52 Welles, "Mr. Lincoln and Mr. Seward," 793; Charles Francis Adams, *Seward and the Declaration of Paris: A Forgotten Diplomatic Episode, April–August, 1861* (Boston: Massachusetts Historical Society, 1912.) See also Lawrence, *The Treaty of Washington*; Burrus Carnahan, *Lincoln on Trial: Southern Civilians and the Law of War* (Lexington: University Press of Kentucky, 2010), 15.

53 Welles, *Diary of Gideon Welles*, 2: 232.

54 Wheaton, *Elements of International Law*, ed. Richard Henry Dana (1866), 71 n. 32. So did War Department solicitor William Whiting. See William Whiting, *The War Powers under the Constitution of the United States* (Boston: Little, Brown, 1864), esp. chapter 5.

55 Wheaton, *Elements of International Law*, ed. William Beach Lawrence (1863), 104–8, 523–25, 597; supplement, 12–33, esp. 32–33. According to Lawrence, the last

each party [is] forming as it were a separate nation, both should be regarded as subject to the laws of war." Treason trials were obviated as soon as the law of war attached, regardless of the outcome of the contest. This was the necessary consequence of such a decision in the first place: the rebels would be dealt with collectively and not as individuals. According to Riquelme, the termination of the war "should be guaranteed by an amnesty ... [because] it is not lawful for any judicial or political authority to proceed for any acts which would not have merited punishment if the cause of those who are admitted to the amnesty had triumphed."[56]

Lawrence also relied on the authority of Andrés Bello, a South American legal scholar who had participated in the Venezuelan independence movement in the 1810s under Simón Bolívar.[57] Bello, like Riquelme, contended that a civil war in which "two parties ... mutually treat each other as enemies" should be recognized under international law, as the insurgent party "is a person in the law of nations." Once international law had attached to the contest, "it is customary [for the parent nation] to concede to [the rebellious party] a general amnesty." But that amnesty extended only so far, wrote Bello; it did not excuse "the authors and chiefs" of the rebellion, who could be "punish[ed] according to the laws."[58] Thus, as the civilian leader of the rebellion, Davis would possibly be subject to punishment even if international law dictated that amnesty be extended to most ordinary participants. Emer de Vattel had also urged the victorious sovereign in a civil war to extend amnesty to the former rebels but exempted "the heads of the party," declaring that the sovereign "may bring them to a legal trial, and punish them, if they be found guilty."[59]

time a victor had meted out such personal punishment against the defeated had been in the aftermath of the Norman Conquest in 1066, when William I redistributed the property of Anglo-Saxons to his own followers.

[56] Don Antonio Riquelme, *Elementos de derecho público internacional* (n.p.: Impr. de don Pedro Vives, 1875), quoted in Wheaton, *Elements of International Law*, ed. William Beach Lawrence (1863), 524 n. 171.

[57] Ivan Jaksic, *Andrés Bello: Scholarship and Nation-Building in Nineteenth-Century Latin America* (New York: Cambridge University Press, 2001.)

[58] Andrés Bello, *Principios de derecho internacional* (Caracas: J. M. De Rojas, 1847), quoted in Wheaton, *Elements of International Law*, ed. William Beach Lawrence (1863), 524 n. 171.

[59] Emer de Vattel, *The Law of Nations* (1758; repr., Northampton, MA: Simeon Butler, 1820), 426.

Even Francis Lieber's close friend, Swiss international law scholar Johann Kaspar Bluntschli, believed that the law of treason could not be applied following a rebellion. Lieber and Bluntschli corresponded throughout the war and its aftermath, and Bluntschli clearly respected Lieber's work.[60] Bluntschli also drew heavily on Lieber's General Orders No. 100 in drafting his own treatise, *Le droit international codifié*, which appeared in 1869. But his work was far more even-handed than Lieber's had been in its treatment of the Confederacy, which earned Bluntschli some negative reviews from Unionist American critics.[61] Bluntschli departed from Lieber in his analysis of treason and belligerency. In this he aligned himself with Jefferson Davis's postwar defenders: if a parent government applied the law of war instead of domestic criminal law to the rebels during the war, it was bound by that decision once the war had concluded. Lieber's view that the United States could apply the laws of war as a matter of *policy* without incurring any obligations therefrom struck Bluntschli as untenable. It gave entirely too much discretion to the U.S. government to determine, on its own, the limits of its duties toward rebels under international law. Bluntschli contended instead that

the party who has the constituted authorities will easily allow itself to treat its adversaries as rebels.... Once the criminal tribunals are no longer respected, and the two parties have de facto started to war against each other, it would be more logical to suspend the application of penal laws, to consider both politically and militarily their adversaries as true enemies, and to recognize their quality as belligerents. Current international law therefore has made progress in according the quality of belligerents to a revolutionary group or to semi-legitimate organizations.[62]

[60] See Richard Henry Dana to Francis Lieber, December 26, 1867; Francis Lieber to Johann Kaspar Bluntschli, February 12, August 23, October 1, 1867, May 29, 1869, Boxes 5, 24, Francis Lieber Papers, HEHL; Francis Lieber to Richard Henry Dana, December 28, 1867, Box 18, Dana Family Papers, MHS. See also Koskenniemi, *Gentle Civilizer of Nations*; Betsy Baker, "The 'Civilized Nation' in the Work of Johann Caspar Bluntschli," in *Macht und Moral*, ed. Markus Kremer (Stuttgart: Verlag W. Kohlhammer, 2007), 343–59; Betsy Baker Roben, "The Method behind Bluntschli's 'Modern' International Law," *Journal of the History of International Law* 4 (2002): 249–92.

[61] "Recent Works on International Law," *Nation*, November 23, 1871.

[62] Johann Kaspar Bluntschli, *Le droit international codifié* (Paris: Librairie Guillaumin, 1874), § 512 n. 3 (originally published 1869). Translation from the French provided by Victoria N. Meyer. See also "Bluntschli's International Law," *American Law Review* 3 (April 1869): 397, 405.

Bluntschli's conclusions found widespread support in the United States, and even within Johnson's cabinet. Treasury Secretary Hugh McCulloch, who visited Davis in prison at the president's behest in 1867, did not believe that Davis should stand trial for treason. For McCulloch, belligerent status had conferred a certain legitimacy on the Confederacy. "It was a revolution which had been attempted by the Southern States," McCulloch wrote. "It was a war in which they had been engaged – war of such proportions that belligerent rights had been accorded to them by foreign nations." As a result of this recognition of the Confederacy's de facto nationhood, McCulloch believed that the U.S. government had waived its opportunity to resort to criminal punishment of individuals' treason after the war. Confederates, he argued, "could not, therefore, be charged with treason, nor could one of their number be singled out and legally convicted of the crime."[63] Robert E. Lee had presented this same view to the Joint Committee on Reconstruction. Treason prosecutions visited the sins of the many upon a single person, and the "state was responsible for the act [of secession], not the individual," according to Lee. George Boutwell, who had served on the committee, wrote later that Lee's "doctrine of State Rights excused the citizen and placed the sole responsibility on the State."[64]

The person of the leader was a stand-in for the state he represented, and it seemed unjust to target such a diffuse and widespread urge for revenge at a single individual. In fact, in circumstances like these President Johnson might have thought back on Lincoln's prescient impulse in April 1865 to let Davis escape his captors and slip out of the country undetected. It was a delicate business, as history had revealed, to decide the fate of a deposed former leader after his fall from grace. English history had demonstrated as much, as nineteenth-century Americans knew. King Charles I had been convicted of treason

[63] Hugh McCulloch, *Men and Measures of a Half-Century* (New York: Scribner's, 1900), 408–9.

[64] As Lee put it, individual citizens' guilt was removed by the state's sovereign decision to secede, a view that Boutwell aptly pointed out came perilously close to endorsing secessionist theory in its insistence on the ultimate sovereignty of the states. George Boutwell, *Reminiscences of Sixty Years in Public Affairs*, 2 vols. (New York: McClure, Phillips, 1902), 2: 82–83. See also Albert Bledsoe, "Review: *Prison Life of Jefferson Davis*," *Southern Review* 1 (January 1867): 233, 246–48; R. E. F., "The Trial of Jefferson Davis," *Law Magazine and Law Review* 21 (1866): 258, 260.

and put to death in 1649, but several earlier deposed monarchs had never actually faced formal charges.[65] Instead, it had been easier for their successors to make sure that Edward II, Richard II, Henry VI, and Richard III each met an informal early demise while in prison.[66] And given that Jefferson Davis himself was never tried for the crime of treason, what "law" emerged from the Civil War with regard to the postwar viability of treason prosecutions against the head of an acknowledged belligerent?

International law scholar Quincy Wright, looking back on Davis's case a century later, did not quite know the answer. On the one hand, "Lieber's Code had insisted that the law of war did not prevent proceeding against rebels for treason after the war," he wrote. On the other, Wright noted, Davis and others were indicted, "but none were tried."[67] For Wright, it was not clear what the Civil War had established on this point. The absence of treason convictions belied Lieber's insistence that Confederate belligerency carried no postwar consequences.

[65] David Lagomarstino and Charles J. Wood, eds., *The Trial of Charles I: A Documentary History* (Hanover, NH: University Press of New England, 1989), 61.

[66] The analogy between deposed kings and the former Confederate president is an imperfect one, as English monarchs were deemed to be the sovereign; they were not merely acting on the sovereign's behalf. Putting a deposed king on trial indirectly impugned the sovereignty of the new monarch. As historian J. G. Bellamy points out, once violent struggles for power no longer pitted "barons versus king as it had been in the fourteenth century but one would-be monarch and his supporters versus another would-be monarch and his supporters," it became difficult for the victorious king to punish a former or putative king and his supporters for treason, as "the leader of neither faction wanted royal authority impugned since he had hopes of using it himself." J. G. Bellamy, *The Law of Treason in England in the Later Middle Ages* (Cambridge: Cambridge University Press, 1970), 99. See also J. G. Bellamy, *The Tudor Law of Treason* (London: Routledge & Kegan Paul, 1979).

[67] Quincy Wright, "The American Civil War (1861–1865)," in *The International Law of Civil War*, ed. Richard A. Falk (Baltimore: Johns Hopkins Press, 1971), 73–74.

13

Two Embattled Presidents

The political power of Andrew Johnson and the Democratic Party was waning by 1867, and the Radical Republicans were gaining ground. President Johnson had never been favorably inclined toward Jefferson Davis, but many of his Radical Republican opponents were committed to the punishment of treason and the hanging of rebels to establish the illegality of secession and the Confederate war effort. In 1867 and 1868, it remained to be seen whether O'Conor could pull off the ultimate coup and ensure that Davis would escape punishment after the Radicals seized political control in Washington.

In the fall of 1867 the prosecutors moved forward – in fits and starts – to secure a new indictment against Davis before the expiration of the statute of limitations in the spring of 1868. Evarts and Dana traveled to Richmond in November to work with U.S. Attorney Lucius Chandler and his assistant H. H. Wells in presenting witness testimony to the grand jury. The new indictment was a much different affair from the one that Chandler had hurriedly drawn up in one afternoon in 1866 at Judge Underwood's insistence. The 1866 indictment had charged Davis with only a solitary count – that of generally "incit[ing] insurrection" in Richmond on May 15, 1864, without mentioning any overt act of treason in which he had participated – whereas the new indictment alleged fourteen specific counts against Davis.[1] The counts were also serious, detailing Davis's actions in carrying out a war of

---

[1] See Chapter 7 for more on the 1866 indictment.

massive proportions against the United States. Several counts charged Davis with sending armies to attack the United States at particular battles, including Manassas, Five Forks, and Petersburg. Others described the organization of his cabinet and the army, his actions in transferring the Confederate capital to Richmond, his acceptance of troops and munitions from the state of Virginia in the Confederate army, and his public speeches, designed to rally the spirit of the Confederate army and the civilian population. Unlike the earlier indictment, which failed to enumerate the statute under which Davis was charged, the new version specified that Davis had violated both the Crimes Act of 1790 and the Treason Act of 1862, with conviction under the first act carrying the certain penalty of death.[2] The indictment was returned at the last possible moment, on the final day of the spring circuit-court session, with the three-year statute of limitations set to expire in a scant few weeks.[3]

Also in contrast to the 1866 indictment, the new indictment was based on the testimony of a number of prominent witnesses: Confederate generals Williams C. Wickham, Thomas Hayward, and Robert E. Lee; Union general John G. Parke; Union lieutenant colonel Horace Porter; Confederate secretary of war James Seddon; Confederate major Charles Duffield; Virginia governor John Letcher and Letcher's deputy George Wythe Munford; Confederate congressman John B. Baldwin; and Virginia state senator Charles W. Wortham all testified against Davis before the grand jury in November 1867. These men confirmed the facts set forth in the indictment, generally describing Davis's involvement in military affairs, their meetings with Davis on specific occasions, and their own involvement in and recollection of particular

---

[2] The indictment was still faulty with respect to the application of the two statutes, however. The second count of the indictment charged Davis with assuming command of the armed forces and seizing Richmond and Henrico County, Virginia, on June 1, 1861, but charged him with violating the Treason Act of 1862.

[3] The government worried that the court might count the limitations period as running from the day Davis had committed his treasonous acts, rather than from the end of the war, so the fourteenth count of the indictment alleged that the limitations period had tolled during the war, as the defendant "was a person fleeing from justice" and not amenable to criminal process in U.S. courts throughout the period of the war. Indictment, U.S. v. Jefferson Davis, at 13, Box 32, Evarts Family Papers, Yale. See Act of July 11, 1864, 13 Stat. 123 (1864) (tolling the limitations period due to the interruption of the Civil War), and Chapter 5, for a discussion of problems with the tolling statute.

battles. Robert E. Lee, James Seddon, and John Letcher spoke about Davis's style of military leadership as commander in chief of the Confederate armed forces. Seddon testified that he "had very frequent personal communications with Prest Davis during all the time I was Secy of War. There were intervals of but few days, whilst he was in the city [of Richmond] that I did not see him. These interviews were mostly relating to the war." Seddon made it clear that Davis had exercised ultimate authority over Confederate military operations, stating that "it was thoroughly understood that he exercised the control, as to military matters, over the Confederate Army, as commander in chief." Seddon also spoke briefly about the planning for certain battles, such as the assaults on Gettysburg and Fredericksburg.

Union generals Horace Porter and John Parke confirmed their presence at the battles of Five Forks, Pittsylvania, the Wilderness, Fort Stedman, Roanoke Island, and Antietam. Former Virginia governor John Letcher and Confederate general Thomas Hayward, who had held state office in Virginia in 1861, testified about transferring the state's troops to Confederate control when the state joined the Confederacy. Letcher also stated that he occasionally met with Davis concerning military affairs, but that Davis rarely "asked my advise [*sic*] or opinion as to the war. He was not a man much given to that sort of thing. He generally acted on his own opinion." Several witnesses also testified about Davis's efforts to rally Confederate troops and bolster Confederate morale. John B. Baldwin, a Virginian who had served in the Confederate Congress and later in the Confederate army, testified that Davis's speeches had sought to "urg[e] [the Confederate people] to renewed effort as to military exertions." Confederate brigadier general Williams C. Wickham confirmed that Davis's speech at the African Church in Richmond in 1865 had "urged the people to prosecute the war with renewed vigor." Thomas Hayward also confirmed that Davis had been determined to secure Confederate independence through the use of force until the very end of the war. According to Hayward, after the conclusion of the Hampton Roads Peace Conference in February 1865, Davis had spoken to him about the need to continue the war, as he "would not agree to peace save upon full absolute independence."[4]

---

[4] "Witnesses ex'd before the Grand Jury at Richmond, November 26, 1867," Box 32, Evarts Family Papers, Yale. (These notes on the grand jury testimony were probably

The most prominent witness to testify against Davis was Robert E. Lee, who described his appearance before the grand jury as a "painful errand."[5] Lee stated that he had very rarely met with Davis personally – he remembered only six such interviews, all of which had taken place in Richmond rather than in the field – and that most of the military decisions had been undertaken by Lee alone, with little input from Davis besides his bare assent. Lee kept his testimony about Davis's involvement in day-to-day military operations very vague. With respect to the Battle of Antietam, for instance, he said that he had "had no conversation with [Davis] touching that that I remember." When speaking of his preparation for the Battle of Fredericksburg, Lee testified that he advised the secretary of war of his plans, and then, "rec[eivin]g no orders to the contrary, I made the move. I received no instructions or order from Mr. Davis, or the Secy of War, to make the move."[6]

None of this testimony accords with historians' assessment of Davis's role as a military leader. By most accounts, Davis was a hands-on commander in chief, even to the point of micromanaging. Although Lee admitted that Davis had necessarily commanded some authority – as he "was President of the Confederacy and commander of the armies and military forces of the Confederacy" – the former general told the grand jury that he had made all military decisions by himself. In addition to testifying that he had had little contact with Davis, Lee said he often received such instructions as he did through the secretary of war, or that he "inferred [Davis's] assent" from his silence in response to Lee's telegraphed proposals. Lee met with Davis in Richmond after delivering this bland testimony and told Davis that he had testified that "he had done with [Davis's] consent and approval only what [Lee] might have done if [Lee] had not consulted [Davis], and that [Lee] accepted the full responsibility for his acts."[7]

---

taken by Lucius Chandler and annotated by Evarts in preparing the indictment several months later.)

[5] Robert E. Lee to Mrs. William H. Fitzhugh Lee, March 10, 1868, in Robert E. Lee Jr., *Recollections and Letters of General Robert E. Lee* (New York: Doubleday, Page, 1909), 304. Lee was in court again in March to testify before the petit jury, but witnesses were never called because the trial was postponed.

[6] "Witnesses ex'd before the Grand Jury at Richmond, November 26, 1867," Box 32, Evarts Family Papers, Yale.

[7] Jefferson Davis, "Robert E. Lee," *North American Review* 150 (January 1890): 65.

Recollecting Lee's turn as a hostile government witness much later in life, Davis wrote: "The evident purpose of [the government's questioning] was to offer to Lee a chance to escape by transferring to me the responsibility for overt acts [of treason]."[8] Lee may also have had in mind the constitutional requirement that treason be proved in court on the testimony of two witnesses to the same overt act. If all meetings on military matters occurred privately between Lee and Davis, Lee would be the sole witness to Davis's acts of treason.[9]

The grand jury that heard testimony in November 1867 and indicted Davis in March 1868 was the first racially integrated federal jury in American history (Figure 13.1).[10] Of the eighteen men who sat

---

[8] "Witnesses ex'd before Grand Jury at Richmond, Nov. 26, 1867, cont'd November 27, 1867," Box 32, Evarts Family Papers, Yale; Davis, "Robert E. Lee," 66. Lee's testimony about Davis's lack of involvement in the day-to-day military operations of the Confederacy was untrue, according to most historians who have studied Davis's role as commander in chief. See William J. Cooper, *Jefferson Davis, American* (New York: Vintage Books, 2000), 457–58; David Potter, "Jefferson Davis and the Political Factors in Confederate Defeat," in *Why the North Won the Civil War*, ed. David Donald (New York: Collier Books, 1960), 104–5. Lee was himself indicted in 1865 for treason by the U.S. Circuit Court, sitting in Norfolk, along with a handful of other Confederates, but had asked General Grant to use his influence to terminate the prosecution on the grounds that Lee's terms of surrender at Appomattox, which granted "parole" to all the soldiers, had included himself. Lee also submitted an amnesty petition, which was not granted but was rendered moot by the same amnesty proclamation that ended Davis's prosecution in December 1868.

[9] U.S. Const. art. III, § 3. There is no external evidence to confirm that this idea motivated Lee's restrained testimony. Many of the witnesses were Davis's friends and confidantes, and several wrote to him expressing their hope and confidence that he would not be convicted. See Robert E. Lee to Jefferson Davis, June 1, 1867, in Jefferson Davis, *Jefferson Davis, Constitutionalist: His Letters, Papers, and Speeches*, ed. Dunbar Rowland, 10 vols. (Jackson: Mississippi Department of Archives and Records, 1923), 7: 110; James Seddon to Jefferson Davis, June 15, 1868, Box 20, Jefferson Davis Papers, MC.

[10] "The First Integrated Jury Impaneled in the United States, May, 1867," *Negro History Bulletin* 33 (October 1933): 134; "Yesterday in Negro History," *Jet*, May 14, 1959, 9; Albert Alschuler, "Racial Quotas and the Jury," *Duke Law Journal* 44 (February 1995): 704, 715. Some black citizens had served earlier on state juries. The *Liberator* reported in 1860 that two black citizens of Worcester – "the first of such instances in Massachusetts" – had been selected as jurors, although it is not clear that they actually served. *Liberator*, June 1860. See www.masshist.org/longroad/03participation/jury.htm (accessed November 1, 2016). Five years later, the *Liberator* reported that a black juror had been impaneled in Rhode Island, when "hitherto it has been customary, when a colored man's name was drawn, to pass it over, but now a new course is to be pursued." *Liberator*, March 17, 1865. Later that year the paper reported

FIGURE 13.1 Jefferson Davis grand jury, 1867–68. Granger Collection.

on Davis's 1868 Richmond grand jury, three were African American; of the twenty-four veniremen selected for the petit jury (which never sat), twelve were black.[11] In part, the heavy representation of African Americans on the Davis jury was a result of the ironclad oath required of federal jurors, which mandated that its adherents swear unbroken loyalty to the Union. Few white Richmonders were eligible. But the Davis prosecution and defense both worried about the effectiveness of the ironclad oath. Evarts and Dana anticipated that a Confederate sympathizer might find his way onto the jury despite the oath, while O'Conor feared that the oath would prove all too efficient in screening

on Robert Johnson, a black man who had served on a jury in Brooklyn. *Liberator*, September 22, 1865.

[11] See "United States Circuit Court," *Staunton Spectator*, May 14, 1867, 1, and photo of the Davis petit jury, Valentine Museum, Richmond, VA.

out those with Confederate leanings. Both sides had good reason for concern.

Many of the African American grand jurors were highly respected in the local community and active participants in Republican politics. Fields Cook, for example, was born a slave and had hired out his time, eventually buying himself and his family out of slavery before the Civil War. After the war, he became a Baptist minister and was counted as one of the most prominent leaders of the Richmond African American community.[12] The members of the petit jury pool were also drawn from the city's African American elite. Joseph Cox may have been born a free man; in the 1850s he worked in a tobacco factory and then at the Tredegar Ironworks as a blacksmith. After the Civil War, Cox participated in the Virginia state constitutional convention of 1867–68, where Judge Underwood served as president. Cox recruited African Americans from rural areas to strengthen the base of Virginia's Republican Party and even attempted to integrate a Richmond street-car in 1867. In 1870 he served as the vice president of the Colored National Labor Union, and five years later he was a delegate to a convention of black Virginians that protested the lack of employment opportunities available to African Americans in the state.[13]

Fellow venireman Albert R. Brooks was born a slave in 1817. Like Fields Cook, he was permitted as a young man to hire out his time to a Richmond tobacco manufacturer and keep part of his earnings. Brooks took a second job as a driver and put aside money to invest in a restaurant and a stable. During the Civil War, Brooks purchased his own freedom for $1,100 and that of his wife, Lucy, and youngest children for $800. His elder children were freed only when the Union army captured the Confederate capital in April 1865. The war wiped Brooks out financially, as Confederate authorities had confiscated much of the equipment from his livery stable. Following the war, Brooks and other black Richmonders faced harassment from the local police, who tried to reimpose slavery's pass and curfew system on the city's

[12] "Fields Cook," in *Dictionary of Virginia Biography*, ed. Sara Bearss, 3 vols. to date (Richmond: Library of Virginia, 1998–), 3: 420–22; "Fields Cook," in *Freedom's Lawmakers*, ed. Eric Foner (Baton Rouge: Louisiana State University Press, 1996), 49.

[13] "Joseph Cox," in *Dictionary of Virginia Biography*, 3: 509–11. See also "Joseph Cox," in *Freedom's Lawmakers*, 52.

freedmen.[14] Brooks protested to the *New York Tribune* and to President Johnson, and the laws were eventually repealed. He and his fellow Republican Richmonders called for universal suffrage and focused on building a biracial Republican coalition in Virginia.[15]

For Albert Brooks and the other African American jurors, service on the Jefferson Davis jury meant a great deal. They were poised to ensure that Davis would not escape punishment for levying war against the United States in order to perpetuate racial slavery. At the same time, they lived and worked among a largely hostile white population in the former Confederate capital. Brooks's family reminiscences provide a small glimpse into his state of mind at the time of his selection as a member of the venire pool for the Davis case. The family recorded that his service was "an honor" and "a recognition" of his social and political prominence. Indeed, the earliest extant family photographs "of this distinguished forbear of the Brooks clan are taken for the group of the petit jury."[16] His great-granddaughter, the historian Evelyn Brooks Higginbotham, noted that her "only visual knowledge of [her] great-grandfather comes from the photograph of him sitting proudly among the black and white members of the [petit] jury in the Richmond courthouse" (Figure 13.2).[17]

The white jurors were subject to great social pressure to acquit Davis. The weight of this pressure could be overwhelming, and the Davis prosecutors doubted whether even committed white Unionists could withstand it. One white grand juror, John Minor Botts, had once, ironically, suffered an eight-week imprisonment in a "negro jail" at the hands of Jefferson Davis's government for the crime of treason against the Confederacy.[18] An outspoken Virginia Unionist throughout the war, Botts had called for the execution of prominent rebels soon after the

---

[14] See Sally E. Hadden, *Slave Patrols: Law and Violence in Virginia and the Carolinas* (Cambridge, MA: Harvard University Press, 2003), 203–20.

[15] "Albert Brooks," *Dictionary of Virginia Biography*, 2: 269–70.

[16] Walter Brooks, Charlotte Brooks, and Joseph Brooks, *A Brooks Chronicle: The Lives and Times of an African-American Family* (Washington, DC: Brooks Associates, 1989), 71–72.

[17] Evelyn Brooks Higginbotham, "The Cost of Remembrance: Reflections on David Blight's *Race and Reunion*," paper presented at Race, Religion, and Nationalism: Three Books Symposium, Amherst College, Amherst, MA, October 27, 2001; available at www3.amherst.edu/~aardoc/Higginbotham.html (accessed November 1, 2016). Albert Brooks appears alone in the front row, seated, in the photo on the right in Figure 13.2.

[18] *Richmond Examiner*, March 8, 1862.

FIGURE 13.2 Jefferson Davis petit jury pool, 1868. The Valentine Museum.

war's conclusion, but he nonetheless put up money for Davis's bail in 1867.[19] That action was alarming enough to Botts's Unionist allies that they demanded a public justification for his sudden about-face. Botts explained that he did not regret his actions in returning the indictment against Davis, but he believed that Davis deserved to be released on bail because of the government's delay in trying the case.[20]

White venireman W. A. Parsons proved even more vulnerable, as his actions later in life revealed. A former Union soldier from New York, Parsons had relocated to Richmond at the end of the war, where he later became a land agent.[21] At a reception at the newly opened Confederate Museum in 1896, Parsons participated in an exchange with the redoubtable Isabel Maury, one of the museum's founders. All of the surviving Davis jurors had been invited to the gathering; Fields Cook, who was present, was described by an observer as a

---

[19] See *Baltimore Gazette*, July 7, 1866, and John Minor Botts, *The Great Rebellion: Its Secret History, Rise, Progress, and Disastrous Failure* (New York: Harper and Brothers, 1866), for Botts's thoughts on the punishment of rebels.

[20] John Minor Botts to Horace Greeley, May 15, 1867, published in *New York Times*, May 21, 1867.

[21] *New York Times*, September 25, 1867; Hennings v. Parsons, 108 Va. 1 (1908); *Southern Planter* 64 (February 1903): 123.

"negro minister a very mild kind of darkey." The same observer chronicled that Parsons's Unionism was shallow indeed.[22] He was clearly
ashamed of his service on the Davis jury. On seeing a photograph of
himself alongside the other Davis jurors, Parsons panicked and "shed
tears and said he was never on the Jeff Davis trial petty Jury." Maury
coldly told him that she would remove his image only if "he would go
before a Court and make oath that he was not of the Jury." Given a
reaction like Parsons's, even years later, it is little wonder that prosecutor Richard Henry Dana worried that "a fear of personal violence or
social retribution may be enough to induce one man to withhold his
assent from the verdict, especially as he need not come forward personally, nor give a reason, even in the jury room."[23]

Davis and his team objected to the integrated panel in highly
racially charged terms. Davis himself described one of the grand jurors
as "a big black negro, whose head had fallen back on the rail of the
bench he sat on; his mouth was wide open, and he was fast asleep."[24]
O'Conor complained about the insult he perceived in trying the case
before a mixed-race panel. "I find it impossible to believe," he told
Varina Davis, "that we are destined to play parts in a farce so contemptible as a trial before Underwood and a set of recently eman-
cipated negroes."[25] He lamented that the "jury [will be] composed
in part of Negroes. Perhaps a majority will wear the favored hue."[26]
O'Conor simply would not risk a trial before an interracial jury. He
told Jefferson Davis, "I think much should be endured to avoid a trial
before a mongrel jury."[27]

At O'Conor's instruction, co-counsel Robert Ould compiled personal and political information about each of the jurors and put

[22] There is no way of knowing who wrote the notes, but the observer was clearly involved
in the founding of the museum. For more on the museum's founders, see Caroline E.
Janney, *Burying the Dead and Not the Past: Ladies' Memorial Associations and the
Lost Cause* (Chapel Hill: University of North Carolina Press, 2008), 167–94.

[23] Handwritten notes, "History of the Jurors who Indicted President Davis for Treason,"
Box 24, Jefferson Davis Papers, MC; Richard Henry Dana to William M. Evarts,
August 24, 1868, Box 18, Dana Family Papers, MHS.

[24] Davis, "Robert E. Lee," 55.

[25] Charles O'Conor to Varina Davis, October 21, 1867, Jefferson Davis Papers, Box
24, MC.

[26] Charles O'Conor to Thomas F. Bayard, October 19, 1867, *Tyler's Quarterly Magazine*
29 (October 1947): 182.

[27] Charles O'Conor to Jefferson Davis, October 29, 1867, Box 24, Jefferson Davis
Papers, MC. See also Charles O'Conor to Jefferson Davis, October 2, 1867, ibid.

together a list of potential veniremen, indicating both their race and his assessment of their "conservatism" – a code word for their sympathy for Davis. Of the fifty-four potential jurors Ould surveyed, he found sixteen to be conservative and four to be "decidedly so."[28] "What will Europe think," Ould queried, "of trying ten imperial states on the law before Underwood, and on the fact before twelve negroes? Will it not make the name of American a badge of abasement in every circle where honor is reverenced?"[29]

By early 1868, the Radical Republicans had determined to impeach President Johnson for his continued efforts to thwart their plans for Reconstruction – and they had gained enough political power to do so. The Davis case was set to collide with the impeachment trial. With the president's removal trial scheduled in the Senate for late February, the cabinet had to consider which lawyers should defend Johnson in the trial. They wholeheartedly approved of hiring former Supreme Court justice Benjamin R. Curtis, and agreed that Attorney General Stanbery would act in the case, although it was unclear whether he would retain the office of attorney general while doing so. Charles O'Conor's name was floated, but he was ultimately rejected because "he was counsel for Jeff Davis, and ... party antipathy would counteract his ability."[30] Secretary Seward urged the president to consider William Evarts for the position, but Secretary Welles was dead set against him, arguing that Evarts had exhibited Radical tendencies and would therefore be inclined toward lackluster representation. Nevertheless, Seward invited Evarts to Washington to confer about the defense without notifying the cabinet in advance. Welles was livid, remarking in his diary that Evarts

---

28 Charles O'Conor to Thomas F. Bayard, April 14, 1868, and Robert Ould to Thomas F. Bayard, April 24, 1868 (with list of jurors enclosed), vol. 12, Bayard Family Papers, LC.

29 Robert Ould to W. W. Corcoran, October 25, 1867, Box 16, W. W. Corcoran Papers, LC.

30 Gideon Welles, *Diary of Gideon Welles*, ed. Edgar Thaddeus Welles, 3 vols. (Boston: Houghton Mifflin Company, 1911), 3: 298. See also Orville Hickman Browning, *Diary of Orville Hickman Browning*, ed. James G. Randall (Springfield: Illinois State Historical Library, 1925), 183, and James C. Kennedy to Andrew Johnson, March 4, 1868, in Andrew Johnson, *The Papers of Andrew*

was "cold, calculating, [and] selfish." In Welles's opinion, he was "destitute of enthusiasm, magnetic power or political influence." Welles also considered Evarts to be a political enemy of Johnson's, more of a Republican than was ideal in this situation. "Ought such a man though unsurpassed as a lawyer ... to be selected in such a case as this?" he queried. President Johnson warned Seward that "his coming here does not insure that Mr. Evarts will be retained," but Seward ultimately prevailed and Evarts became junior counsel for the president.[31]

Although Evarts had initially believed that he would not have a major role to play in the impeachment trial, Henry Stanbery fell ill, shifting much of the responsibility for Johnson's defense to him. Evarts, writing to his friend and fellow New York attorney Edwards Pierrepont, said that he would "get through it somehow, but [would] be glad when it is over."[32] Johnson's impeachment trial put severe limits on Evarts's time and his ability to devote himself to the Davis case. After the impeachment began in late February, Evarts's involvement in the drafting of Davis's indictment was minimal, as most of his time was spent on the Johnson defense. Evarts's schedule was exhausting. According to a European visitor several years later, Evarts recounted that "one night he was closet[ed] till 11 with President Johnson advising him about his impeachment and from 11 to 1 consulting with other law officers on the impeachment of President Davis," a situation the visitor found to be "a sufficiently curious experience."[33]

The contrast between his actions on behalf of the two embattled presidents did not escape the notice of Evarts's Southern cousin, S. A. Tiffany, who wrote from Charlottesville to chastise him for his

Johnson, ed. Paul Bergeron, 16 vols. (Knoxville: University of Tennessee Press, 1967–69), 13: 609.

[31] Welles, *Diary of Gideon Welles*, 3: 298, 307. Seward had obviously tipped off Evarts about the possibility of his being retained by March 3, as Evarts mentioned it confidentially to Dana on that date. William Evarts to Richard Henry Dana, March 3, 1868, Box 18, Dana Family Papers, MHS.

[32] William Evarts to Edwards Pierrepont, April 21, 1868, folder 28, Box 1, Edwards Pierrepont Papers, Yale.

[33] Archibald Philip Primrose [Earl of] Rosebery, *Lord Rosebery's North American Journal, 1873*, ed. A. R. C. Grant and Caroline Combe (London: Sidgwick & Jackson, 1967), 32–33.

lack of empathy for Davis in light of his advocacy on behalf of the beleaguered Johnson. After praising him for his work in the Johnson impeachment trial, she reminded him, "You have a Virginian's name. I can't help wishing you were for not against a certain other President (that was)."[34] In March, Richard Henry Dana stopped in Washington on his way to Richmond to confer with Evarts on their plans for the Davis trial.[35] Although Dana urged Evarts to try to convince prominent Republicans of the wisdom of dropping the prosecution, the more immediate issue was the drafting of the indictment.[36] Taking precious time away from his work on Johnson's impeachment, Evarts personally reviewed Dana's draft and changed some of its wording to read that Davis had "levied" rather than "waged" war against the United States, so as to conform to the exact specifications of the crime of treason as set forth in the U.S. Constitution.[37]

Davis's trial had already contributed to Johnson's difficulties with the Republicans in Congress. For the previous year and a half, Representative George Boutwell, chairman of the House Committee on the Judiciary, had sought to prove that the administration's failure to prosecute Davis was an impeachable offense.[38] As a Radical Republican, Boutwell objected to Johnson's lenient plan for Reconstruction, particularly his liberal distribution of presidential

[34] S. A. Tiffany to William Evarts, May 4, 1868, Box 1, William Evarts Papers, LC. Evarts's father, Jeremiah, had named him after a Yale classmate, William Maxwell, a Virginian who became a lawyer and eventually the president of Hampden-Sydney College. Chester L. Barrows, *William M. Evarts: Lawyer, Diplomat, Statesman* (Chapel Hill: University of North Carolina Press, 1941), 5.

[35] William Evarts to Richard Henry Dana, March 3, 1868, Box 18, Dana Family Papers, MHS.

[36] Dana diary, March 27, 1868, vol. 160, Dana Family Papers, MHS; Richard Henry Dana to Ebenezer Rockwood Hoar, August 3, 1869, Jefferson Davis Case File, NA-CP.

[37] Davis indictment of 1868 (with Evarts's notations), Box 32, Evarts Family Papers, Yale. There is no evidence that Evarts had O'Conor's argument about the legal distinction between waging and levying war in mind in drafting the indictment.

[38] *Impeachment Investigation: Testimony Taken before the Judiciary Committee of the House of Representatives in the Investigation of the Charges against Andrew Johnson* (Washington, DC: Government Printing Office, 1867), 781. Charles Sumner agreed with Boutwell's assessment, writing to Gideon Welles about the president's alliance with the Democrats and ex-Confederates. See Charles Sumner to Gideon Welles, June 15, 1865, Reel 79, Charles Sumner Papers, HU.

pardons to ex-Confederates and his insistence on the premature political reintegration of the still-rebellious Southern states into the Union.[39]

In July 1866, Boutwell had told a crowd in Weymouth, Massachusetts, that Davis and Lee ought to be tried and executed for treason, insisting that "those two men, above all others, deserve to pay the highest forfeit ever exacted by human tribunals from those who have violated the law.... They are peculiarly responsible to the army of the republic, to the country, and to mankind, for this great crime."[40] Writing in the *Atlantic Monthly*, Boutwell condemned Johnson for his failure to follow through on his promise to make treason odious by prosecuting Jefferson Davis.[41] In his opinion, Johnson had refrained from trying Davis in order to cultivate the political support of Southern Democrats, and he was flouting his duty to enforce the laws of the United States.[42]

During the impeachment investigation the following year, Boutwell's Judiciary Committee tried to elicit information from those closely involved in the Davis prosecution that would demonstrate that Johnson had acted improperly in failing to bring Davis to justice. Just prior to convening the committee, Boutwell asked former prosecutor

---

[39] See Gregory Downs, *After Appomattox* (Cambridge, MA: Harvard University Press, 2015), for an account of the disagreement between Johnson and Congress on the legal issue of the war's conclusion. As historian Eric McKitrick pointed out more than a generation ago, Johnson saw the executive pardon as his most powerful tool for effecting Reconstruction, and his liberal use of the privilege incensed his opponents in Congress. See Eric L. McKitrick, *Andrew Johnson and Reconstruction* (Chicago: University of Chicago Press, 1960), 142–52, for an analysis of the problems with Johnson's pardon policy; Jonathan T. Dorris, *Pardon and Amnesty under Lincoln and Johnson* (Chapel Hill: University of North Carolina, 1953). In fact, Charles Sumner and legal academic Joel Bishop discussed Johnson's perceived abuse of the pardon as a possible ground for impeachment. Joel Bishop to Charles Sumner, January 5, 1866, Reel 35, Charles Sumner Papers, HU. Bishop ruminated on the possibility of passing legislation to prevent the president from pardoning someone who had been convicted of a violation of the law of war. But he ultimately concluded that the proposal was likely unconstitutional and the best course of action was to remove an unsatisfactory president through impeachment.

[40] George Boutwell, "Reconstruction: Its True Basis. Speech Delivered at Weymouth, Mass, July 4, 1865," in *Speeches and Papers Relating to the Rebellion and the Overthrow of Slavery* (Boston: Little, Brown, 1867), 399.

[41] George Boutwell, "The Usurpation: From the 'Atlantic Monthly,' October, 1866," in *Speeches and Papers Relating to the Rebellion*, 489.

[42] Boutwell, "Reconstruction: Its True Basis" and "The Usurpation," in *Speeches and Papers Relating to the Rebellion*, 399–400, 497–98. See also Thomas Domer, "The

John H. Clifford for an explanation as to "why [he] retired from the Davis case."[43] Clifford saw no reason to dissemble, explaining frankly, "I withdrew because I was satisfied that his trial before any Jury in Virginia would only result in the humiliation of the Govt, with entire impunity to the prisoner." Clifford said he had been unwilling to participate in "the enactment of a judicial farce, the result of which was a foregone conclusion."[44] Apparently unsatisfied with Clifford's answer, Boutwell and the other members of his committee grilled Davis's prosecutors about the administration's foot-dragging.

Among the topics the Judiciary Committee singled out for deeper investigation was Davis's release on bail in May 1867 and the decision of the military commander at Fort Monroe to relinquish Davis into civil custody under a writ of habeas corpus. Lucius Chandler testified that he had conferred with William Evarts and Attorney General Stanbery on the appropriateness of granting bail in a potentially capital case, and that they had determined, after some research, that bail was up to the judge's discretion.[45] Judge Underwood told the committee that he had granted bail because its acceptability had already been agreed on by opposing counsel. When pressed by the committee about whether he would have chosen to bail Davis if the prosecution had not acquiesced, Underwood stated that he probably would have, as the government's "default ... for no good excuse" outweighed the magnitude of Davis's offenses.[46] Secretary of War Edwin Stanton told

Role of George S. Boutwell in the Impeachment and Trial of Andrew Johnson," *New England Quarterly* 49 (December 1974): 596, 597.

43 Clifford and Boutwell knew each other fairly well, as Clifford had served as attorney general when Boutwell was governor of Massachusetts and then succeeded Boutwell as governor. See George Boutwell, *Reminiscences of Sixty Years in Public Affairs*, 2 vols. (New York: McClure, Phillips, 1902), 1: 124.

44 George S. Boutwell to John H. Clifford, June 27, 1867, and John H. Clifford to George Boutwell, June 30, 1867, Papers 1867–1869, John Clifford Papers, MHS.

45 *Impeachment Investigation*, 504–5 (testimony of Lucius Chandler). The three had consulted Alfred Conkling's federal courts treatise on the question of whether the Judiciary Act of 1793 prevented granting bail in a capital case. See Judiciary Act of 1789, § 33, 1 Stat. 73 (1789), and Judiciary Act of 1793, § 41, 1 Stat. 333 (1793). See also Alfred Conkling, *Treatise on the Organization Jurisdiction and Practice of the Courts of the United States* (Albany: W. C. Little, 1856), 627–28. Two early cases in which the federal courts found bail to be discretionary under the 1793 act were United States v. Stewart, 2 U.S. 343, 27 F. Cas. 1338 (C.C.D. Pa. 1795) (No. 16,401), and United States v. Robins, 27 F. Cas. 825 (D.S.C. 1799) (No. 16,175).

46 *Impeachment Investigation*, 578–79 (testimony of John C. Underwood).

the committee that he had willingly released Davis from military custody into civil in May 1867 and that "from the period that it was determined Davis should be brought to trial before a civil tribunal, I was anxious to be relieved from his military custody."[47] They had all acted in good faith, they declared, and had had good reasons for not pursuing Davis's prosecution more aggressively.

As Boutwell probed for evidence that the failure to prosecute Davis rested with President Johnson, quite a different picture emerged from the testimony of Davis's prosecutors. Evarts and Chandler spoke frankly of their bewilderment with regard to the case and their desire for clear instructions on how to proceed with Davis's prosecution. Speed and Stanbery detailed their frustrated efforts to find a satisfactory solution to the problems the case presented. Rather than placing the blame for the uncertainty and delay on the president, Johnson's advisers and subordinates described the Davis prosecution as a minefield fraught with dangers and difficulties that Johnson had attempted to proceed through with caution. The intractable problems associated with the trial and its potential to exonerate rather than condemn Davis – rather than Johnson's "softness" on treason – had caused the delays, they said. In light of such testimony, Boutwell had no choice but to abandon the stalled proceedings in the Davis trial as a possible ground for impeachment.

In the early months of 1868, the Davis prosecution viewed the convergence of the Johnson impeachment and the finding of the Davis indictment as simply a somewhat unfortunate coincidence. William Evarts and Chief Justice Chase, who would preside over the impeachment trial in the Senate, would both necessarily be distracted from the Davis case by their duties in Johnson's trial. Their attention would be diverted away from Richmond and toward Washington for the time being. Furthermore, because Johnson's political future was uncertain, Evarts and Dana could not predict who the next attorney general would be – and whether he would be receptive to their proposal that the case against Davis should be abandoned in light of an uncertain conviction.[48]

---

[47] *Impeachment Investigation*, 396–98 (testimony of Edwin Stanton).
[48] William Evarts to Richard Henry Dana, March 3, 1868, Box 18, Dana Family Papers, MHS.

From their perspective, these concerns meant that the case should be delayed – again – until the conclusion of Johnson's impeachment trial.

Charles O'Conor saw far more sinister possibilities lurking in Johnson's impeachment. The first sign of trouble came when the grand jury in Richmond returned the new indictment against Davis on March 26, 1868. This was the indictment that had given the prosecution so much trouble to produce, but to O'Conor it was written with a seriousness of purpose that the shoddily drafted 1866 indictment had lacked and seemed to indicate that the prosecution truly intended to proceed against Davis. If the earlier indictment had been an absolute mess, failing even to specify under which statute Davis was charged, the new version was well drafted and designed to hold up in court. And it charged Davis with treason under the Crimes Act of 1790, which, if he were convicted, carried the certain penalty of death.[49]

O'Conor was generally inclined to view potential threats against Davis with equanimity. In 1865 he had reassured Varina Davis and Jeremiah Black, whom he judged to be not "particularly weak of nerves," that it was unlikely that Davis would ultimately face trial by military commission.[50] In early 1867 he had casually dismissed Varina's worries about John Surratt's return to the United States and the renewed potential to link Davis to the Lincoln assassination. Later that year, on hearing of a somewhat credible plot to assassinate Davis as he traveled from Canada to Richmond to attend court in November, O'Conor merely warned his client to take care and to travel under an assumed name.[51]

---

[49] This was in addition to the Confiscation Act of 1862. The Confiscation Act did not preclude prosecutors from charging Davis under the earlier statute for acts that had taken place in 1861 and early 1862. The 1862 act provided that it "should not be construed in any way to affect or alter the prosecution, conviction, or punishment of any person or persons guilty of treason against the United States before the passage of this act, unless such person is convicted under this act." Confiscation Act, § 4, 12 Stat. 589 (1862).

[50] Charles O'Conor to Jeremiah Black, September 29, 1865, Reel 22, Jeremiah Black Papers, LC [microfilm edition].

[51] Jefferson Davis to William F. Howell, November 6, 1867, Jefferson Davis Papers, Beauvoir, Jefferson Davis Presidential Library, Biloxi, MS; Charles O'Conor to Jefferson Davis, November 5, 13, 1867, Jefferson Davis Papers, MC; Varina

But the new indictment worried him immediately. An official copy reached O'Conor on April 9, and after perusing it in haste, he wrote Davis of his concerns amid "a crowd of persons and multitude of occupations." The indictment's soundness convinced O'Conor that it was handiwork of Richard Henry Dana, whose abilities as a lawyer O'Conor respected. It was arresting, to say the least, given that the administration had loped along for so long without any serious commitment to the enterprise of trying Davis. O'Conor suspected that Seward – "to whom I impute the direction of all that has been done against you" – had managed to convince his friend Evarts, who was now living in close proximity while working on the impeachment in Washington, to pursue the prosecution against Davis in a serious way. Still, O'Conor cautiously reassured Davis that his "life [was] in no serious peril."[52]

By the following day, having taken more time to study the indictment, O'Conor had changed his mind. The indictment was nothing short of alarming. In O'Conor's opinion, the carefully drafted indictment reflected the growing political power of the Radical Republicans.[53] The Radicals in Congress had dusted off their plans to make Davis's conviction a virtual certainty, and O'Conor reported that "a bill has passed the Senate to facilitate the packing of the

---

Davis, *Jefferson Davis, Ex-President of the Confederate States: A Memoir*, 2 vols. (New York: Belford, 1890), 2: 805.

[52] Charles O'Conor to Jefferson Davis, April 9, 10, 1868, Box 24, Jefferson Davis Papers, MC.

[53] Although he believed the indictment to be well drafted, O'Conor still found it be flawed in its clumsy attempt to avoid a potential statute of limitations problem. Under the Crimes Act of 1790, an indictment for treason had to be brought "within three years next after the treason or capital offense … shall have been committed," but the act allowed an exception if the accused was "a person … fleeing from justice." Crimes Act of 1790, § 32, 1 Stat. 112 (1790). The Civil War tolling statute also permitted the delay of prosecutions during hostilities. Act of July 11, 1864, 13 Stat. 123 (1864). The fourteenth clause of the indictment thus recited that Davis had, from 1861 to May 10, 1865, been "a person fleeing from justice within the intent and meaning of the statute," because the "resistance to the execution of the laws of the United States, and the interruption of the ordinary course of judicial proceedings" made it impossible to serve process on Davis. O'Conor pointed out that the attempt to preempt the limitations objection was "an instance of the blunder commonly designated, leaping before you come to the stile." Pleading the statute of limitations is a defense to be raised only in an answer, and O'Conor maintained that the prosecutor "should have awaited our plea and then *replied* this matter in section 14." Charles O'Conor to Jefferson Davis, April 18, 1868, Box 24, Jefferson Davis Papers, MC.

jury."[54] But the most sinister development was the Radicals' success in impeaching Johnson in February 1868, a move that could very well result in the president's removal. In fact, it seemed likely that the conclusion of the president's impeachment trial would coincide with the date Davis had been called to appear personally in court or forfeit his recognizance: May 2.[55] O'Conor regarded this coincidence as potentially lethal. If Johnson should be convicted, O'Conor speculated to Davis that the impeachment prosecutor Benjamin Butler – "the foremost man among the black-republican leaders" – would next turn his attention toward Davis and, "beyond all peradventure, demand your life."[56]

Moreover, Senator Benjamin Wade, who was slated to become president in the event of Johnson's removal, had also already denounced former rebels. Indeed, he had vowed to transcend the limits of the law to see them convicted. In the course of debate over the Second Confiscation Act in 1862, Wade had declared himself to "have no scruples about the Constitution of the United States as wielded against traitors in this time of violent revolution. You have seen that the ordinary course of the common law and the Constitution cannot be followed [in the prosecution of treason]." Wade's determination had not expired at the end of the war. He had counseled President Johnson to "either force into exile or hang ten or twelve of the worst of these fellows.... We would all agree on Jeff Davis."[57]

Even if the president managed to avoid conviction, O'Conor believed that Davis's life was still in danger. Johnson would be weakened by his own narrow escape, and the Republicans empowered,

---

[54] Such a bill had been introduced in the Senate in 1865 but had not passed. It was taken up again in 1868 and passed the Senate but not the House. See Chapter 5 for a discussion of this bill, introduced by Senator Doolittle.

[55] This date had been pushed back from April 14. See Order of Judge Underwood, March 12, 1868, Federal Records, U.S. v. Jefferson Davis, LVA.

[56] Butler had met with President Johnson in 1865 about Davis's trial and had urged the president to try Davis for treason before a military tribunal. See Benjamin Butler, *Butler's Book: Autobiography and Reminiscences of Major-General Benjamin F. Butler* (Boston: A. M. Thayer, 1892), 915–18.

[57] *Congressional Globe*, 37th Cong., 2d sess., April 21, 1862, 1737; Albert G. Riddle, *The Life of Benjamin Franklin Wade* (Cleveland: W. W. Williams, 1886), 268–69.

such that he would be impelled to appease them by offering up Davis. According to O'Conor, Seward – "the mean viper who counsels the executive" – would necessarily gain power within the administration because of his Republican credentials and "will be apt to advise the sacrifice [of Davis's life] as an impressive proof of fidelity" to congressional authority. O'Conor judged that Davis's life would be in serious jeopardy – whether the president was convicted or acquitted. He counseled a third option: Davis should forfeit his bail and refuse to return to the United States for trial.[58]

In recommending such a drastic measure, O'Conor assured Davis that his "personal honor" would not be compromised by failing to appear for a trial when the stakes were so high and the odds so stacked against him. Davis's sureties would have to be reimbursed for the bail money they would forfeit, but O'Conor pledged to indemnify them out of his own very considerable personal fortune.[59] The choice boiled down, he wrote, to "incurring risks of the most serious moment [or] a mere pecuniary loss [and] it seems to me that any discreet man set to determine between these alternatives would choose the latter." Davis should not concern himself about the money his lawyer would

[58] In fact, James Gordon Bennett's *New York Herald* had been advocating this solution to Davis's problem for a few weeks, for the same reasons as O'Conor. O'Conor enclosed some *Herald* clippings on the topic in his letters to Davis, wryly noting that "the cunning Scot whose slip I sent seems to have got upon [our] same track. But he was *late*." Charles O'Conor to Jefferson Davis, May 4, 1868, Jefferson Davis Papers, MC. Bennett had been born in Scotland and moved to the United States in his twenties. Bennett and O'Conor were close neighbors in Fort Washington, New York. The two even attended the same church, and both had contributed substantial sums for the church's construction. Henry A. Brann, "A Few Chapters in Church History: St. Elizabeth's Church," *United States Catholic Historical Society: Historical Records and Studies* 6 (February 1911): 63, 64–65.

[59] Under the initial bail arrangement, Davis himself was personally bound for $100,000 and his sureties for $110,000. In advising Davis to jump bail, O'Conor also recommended that Davis sell or mortgage any real property he owned in the United States, if possible, before forfeiting his bond. When Davis's bail was renewed on May 2, 1868, O'Conor arranged that Davis would no longer be personally liable on his bail, that the amount of bail for the sureties was dropped to $100,000, and that only three of his wealthiest supporters, Horace Greeley, Gerrit Smith, and Cornelius Vanderbilt, would be liable on the bond. These sureties could well afford the loss of that sum, and might not immediately demand repayment from O'Conor and Davis. See Charles O'Conor to Jefferson Davis, April 19, 26, May 4, 13, 1868 (newspaper clipping from *New York Herald*, May 3, 1868, enclosed in May 4 letter), Box 24, Jefferson Davis

lose, because O'Conor believed that avoiding such an unjust trial was worth the price to be paid: "I never bargained for a trial before a jury of negroes and I have a great repugnance to figuring in such a filthy transaction." O'Conor maintained that Davis's first concern should be the personal hardships in store for his family should he be sentenced to death, rather than his public duty. "For what I have done or may do in endeavoring to defeat the attempt upon your life you owe me nothing," he told Davis. "You owe your wife and young children solace and protection: you are not at liberty wantonly to deprive them of either."[60]

Finally, O'Conor insisted that Davis must not become a martyr in a futile attempt to vindicate the Confederate cause and the right of secession. He told his client that "perhaps public considerations should not be wholly left out of view" but that "suicide is the least heroic of actions."[61] In any event, O'Conor proposed that Davis could fulfill his public duty by publishing an explanation for his actions, which O'Conor and Davis would write together in Montreal.[62] For Davis's own safety, O'Conor warned his client not

---

Papers, MC. O'Conor's personal wealth (including both personal and real property), was valued at $450,000, at a time when the wealth of the average American household totaled about $3,000. See Joshua L. Rosenbloom and Gregory W. Stutes, "Reexamining the Distribution of Wealth in 1870," Working Paper 11482, available at www.nber.org/papers/w11482 (accessed November 3, 2016); Lee Soltow, *Men and Wealth in the United States, 1850–1870* (New Haven: Yale University Press, 1975), 112–13.

[60] Charles O'Conor to Jefferson Davis, April 19, 1868, Box 24, Davis Papers, MC.

[61] Charles O'Conor to Jefferson Davis, April 19, 1868, Box 24, Davis Papers, MC.

[62] O'Conor's advice to Davis raises a deep ethical concern. Although recommending (and facilitating) a client's flight would certainly be unethical (and illegal) on the part of a defense attorney today, there were no formal rules of legal ethics in O'Conor's day. While no rules of professional conduct had been enacted in the late 1860s, there were still canons of ethical behavior for attorneys. In 1854 Pennsylvania lawyer George Sharswood gave a highly influential address to the law students at the University of Pennsylvania on the topic of legal ethics that formed the basis of later codes. Sharswood emphasized the lawyer's duties to both the court and his client, and concluded that two were often difficult to balance. Sharswood accordingly insisted that "high moral principle is his [the lawyer's] only safe guide; the only torch to light his way amidst darkness and obstruction." George Sharswood, *A Compend of Lectures on the Aims and Duties of the Profession of the Law Delivered before the Law Class of the University of*

to disclose the substance of this secret arrangement to anyone other than Varina.[63]

O'Conor kept his counsel, declining even to reply when William B. Reed sent letters warning of the very political concerns O'Conor had raised with Davis with respect to the president's impeachment.[64] Indeed, when another associate visited O'Conor's office and urged him to recommend that Davis not appear at trial, O'Conor later reported to Davis that he had managed to sit through the meeting "keeping on a stolid inexpressive face ... look[ing] out upon him as from a chamber of dull nothingness."[65] Davis may have chafed at the notion of fleeing his trial, but he eventually accepted O'Conor's advice, telling his friend James M. Mason that "if A[ndrew] J[ohnson] is removed by the pending impeachment, things cannot be worse for me."[66]

Before embarking on this secret plan, O'Conor made one last trip to Washington to try to convince the administration to drop the

---

Pennsylvania (Philadelphia: T. & J. W. Johnson, 1854), 55. In the Davis case, it seems that O'Conor weighed his duty to court and client according to his own conscience and ultimately decided that avoiding the risk to Davis's life trumped all other considerations, including potential harm to his own professional reputation. In this, O'Conor – like lawyers past and present – mediated as best he could through competing concerns to achieve the best outcome, according to his own sensibilities. See Robert W. Gordon, "The Citizen-Lawyer – A Brief Informal History of a Myth with Some Basis in Reality," *William and Mary Law Review* 50 (2009): 1169, 1185–86, and Norman W. Spaulding, "The Myth of Civic Republicanism: Interrogating the Ideology of Antebellum Legal Ethics," *Fordham Law Review* 71 (2003): 1397, 1452.

[63] O'Conor did not even tell his co-counsel of the plan, and he used misdirection with his colleagues, bewildering James F. Bayard when he told him that he no longer desired a postponement and that his only concern was procuring a fair jury. Charles O'Conor to Thomas F. Bayard, April 14, 1868, and Thomas F. Bayard to James A. Bayard, April 17, 1868, vol. 12, Bayard Family Papers, LC.

[64] William B. Reed to Charles O'Conor, April 2, 1868, appended to William B. Reed to Robert Ould, April 2, 1868, "Correspondence, Letters 1865–1873," Isaac Carrington Papers, DU.

[65] Charles O'Conor to Jefferson Davis, May 4, 1868, Box 24, Jefferson Davis Papers, MC. See also Charles O'Conor to Thomas F. Bayard, April 14, 1868, and Thomas F. Bayard to James Bayard, April 17, 1868, vol. 12, Bayard Family Papers, LC.

[66] Jefferson Davis to James M. Mason, April 16, 1868, in Jefferson Davis, *The Papers of Jefferson Davis*, ed. Lynda L. Crist, 14 vols. (Baton Rouge: Louisiana State University Press, 1971–2014), 12: 289.

prosecution against Davis, or at least to postpone it until well after the impeachment trial. In Washington he planned to meet with Seward, whom he would confront on the subject of his secret supposed machinations against Davis "in a plain, blunt, home-spun style that would do no discredit to the taste of the Chief Impeacher [Benjamin Butler]." Next he would move on to the second "act in my contemplated drama … an interview with the Great Impeached [Johnson]." In preparation for this trip, O'Conor wrote a deliberately misleading letter to Horace Greeley, telling Greeley that his own annoyance with the delays in the case (rather than his concern for Davis's life) was driving him to try to settle the court date definitively.[67] O'Conor asked Greeley for a letter of introduction to influential Republicans who might aid his cause in Washington, while sounding an appropriate note of professional frustration with the case. "There is something very contemptible in the way this case is treated by those who direct the prosecution," he groused. "It is at once oppressive and humiliating to be kept playing tail to the kite of some persons of little significance who have a control over it. I am pretty patient always, have been extremely so in this case, but my patience is exhausted and I want to have a definite understanding."[68]

The trip turned out to be fortuitous. Beforehand, O'Conor had considered it unlikely that he would accomplish anything in Washington. He viewed the trip merely "as a suitable effort to save a large sum of money," but he ended up bumping into William Evarts on the street when he reached Washington on April 25. After this unexpected meeting, he, Evarts, and U.S. Attorney Chandler arranged another postponement. Davis would not be called to appear at trial until the fall. With Davis's safety thus assured for the immediate future, and

---

[67] O'Conor disclosed to Davis that "in a note to H. G. [Horace Greeley] and at the outset of my conversation with Mr Evarts I expressed some indignation at the trouble and inconvenience they were imposing on me. There was no deception in this; as to the rest is our privileged secret." Charles O'Conor to Jefferson Davis, April 26, 1868, Box 24, Jefferson Davis Papers, MC. See also Charles O'Conor to Horace Greeley, April 24, 1868, Horace Greeley Papers, Reel 2, NYPL.

[68] Charles O'Conor to Jefferson Davis, April 19, 1868, Box 24, Jefferson Davis Papers, MC; Charles O'Conor to Horace Greeley, April 24, 1868, Horace Greeley Papers, Reel 2, NYPL. William Cooper's biography of Jefferson Davis takes the letter at face value. See Cooper, *Jefferson Davis, American*, 620.

with the Johnson impeachment due to wrap up, O'Conor believed that the threat to Davis's life had passed. As he told Davis, "Your person in the power of either party at the precise instant of triumph was the thing dreaded." When the president was acquitted on May 16, with Davis not due to appear in court for another four months, O'Conor resumed his default position of negotiating for an abandonment of the prosecution.[69]

---

[69] Charles O'Conor to Jefferson Davis, April 19, 26, May 4, 13, 19, 1868, Box 24, Jefferson Davis Papers, MC.

14

O'Conor's Triumph

Even though the immediate danger had passed and it was clear that Davis's trial would not take place on the heels of the Johnson impeachment trial, O'Conor still felt uneasy about the March 1868 indictment. Perhaps, he feared, its cogency signaled that the prosecution intended to move forward with the case.[1] O'Conor also contemplated the potential impact of a shakeup in the prosecution team: William Evarts became the new U.S. attorney general in July. Thereafter, Evarts moved to Washington from New York to become a member of the Johnson cabinet. O'Conor predicted that Evarts's close proximity to the political situation in Washington and more frequent communications with his friend (and Davis's foe) William H. Seward would make him more inclined to pursue the case than he had been previously, as he would be in "full possession of his friend's views."[2]

O'Conor's worries were unfounded. Evarts's skepticism about the wisdom of conducting the trial remained unchanged. Johnson had offered Evarts the attorney general post as a reward for his impressive performance as defense counsel in the impeachment trial, but Evarts was lukewarm about the promotion. Being associated with Johnson

---

[1] See Jonathan W. White, "The Trial of Jefferson Davis and the Americanization of Treason Law," in *Constitutionalism in the Approach and Aftermath of the Civil War*, ed. Paul D. Moreno and Johnathan O'Neill (New York: Fordham University Press, 2013). White argues that the specificity of Davis's indictment reflected a newfound insistence on real episodes (overt acts) of treason.

[2] Charles O'Conor to Jefferson Davis, April 26, 1868, Box 24, Jefferson Davis Papers, MC.

in the difficult political climate of 1868 was fraught with peril. Evarts told his friend Edwards Pierrepont that the impeachment trial "is little suited to make further public station an object of desire," and Evarts's cousin Rockwood Hoar communicated his condolences on hearing the news.[3] Hoar said he could not "offer many congratulations, or indeed to know what to say."[4]

Despite its numerous drawbacks, Evarts's new position gave him and Richard Henry Dana a bit more breathing room to conduct Davis's prosecution. In May, Evarts traveled to Boston to meet with Dana about urging the administration to drop the case. Back in February they had drafted a letter to Attorney General Stanbery, setting forth their reasons for urging an abandonment of Davis's case. At Evarts's suggestion, they had postponed sending the letter because of their uncertainty about who might hold the position of the nation's chief law officer after Johnson's impeachment. If the president was removed from office and Ben Wade should take his place, Evarts and Dana reasoned, they did not want to have an official record of their doubts about the Davis prosecution before a Radical Republican cabinet determined to convict Davis at all costs.[5]

Holding the attorney general's office himself made things much easier. Now Evarts could safely present a statement to the cabinet detailing the problems with the case. Less than a month after taking office, he asked Dana to dust off the letter they had planned to send to Attorney General Stanbery back in February. "I think you had better write me a spontaneous letter in regard to the case of Davis, and I will give the matter prompt attention," he told Dana in August.[6] Dana spent a considerable amount of time carefully revising the lengthy missive and sent it to Washington about a month later.[7]

[3] William Evarts to Edwards Pierrepont, April 16, 1868, Edwards Pierrepont Papers, folder 28, Box 1, Yale.

[4] E. R. Hoar to William Evarts, July 18, 1868, Ebenezer Rockwood Hoar Papers, University of Michigan Library, Ann Arbor. Hoar became U.S. attorney general under President Grant the following year, succeeding Evarts.

[5] William Evarts to Richard Henry Dana, June 21, 1868, Box 18, Dana Family Papers, MHS.

[6] William Evarts to Richard Henry Dana, August 10, 1868, Box 18, Dana Family Papers, MHS.

[7] See Richard Henry Dana to William Evarts, August 24, 1868, Box 18, Dana Family Papers, MHS. Dana's papers contain quite a few drafts of the letter, some with extensive editing.

Evarts waited more than a month before forwarding it to the president. He told Dana that he wanted to familiarize himself with the details of the present indictment pending against Davis before sending the letter to Johnson. When Evarts finally introduced Dana's letter in the cabinet in October, he informed the other officers that he shared Dana's misgivings. He was equally convinced, he said, that Davis's trial could easily result in acquittal and consequent humiliation for the government, and noted that "the opinions which Mr. Dana expresses were a subject of conference between him and myself while we occupied the common relation of counsel for the Government." If he had "remained in a private professional relation to the case and to the Government, [Dana's] communication probably would have borne my signature also," Evarts explained.[8]

Along with Dana's letter, Evarts also presented a recommendation that the president issue a proclamation of amnesty that would cover all of the Confederates still under indictment, including Davis. According to Interior Secretary Orville H. Browning, Evarts made it clear to the cabinet "that he did not think, and had not for the last two years thought any good end was to be attained by trying [Davis] – that if tried there was no likelihood whatever [of conviction], and if convicted he would not be, and at this day ought not to be punished. It would be but a moot trial, and to such he had always been opposed." Despite these strong statements, however, the cabinet was still divided about the wisdom of pursuing Davis's trial and postponed the matter again.[9]

Frustrated by this outcome, Dana and Evarts discussed the idea of going public with their objections to trying Davis. The very real possibility that they might be blamed for an acquittal remained at the forefront for Dana. In the fall of 1868 Dana was embroiled in an electoral contest against General Benjamin Butler for a seat in Congress from Essex County, Massachusetts, where Dana kept a summer home. Butler had supported Jefferson Davis for president in 1860, but after the war he had become one of Davis's fiercest critics, calling repeatedly for his trial before a military commission. Dana's perceived laxity in pursuing

---

[8] William Evarts to Andrew Johnson, October 9, 1868, included in William Evarts to Richard Henry Dana, October 9, 1868, Box 18, Dana Family Papers, MHS.

[9] Orville Hickman Browning, *Diary of Orville Hickman Browning*, ed. James G. Randall (Springfield: Illinois State Historical Library, 1925), 225–27.

the Davis prosecution had now become an issue in the congressional campaign. Butler had gone so far as to suggest that Dana, a moderate Republican, harbored Confederate sympathies and had purposely refrained from trying Davis.[10] But Evarts's support for Dana in his electoral bid did not extend to endorsing a plan to expose the attorneys' deep-seated reservations about conducting the trial. It was Evarts's strongly held view that "nothing should be publicly said about the Davis trial until after the elections."[11] Evarts feared that speaking out against Davis's trial prior to the election would undercut their ability to persuade the president to drop the case, as their motives might be thought of as political and personal rather than considered and genuine.

Meanwhile, O'Conor decided to pursue new avenues for a dismissal other than his standard tactic of delay and renegotiation with Evarts. Chief Justice Chase proved to be an unlikely, though invaluable, resource for the Davis defense team in 1868. A perpetual candidate for the presidency, Chase was seeking the Democratic nomination in 1868, although he had tried to run as a Republican twice previously. This ambition meant that Chase badly needed to win Democratic allies. As the 1868 Democratic convention approached, which was to be held in New York City, Chase received encouragement from Charles Halpine, author of the popular pro-Davis polemic *The Prison Life of Jefferson Davis*. Halpine assured Chase of the support of the New York Democrats, telling him that "there are 25,000 Democrats in this city who would vote for Chase, myself included." The chief justice's appeal for Democratic support, O'Conor reasoned, could possibly be channeled into an incongruous alliance with Jefferson Davis. As O'Conor pointed out to his client: "Chase has the presidential mania in the most spasmodic form and is deeply incensed at the evident intent of the radicals to set him aside. The quarter from which under normal circumstances, nothing good could be expected, might, on this account, send forth a gentle breeze with healing and safety upon its wings."[12]

[10] Samuel Shapiro, "'Aristocracy, Mud, and Vituperation': The Butler-Dana Campaign in Essex County in 1868," *New England Quarterly* 31 (September 1958): 340, 349.

[11] William Evarts to Richard Henry Dana, October 17, 1868, Box 18, Dana Family Papers, MHS.

[12] Charles G. Halpine to Salmon P. Chase, April 1, 1868, Charles Halpine Collection, UVA; Charles O'Conor to Jefferson Davis, April 26, 1868, Box 24, Jefferson Davis Papers, MC.

At some point during the summer of 1868, Chase shared his thoughts on the Davis trial with O'Conor's deputy counsel, George Shea. Over tea, Chase became "very communicative," getting out his copy of the newly ratified Fourteenth Amendment to the Constitution. Chase read aloud from Section Three to Shea:

No person shall ... hold any office, civil or military, under the United States, or under any State, who, having previously taken an oath, as a member of Congress, or as an officer of the United States, or as a member of any State legislature, or as an executive or judicial officer of any State, to support the Constitution of the United States, shall have engaged in insurrection or rebellion against the same.[13]

The chief justice then told Shea that he believed the clause "seems to make doubtful the liability to further punishment for treason of persons engaged in the rebellion."[14] In Chase's opinion, the clause exonerated prominent Confederates from any punishment other than an inability to hold public office. Shea was startled – but motivated – by this strained reading of the clause. "This meaning was certainly new to me," he wrote, "but, of course, whether the reading was intended as a suggestion or not, it has left a deep impression."[15]

It was indeed intended as a suggestion. As O'Conor began to worry in the summer and fall of 1868 that Evarts might decide to try Jefferson Davis, he seized on Chase's encouraging comments as a ray of hope. He dispatched co-counsel Robert Ould to meet with Chase and verify that the chief justice's views on the Fourteenth Amendment remained unchanged. After receiving such assurances, O'Conor "determined at once to give him a chance of making a judicial determination accordingly."[16]

[13] U.S. Const. amend. XIV, § 3.
[14] George Parsons Lathrop, "The Bailing of Jefferson Davis," *Century Magazine* 33 (February 1887): 636, 639. See also David K. Watson, "The Trial of Jefferson Davis: An Interesting Constitutional Question," *Yale Law Journal* 24 (1915): 669, 674. Watson called Chief Justice Chase's reading of the amendment "exceedingly novel, interesting, and important."
[15] Lathrop, "The Bailing of Jefferson Davis," 639. Lathrop's article says that this meeting took place in 1865, but the fact that Chase supposedly read the Fourteenth Amendment aloud means that the meeting could only have taken place in 1868. The amendment was ratified on July 9 of that year. Lathrop received his information from discussions with George Shea. See G. P. Lathrop to George Shea, November 21, 1885, Box 1, Bryan Family Papers, LVA.
[16] Charles O'Conor to Jefferson Davis, December 7, 1868, Box 24, Jefferson Davis Papers, MC. Chase's instigation of defense counsel's argument in the motion to quash

O'Conor could not quite fathom *why* Chase had made the suggestion to the defense team of arguing an unlikely interpretation of the Fourteenth Amendment. As always, O'Conor was suspicious of Chase's motives. He believed the chief justice to be ruled by political ambition, but did not know how to interpret his actions in this instance, telling Davis: "What may be the real objects of this practiced politician I know not." Although he had not yet managed to extricate himself entirely, Chase could have simply continued to avoid the case. Pondering Chase's actions led O'Conor to the conclusion that the chief justice was trying to use Davis's case as a means by which to win white Southern support for the newly ratified Fourteenth Amendment. He could do this by offering an interpretation that afforded protection to Davis. O'Conor himself had voiced serious objections to the new Reconstruction amendments, both as to form and content, as had many ex-Confederates.[17] Perhaps such objections would cease if the

the indictment became an open secret, although the prosecutors remained ignorant of the chief justice's behind-the-scenes involvement while the case was pending. Although Chase's ex parte discussions with defense counsel would certainly transgress the bounds of judicial ethics today, his behavior was more ethically uncertain by nineteenth-century standards. Chase certainly did not want to publicize his involvement in the formulation of defense counsel's argument in the case, but he did not take great pains to keep his actions hidden, which suggests that his behavior was ethically dubious but did not rise to the level of blatant misconduct. George Sharswood's precepts of judicial ethics frown on ex parte communications between attorney and judge because "such conduct is wrong in itself and has a tendency to impair confidence in the administration of justice." George Sharswood, *A Compend of Lectures on the Aims and Duties of the Profession of the Law Delivered before the Law Class of the University of Pennsylvania* (Philadelphia: T. & J. W. Johnson, 1854), 66. For more on judicial ethics in the nineteenth century, see G. Edward White, *The Marshall Court and Cultural Change, 1815–1835* (New York: Macmillan, 1988), 197–99.

[17] O'Conor believed the amendments to be unconstitutional because they altered the basic form of government set forth in the Constitution by sapping state sovereignty and creating federal oversight of states. He also objected to the process by which they were ratified, because the assent of the Southern states was coerced. For more on his opposition, see Cynthia Nicoletti, "Strategic Litigation and the Death of Reconstruction," in *Signposts: New Directions in Southern Legal History*, ed. Sally E. Hadden and Patricia H. Minter (Athens: University of Georgia Press, 2013). See also John Harrison, "The Lawfulness of the Reconstruction Amendments," *University of Chicago Law Review* 68: 375 (2001), and Bruce Ackerman, *We the People: Transformations*, 2 vols. (Cambridge, MA: Belknap Press of Harvard University Press, 1998), for more on the procedural irregularities associated with the ratification of the amendments, and Michael Vorenberg, *Final Freedom: The Civil War, the Abolition of Slavery, and the Thirteenth Amendment* (Cambridge: Cambridge University Press, 2001), for discussion of the idea of the unamendable fundamentals of the Constitution.

amendment now undergirded Jefferson Davis's freedom. It was a plausible theory. As O'Conor told Davis, "Whether this 14th Amendment has ever been adopted in such a perfect and effectual manner as to form a part of the Constitution is a question. Perhaps [Chase] hopes that a decision of the Supreme Court in this case might conclusively and finally determine that question in the affirmative."[18]

Although they may have disapproved of Chase's motives, Davis's attorneys wasted no time in presenting his argument to the court in Richmond. The prosecuting lawyers received notice of the defense's motion to quash the indictment on November 28. A couple of weeks earlier, Evarts had again urged Johnson to act on his proposed amnesty proclamation before the circuit court met in November, but again "the President replied that he had not yet reached a conclusion."[19] S. Ferguson Beach, a young Republican lawyer who had replaced the problematic Chandler as U.S. attorney in the summer of 1868, was not worried about the defense's motion. The argument, he noted, was grounded in the unlikely proposition that the Fourteenth Amendment prevented Davis's prosecution. In his opinion, it was untenable. "I do not myself see anything very formidable in the position upon which the motion will be grounded," he told Evarts.[20]

And yet, he confessed to a certain queasiness about the motion, admitting that he did "not feel willing now to proceed with the argument of it [because] the distractions of many other matters preclude anything like a calm examination of the questions which may arise." Half-heartedly, Beach suggested to Evarts that the prosecution should object to the motion on the grounds that Davis would be absent from the hearing. But he was untroubled by the prospect of the motion's success and calmly planned to use the upcoming hearing to ask the defense to agree to another postponement of the case once their motion failed.[21]

Beach mentally dismissed the merits of the motion to quash almost immediately, but Evarts, who had had far more experience in battling

[18] Charles O'Conor to Jefferson Davis, December 7, 1868, Box 24, Jefferson Davis Papers, MC.

[19] Browning, *Diary of Orville Hickman Browning*, 225–27.

[20] S. Ferguson Beach to William Evarts, November 28, 1868, Jefferson Davis Case File, NA-CP.

[21] S. Ferguson Beach to William Evarts, November 28, 1868 (two letters), Jefferson Davis Case File, NA-CP.

his opposing counsel in court, had an inkling that the argument might indeed succeed. He instructed Beach not to object to the motion on the weak ground that Davis would not be personally present at the hearing, but to allow the motion to be assigned for argument the following week. Evarts did not find the defense's reading of the Fourteenth Amendment to be absurd, and he warned Beach not to treat it lightly. He wrote, presciently, "although I have received no intimation to this effect, yet it has occurred to me as possible that there may be an expectation that this question, raised in this manner, may be promptly brought up for determination in the Supreme Court, at its approaching session."[22]

As it turned out, Evarts was correct. Alerted to the fact that Chief Justice Chase was finally to appear in court, Dana came down to Richmond to argue the motion in Evarts's absence and stopped in Washington on the way to confer with Evarts about the possible merits of the defense's argument.[23] In court on December 3, O'Conor and his co-counsel Ould presented Chase and Underwood with an affidavit stipulating that Davis had taken the oath of office in the U.S. House of Representatives in 1845. On Davis's behalf, Ould argued that the Fourteenth Amendment set forth an exclusive punishment for treason: banning anyone who "engaged in insurrection or rebellion against the [United States]" from holding public office. Relying on the Supreme Court's recent decisions in *Ex parte Garland* and *Cummings v. Missouri*, Ould contended that "disqualification from office-holding is punishment" for a criminal offense, and that the Fourteenth Amendment therefore superseded previously specified penalties for committing treason.[24]

Dana was quickly faced with the unpleasant realization that Chase seriously entertained the defendant's motion, although he remained unaware that the impetus for the argument had come from the chief

[22] William Evarts to S. Ferguson Beach, November 29, 1868, Letterbook G, Microfilm M 699, Attorney General's Records, Record Group 60, NA-CP.
[23] William Evarts to Richard Henry Dana, November 28, 30, 1868 (second letter misdated 1867); S. Ferguson Beach to William Evarts, November 30, 1868, Boxes 18, 17, Dana Family Papers, MHS.
[24] Ex parte Garland, 71 U.S. 333; Cummings v. State of Missouri, 71 U.S. 277 (1867). Case of Davis, *Reports of Cases Decided by Chief Justice Chase*, ed. Bradley Johnson (New York: Diossy, 1876), 87 (hereafter cited as *Chase's Reports*).

justice himself.[25] Bewildered by this development, Dana claimed that "the counsel for the United States had had no opportunity to confer, and as the motion had been on a point unexpected to them, and probably to the court, they desired time to look over authorities."[26] This was untruthful, given that Beach and Evarts had discussed the merits of the argument several days earlier, and, indeed, Dana and Evarts had met briefly about the motion in Washington. Unimpressed, Chase ignored Dana's objections and remarked blandly that "the court had not been surprised, as intimated by Mr. Dana, at the ground taken by the defendant." Chase said he had anticipated that the argument would center on "the common principle of constructive repeal."[27] Dana then requested a continuance to formulate a counterargument, which Chase denied. Instead, he allowed Beach and Dana one hour to prepare their argument.

When the court convened again that afternoon, Ould and O'Conor made the extraordinary claim that Section Three of the Fourteenth Amendment embodied an understanding that the legality of secession had been resolved on the battlefield and could not get a second hearing in a court of law. It had seemed clear to Congress, O'Conor argued, that the question of whether Davis had committed treason by engaging in secession and war to enforce the right to secede could not be decided in a *judicial* forum. In drafting the amendment, Congress had comprehended the impossibility of impaneling juries in formerly Confederate territory that would convict their former leaders of treason. The amendment had thus attempted to correct this problem and remove the issue from the courts by setting forth a distinct punishment for engaging in the rebellion.[28] Section Three, he contended, had preempted treason prosecutions against rebels and enacted a policy of amnesty toward Confederates.

[25] In an anonymously written article of dubious veracity, published long after the fact, Virginian J. Wilcox Brown suggested that Beach had been present when Chase suggested the Fourteenth Amendment argument to Davis's attorneys, but the prosecution's lack of preparedness belies that statement. See "Why Jefferson Davis Was Never Tried," *Richmond Times-Dispatch*, February 19, 1911, and in *Southern Historical Society Papers* 38 (1910): 347.

[26] Case of Davis, *Chase's Reports*, 91.

[27] Case of Davis, *Chase's Reports*, 91.

[28] See William A. Blair, *With Malice toward Some: Treason and Loyalty in the Civil War Era* (Chapel Hill: University of North Carolina Press, 2014), on the idea that Americans believed that treason was not a matter only for courts to resolve.

Dana and Beach insisted that Congress had had no such intention in enacting the amendment. If Section Three did in fact set forth a punishment for a specific criminal offense, Dana contended, then it was in tension with other sections of the Constitution – such as the ban on bills of attainder, which prevented the legislature from punishing individuals for crimes without a judicial determination of guilt.[29] Ould countered that the Fourteenth Amendment was unlike an attainder because it mitigated criminal penalties rather than creating them.[30] Dana also claimed that the defense's construction of the amendment bordered on the nonsensical, because nonofficeholding Confederates were thereby left open to more severe punishment than their leaders who had served in Congress or other positions of honor before the war. O'Conor refuted this argument, insisting that Congress had been well aware of the executive branch's policy to prosecute only well-known officials for their participation in the war.[31]

The next day, the court announced that the judges had split on the merits of the motion, with Chase voting to quash and Underwood voting to sustain the indictment. As a result, the question was certified to the Supreme Court for resolution. With their hand thus unexpectedly forced by the defense counsel's motion and the court's surprising willingness to entertain it, Johnson and his cabinet finally decided on a definite course of action in the Davis matter. On Christmas Day 1868, President Johnson issued a proclamation granting universal amnesty to "every person who, directly or indirectly, participated in the late insurrection or rebellion," thereby forestalling a resolution of Davis's motion in the Supreme Court.[32] The

[29] A bill of attainder is the punishment of a crime by a legislature, without the benefit of a judicial trial. Article I, Section 9, of the U.S. Constitution prohibits bills of attainder, but presumably a constitutional amendment would not be bound by that stricture. Bryan A. Garner, ed., *Black's Law Dictionary*, 8th ed. (St. Paul: Thomson/West, 2004), s.v. "bill of attainder"; U.S. Const. art. I, § 9.

[30] Case of Davis, *Chase's Reports*, 86. See also Eberhard P. Deutsch, "*United States v. Jefferson Davis*: Constitutional Issues in the Trial for Treason," *American Bar Association Journal* 52 (February 1966): 264–65.

[31] Case of Davis, *Chase's Reports*, 86–122.

[32] The proclamation granted "unconditionally, and without reservation, to all and every person who directly or indirectly participated in the late insurrection or rebellion, a full pardon and amnesty for the offence of treason against the United States, or of adhering to their enemies during the late civil war, with restoration of all rights, privileges, and immunities under the Constitution and the laws which have been made in pursuance thereof. Proclamation of December 25, 1868, 15 Stat. 711 (1868).

prosecution subsequently formally withdrew the indictment against Davis in the early months of 1869.

After his success in Richmond, O'Conor returned, jubilant, to New York. His satisfaction was marred only by a pickpocket on the boat trip north.[33] A few weeks later, in the wake of Johnson's amnesty proclamation freeing Davis from the threat of prosecution, O'Conor realized that he had accomplished his paramount goal of saving Davis's life. On New Year's Day 1869, he exulted that universal amnesty "is an accomplished fact at last and our long agony is over!"[34] Davis's freedom was now assured.

Over the course of the past four years, O'Conor's objectives for the Davis case had changed subtly. He had started out as something of a cause lawyer for the Lost Cause, striking out against the hegemony of postwar Unionist thinking to defend secession and attack Reconstruction. Winning legal victories was less important to him than standing up for unpopular beliefs, or "saving his country from the reproach of unanimity," as he had phrased it back in the summer of 1865. But the case – or perhaps the reality of contemplating his client's death – transformed him from a lawyer for a particular ideological cause into a lawyer for the cause of a particular person, Jefferson Davis. Over time, it became increasingly apparent to a savvy observer like O'Conor that secession would never be vindicated in court. At best, the courts would leave the issue untouched. It could, however, be strategically deployed to save Jefferson Davis. As the Davis case wore on, secession's vindication increasingly took a back seat to preserving Davis's life, so much so that O'Conor could argue in 1868 that the battlefield's determination against secession was a fitting resolution of the issue. In 1869 he could take great pride in his success in leveraging his initial goal of vindicating secession to achieve his secondary, more realistic aim of saving Jefferson Davis.

The most remarkable thing about O'Conor's strategy was the fact that it was so successful. It convinced the prosecutors that he actually intended to use Davis's trial to vindicate secession. They took seriously O'Conor's declaration that he expected to win a victory for secession, and his bluff ensured that Davis's life was not in jeopardy. This would

---

[33] Charles O'Conor to Samuel L. M. Barlow, December 2, 7, 1868, Box 67, Samuel Barlow Papers, HEHL.

[34] Charles O'Conor to George Shea, January 1, 1869, Box 1, Bryan Family Papers, LVA.

probably not have been true if a less shrewd lawyer had directed Davis's defense. In the fragile aftermath of Appomattox, the strange intersection of secessionist theory with Radical Reconstruction, together with the pressing need to restore the rule of law in the United States, allowed an adroit lawyer to raise the secession question and thus win Davis's freedom. The unique circumstances of the late 1860s made it possible, but O'Conor's particular ability to exploit those circumstances made it happen.

At the same time, the historian has to ask *why* the prosecutors were so willing to believe O'Conor's statements about his eagerness to bring the case to trial. Had anyone cared to look, signs that O'Conor's stated purposes might be less than forthright fairly abounded. Evarts and his associate counsel did not doubt that Davis wanted nothing more than his day in court to prove the legality of secession. They never even considered the possibility that O'Conor only feigned confidence in order to undermine theirs.[35] In court, O'Conor and his associates claimed to abhor the delay in bringing Davis to justice, but, as the prosecution discovered, O'Conor always agreed to the government's endless series of continuances. O'Conor might fulminate in open court about the inhumanity of leaving his client to twist in the wind without a resolution of his guilt, but behind the scenes, he was amenable to delays.

An appearance in court thus became an orchestrated performance on O'Conor's part – a performance with high stakes, to be sure, as his client's fate depended on his ability to convince the prosecutors and the general public of his sincerity. As O'Conor once instructed his co-counsel William B. Reed, the defense attorneys "should appear in the case at the opening of the court [to] tender a readiness for trial and in case the government declined to proceed immediately urge an assignment of the earliest day for that purpose." But, O'Conor reminded Reed, such a policy was safe solely because "I think we were all of the opinion that the government would not proceed and that the court would pay no particular attention to our urgency, leaving the matter to go over with the other business of the Court until the autumn."[36] The *Baltimore Gazette*, whose editor, William Wilkins Glenn, was privy to

---

[35] For more on the general idea of feigning confidence in one's own case as a trial strategy, see Gary Goodpater, "Lawsuits as Negotiations," *Negotiation Journal* 8 (1992): 221, 229–34.

[36] Charles O'Conor to William B. Reed, June 5, 1866, Box 43, Edridge Collection, HEHL.

O'Conor's strategy in the case, reported that O'Conor pressed for an immediate trial in 1867 before making an application for Davis's bail, but also took care to note that "the general opinion is that no trial will take place now," as the government was not ready to proceed.[37]

O'Conor's misdirection extended to his obsequious attitude toward Judge Underwood in the courtroom, which raised eyebrows among Davis supporters. On one occasion when he appeared before Underwood, O'Conor declared himself "exceedingly anxious to receive the advantages, and enjoy the rights which your honor has so eloquently and justly eulogized ... the blessings and advantages of a just, equal, fair, and I may say, benign (for that becomes the occasion) administration of law."[38] In spite of O'Conor's sycophancy in the courtroom, that same day he described the judge in a letter to his wife as a "shocking beast" who could be prevailed upon to conduct himself with dignity in court only by the "grace and good manners of his company."[39] Witnessing O'Conor's public display in the courtroom, William Wilkins Glenn confided to his diary that O'Conor "to my surprise said things that were at least undignified. To be sure he knew that Underwood might play false at the last moment.... But that was no reason why he should praise Underwood and applaud the Government. Fortunately he spoke so low that but few heard him. Near as I was, I did not know what he said until I read it in print the next day."[40]

After Glenn informed him of O'Conor's behavior in court, exiled Confederate diplomat James Mason surmised that O'Conor's repugnant speech must have been a performance on O'Conor's part, the product of behind-the-scenes negotiations between defense and government counsel. Otherwise it would have been a disgrace. "I take for granted that counsel was told at Washington," Mason wrote, "[that] your client shall be bailed, provided you will adopt our programme, and speak the speech that will be written for you – their acquiescence

---

[37] *Baltimore Gazette*, May 13, 1867.

[38] Case of Davis, *Chase's Reports*, 47–48.

[39] Charles O'Conor to Cornelia O'Conor, May 13, 1867, Freeman's Auction Lot 424, January 25, 2007, digital copy available at www.freemansauction.com (accessed November 2, 2016).

[40] William Wilkins Glenn, *Between North and South: A Maryland Journalist Views the Civil War*, ed. Bayly Ellen Marks and Mark Norton Schatz (Cranbury, NJ: Associated University Presses, 1976), 287.

was in accordance with the scriptural advise, 'answer a fool according to his folly.' "[41]

The discrepancy between O'Conor's public and private behavior should have been readily apparent to Evarts. In November 1867, Evarts blithely reported to Dana that "my interview with Mr. O'Conor was not unsatisfactory," as O'Conor had "concur[red]" in Evarts's suggestion that the trial be postponed until the chief justice would appear at trial.[42] After prearranging the continuance, when O'Conor and Evarts appeared in court later that month, O'Conor "reluctantly" consented to delay the date, but protested that the "personal wishes and convenience" of Davis and his defense counsel "would have been greatly promoted by a trial when Mr. Davis was first brought before the court, in May last; and in a greater degree was it true that their personal wishes and convenience would be consulted by proceeding at this time." O'Conor acted the part of distressed innocent to perfection, lamenting that "the defendant and his counsel would be subjected to a renewal of the inconvenience which they had been compelled to suffer, and had suffered uncomplainingly on two occasions," but then agreed to wait on the chief justice's attendance, just as he had arranged with Evarts ahead of time.

Similarly, in April and May of 1868, O'Conor and Evarts privately agreed to continue the case until November because of O'Conor's fears about the temporal proximity of Davis's trial to Andrew Johnson's impeachment trial. O'Conor had hurried to Washington to secure such a delay. There he bumped into Evarts outside his hotel and secured a pledge that the case would be delayed until well after the conclusion of the impeachment trial. O'Conor privately had considered the negotiation with Evarts the last step before advising his client to flee the court's jurisdiction, but "at the outset of my conversation with Mr. Evarts I expressed some indignation at the trouble and inconvenience [the prosecutions' delays] were imposing on *me*," so as to mislead Evarts about their desire to secure a delay.[43] O'Conor confirmed a week or so

---

[41] James Mason to William Wilkins Glenn, May 23, 1867, Box 3, John Glenn Papers, MdHS.

[42] William Evarts to Richard Henry Dana, November 15, 1867, Box 17, Dana Family Papers, MHS.

[43] Charles O'Conor to Jefferson Davis, April 26, 1868, Box 24, Jefferson Davis Papers, MC.

later that his tactics were effective, as "the enemy indulges not in the slightest doubt, I presume; And it is certainly to our advantage to keep up that condition." In his judgment, "from my utter silence, [observers] have probably induced the belief that I am rather phlegmatic or over-confident."[44]

As O'Conor reported to Davis, his negotiations with Evarts about delaying the trial aroused no suspicion on Evarts's part.[45] O'Conor gathered that Evarts left the details about setting particular days to U.S. Attorney Chandler and to Underwood, who endeavored to schedule numerous court appearances because "they like to have the thing up as frequently as possible: they live upon its éclat."[46] Evarts's communications with Dana reveal that he did not find O'Conor's amenability to postponements to be at all troubling. He told Dana in May 1868 that delaying Davis's case until the fall would "suit all concerned," with the only possible objections to come from the bench rather than their opposing counsel.[47]

To anyone familiar with deception as a litigation tactic, the prosecution's trust in O'Conor's candor is surprising.[48] Evarts's and Dana's faulty assessment of O'Conor's strategy stemmed from different sources. First, although Richard Henry Dana was well aware of O'Conor's sterling reputation at the New York bar, Dana's New England snobbery led him to discount O'Conor's abilities. Dana's friend and fellow Bostonian Charles Sumner told Dana that O'Conor's strengths as a litigator had been greatly exaggerated. In January 1868, Sumner boasted of the superiority of New England attorneys to those from New York, specifically contrasting O'Conor's supposedly

44 Charles O'Conor to Jefferson Davis, May 4, 1868, Box 24, Jefferson Davis Papers, MC.
45 William Evarts to Charles O'Conor, April 14, 1868 (included in Charles O'Conor to Jefferson Davis, April 17, 1868), and October 15, 186[8] (O'Conor's clerk misdated the copy in enclosing it to Davis); Charles O'Conor to Jefferson Davis, October 16, May 19, 27, 1868, Box 24, Jefferson Davis Papers, MC.
46 Charles O'Conor to Jefferson Davis, May 13, 1868, Box 24, Jefferson Davis Papers, MC.
47 William Evarts to Richard Henry Dana, May 31, 1868, Box 18, Dana Family Papers, MHS.
48 For more, see Roger Fisher, "Negotiating Power: Getting and Using Influence," *American Behavior Science* 27 (1983): 149, 150–65.

unimpressive courtroom presence with the oratorical skill of Harvard-educated Boston lawyer Sidney Bartlett.[49]

Dana scorned the immigrant classes of New York, especially Irish Americans, whom he regarded with particular distaste. During a trip to New York to visit Evarts in July 1857, Dana had ventured out into the city streets in anticipation of a duly inspiring celebration of Independence Day, and had suddenly found himself in the midst of the famed Metropolitan Police Riot, in which the Irish "Dead Rabbits" gang battled the native "Bowery Boys" in the Five Points.[50] Witnessing the violence in the streets, Dana noted that "the people of this neighborhood were chiefly Irish, & of a very low character." Because he was "[un]willing to be either hurt or caught in such a crowd," Dana fled the scene. The next day he returned to the Five Points to observe the neighborhood, and he recorded in his diary that the experience had impressed on him the notion that the Irish simply could not be civilized. "The men seem so brutalized," he wrote, "as to be beyond hope of recovery.... The effect upon my spirits was most depressing. Is there hope for man? Can the race be redeemed?" In Dana's opinion, it "seemed ... easier & more encouraging to destroy the whole race to begin anew with a grafting of humanity upon dogs & horses, or even bears and tigers" than to attempt to refine the population he observed. Disheartened by what he had seen in lower Manhattan, Dana escaped to the sanctuary of Evarts's new house uptown.[51]

Dana's low opinion of Irish American New Yorkers persisted during and after the Civil War. Writing to Charles Francis Adams, a fellow member of Boston's upper crust, soon after the war, Dana railed against the New York Irish as "northern rebel sympathizers ... the non reading & writing class, the vagabonds & the ignorant vicious & dangerous classes in the great cities." Dana had not a doubt that the Irish American population in New York had no interest in sustaining the fruits of Northern victory, telling Adams that "in the Five Points, the

---

[49] Charles Sumner to Richard Henry Dana, January 14, 1868, Box 18, Dana Family Papers, MHS. Another copy of this letter can be found on Reel 80, Charles Sumner Papers, HU.

[50] On the riot, see J. T. Headley, *The Great Riots of New York* (New York: E. B. Treat, 1873), 129–34. On the Five Points, see Tyler Anbinder, *Five Points: The 19th-Century New York City Neighborhood That Invented Tap Dance, Stole Elections, and Became the World's Most Notorious Slum* (New York: Plume, 2001).

[51] Richard Henry Dana, *The Journal of Richard Henry Dana*, 2 vols. (Cambridge, MA: Belknap Press of Harvard University Press, 1968), 2: 823–26.

'conservative' party had every vote but five, & those were missionaries at the House of Refuge." Dana contrasted the amoral, degenerate, and ignorant attitude of Irish Americans with the "moral & religious conviction" that "runs through the thinking, feeling, praying, working, churchgoing, reading, child-instructing classes" of New England.[52]

Dana's disdain for Irish Americans included their adherence to Catholicism. When Dana's sister Charlotte converted to Catholicism in 1846, her religion became a source of family embarrassment. Dana's biographer Samuel Shapiro noted that Dana was himself drawn to the rituals and doctrines of the Catholic Church, and at times flirted with the possibility of converting, but ultimately rejected the faith because of its association with the working-class Irish. As Shapiro argued, "Romanism, with its alien priests and congregations of Irish workingmen, was socially unacceptable to Dana."[53]

While prejudice may have led Dana to underestimate O'Conor, the same cannot be said of William Evarts. Although Evarts shared Dana's elite New England pedigree, as a prominent member of the New York bar, he knew O'Conor personally. He had faced O'Conor as an antagonist in a number of cases, and in fact, while the Davis case was pending, O'Conor and Evarts worked on four other reported cases together, two as opposing counsel, and two as co-counsel.[54] In the course of the Parish Will litigation in the New York surrogate's court in the early 1860s, Evarts took full advantage of his opportunity to observe O'Conor hawkishly.[55] Seated across the aisle from him, Evarts filled no fewer than three notebooks with his notes on O'Conor's courtroom remarks.[56] Because of his personal acquaintance with his opponent, his assessment of O'Conor differed markedly from Dana's.

[52] Richard Henry Dana, Jr., to Charles Francis Adams, April 14, 1867, Reel 175, Adams Family Papers, MHS.
[53] Samuel Shapiro, *Richard Henry Dana Jr., 1815–1882* (East Lansing: Michigan State University Press, 1961), 24.
[54] Brown v. Pacific Mail S.S. Co., 4 F. Cas. 420 (C.C.S.D.N.Y. 1867) (No. 2,025); Lovett v. Gillender, 35 N.Y. 617 (1866); People ex. rel. Kennedy v. Commissioners of Taxes, 35 N.Y. 423 (1866); New York & New Haven R.R. Co. v. Schuyler, 34 N.Y. 30 (1865). O'Conor and Evarts opposed each other in *Lovett* and *People v. Commissioners of Taxes*, and were co-counsel in *Brown*. The two attorneys represented different defendants in *New York & New Haven R. R. Co.*
[55] Delafield v. Parish, 25 N.Y. 9 (1862).
[56] Notebooks, "Parish Will Case: Memorandum of Mr. O'Conor's Argument," folder 68, Box 57, Evarts Family Papers, Yale.

Recalling his initial impressions of the elder lawyer on O'Conor's death, Evarts remembered being somewhat in awe of him when he first entered the profession in New York. He took the opportunity to reflect on "the respect and regard which I always felt and exhibited towards him." Evarts clearly believed that O'Conor deserved his reputation as a great attorney, telling the members of the New York bar that "no cause which he represented suffered, in its defense or in its prosecution, in any of the qualities, mental, moral or personal, that should be at the service of clients, that should be at the service of the administration of justice, and the maintenance of the law." Evarts acknowledged that O'Conor's "aversion to, and distrust of, the new political authorities that were put in charge of the National Government" in 1860 conflicted with the political sentiments of the vast majority of the distinguished men in New York, including Evarts himself. But he also respected that O'Conor had maintained his "fidelity to himself and his views," even at the risk of social ostracism. Unlike Dana, Evarts did not denigrate O'Conor's Irish Catholic heritage and impoverished childhood but instead eulogized O'Conor as "the son of an Irishman expatriated for his patriotism, himself at home a gentleman and a man of good estate, and overpowered by some disastrous reverse of fortune."[57]

Evarts's blindness to O'Conor's misdirection in the Davis case cannot therefore be attributed to an underestimation of his abilities. Rather, his inattention to the day-to-day developments were to blame. At the conclusion of the Civil War, Evarts's law practice had exploded dramatically. Evarts participated in no fewer than forty *reported* cases between 1865 and 1869, ten of those in the U.S. Supreme Court.[58] He was plainly stretched thin during the pendency of the Davis case, and as his correspondence reveals, his time and attention were often claimed by other legal matters. While working on the Davis indictment and preparing for the Johnson impeachment trial in February 1868, Evarts was simultaneously caught up in a "long trial for the Govt … in

[57] *In Memory of Charles O'Conor* (New York: n.p., 1884), 42, 46, 43.

[58] Included among Evarts's unreported cases were major controversies, including Johnson's impeachment trial and the *Alabama Claims* case in England. A search of Lexis reveals that Evarts participated in about half that number of reported cases in the four-year period between 1856 and 1860, and again between 1861 and 1864.

the Sherry Wine cases."[59] Despite Evarts's familiarity with O'Conor, he simply failed to recognize that his opponent's wariness about the case's outcome equaled or exceeded his own.

It was a testament to O'Conor's success that Davis's prosecution ended in late 1868 with a carefully orchestrated whimper rather than an explosive bang, more than three and a half years after his ignominious capture at Irwinville. By that point, it seemed to the American public that pursuing a judicial confirmation of the verdict of the battlefield by trying Jefferson Davis was a futile endeavor. American newspapers voiced the nation's frustration with the unending delays in the ultimately hopeless task of convicting Davis. In December, the *New York World* declared that "the interest in the 'Great Treason Trial,' as it was once rhetorically called, has very much faded away." When the president's Christmas amnesty proclamation freed Davis, the paper remarked wearily, "The wonder is not that this proclamation has come out now, but that it has been delayed so long. There is no consideration to warrant the issuance of this proclamation now that was not equally strong two years ago. Had it been given to the world then, we should have been spared the absurd national farce known as the Jeff. Davis trial."[60]

The *Boston Daily Advertiser* also welcomed the end of the case, even while lamenting that the government had not put Davis on trial immediately after his arrest in 1865. It would have been easier then to ensure that the law would conform to the results of the battlefield, the paper's editors said. Davis should have been "dealt with like other criminals ... swift punishment should [have been] dealt out to the greatest offender in modern times." After detailing many of the bizarre occurrences that had taken place in the trial, including Chase's unwillingness to preside, Attorney General's Stanbery's refusal to participate, and Horace Greeley's strange advocacy on Davis's behalf, all of which gave "an absurd turn to the case," the paper declared, "Now we submit that the country has had about enough of this thing. ... The government cat has played with this helpless and insignificant mouse full

[59] William Evarts to Richard Henry Dana, February 18, 1868, Box 18, Dana Family Papers, MHS. The case was In re Twelve Hundred and Nine Quarter Casks, etc., of Wine, 24 F. Cas. 398 (S.D.N.Y. 1868) (No. 14,279).
[60] *New York World*, December 9, 25, 1868.

enough." Holding "trial at this late date would settle nothing which history has not irrevocably settled already."[61]

Like many Northern papers, the *Charleston Courier* celebrated Chase's decision to quash the indictment against Davis. But the paper also interpreted the outcome as a silent victory for the cause of secession and saw it as tantamount to an acknowledgment of the merit of Davis's case. The war had settled "as far as the sword can, these questions. But it might well be that an appeal to the fundamental law and the true history of the Union would result in the reversal of the decision of arms by the Supreme Court. The judgment of war might not be that of the tribunal of justice." The paper argued that the government had decided to leave these questions untouched because the "hour of vengeance has passed" and the people no longer clamored for Davis's punishment.[62]

Indeed, Chief Justice Chase's official reporter of decisions, Bradley Johnson, wrote his volume of *Chase's Reports* (published after the chief justice's death in 1873) to reveal that Chase's evasive actions in the Davis case were borne of the chief justice's deep fear of the wrong outcome. Johnson was a former Confederate general from Maryland, and his report was, by his own admission, a partisan document.[63] Johnson exposed Chase's ex parte communications with defense counsel, even though he did so somewhat cryptically. Although Chase's role in crafting the defense's case was not publicly known in 1868, the official report highlighted that defense counsel's arguments in the motion to quash the indictment "were inspired and suggested from the highest official source – not the President of the United States."[64]

Johnson was more explicit about Chase's dealings with Davis's counsel in his private correspondence. The "final conclusion of the case," he wrote, "came from a private suggestion of the Ch. Justice – that the constitutional amendment operated as a general amnesty. He

[61] *Boston Daily Advertiser*, December 7, 1868.
[62] *Charleston Tri-Weekly Courier*, December 8, 1868.
[63] Bradley T. Johnson to W. T. Walthall, October 19, 1877, Box 28, Jefferson Davis Papers, MC. The report was also a strange hodgepodge of Johnson's own thoughts and notes about continuances and the state of the country at the time. It did not resemble most official case reports.
[64] Case of Davis, *Chase's Reports*, 81.

was the originator of that idea." His own goal in producing the report of Davis's case, Johnson admitted, "was to put on record in a permanent form, the fact that the Govt was afraid to try the legal issue 'rebel vel non.' All the facts show it."[65]

Johnson's volume of *Chase's Reports* (the sole volume) was designed to promote Johnson's own personal view that engaging in the Confederate war effort did not amount to treason. In the 1880s, before a crowd of Confederate veterans, he sought to refute the larger implications of Chase's *Shortridge* ruling. Johnson still smarted from the imprisonment he had briefly suffered in 1865 when he faced a treason charge for (as he characterized it) "committing acts of war in the Sharpsburg and Gettysburg campaigns." In Johnson's opinion, the government's decision to punish former Confederates individually for their actions during the war was invalid, given that the U.S. had recognized the Confederacy's belligerent status during the war. "War is a status between nations, countries, or parties," he told the crowd. "As soon as it occurs, it changes at once the relation of every person subject to either party; each one becomes bound to obey his own country, and ceases to be personally responsible for actions committed by command of its civil authority." Individuals could not be personally liable for acts of treason, Johnson insisted, because if the dealings of Confederate officials had not been cloaked with some kind of governmental authority, all actions "would have been void and everything would have been in chaos." Instead, he maintained, the world had recognized Confederate belligerency, thus signifying that "no personal responsibility [should attach] for acts of lawful war."[66]

Indeed, Johnson insisted that the chief justice had come around to the idea that the vast scope of the war excused treason, presumably after issuing the *Shortridge* opinion.[67] Chase's clandestine actions in

---

[65] Bradley T. Johnson to W. T. Walthall, October 19, 1877, Box 28, Jefferson Davis Papers, MC. Walthall was Jefferson Davis's writing assistant for his *Rise and Fall of the Confederate Government* (1881).

[66] Bradley T. Johnson, "The Maryland Confederate Monument at Gettysburg," *Southern Historical Society Papers*, 14 (1886): 429, 430–31.

[67] See also the preface to *Chase's Reports*, in which Johnson argued that *Shortridge* was undercut by Chase's decision in *Keppel's Administrators,* 14 F. Cas. 357 (C.C.D. Va. 1868) (No. 7,722). This was not an unbiased reading of *Keppel.*

providing defense counsel with a winning argument – thereby ridding himself of the explosive potential of the Davis case – proved this. In 1868 O'Conor and others had argued repeatedly that the United States had bound itself to treat the actions of individual Confederates only under international law and not the domestic law of treason.

The law of the United States … had settled the fact that resistance by any great body of people, controlling a large territory for a considerable time against the government which they were endeavoring to throw off, was war and not rebellion, and must be treated as a war, with all the legal consequences of war. As O'Conor said, "Washington might have failed, Kosciusko did fail," but neither of them could have been tried, under the civilized code of nations, as traitors.[68]

Johnson maintained that the failure to prosecute Davis represented a legal victory because it signaled that the government and the judiciary understood that "we had not been rebels nor traitors, and could not, under the law, be held responsible as such."[69]

Jefferson Davis agreed that his aborted trial constituted a precedent of sorts. After reading Johnson's published report sometime in the late 1870s, he reflected on the meaning of his case. To Davis, the government's unwillingness to try him signified that individuals could not be held accountable for secession. "A sovereign state cannot commit treason," he wrote. "The Government early discovered that if this issue came before the Supreme Court, it would lose its case & I should be acquitted.... So none of the indictments were ever tried."[70] In Davis's mind, his abandoned prosecution thus stood for the proposition that treason would not lie against Confederates and that the constitutionality of secession had been settled only on the battlefield.

This was a highly slanted – and grandiose – interpretation of what was, after all, merely a decision to drop a case pending appeal, particularly in light of the Supreme Court's condemnation of secession in *Texas v. White* a few months later. At ten years' remove, Davis and Bradley Johnson were able to discuss Davis's case and its bearing

[68] Johnson, "The Maryland Confederate Monument," 430–31.
[69] Johnson, "The Maryland Confederate Monument," 431.
[70] Jefferson Davis, undated memo, written sometime after 1876 [probably 1878], Jefferson Davis Collection, Tulane University Library, New Orleans.

on secession without even mentioning *Texas v. White*. Their incomplete analysis was partially a result of their focus on belligerent status and the difference between an individual's and a state's acts of disloyalty, distractions that were not present in *Texas v. White*. But it also reflected the fact many contemporaries believed *Texas v. White*'s seemingly definitive pronouncement against secession could be easily dismissed.

Epilogue

Texas v. White and the "Settlement" of Secession's Constitutionality

In the end, Chief Justice Salmon P. Chase ensured that the verdict of the battlefield was not the last word on secession. Chase had avoided the question in the explosive context of Davis's case. Instead, he took the opportunity to pronounce secession unconstitutional in *Texas v. White* in April 1869, just a few months after the government dropped its case against Davis. An original suit in the Supreme Court, *Texas v. White* involved Texas's attempt to block payment on U.S. government bonds sold by the state during the Civil War. The Reconstruction government of Texas sought an injunction to prevent the parties from receiving payment from the United States on the bonds and to compel the bonds' return to the state.[1] The United States had given the bonds over to the state as part of the Compromise of 1850.[2] They became payable beginning in the late months of 1864, and the state had sold them soon thereafter to George W. White and his codefendant John Chiles in order to procure medicines and other goods to be used "in aid of the rebellion."[3] The threshold issue was a basic but difficult jurisdictional question: was Texas, in its current configuration under military Reconstruction, one of the United States, and thus capable of bringing an original action in the Supreme Court?

---

[1] As Justice Grier's dissent pointed out, the U.S. government was not a party to the suit, and in fact was wholly uninterested in the question of which party (Texas or White) would be paid. Texas v. White, 74 U.S. 700, 728 (1868).
[2] Act of September 9, 1850, § 1, cl. 49, 9 Stat. 446 (1850).
[3] Texas v. White, 74 U.S. at 734.

Counsel for the bondholders hoped to catch the Court on the horns of a dilemma, because the jurisdictional question implicated both the validity of secession and the constitutionality of military Reconstruction. If Texas had not legally seceded from the United States in 1861, they contended, it was still in the Union. But if the state remained in the Union throughout the Civil War – because it was incapable of seceding – then Reconstruction was unconstitutional. Military Reconstruction subjected the states of the former Confederacy to direct federal supervision under a military governor, excluded representatives from those states from Congress, and forced the states to ratify the Fourteenth Amendment to qualify for readmission.[4] As Texas was still subject to military Reconstruction, the lawyers argued, it could not file an original action in the Supreme Court – because it was not a "state." In fact, White's lawyer Philip Phillips told White that he had the utmost "confidence in the opinion that the Court will not take jurisdiction of the case" and asked, accordingly, for a bonus.[5]

Phillips underestimated Chase's ingenuity in tackling such difficult questions. Writing for the Court, Chase threaded the needle carefully and crafted an opinion that acknowledged Texas's unbroken status as a state in the Union, while simultaneously sustaining Reconstruction. Chase did this by decoupling statehood and governmental status.[6] Texas had never ceased to be a state, he decided, because secession was unconstitutional and therefore ineffective. But during the war there

---

[4] For more on this contradiction and various constitutional theories to sustain it, see Akhil Amar, "The Lawfulness of Section 5 – and Thus of Section 5," *Harvard Law Review Forum* 126 (2013); Bruce Ackerman, *We the People: Transformations*, 2 vols. (Cambridge, MA: Belknap Press of Harvard University Press, 1998); Jack M. Balkin, "The Reconstruction Power," *New York University Law Review* 85 (December 2010); and Gregory Downs, *After Appomattox* (Cambridge, MA: Harvard University Press, 2015).

[5] Phillips to George W. White, September 28, 1868, and January 13, 1869, Philip Phillips Letterbook, 1867–69, Philip Phillips Papers, LC.

[6] In his brief, Phillips characterized the contention that a distinction existed between "the *State government* and the *State*" as patently ridiculous. "Without intending to deal harshly with this proposition," he wrote, "I may be permitted to quote the language of this Court on a former occasion: 'A state can only act through its agents, and it would be absurd to say that any act was not done by the State which was done by its authorized agents.' " Reply Brief of G. W. White, Texas v. White, 74 U.S. 700 (1868), in Philip B. Kurland and Gerhard Casper, eds., *Landmark Briefs and Arguments of the Supreme Court of the United States: Constitutional Law*, 100 vols. (Washington, DC: University Publications of America, 1978), 5: 582, 583.

had been no valid government in the state. The illegal Confederate government in Texas had "immediately disappeared" at the war's conclusion, and thereafter the federal government had stepped in to provide a new, "republican" government as required by the Guarantee Clause. At the war's conclusion, "there being then no government in Texas in constitutional relations with the Union," Chase declared, "it became the duty of the United States to provide for the restoration of such a government," which it had done through Reconstruction.[7] Thereafter, the state of Texas possessed a valid government and was thus capable of sustaining the Court's original jurisdiction.[8]

The case is remembered today for its pithy declaration of secession's unconstitutionality. The issue of the bond repayment has largely faded from historical memory, as has the complicated distinction Chase drew between a state and a government in *Texas v. White*. As Charles Fairman noted, "*Texas v. White* is celebrated by reason of one memorable sentence – the most enduring thing Chase ever said: 'The Constitution, in all its provisions, looks to an indestructible Union, composed of indestructible states.'"[9]

The secession issue was hardly touched on by counsel, who focused their attention on the case's implications for Reconstruction instead of on the jurisdictional basis for the suit. Rather, the unspoken assumption of both plaintiff's and defendants' briefs was that secession had no basis in the U.S. Constitution. Texas's brief disclaimed the actions of the state's wartime government, an "unlawful combination of individuals," while White's brief reasoned from the disabilities imposed on Texas during Reconstruction to declare that "she is not a member

---

[7] Chase punted on the question of whether the president was constitutionally able, through his power as commander in chief, to set up a new republican government without Congress's input, as Andrew Johnson had done prior to the passage of the Military Reconstruction Acts in 1867. Chase's opinion *suggested* that congressional action was necessary to restore a republican form of government in the state of Texas. See Texas v. White, 74 U.S. at 729. See also Luther v. Borden, 48 U.S. 1 (1849).

[8] Finally, Chase granted Texas's requested injunction because the contract with the bondholders had been in furtherance of the war and therefore was illegal. Neither the original parties to the contract nor subsequent holders of the notes could recover, because there had been sufficient notice that the prospect of recovering on them was doubtful. They sold well below market value, and "the purchasers took the risk of a bad title." Texas v. White, 74 U.S. at 736.

[9] Charles Fairman, *Reconstruction and Reunion*, 2 vols. (New York: Macmillan, 1971), 1: 628, quoting Texas v. White, 74 U.S. at 724.

of this Union and that she is not a state in the sense of this jurisdictional provision."[10] Albert Pike, counsel for defendant John Chiles,
touched on the constitutional and historical argument for secession in
his brief, but carefully distanced himself from those ideas. "We state
[these arguments]," Pike maintained, "not for discussion, but for the
single purpose of showing the nature of the great movement of States,
under solemn, deliberate, and emphatic claim of right of separation
and withdrawal from the Union, and to represent which as a rebellion or insurrection was to de naturalize it."[11] Pike emphasized the
sincerity of ex-Confederates' good-faith belief in the constitutionality
of secession, but did not claim that their adherence to this theory was
determinative in the case.

And so the momentous constitutional question that had animated
the Civil War was never actually argued before the Supreme Court.

Chief Justice Chase's pronouncement on secession was perfunctory.
He found it "needless to discuss at length the question whether the
right of a State to withdraw from the Union for any cause regarded by
herself as sufficient is consistent with the Constitution of the United
States." He had given a small nudge, in the *Shortridge* case two years
earlier, to idea that the battlefield had given a "practical ... answer" to
that "theoretical question," but *Texas v. White*'s analysis was far more
formal and legalistic.[12] It gave no indication that the outcome of the
Civil War had any bearing on the question. Chase's reasoning drew on
the logic Abraham Lincoln had put forth in his First Inaugural Address
eight years earlier.[13] The Union was an organic creature, formed out
of the "common origin, mutual sympathies, kindred principles, similar

---

[10] For Texas's brief, see Bill of Complaint at 5, Texas v. White, 74 U.S. 700 (1868);
Complainant's Brief at 9, Texas v. White, 74 U.S. 700 (1868), in Kurland and Casper,
Landmark Briefs and Arguments of the Supreme Court , 5: 414. For White's, see
Brief for Defendant, White at 5, Texas v. White, 74 U.S. 700 (1868), in Kurland and
Casper, *Landmark Briefs and Arguments of the Supreme Court*, 5: 582.

[11] Brief for Defendant, John Chiles, at 27, Texas v. White, 74 U.S. 700, in Kurland and
Casper, *Landmark Briefs and Arguments of the Supreme Court*, 5: 460. The secession
argument is set forth on 17–26 of the brief. Ibid., 450–59.

[12] Shortridge v. Macon, 22 F. Cas. 20 (C.C.D.N.C. 1867) (No. 12,812). In *Shortridge*,
Chase came much closer to endorsing Justice Grier's approach to secession in the
Prize Cases and in dissent in *Texas v. White*. See Chapter 9.

[13] Abraham Lincoln, "First Inaugural Address," in Lincoln, *This Fiery Trial: The Speeches
and Writings of Abraham Lincoln*, ed. William E. Gienapp (New York: Oxford
University Press, 2002), 88.

interests, and geographical relations" of the colonies. Those colonies had banded together during the Revolution, and their Union had taken "definite form" under the Articles of Confederation in 1781. The Articles of Confederation had declared the Union to be "perpetual," Chase argued, and though the Constitution was silent on the permanence of the arrangement, the preamble described the Union as "more perfect" than under the Articles. To be "more perfect," the Union must have remained indissoluble, Chase declared. The Constitution mandated that the states could not be separated from the Union.

Short on analysis, *Texas v. White*'s declaration against secession seemed like an afterthought, but it was surely the product of calculation. Here, in a case that had none of the difficulties that had plagued Davis's prosecution, Chase reached for the issue and imprinted his quotable formulation of the Unionist vision of national structure onto the *U.S. Reports*, where it would reside in posterity.[14] Historian Charles McCurdy noted that Chase's famous sound bite "quickly supplanted *e pluribus unum* as the motto of choice for conveying the essence of American federalism."[15] In writing his most memorable paragraph, we might say that Chase was doing what was necessary to ensure that the law as made by the courts fit with the ruling already issued on the battlefield. After all, Chase had little choice in the matter, and it is true that he faced enormous pressure to ensure that the battlefield's determination was ratified by law.

But Chase's view of the ways in which the law had to be reconciled with the war is still troubling. Unlike every other major player in Davis's postwar drama, Chase never acknowledged – even in private – that accommodating war and law in the postbellum world was a painful task for an introspective American. Unlike O'Conor, Evarts, Dana, Johnson, Speed, Lieber, Stevens, Underwood, and even Davis, Chase did not reflect on the internal struggle Americans faced in molding the law to conform

---

[14] The status of the former Confederate states had been an issue percolating below the surface in *Mississippi v. Johnson*, 71 U.S. 475 (1867) and *Georgia v. Stanton*, 73 U.S. 50 (1868), both original suits in the Supreme Court, brought in 1867 and 1868, respectively, but both were dismissed on other grounds. The same issue of statehood was implicated in those cases, but Chase did not seize on it then.

[15] Charles McCurdy, "Federalism and the Judicial Mind in a Conservative Age: Stephen Field," in Harry Scheiber, ed., *Federalism and the Judicial Mind: Essays on American Constitutional Law and Politics* (Berkeley: Institute of Governmental Studies Press, University of California, 1992), 33.

to the realities of life in a hardened post-Appomattox world. Except for his one, fleeting acknowledgment in *Shortridge* that the results of the war might have had something to do with the constitutional understanding of secession, quickly retracted in *Texas v. White*, Chase professed to act as though legal outcomes were wholly divorced from the world around them. Justice Grier's *Texas v. White* dissent pressed on this very nerve, and Grier challenged Chase by declaring that the issue in the case "was to be decided as a *political fact*, not as a *legal fiction*. This court is bound to know and notice the public history of the nation."[16]

Chase's actions belied his public and private insistence that he simply followed logic in making the law. His invocation of procedural technicalities did not convince anyone that he had not deliberately avoided the messiness of Davis's case. He had thrust that responsibility upon Judge Underwood until he found a neat solution to the problems Davis's trial presented, while carving a pathway for his own easy declaration against secession in *Shortridge* and *Texas v. White*. Chase manipulated the law to serve the needs of his society in the same way that his contemporaries did, but his silence on – or denial of – the difficulty of coming to terms with these compromises was singular.

Texas v. White attracted very little attention in 1869. Legal periodicals noted the substance of the decision but provided no additional commentary.[17] The world had not been expecting the Court to rule on the great question that had animated the war, and its conclusion – that there was no right of state secession in the U.S. Constitution – was hardly a surprise. The case also was eclipsed in the national media by *Ex parte McCardle*, which was handed down the same day as *Texas v. White*.[18] *McCardle* sustained Congress's decision to remove the Supreme Court's appellate jurisdiction over habeas challenges to military trials conducted under the authority of the Military Reconstruction Act.[19] Congress had sought to prevent constitutional challenges to military trials from reaching the Court, and the Court's

---

[16] Texas v. White, 74 U.S. at 737 (Grier, J., dissenting).

[17] "Legal Notes," *American Law Register* 17 (1869): 371–76; "Summary of Events," *American Law Review* 3 (1868): 784; *American Law Review* 4 (1869): 170; "Recent American Decisions," *American Law Register* 18 (1870): 272; *Canada Law Journal* 5 (1869): 113.

[18] Ex parte McCardle, 74 U.S. 506 (1868).

[19] Act of March 27, 1868, 15 Stat. 44 (1868).

refusal to examine Congress's motives attracted far more attention than the relatively sleepy issue of Texas's responsibility to pay back its creditors.

Newspaper coverage of the case was also sparse, and focused on Reconstruction rather than secession. Chase's lone paragraph about secession was perhaps the least publicized aspect of the decision. The press was more interested in discussing the fine distinction Chase had drawn between a state and the government thereof. Most Court observers found Chase's analysis baffling – so much so that they were not certain on first reading whether *Texas v. White* had upheld military Reconstruction or struck it down.

How had Chase squared the circle in declaring secession unconstitutional, finding that Texas was a state, and yet upholding federal supervision of the state under military Reconstruction? The *Milwaukee Daily Sentinel* declared the opinion to be so confusing that it was rendered useless. The paper surmised that Chase's tortured analysis arose from the Court's "attempts to reconcile the irreconcilable."[20] Other papers completely misunderstood the decision as a blow against the Republican Party. The *Harrisburg Weekly Patriot* wrongly reported that the opinion "virtually annul[ed] the Reconstruction Acts," because of its insistence that the Confederate states had never left the Union.[21] Chicago's *Pomeroy's Democrat* followed suit, assuming that Chase's strike against secession meant that the Court must necessarily have also condemned Reconstruction.[22]

Those who did comprehend that the Court had sustained military Reconstruction were dumbfounded by Chase's distinction between the state and government of Texas. Defense lawyer Albert Pike was disgusted with what he termed the "judicial folly" of the Court's decision. "All the people of Texas were not Texas!" he wrote. "There was no secession government de facto of Texas! Such nonsense the Court gravely gabbled."[23] Pike was not alone. The *Macon Weekly Telegraph* criticized Chase for hypocrisy in finding that the state of Texas had never left the Union and yet was rightfully subject to Reconstruction.

[20] *Milwaukee Daily Sentinel*, April 17, 1869.
[21] *Harrisburg Weekly Patriot* (Pennsylvania), April 22, 1869.
[22] "The Dreaded Decision Given," *Pomeroy's Democrat*, April 21, 1869.
[23] Quoted in Walter Brown, *A Life of Albert Pike* (Fayetteville: University of Arkansas Press, 1997), 446.

The Chief Justice had had to summon a great deal of "ingenuity to harmonize these two points," the editors wrote.[24] The *New Hampshire Patriot* marveled at the Court's ability to view Texas as a state and a nonstate at the same time. In spite of Texas's statehood, it said, the Court had permitted the "Radicals in Congress [to] persist in excluding this legal State from all of its rights and privileges as a State."[25] The *Missouri Democrat* described the distinction Chase had drawn between the "legal" and "political" existences of a state as "lame nonsense.... But if it pleases any hair-splitting lawyer to imagine that a State can exist and not exist at the same time, we know of no particular harm in his indulging the notion."[26]

When the press did discuss the opinion's pronouncement against secession, they treated *Texas v. White* as the continuation of a conversation that had begun on the battlefield. In the opinion, Chase had sought to distance himself from the idea that the war had any bearing on the legality of secession. Although Chase did not acknowledge it, and based his scant analysis solely on constitutional logic, others understood that the verdict of the war undergirded the decision.

Republican papers celebrated the decision for gilding the verdict of the war with gloss of judicial legitimacy. The *Houston Union* commended the Court for its "settlement of constitutional questions arising from the war."[27] Horace Greeley's *New York Tribune* declared that the decision had put the "much-vexed questions ... of Secession and Rebellion" to rest with "lucidity of thought and terseness of expression."[28] The *San Francisco Bulletin* praised *Texas v. White* for "justifying the theory on which the Government resorted to coercion to maintain the Union" and welcomed the news that the "Court is gradually giving judicial expression to the principles contended for by the Government in the struggle against secession." According to the *Bulletin*, the decision signified that "the Republican idea on this subject may now be regarded as constitutionally vindicated."[29]

[24] *Macon Weekly Telegraph*, April 16, 1869.
[25] *New Hampshire Patriot*, April 21, 1869.
[26] *Missouri Democrat*, reprinted in *Des Moines Daily Register*, April 22, 1869. See also *New York Express*, reprinted in the *Milledgeville Southern Recorder*, April 27, 1869.
[27] *Houston Union*, April 21, 1869.
[28] *New York Tribune*, April 13, 1869. See also *Baltimore Sun*, April 13, 1869; *Little Rock Morning Republican*, April 22, 1869.
[29] *San Francisco Daily Bulletin*, April 22, 24, 1869.

On the other side of the political spectrum, the *New Orleans Times-Picayune* expressed disappointment with the Court's perfunctory treatment of the secession question. "The court made short work of that doctrine," the paper remarked, "without bestowing any attention on the arguments in its favor drawn from the history of the making, and the analogies of the constitution. It is stated as a dogma – for which no argument is thought to be necessary" that the Union was perpetual. The flimsiness of the reasoning actually implied that the Unionist argument was weak, the editors contended: "The Court weakens its own position, and the original argument against secession by the feebleness of the only point it reproduced in the way of authority." As the *Picayune* put it, "the right of secession may *not* have existed, but it is not by such reasoning that the doctrine is to be refuted." All that the decision proved, the paper's editors concluded, was that the Court felt obligated to rubber-stamp the results of the war. "The roots of the doctrine of secession were cut out of the constitution by the sword," the paper declared. "The end of the old debate may as well be recognized as having been come at in that way."[30]

The *New York Herald* echoed this conclusion. Chase's ruling proved that "the preservation of the government and to prevent dangerous complications or serious embarrassments to it seem to be the highest object of the Supreme Court." According to the *Herald*, *Texas v. White* "shows that not logic, abstract right or abstract principle governs the highest tribunal of the country so much as the law of necessity."[31] As the *Herald*'s editorial pointed out, the Court's opinion was the one that had to be written. It served only to save the country from disturbing what the war had wrought.

Following Jefferson Davis's release on bail in May 1867, the *Army and Navy Journal* had forecast that there would be no final disposition of the secession question. It would "probably go undecided into history. Or, if it be exhumed at some distant day, it will appear in some dry, legal dictum, interesting as a professional opinion, but taking no vital hold as a fact upon the people of the Republic," the paper said.[32] *Texas v. White* confirmed that prediction. Chief Justice Chase's throwaway

---

[30] *New Orleans Times-Picayune*, April 21, 1869.
[31] *New York Herald*, April 14, 1869.
[32] "The Release of Davis," *Army and Navy Journal*, May 18, 1867.

paragraph on secession has stood as the judiciary's most definitive pronouncement on the constitutional theory that animated the Civil War, but that is not to say it was truly definitive. It failed to sort out the weighty legal issues the war left not quite resolved.

In the remaining years of the nineteenth century, *Texas v. White* enjoyed a curious status. The courts treated Chase's opinion as the law of the land – in the sense that judges and lawyers relied on it as legal precedent, and that its holding was not open to reexamination. But it differed in kind from other cases. It was viewed, even by the courts, as reliant on the force of events rather than the force of logic. The case was treated more as a necessary pronouncement for the courts to make than a careful exposition of the law that sounded in reason. Tellingly, in the 1878 Supreme Court case *Keith v. Clark*, involving a Contracts Clause challenge to an amendment to the Tennessee constitution, Justice Samuel Miller suggested that *Texas v. White* and its progeny had bound the courts, but they had not ended the larger national discussion about the merits of the secession question. "These cases," Miller wrote, "and especially that of *Texas v. White*, have been repeatedly cited in this court with approval, and the doctrine they assert must be considered as established in this forum at least."[33] Miller intimated that *Texas v. White* had established law for the courts, but not beyond them.

Miller's somewhat cryptic commentary on the relationship between the death of secession and the Court's ruling in *Texas v. White* received fuller explication in legal scholar John Codman Hurd's *Theory of Our National Existence*. Published in 1881, Hurd's book focused on the relationship between the law as made on the battlefield and law established in the courtroom. Hurd opened with a discussion of *Texas v. White*, arguing that the Court's ruling memorialized the fact that the

---

[33] Keith v. Clark, 97 U.S. 454, 462 (1878). A great many cases relied on *Texas v. White* in sorting out legal problems that turned on the legitimacy of government acts undertaken in the Confederate states during the war. Others involved the ability of state governments to repudiate wartime actions. See, e.g., The Legal Tender Cases, 79 U.S. 457 (1870); Morgan v. U.S., 113 U.S. 476 (1885); In re Chiles, 89 U.S. 157 (1874); Ex parte Virginia, 100 U.S. 339 (1879); Dodge v. Freeman's Savings & Trust Co., 93 U.S. 379 (1876); Thomas v. City of Richmond, 79 U.S. 349 (1870); U.S. v. Reese, 92 U.S. 214 (1875); Dewing v. Perdicaries, 96 U.S. 193 (1877); Taylor v. Thomas, 89 U.S. 479 (1874); Christmas v. Russell, 81 U.S. 69 (1871); U.S. v. Home Ins. Co., 89 U.S. 99 (1874); Vermile & Co. v. Adams Express Co., 88 U.S. 138 (1874).

locus of sovereignty within the United States had been altered by the Civil War. "It is common to speak of some battles as having decided the fate of empires," he wrote on the opening page. But in America, he said, where the rule of law reigned supreme, Union victory was incomplete without a corresponding endorsement by the courts. In a section titled "How Revolution Is Accepted by a Court," Hurd argued that the war had established every citizen's obligation to "obey [the national] Government as the only sovereign."[34]

Hurd maintained that "when a revolution is recognized, there should be an end of all controversies based on an earlier history. There is no question of constitutionality or unconstitutionality in a revolutionary change." In the postbellum world, he said, the Supreme Court had a duty to recognize the "new state of political facts" that the war had produced. In so doing, the justices did not betray any obligation they possessed to uphold neutral principles of law. On the contrary, Hurd argued, the justices' oath to support the Constitution of the United States created an "allegiance to" the sovereign, even though the identity of the sovereign could shift "at any moment," as it had during the Civil War. The war itself had solved the persistent antebellum dispute about the nature of sovereign power within the United States "by the only evidence which settles such a question." Thereafter, the Court was bound to support that sovereign unquestioningly, as "an instrument for the execution of its will." The courts had to declare the Union unbreakable "if they consent to be courts of law at all." For this reason, it made sense that Chief Justice Chase had dismissed secession so easily in *Shortridge v. Macon* and in *Texas v. White*. And the government had been right to avoid the issue in the Davis case because it would have forced the jury to confront secession too directly. "Is it to be inferred that, if Mr. Davis's indictment had gone to the jury, the judge would have charged that the question was 'theoretical' or settled by the 'issue of battle' only?" Hurd queried.[35]

Hurd took this argument one step further, insisting that the courts also possessed a duty to disguise the reality that the secession question had been resolved by force of arms. Indeed, in the postwar world, the

[34] John Codman Hurd, *The Theory of Our National Existence* (Boston: Little, Brown, 1881), 3, 357.
[35] Hurd, *Theory of Our National Existence*, 351, 357, 80 n. 1.

formal lawmaking bodies of the United States were bound to erase the fact that the nature of the federal Union had ever seriously been in dispute. The Court's decision in *Texas v. White* was designed to do precisely that, Hurd said. The Court intended its decisions to operate as "precedents," such that "it will appear to any inquirer that no positive discrimination of a revolutionary political change has been made by any member of the court." Looking back, future observers would not be able to discern a difference between the Court's opinions ratifying the results of the war and any others. The Court pretended that the Unionist formulation of the sovereignty of the people in the aggregate stretched back to the founding. "Whatever political condition the Supreme Court may have accepted as the basis of its decision," Hurd wrote, "they have in all their opinions stated [that political condition] as one continuously existing from the time of the adoption of the Constitution in 1787."[36]

As it turned out, Hurd's predictions proved to be largely accurate. Some late nineteenth-century legal scholars treated *Texas v. White* as a regular example of judicial decision making, but others acknowledged that the decision was a form of legal wallpaper that camouflaged the Court's extraordinary efforts to reconcile the war with the law.[37] Today, by contrast, this closer degree of scrutiny has largely faded. As the memory of the Civil War receded into the background of our consciousness, *Texas v. White*'s perfunctory analysis of secession became – in the eyes of the legal academy – dogma.[38]

---

[36] Hurd, *Theory of Our National Existence*, 425.

[37] For a general discussion of this issue in late nineteenth-century constitutional law treatises, see Charles Larsen, "Nationalism and States' Rights in Commentaries on the Constitution after the Civil War," *American Journal of Legal History* 3 (1959): 360, 364. For examples of legal scholars who acknowledged the political underpinnings of the Court's decision, see John Randolph Tucker, *The Constitution of the United States* (Chicago: Callahan, 1899), 1: 338–40; Henry Campbell Black, *Constitutional Law* (St. Paul: West Publishing, 1895), 27–28.

[38] Modern law reviews treat the Court's decision as a definitive analysis that settled the issue of the legality of secession. See, e.g., Francisco Forrest Martin, "Our Constitution as Federal Treaty: A New Theory of United States Constitutional Construction Based on an Originalist Understanding for Addressing a New World," *Hastings Constitutional Law Quarterly* 31 (2004): 269; Steven Calabresi, "We Are All Federalists, We Are All Republicans: Holism, Synthesis, and the Fourteenth Amendment," *Georgetown Law Journal* 87 (1999): 2273; Raymond Friel, "Secession from the European Union: Checking Out of the Proverbial 'Cockroach Motel,'" *Fordham International Law Journal* 27 (2004): 590; Craig S. Lerner, "Saving the Constitution: Lincoln, Secession, and the Price of Union," *Michigan Law Review* 102 (2004): 1263.

Writing in the 1980s, historian David P. Currie remarked with some degree of frustration on the inadequacy of Chase's declaration against secession, which, he noted, took up only "a single paragraph." Currie found Chase's discussion "hardly ... an adequate treatment of an issue on which reasonable people had differed to the point of civil war. It was an act of considerable audacity to treat the mere statement of purpose in the preamble as if, contrary to its natural reading, it imposed legally binding limitations on the states."[39]

Those who have examined the case have always understood that the Court's decision was undergirded, if not directly dictated, by the results of the war. Chief Justice Chase "answered" the secession question in the Union's favor without really considering it, because an answer that contradicted the outcome of the war would have been unbearable. Human sacrifice on such a large scale – 700,000 deaths – *had* to hold meaning, even if *Texas v. White* was not the true "test" of secession that Davis's case had threatened to be for a time.

Would the world look different today if Davis's case had gone to trial and he had won an acquittal? Would such a thing really have been possible, or is our inability to envision that outcome just a product of 150 years of collective amnesia about such an unpleasant prospect? No wonder none of the parties involved in the Davis matter (except Davis himself) wanted to see the case through. It had the potential to strike too deeply at our notion of an acceptable amount of distance between law and political and social reality.

If the verdict in the case had not matched the results of the war, Americans might have been forced to acknowledge that war was ultimately more powerful than law. Or, on the other hand, they might have allowed law the power to reverse the most desperate of human struggles, and learned to live with an outcome that condemned the war. Given that both possibilities were so unpalatable for the war's survivors, it has been easier for historians to assume that the law *had* to follow the results of the battlefield, because law is simply politics by another name, especially in the aftermath of a political event so cataclysmic as the Civil War. Nineteenth-century Americans' answers, and

---

[39] David P. Currie, *The Constitution in the Supreme Court: The First Hundred Years, 1789–1888* (Chicago: University of Chicago Press, 1985), 311–12.

ours, to the legal questions raised by the war were reflexive rather than profound, because it was – and is – too disturbing to contemplate the alternative. It has been easier for Americans to forget that secession's unconstitutionality was ever seriously in doubt after Appomattox. It has been easier to forget that the judgment of the law ever threatened to disrupt the judgment of the battlefield.

Important Participants in the Davis Case

Prosecutors

S. Ferguson Beach, U.S. attorney
Lucius Chandler, U.S. attorney
John H. Clifford
Richard Henry Dana Jr.
William Evarts, attorney general
John Hennessey, Beach's assistant
E. Rockwood Hoar, Evarts's cousin and attorney general
Andrew Johnson, president of the United States
Lovell Rousseau
James Speed, attorney general
Henry Stanbery, attorney general
H. H. Wells, Chandler's assistant

Other Davis Opponents

James Doolittle, Wisconsin senator
Joseph Holt
Francis Lieber
William Seward, secretary of state

Defense Attorneys

James T. Brady
George William Brown
R. H. Gillett
Burton Harrison
Giles Hillyer
C. E. Hooker
Robert Lowry
James Lyons
Charles O'Conor
Robert Ould
Thomas G. Pratt
George Pugh
William B. Reed
B. J. Sage
George Shea
John Randolph Tucker

Other Davis Allies

Thomas F. Bayard
Jeremiah Black, former attorney general
Caleb Cushing
Varina Davis
Robert Garrett
William Wilkins Glenn
Horace Greeley
Bradley Johnson
Reverdy Johnson
Philip Phillips
Franklin Pierce, former president
Gerrit Smith
Thaddeus Stevens

Judges

Salmon P. Chase, chief justice of the United States
John C. Underwood

Archival Collections Consulted

Abbreviations used in the notes appear in parentheses.

Alabama Department of Archives and History, Montgomery (ADAH)
    Jefferson Davis Papers
    Colin McRae Papers
University of Alabama Library, Tuscaloosa, Alabama
    Jefferson Davis Papers
Beauvoir, Jefferson Davis Presidential Library, Biloxi, Mississippi
    Jefferson Davis Papers
Boston Athenaeum, Boston
    John Codman Hurd Papers
University of Chicago Library, Chicago (UChi)
    Jefferson Davis Trial Papers
Duke University Library, Durham, North Carolina (DU)
    Isaac Carrington Papers
    Clement Clay Papers
    Bradley T. Johnson Papers
Filson Historical Society, Louisville, Kentucky
    Breckinridge-Marshall Papers
Georgetown University Special Collections Library, Washington, DC
    Joseph Maria Finotti Papers
Harvard Law School, Special Collections Library, Cambridge,
  Massachusetts
    William Evarts Papers

Houghton Library, Harvard University, Cambridge,
    Massachusetts (HU)
        Charles O'Conor Papers
        Charles Sumner Papers
Schlesinger Library, Harvard University, Cambridge, Massachusetts
        Ellis Gray Loring Papers
Huntington Library, San Marino, California (HEHL)
        Samuel Barlow Papers
        Edridge Collection
        William Evarts Papers
        Ward Hill Lamon Papers
        Francis Lieber Papers
        Stowe Manuscripts
Johns Hopkins University, Baltimore
        James Roberts Gilmore Papers
Manuscripts Division, Library of Congress, Washington, DC (LC)
        Bayard Family Papers
        Jeremiah Black Papers
        James Buchanan Papers
        Salmon P. Chase Papers
        W. W. Corcoran Papers
        Caleb Cushing Papers
        James R. Doolittle Papers
        William Evarts Papers
        Robert Garrett Papers
        Burton Harrison Papers
        Joseph Holt Papers
        James M. Mason Papers
        Edward McPherson Papers
        Philip Phillips Papers
        Franklin Pierce Papers
        Samuel Chester Reid Papers
        Gerrit Smith Papers
        William Seward Papers
        Edwin Stanton Papers
        John Underwood Papers
Library of Virginia, Richmond (LVA)
        Bryan Family Papers

Indictments against Various Confederate Leaders
Federal Records, U.S. v. Jefferson Davis
Maryland Historical Society, Baltimore (MdHS)
Brune-Randall Papers
John Glenn Papers
Massachusetts Historical Society, Boston (MHS)
Adams Family Papers
John Clifford Papers
Dana Family Papers
Miami University of Ohio, Oxford, Ohio
Samuel Richey Collection
University of Michigan Library, Ann Arbor
Ebenezer Rockwood Hoar Papers
Mississippi Department of Archives and History, Jackson
Jefferson Davis Papers
Museum of the Confederacy, Richmond, Virginia (MC)
Jefferson Davis Papers
National Archives, College Park, Maryland (NA-CP)
Attorney General's Records, Record Group 60
Jefferson Davis Case File, Record Group 60
National Archives, Washington, DC (NA-DC)
Case Files of Applications from Former Confederates for
Presidential Pardons ("Amnesty Papers"), 1865–1867,
Record Group 94
Jefferson Davis Amnesty Papers, Record Group 94
Records of the Senate, Record Group 46
New-York Historical Society, New York (NYHS)
Horace Greeley to George William Blunt, John Alexander
Kennedy, and John O. Stone (broadside)
Thomas O'Conor Miscellaneous Manuscripts
Kenneth Rayner Papers
Gerrit Smith to Salmon P. Chase (broadsides)
Manuscripts Division, New York Public Library, New York (NYPL)
Charles P. Daly Papers
Horace Greeley Papers
Thomas F. Madigan Papers
Charles O'Conor Papers, Miscellaneous Manuscripts
Samuel J. Tilden Papers

Maps Division, New York Public Library, New York (NYPL)
    Major and Crapp, "Map of that Part of the City of New York
      North of 155th Street" (New York, 1865)
University of Notre Dame, South Bend, Indiana
    James A. McMaster Papers
Pennsylvania Historical Society, Philadelphia
    Salmon P. Chase Papers
University of Pennsylvania, Philadelphia (UPenn)
    Henry C. Lea Papers
Princeton University Library, Princeton, New Jersey
    Blair-Lee Papers
Public Archives of Canada, Ottawa, Ontario
    Dispatches from U.S. Consuls in Toronto
Southern Historical Collection, University of North Carolina, Chapel
  Hill (SHC)
    Campbell Family Papers
    James Speed Papers
    Tucker Family Papers
Transylvania University, Lexington, Kentucky
    Jefferson Davis Papers
Tulane University Library, New Orleans
    Jefferson Davis Collection
Virginia Historical Society, Richmond (VHS)
    Lyons Family Papers
    Saunders Family Papers
    Indictment, U.S. v. Jefferson Davis, U.S. District Court,
      Washington, DC
Small Special Collections Library, University of Virginia,
  Charlottesville (UVA)
    Albert T. Blesdoe Papers
    Bradley T. Johnson Papers
    Charles Halpine Papers
    Morton-Halsey Papers
Beinecke Library, Yale University, New Haven, Connecticut (Yale)
    Evarts Family Papers
    Edwards Pierrepont Papers

Index

former Confederates' view of, 86,
92–98, 100–1
historical definition of, 87
Hurd on, 117–18
Lea's view of as obsolete, 107, 108–11
loss of legitimacy of, 118–19
medieval revival in Antebellum
America and, 89–90
Northerners' view of, 92
O'Conor's view of as providing an
as alternative resolution to the
secession question, 84, 85
Prize Cases (1863) and, 103–6
Southern interest in writings of Scott
and, 90
Spooner's condemnation of, 115–16
Stephens (Alexander) on, 100–1
Stevens (Thaddeus) on, 105–6
Sumner on, 89
Texas v. White (1869) and, 103–6
Unionist thinkers on, 100, 111
view of as as a terrible medieval
superstition, 107–8
West Virginia Supreme Court of
Appeals on, 107
Whitman on, 118
Trigg, Connally F., 145, 146
Two Years Before the Mast (Dana), 228

U.S. attorneys, 27, 29, 32, 38, 39, 40, 43,
47, 49, 51, 60, 90, 123, 243, 307
U.S. Constitution
requirement that a crime be tried in
state where the crime was committed
and, 231
right of secession in Articles of
Confederation and, 15–16
U.S. v. Burleigh, 81
U.S. v. Greathouse (1863), 80, 216–17
U.S. v. Hanway, 145
Underwood, John C., 130
desire to pack pro-Union jury in
Virginia by, 186
eagerness to try Confederates for
treason, 184–85
grand jury in 1866 and, 165–66

public wariness towards, 186–87
radicalism of as potential advantage to
Davis defense, 180–81
rejection of O'Conor's bail request in
1866 by, 167–70
release of Davis on bail by in
1867, 187–89
self-dealing via Second Confiscation
Act of, 183–84
suspects Chandler of being a
Confederate sympathizer, 185
Union, idea of perpetual. *See* perpetual
Union, idea of

Vanderbilt, Cornelius, 161
Varennes, John, 26–27
Vattel, Emerich de, 206, 208, 262
violence, 10, 62, 84, 86, 91, 92, 108, 114,
115, 117, 120
treason and, 32, 140, 141, 166

Wade, Benjamin, 284
war and law, links between, 317, 322–24.
See also international law; law of
war; secession's constitutionality;
trial by battle
Washington National Intelligencer, 247
Washington, DC, as venue for Davis
trial, 140–41
Webster, Daniel, 17
Welles, Gideon, 34–35, 47, 194,
260–61, 276, 277
West Virginia Supreme Court, 107
Wheaton, Henry, 88, 208, 227,
249–51, 261
white supremacy, 13, 14, 230n. 12
Whiting, William, 70, 216
Whitman, James Q., 118
Wiebe, Robert, 4
Winder, John, 75–76
Wirz, Henry, 75–76
Witt, John Fabian, 252, 260
Wood, Fernando, 11
Woodman, Horatio, 121
Woodward, George Washington, 28
Wright, Quincy, 265